HUNT COUNTY, TEXAS CEMETERIES

Volume 4

Kathy Lynn Penson
Robert Lee Thompson

Heritage Books
2024

HERITAGE BOOKS

AN IMPRINT OF HERITAGE BOOKS, INC.

Books, CDs, and more—Worldwide

For our listing of thousands of titles see our website
at
www.HeritageBooks.com

Published 2024 by
HERITAGE BOOKS, INC.
Publishing Division
5810 Ruatan Street
Berwyn Heights, MD 20740

International Standard Book Number
Paperbound: 978-0-7884-7769-0

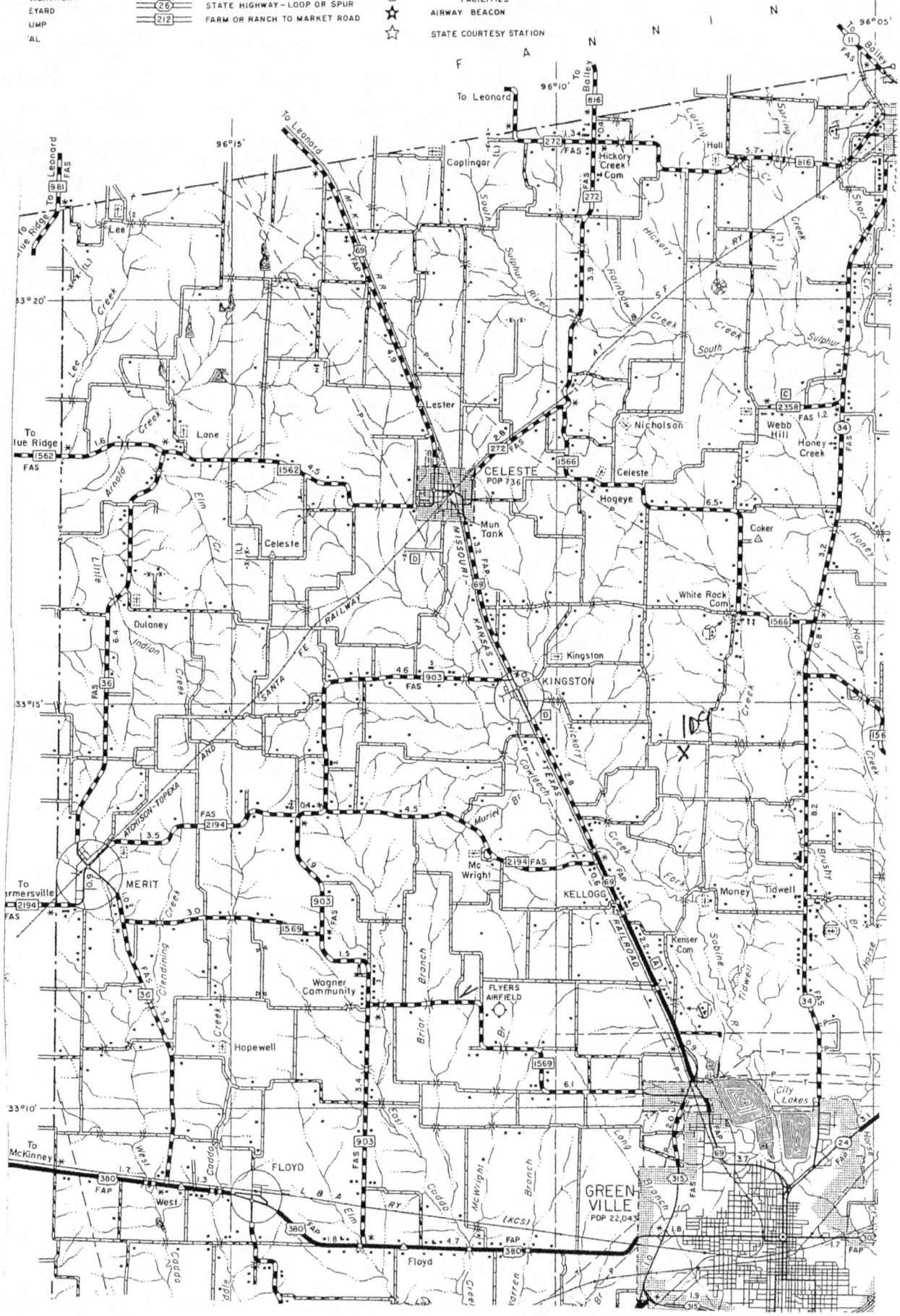

CELESTE
POP 736

KINGSTON

KELLOGG

MERIT

GREENVILLE
POP 22,043

FLOYD

Lee

Lane

Lester

Nicholson

Webb Hill

Honey Creek

Celeste

Hogeye

Coker

White Rock Com.

Coplinger

Hickory Creek Com.

Lotty Hall

Mun Tank

Dulaney

Kingston

Mc Wright

Money

Tidwell

Kenser Com.

Wagner Community

Hopewell

FLYERS AIRFIELD

West

City Lakes

To Leonard

To Bailey

To Blue Ridge

To Farmersville

To McKinney

South Sulphur River

Hickory Creek

Sulphur Creek

Honey Creek

Caddo Creek

Indian Creek

Sabine River

Long Branch

MISSOURI KANSAS TEXAS RAILROAD

ATCHISON-TOPEKA AND SANTA FE RAILWAY

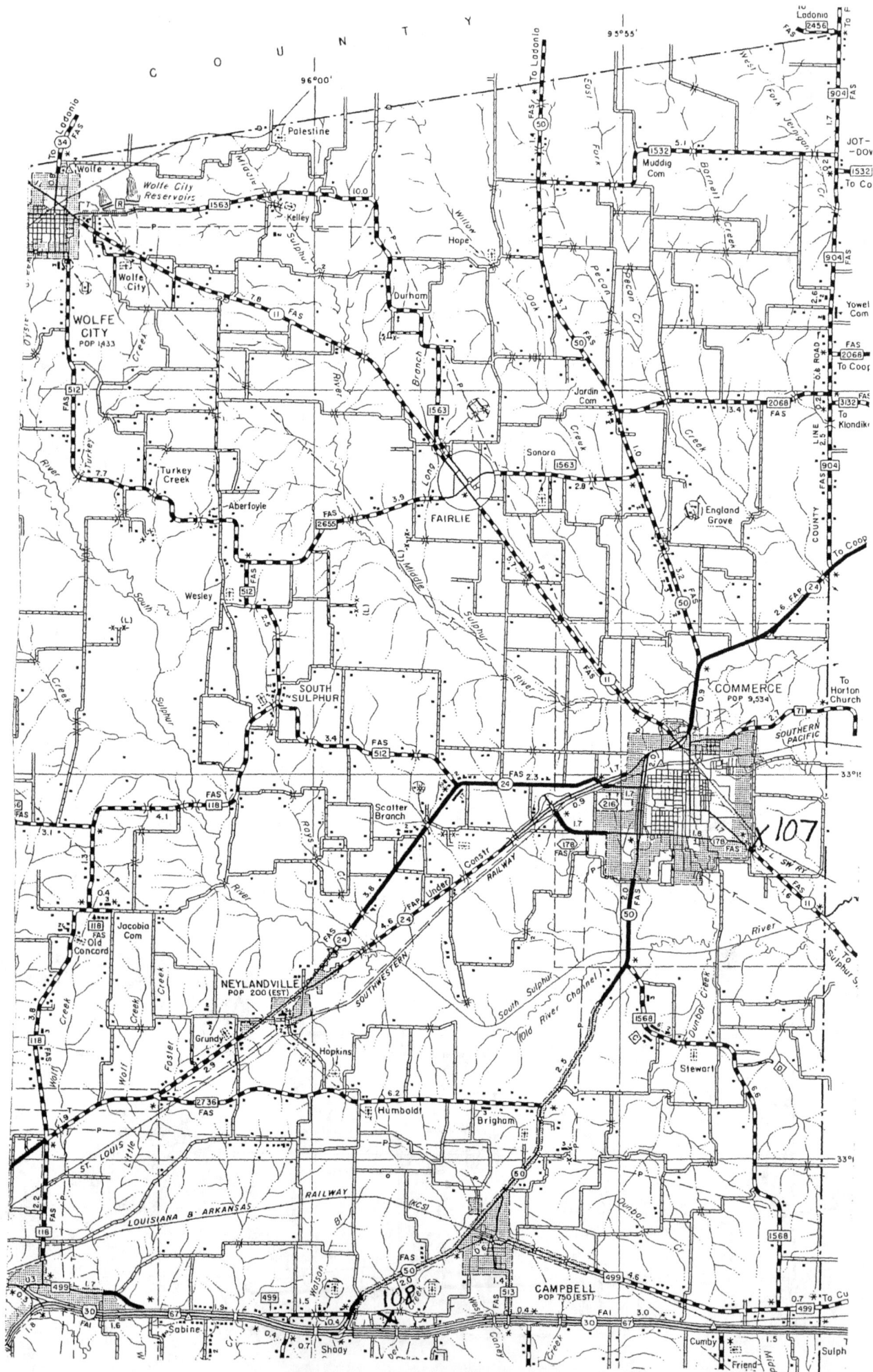

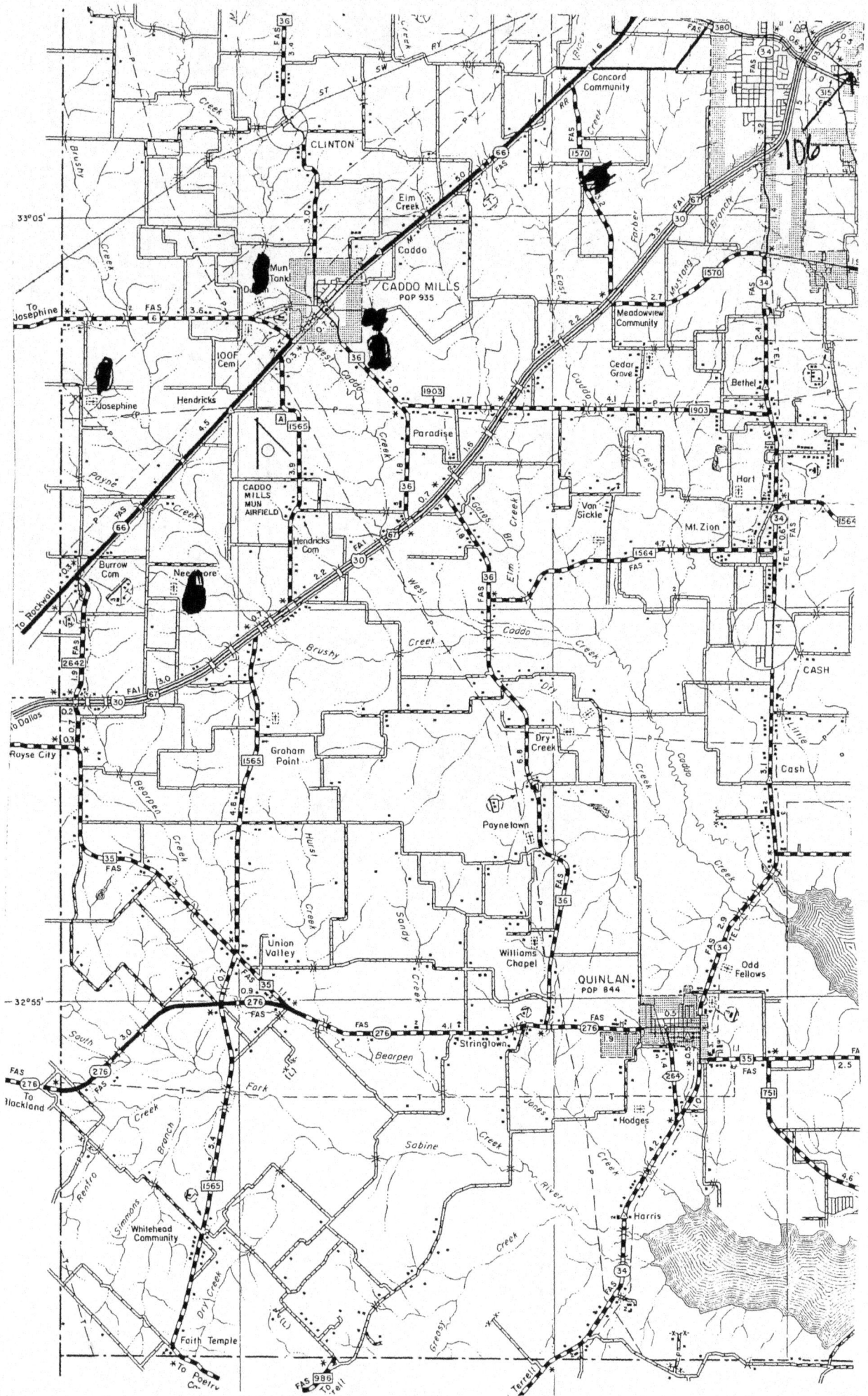

CLINTON

Concord
Community

CADDO MILLS
POP 935

Meadowview
Community

Cedar
Grove

Bethel

Hart

Mun
Tank

IOOF
Cem

To Josephine

Josephine Hendricks

Paradise

Van
Sickle

Mt. Zion

CADDO
MILLS
MUN
AIRFIELD

Hendricks
Com

CASH

Burrow
Com

Needmore

To Rockwall

Graham
Point

Dry
Creek

Paynetown

Cash

To Dallas

Royse City

Union
Valley

Williams
Chapel

QUINLAN
POP 844

Odd
Fellows

To
Blackland

Stringtown

Hodges

Harris

Simmons
Community

Whitehead
Community

Faith Temple

To Poetry

To Terrell

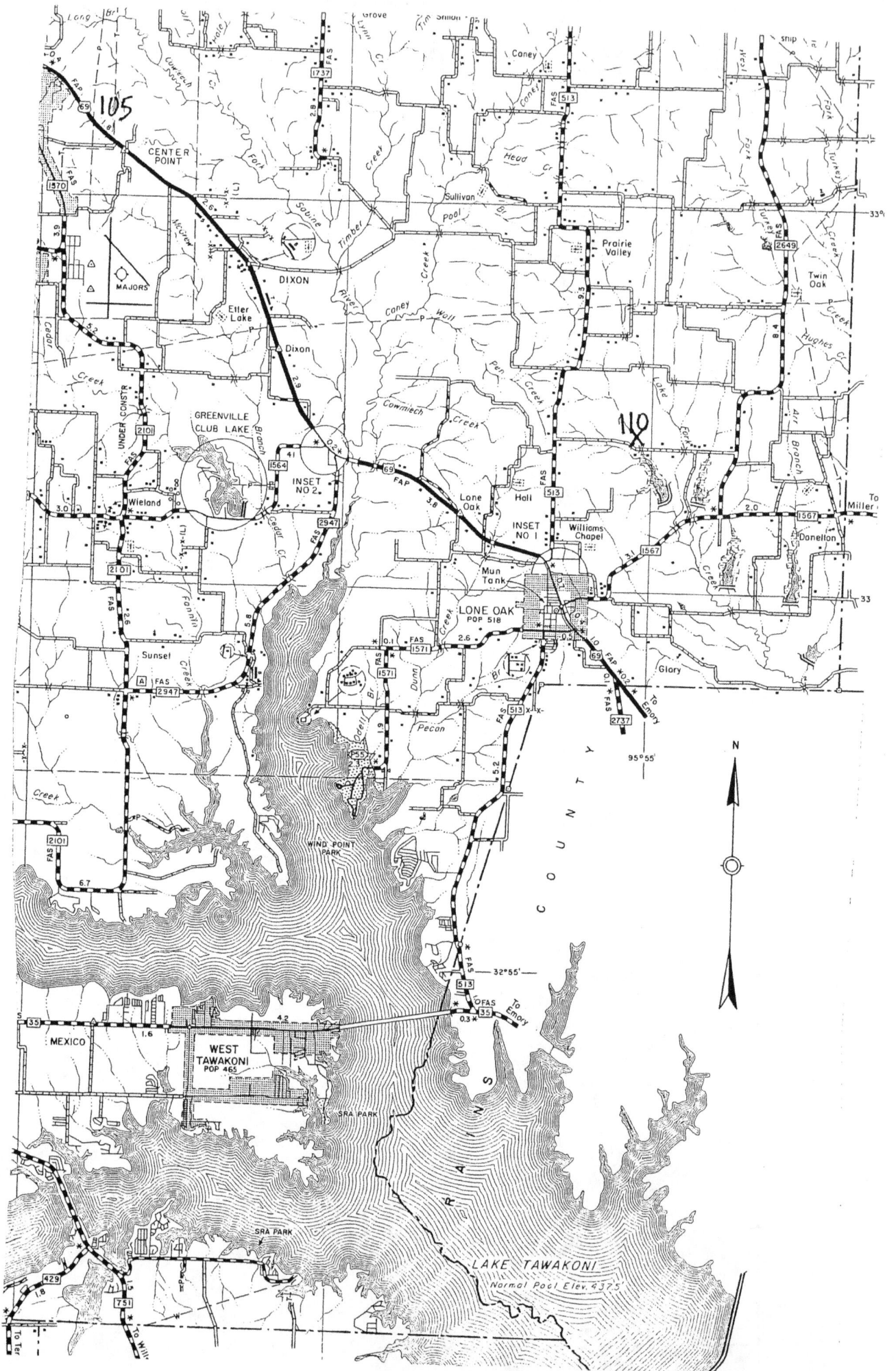

TABLE OF CONTENTS

DEDICATED

TO

RICHARD HARRELL   MY GREAT GREAT GRANDFATHER
(1813-1895)

FOUNTAIN E. PITTS HARRELL   MY GREAT GRANDFATHER
(1842-1911)

FRANCES EDWIN (ED) HARRELL   MY GRANDFATHER
(1870-1948)

ANNIE LAURA (HARRELL) THOMPSON   MY MOTHER
(1906-1978)

BY ROBERT LEE THOMPSON

PERKINS, Minnie L., 12-8-1877   4-2-1964
PERKINS, John L., 1-16-1870 6-13-1950
NICHOLS, Jack R., 1927-1951
KINCER, Infant, died 5-19-1909
KINCER, Elizabeth H., 1878-1949
KINCER, George P., 1874-1938
KINCER, June, 9-20-1869 11-1-1959
KINCER, William, 1-9-1866 3-3-1926
KINCER, Hiram, 6-2-1825 3-13-1910
KINCER, Lizzie, wife of Hiram, 12-23-1836 8-18-1904
NICHOLS, Edward E., 1898-1974
PORTWOOD, Russell, 1894-1969
CURFMAN, Gladys M., 1-28-1899 1-24-1972
SCOTT, Frances "Frenchie", 4-15-1920 12-6-1955
SCOTT, William Patrick, born and died 1955
CAUSEY, Edgar Zeff, 1892-1958
HEMSELL, Dave L., 10-31-1869 1-12-1959
HEMSELL, Minnie A., 12-13-1870 5-13-1955
HEMSELL, Clorine J., 12-18-1906 4-27-1974
MIZE, James Willard, 8-12-1913 1-13-1953
WOOD, Lucy A., 12-30-1888 No Date
WOOD, O. Marvin, 2-4-1881 8-25-1960
YOUNG, Mattie E., 1886-1957
YOUNG, Jim R., 1882-1958
MIZE, Donald D., 5-11-1911 10-3-1954
PAYNE, Melvin W., 1908-1958
NICHOLSON, Roland O., 1890-1956
NICHOLSON, Beulah B., 1893-No Date
LIGHTFOOT, G. W., 6-14-1910 No Date
LIGHTFOOT, Mary Lou, 10-11-1914 6-27-1963
WOODALL, A. J., 1915-1960
WOODALL, John R. "Bob", 8-31-1888 11-25-1951
WOODALL, Birdie C., 9-30-1895 No Date
WHITE, Willie Minus, Cpl., U. S. A., W. W. I., 8-20-1892 10-28-1971
WHITE, Susan E., 6-28-1898 No Date
JORDAN, Julia E., 3-8-1913 7-31-1974
HOLLIDAY, Bettie, 10-29-1872 4-25-1957
MARSHALL, Donia C., 1894-1950
MARSHALL, Jesse, 1914-1951
TAYLOR, Cora E., 1876-1961
TAYLOR, Henry M., 1868-1951
HAWTHORNE, Everett W., 12-9-1883 6-6-1964
HAWTHORNE, J. Elgin "Bue", 9-24-1915 12-3-1951
GOODWIN, Thomas D., 6-2-1883 5-17-1962
GOODWIN, Maud E., 9-25-1888 9-14-1965
NICKELS, Charles F., 11-22-1865 8-1-1957
NICKELS, S. A., 2-23-1868 2-2-1958
KEY, Charlie R., 3-8-1903 9-2-1920
KEY, Lula E., 6-15-1880 5-17-1952
KEY, J. Wallace, 11-26-1879 2-16-1960

PETTY, Burley A., 1880-1966
PETTY, Anna Y., 1888-1952
EWING, Jerry Bob, 3-5-1944 1-2-1952
FRYER, Ruby, 1901-1951
FRYER, Jim H., 1898-1961
ERWIN, Allen L., 1881-1967
ERWIN, Rosa E., 1882-1961
FOSTER, Martin I., 1877-1950
FOSTER, Evy, 1883-No Date
FLENNIKER, Davis C., 1903-1951
LOCKHART, Robert F., Jr., 1947-1951
PARKER, Bob Wren, 1-23-1936 3-28-1953
PARKER, J. Tom, 9-6-1891 3-5-1951
DEES, Earl, 9-9-1921 9-10-1952
DEES, Mrs. Nell, 5-13-1894 10-14-1960
DEES, Margin T., 10-6-1896 7-26-1962
STEVENS, Gertie, 1900-1957
NEELY, Frank I., 1889-1974
NEELY, Lola H., 1892-1952
BACK, Edgar, 4-21-1893 5-11-1955
BACK, Genia, 11-25-1899 10-27-1952
BACK, Edgar, Tex., Pfc., 130 BN, MPC., W. W. I., 4-21-1893 5-11-1955
RAMSAY, Malcolm, 1880-1952
RAMSAY, Alice, 1895-No Date
HYDEN, Samuel Ray, 8-28-1900 8-29-1951
HYDEN, Rosa Mae, 4-30-1902 No Date
SANDERS, James B., 10-8-1885 5-23-1967
SANDERS, Bertha E., 10-9-1886 12-18-1958
TANTON, William W., 1887-1951
TANTON, Carrie Z., 1888-No Date
LEAKE, Herman, 1896-1972
LEAKE, Avis L., 1909-1953
ROW, Mrs. W. H., 1882-1964
TANTON, Morris E., Tex., Pfc., 38 Inf., 2 Inf. Div., Korea, PH
                                        12-3-1930 3-15-1951
DENNEY, Ella C., 1885-1953
AMMONS, E. Christine, 3-9-1909 12-29-1962
AMMONS, W. Harold, 8-26-1909 1-4-1974
THOMASON, Jimmy Lynn, 12-25-1952 5-4-1953
DELCORE, Sheila D., 1973-1973
MANSFIELD, Henry A., 2-25-1868 9-21-1957
MANSFIELD, Bennie Ann., 1-16-1882 8-22-1972
RAGLAND, Joseph Harden, 1872-1953
RAGLAND, Sallie, 1878-1970
FORD, Walter Harris, Sr., 8-25-1881 7-6-1953
HENDERSON, George B., Jr., 2-15-1949 9-26-1953
THOMASON, J. B., 4-3-1897 9-3-1962
THOMASON, Edith Ann, 3-2-1903 No Date
THOMASON, J. B., Tex., Pfc., Motor Trans. Corps, W. W. I.,
                                        4-3-1897 9-3-1962
TAYLOR, William B., 1880-1953
1 - Stump
JENKS, Dr. Ralph W., 8-5-1893 10-21-1959
JENKS, Edith N., 5-3-1920 11-29-1964

NEVILL, Charles P., Jr., 4-28-1912 2-25-1958
WRIGHT, Frank R., 1935-No Date
WRIGHT, Frank A., 1915-1970
          married 2-2-1935
WRIGHT, Alyne L., 1915-No Date
SHAW, Pearl, No Dates (Funeral Marker)
SHAW, Roy P., Tex., Pvt., Btry A., 241 F A BN, W. W. II.,
                    8-24-1901 7-1-1971

GILLILAND, John V., 1873-1954
GILLILAND, Mary A., 1883-1960
BEARDEN, John I., 1892-1954
ETHRIDGE, Aubrey S., 1918-1954
WALLACE, Clinton, 1905-1953
LINDLEY, Rilla C., 12-14-1888 12-10-1969
LINDLEY, Edgar William, 6-17-1886 12-23-1954
LINDLEY, James Edgar, 1-18-1917 8-19-1962
LINDLEY, Infant of E. W. & R. C., 6-21-1909 7-25-1909
HINO, Jose Ella MARONEY SMITH, 7-10-1901 10-10-1968
MARONEY, W. L., 1876-1955
SWAFFORD, George S., Tex., Pfc., U. S. A., W. W. I., 8-24-1895 1-22-1968
PARKER, John T., 1889-1952
PARKER, Dora M., 1914- No Date
ULMER, Norman D., Tex. Pvt., 1550 Serv. Unit, W. W. II.,
                    7-13-1920 9-12-1952

LAMBERT, Doris, 2-24-1931 11-7-1956
MATHIS, Elener, 1901-1960

SECTION "F"

LEWIS, Larry Phillip, 9-21-1941 10-2-1960
LEWIS, Annie Marie, 1910-No Date
LEWIS, Benton L., 1909-No Date
JOHNSON, Henry, 8-17-1888 2-1-1961
JOHNSON, Pearl, 11-15-1891 6-11-1966
TILLERY, Zentih M., 1897-No Date
TILLERY, Roy, 1901-No Date
PRINCE, Jesse E., 1-22-1888 2-25-1961
1 - Unmarked Grave
WOLFE, Margaret Frances, 7-30-1872 12-31-1960
WOLFE, Ben Benton, 10-26-1898 9-8-1972
WOLFE, Mary Sue, 3-25-1902 No Date
HUNT, David A., 10-21-1887 7-26-1958
PRUITT, Charles Edmond, 10-16-1877 1-1-1961
PRUITT, Mary EVANS, 12-29-1879 7-24-1966
TERRY, Mrs. David D., 10-20-1889 2-21-1967
TERRY, William Camp, 9-16-1923 10-14-1960
LANDRETH, Ralph Lynn, 1908-1946
LANDRETH, Mrs. Evelyn, 1922-1952
LANDRETH, C. D. "Johnny", 1918-1952
BRUNDIDGE, James W., 1903-1960
WILSON, Emma D., 1896-1971
WILSON, T. Protus, 1880-1960
CURTIS, Dennis Joe, 11-15-1944 9-18-1960
LITTLE, Joseph E. "Buster", 11-11-1931 2-16-1961

LITTLE, Frank O., 1900-1968
LITTLE, Frank O., Jr., 1924-1949
CLINTON, Janie, 11-9-1884 5-20-1960
CLINTON, James Robert, 3-26-1913 5-30-1966
CLINTON, Sidney W., Tex., S-Sgt., U. S. Army, W. W. II
                                    7-7-1908 6-21-1970
MC WHIRTER, Ella Irene SHEFFIELD, 1910-1949
LANDRETH, Jamie, son of T. C. & Caroline, 1962-1967
JACOBS, Mary F., 1875-1965
JACOBS, W. L., 1878-1957
HUNT, David A., 10-21-1887 7-26-1958
SMITH, Mary Ella, 9-17-1862 6-1-1934
SMITH, Lawrence Samuel, 6-19-1855 4-28-1920
ARMSTRONG, Lura W., 10-22-1883 10-10-1971
ARMSTRONG, Alger H., 7-30-1875 8-6-1961
WINTON, Atlee, 11-10-1889 2-1-1960
WINTON, Lillie, 10-31-1890 2-11-1973
SMITH, Garnett, 1893-1964
REAVIS, Mary Jane, 1868-1963
REAVIS, Mack S., 1865-1946
REAVIS, H. Eddgar, 1898-1948
REAVIS, Esma J., 1900-1956
GRIMES, Wilson A., Jr., 7-3-1915 3-15-1968
GRIMES, Wilson A., 7-22-1882 6-27-1961
NICHOLSON, Roland G., Tex., Tec-5, 48 General Hospt., W. W. II
                                    1-24-1912 2-19-1955
SMITH, Margie Elizabeth, 7-10-1893 11-6-1930
SMITH, Edward Olin, 6-6-1886 2-1-1957
BAKER, Alfred T., Tex., Sm-Sgt., U. S. A. F., W. W. II
                                    6-20-1923 12-22-1968
BAKER, Alfred Thomas, Tex., Pfc., Hq. Co. 144 Inf., W. W. I
                                    11-10-1890 4-24-1961
BAKER, Evie May, 6-25-1900 NO DATES
COLLINS, David A., 1873-1946
COLLINS, Lula, 1876-No Date
BUSBY, Henry Gordon, 5-3-1886 4-19-1946
BROOKS, Jesse Elmer, 1-6-1886 1-12-1965
BROOKS, Freddie Ende, 8-25-1882 1-25-1957
BROOKS, Pheobe Ann, 10-8-1852 1-23-1933
BROOKS, Samuel Jenkins, 9-17-1850 2-23-1934
BROOKS, Ester Sammie, 9-11-1880 5-2-1931
BROOKS, Maude, 8-11-1884 8-14-1884
MILNER, Jewel BROOKS, 11-18-1891 No Date
MILNER, Oscar Bradley, 10-15-1886 1-13-1974
SMITH, John Henry, 8-2-1863 11-20-1955
SMITH, Julia FOX, 2-16-1866 7-12-1946
HOLDNER, Henry B., 6-3-1886 11-12-1964
HOLDNER, Halie Be Be, 9-24-1891 1-4-1945
LAFAVERS, Essie Ray, 3-16-1943 4-6-1945
LAFAVERS, W. J., 1910-No Date
LAFAVERS, George Louie, 1916-No Date
LAFAVERS, Mc Michael, 1920-1963
HOUSTON, Mrs. Edga M., 1886-1950
HOUSTON, Edga M., 1882-1944

LAMBERT, _____, 1897-1948
LAMBERT, Tommie, 1895-1966
RUCKER, Lila VAN CLEAVE, 1871-1950
RUCKER, Solomon, 1861-1939
SUMROW, Ava L. RUCKER, 1891-1968
SUMROW, Luther D., 1888-1937
SIMPSON, Allan S. "Jack", 1875-1964
SIMPSON, Clyde STAPP, 1891-No Date
MORROW, Katie STAPP, 1881-1956
MORROW, Willie C., M. D., 1877-1951
STRAWN, Lois Ann, 4-19-1933 5-10-1953
STRAWN, Dorothy Mae, 2-8-1924 3-9-1943
STRAWN, Chester C., 3-15-1887 10-12-1964
STRAWN, Levena, 10-18-1900 No Date
MORRIS, Mrs. C. V., 1-8-1889 2-9-1948
HATAWAY, Sallie Elizabeth, 1883-1945
HATAWAY, J. L., 1871-1964
FITZGERALD, Ronald Lynn, 5-12-1947 12-26-1947
FITZGERALD, William Clark, 1881-1961
FITZGERALD, Sallie, 1876-1966
MORRISON, Travis B., 8-4-1887 10-31-1948
MORRISON, Durward D., Tex., 2nd. Lt., Infantry, W. W. II.,
                                3-25-1922 7-13-1944

HAMILTON, James T., 1872-1951
HAMILTON, Lena G., 1881-1970
WOODARD, Johnnie J., 10-11-1899 8-19-1926
WOODARD, Marie, 12-13-1900 No Date
WOODARD, Charles Elliott, Tex., S-Sgt., W. W. II., 10-26-1923 12-26-1944
BARHAM, George L., 1865-No Date
BARHAM, Loise TATE, 1872-1946
BRIGGS, Rudd C. L. "Bucky", 1880-1960
BRIGGS, Emma Lou, 1886-1970
BOGGS, Oma Lea, 4-19-1907 No Date
BOGGS, Warren, 11-27-1904 11-8-1948
MARTIN, Myrtle Lee, 4-10-1915 4-3-1970
CLAIR, Maggie B., 6-17-1881 2-5-1946
CLAIR, Cullen M., 4-10-1870 5-14-1963
GREER, Marion Lou, 12-12-1948 (Died)
EILAND, Bedford B., 1878-1958
EILAND, Grace S., 1888-No Date
HAWKINS, W. E., 1880-1947
HAWKINS, Ellen, 1887-1963
MASON, Walter Lee, 3-18-1897 10-1-1963
        married 2-4-1917
MASON, Tommie Lillian, 8-8-1899 No Date
WOOD, Lola Mae, 1903-1969
JAMES, Annie E., 12-10-1893 9-6-1974
JAMES, Elbert L., 2-29-1886 3-9-1946
RODDAM, Lawrence C., 1860-1951
RODDAM, Callie D., 1859-1946
ENDE, Von Elard F-, 1863-1948
ENDE, Ola FORD, 1872-1953
HELM, H. D., 1896-1948
HELM, Eula Lee, 1892-1954

WARREN, Alexander T., 1879-1958
WARREN, Mary L., 1875-1948
GARRETT, Henry R., 10-5-1874 8-10-1944
GARRETT, Lucy M., 11-29-1876 11-12-1955
BRASHER, Homer D., 1898-1923
BRASHER, Addie, 1901-No Date
MANNING, Mary R., 2-1-1868 6-1-1953
MANNING, J. W., 7-26-1866 10-24-1918
MANNING, Jack W., 12-23-1898 2-17-1940
WHITEHEAD, Alvin O., Tex., Sgt., 805 AAF Base Unit W. W. II
                                    1-22-1914 8-13-1950
WHITEHEAD, Nancy K., died 6-17-1946
WHITEHEAD, Nelda Fay, died 6-17-1946
WHITEHEAD, John G., 1864-1945
WHITEHEAD, Maggie A., 1870-1953
JOURNER, James E., 2-14-1880 5-16-1947
JOURNER, Rosa B., 1881-1971
JOURNER, John B., 8-28-1911 2-21-1964
EDWARDS, Lewis N., 3-23-1914 1-28-1948
EDWARDS, Moody C., 9-7-1893 1-25-1967
SHIELDS, Caleb A., 1881-1945
SHIELDS, Lena M., 1886-1962
LEWIS, Erin H., 1913-1948
MAULDIN, J. Claude, 1901-No Date
MAULDIN, Florence L., 1900-1965
BEAN, T. Maurice, 5-28-1905 12-27-1968
BEAN, Hellen J., 4-25-1906 No Date
VAN CLEAVE, Rita Mae, 1901-1973
VAN CLEAVE, George L., 1873-1946
VAN CLEAVE, Olive V., 1875-1956
BRADFORD, Harry Milton, M. D., 4-8-1869 11-1-1962
BRADFORD, Annie GOOD, 3-13-1875 7-12-1966
BRADFORD, Harry M., Jr., 2-11-1897 1-8-1973
BRADFORD, Fannie HOWELL, 9-21-1903 No Date
HARRIS, C. Pearl, 1883-1973
HARRIS, C. Silvey, 1879-1940
HARRIS, M. Maurine, 1904-No Date
HARRIS, Melba L., 1906-No Date
GRADY, Carroll Lloyd, 1930-1947
JONES, Jarrod Glenn, 1975-1975
LONG, Alfred, 1885-1947
LONG, Elta TAYLOR, 1890-1975
TAYLOR, P. R., 1866-1946
WOOD, Stephen D., 1879-1946
WOOD, Leona V., 1882-1971
KIRK, Neppie S., 4-1-1901 7-15-1947
KIRK, Jo Ellen, 1927-1946
ELLIOTT, Mrs. Jim, 1877-1946
ELLIOTT, Jim L., 1874-1948
PAYNE, Arlean Ruth, 11-11-1921 2-27-1972
JONES, Clara Lea, wife of J. L., 7-26-1912 5-12-1959
STEVENS, Mary Maude, 10-7-1879 11-26-1960
STEVENS, B. B., 12-3-1879 8-20-1965
SNEAD, Lea PAYNE, 7-31-1925 6-21-1946

SNEAD, H. Lauerl, C.G.M., U. S. N., W. W. II., 4-30-1921 2-9-1974
SNEAD, Raymon, No Dates
MONTGOMERY, Frances Audelia, 12-18-1911 2-23-1946
MONTGOMERY, Lottie NORMAN, wife of F. C., 6-11-1879 10-31-1957
MONTGOMERY, Fannin Cawood, 10-21-1875 4-30-1972
ORME, James Edgar, 1880-1945
ORME, Jeffie B., 1886-1966
BRANCH, Pearl S., 1-8-1893 No Date
BRANCH, J. Wesley, 9-15-1893 12-2-1946   married 8-3-1912
BRAZIEL, Judge Sam, 12-2-1902 11-11-1964
CREEL, James E., Tex., Pfc., Inf., W. W. II., 7-31-1908 2-26-1945
CATHEY, Charles Wayne "Tubby", 1909-1953
CATHEY, Truman Ward, -8-25-1906 5-21-1971
GIDEON, Thomas G., 12-11-1872 3-21-1947
GIDEON, Maggie B., 2-2-1879 8-31-1955
GIDEON, Clifton H., 9-8-1897 No Date
GIDEON, Dorotha M., 9-15-1921 No Date
MC WHIRTER, Lillie E., 1879-1948
BOWDEN, Dewey H., 1899-1963
BOWDEN, Mary F., 1899-No Date
BOWDEN, Dewey H., Texas, S-2, U. S. Navy, W. W. I., 1-29-1899 3-3-1963
GRESHAM, Clara L., 1889-1968
GRESHAM, Eugene, 1883-1944
LYNCH, Eugie, 7-10-1892 10-18-1949
BEDDINGFIELD, Bobby Glenn, (Son), 11-26-1936 12-23-1945
BEDDINGFIELD, Cora Leah, (Daughter), 4-6-1944 7-15-1944
CROUCH, Emmet O., 9-5-1887 12-27-1973
CROUCH, Lola N., 7-11-1888 No Date
JORDAN, Roy, 1901-1951
JORDAN, Clara, 1901-1949
PAYNE, Nathan, 1881-1960
PAYNE, Mrs. Bernie, 2-22-1895 12-2-1972
1 - Funeral Marker
LUCAS, William E., 1873-1946
LUCAS, Cora A., 1873-1947
STINEBAUGH, Arch L., 12-25-1900 5-31-1950
STINEBAUGH, Celina K., 12-17-1945 5-31-1950
MC GARRY, William J., 6-23-1888 5-13-1957
MC GARRY, Oma, 10-22-1892 7-3-1943
OSTER, Grant, 7-12-1863 10-19-1946
OSTER, Ida, wife of Grant, 11-12-1872 11-10-1942
SMITH, Theresa, dau. of O. & Minnie E., 12-27-1899 5-22-1924
SMITH, Minnie E., wife of Dr. O., 1-12-1869 2-22-1924
SMITH, Dr. Oscar, 2-27-1855 10-9-1948
SMITH, M. Dixon, 1-5-1888 8-17-1961
SMITH, Ethel, wife of G. S. BERRY, 4-26-1886 11-5-1969
BERRY, Mary L., wife of G. S. & Ethel, 10-7-1910 12-17-1910
BERRY, Garland Saddine, 2-18-1881 1-27-1972
HALL, Jack B., Texas, Sgt., 52 Field Arty., 18 Div., W. W. I.,
                                        2-11-1896 3-1-1949

MOSELEY, Earnest, 11-10-1889 4-4-1961
BEENE, Sim, 1883-1966
BEENE, May, 1887-1942
BONE, William Andrew, 9-1-1891 1-3-1973

BONE, Mary Ellen, 7-28-1892 No Date
BRYAN, Jess A., 11-25-1887 12-21-1945
BRYAN, Lula B., 6-15-1888 No Date
BLOUNT, Mollie Lee, 1895-1947
BLOUNT, Billie, 1895-1970
BLOUNT, Anabel, 1897-1945
MONROE, John O., 1871-1930
MONROE, Minnie A., 1869-1958
DODD, Robert L., 1879-1931
DODD, Myrtle W., 1882-1967
BENNETT, Herman H., 2-9-1900 12-23-1972
          married 2-15-1920
BENNETT, Mabel A., 9-11-1898 No Date
BENNETT, Everett M., Lieut., A. A. F., 11-28-1923 7-4-1944
BURNETT, Robbie Kate, 12-6-1942 5-19-1944
GREENWADE, James F., 1889-1948
GREENWADE, Lena, 1890-1969
GREENWADE, Lt. Billy R., Killed in Action, 1921-1944
HILTON, William Collins, 11-11-1947 11-14-1947
COLLINS, Tilford, Sr., 5-31-1893 3-2-1968
GARY, C. D., Jr., Tex., Pfc., U. S. Army, W. W. II., 8-12-1913 6-14-1972
PINER, Dr. R. G., Jr., 1896-1944
PINER, Thelma M., 1897-1949
PINER, Robert G., Jr., Cpl., 4th. Texas Inf., N. G., 2-10-1896 8-26-1944
PHILLIPS, Chester L., Jr., Capt., A. A. F., 1-26-1918 5-14-1943
1 - Funeral Marker
BAGWELL, William J., 1889-1975
RIDDELES, Rufus W., 6-12-1876 12-22-1942
RIDDELES, Billie O., 8-10-1883 3-27-1964
CARAWAY, Michael E., died 3-1-1944
SHELTON, Lawrence C., 1881-1943
SHELTON, Nora L., 1880-1974
GARY, Claude D., 8-1-1889 9-15-1951
DULANY, Hillie, 11-3-1882 7-30-1943
DULANY, Cesscy, 11-11-1890 5-29-1972
HALL, Clarence S., 1-28-1890 2-18-1943
HALL, Fay MERRICK, 7-6-1893 4-8-1956
BOYCE, Willis Dean, 4-22-1942 2-21-1944
SMITH, Lt. Comdr. Virgil A., 1900-1944
SMITH, Winnie Lee, 1900-1959
SMITH, Virgil A., Jr., Tex., Pvt., 403 TNG G.P. A. A. F., W. W. II.,
                          6-23-1923 7-31-1967
BURNSIDE, Charles S., 1-7-1876 1-4-1957
BURNSIDE, Emma F., 8-27-1875 8-5-1950
THORNTON, Lt. Cordus H., 4-24-1916 11-1-1950
THORNTON, Mabel C., 6-21-1908 No Date
PARKER, Steve Ed., 11-9-1878 1-12-1944
WILLIAMS, Lillie PARKER, 10-4-1892 11-1-1963
CROSSKNO, Lecy Jane, 3-12-1875 10-1-1953
CROSSKNO, Maurine, 8-18-1914 11-25-1943
SOCKWELL, Lorene PAGE, 9-24-1911 7-19-1972
LE FAN, Kenneth J., 12-4-1903 6-21-1944
LE FAN, Lolita M., 1-19-1906 8-2-1968
HUNT, Alvin, 11-4-1875 1-14-1959

HUNT, Lula, 2-15-1880 2-2-1948
SKINNER, Pearl, 7-30-1892 2-24-1960
CHAMBLISS, T. W., 2-5-1886 8-28-1971
SMITH, Oscar J., 1891-1954
SMITH, Evan, 1897-1958
SMITH, Loyd, 1915-No Date
LE FAN, William J., 5-9-1860 7-12-1942
LE FAN, Joanna, 11-20-1864 8-26-1948
PAYNE, James M., 6-10-1875 3-24-1955
PAYNE, Sarah J., 11-28-1872 9-25-1943
BOWEN, Henry T., 1886-1953
GLENN, Kenneth Lesley, 9-30-1944 3-12-1945
BOWERS, Henry Mc Kinley, 11-26-1893 1-22-1945
BOWERS, Essie CLara, 2-14-1900 No Date
BRIGGS, Dale, Texas, Pvt., Co. B., 144 Inf., W. W. I, 9-12-1893 2-2-1960
JONES, Althis, 1887-1970
JONES, Loceile, 1892-1973
LE FAN, Foy R., 1906-1957
LE FAN, Alma L., 1909-No Date
PHILLIPS, James S., 1881-1954
PHILLIPS, Alice L., 1887-No Date
TREDWAY, William C., Tex., Sgt., 422 Base Hq. & AB Sq., A. A. F., W.W. II
                        7-7-1918 4-25-1953

TREDWAY, Albert, 1-25-1875 10-20-1959
          married 8-29-1915
TREDWAY, Hazel, 1-5-1896 No Date
TREDWAY, George E., 1886-1964
TREDWAY, Viola C., 1896-1972
HARTLEY, O. M., 1882-No Date
HARTLEY, Nettie, 1881-1964
KELLY, Martha Ann, 11-5-1868 8-28-1922
KELLY, Jesse Slavin, 2-27-1861 3-28-1945
HORN, Eliza STEELE, 1882-1968
HORN, William Newton, 1875-1939
RENEAU, Marguerite KELLY, 3-2-1901 No Date
RENEAU, William Wayne, 9-2-1901 5-6-1961
THOMPSON, James Allen, 6-15-1881 6-27-1956
THOMPSON, Lula Mae, 4-29-1882 6-6-1952
LANCASTER, Claude, 3-27-1889 9-15-1967
LANCASTER, Annie, No Dates
1 - Unmarked Grave
ECK, Lt. Col. Samuel K., 4-19-1903 10-19-1947
2 - Unmarked Graves
ECK, Samuel Kroninger, North Dakota, Lt. Col., A. Corps, W. W. II.,
                        4-19-1903 10-19-1947
MC NATT, Idella A., 1-24-1885 11-14-1949
MC NATT, Alvin S., 12-17-1883 5-4-1970
MC NATT, Lula, 5-24-1867 5-29-1954
MC NATT, J. F., 2-9-1860 3-25-1950
2 - Unmarked Graves
PRIESTER, J. Charles, 1898-1947
PRIESTER, Myrtle E., No Dates
HEED, Sarah A., 2-9-1849 11-16-1928
FAULKNER, Frances F., 7-22-1881 1-11-1946

FAULKNER, Le Land H., 9-7-1875 2-21-1959
FAULKNER, Allie Mae, 2-4-1904 11-11-1963
STUART, Allie J., 9-27-1867 11-6-1943
STUART, John D., 9-26-1869 6-22-1943
PRICE, Caroline STUART, 10-25-1922 1-8-1950
STUART, John W., Texas, 1st. Lt., 809 Pioneer Inf., W. W. I.
                                    10-19-1889 5-30-1968
STUART, Caroline CAMPBELL, 11-26-1893 No Date
AREY, Donald Ray, son of Mr. & Mrs. L. L., 11-20-1933 11-21-1933
AREY, Lonnie L., 1912-1963
PRICE, Eppsy SMITH, 7-2-1880 12-23-1967
PRICE, John E., 9-26-1877 2-15-1954
PRICE, Hobert, 7-9-1899 6-20-1965
DOOLEY, Winona Fay, died 9-18-1942
ROSS, Audrey, No Dates
SMITH, Willie BINGHAM, 3-5-1881 4-5-1943
SMITH, Edward Finley, 12-5-1879 12-27-1941
FURGUERON, Edward A., Tex., 1st. Lt., U. S. Marines Corps, 1-14-1935
                                                    10-31-1972

SOCKWELL, Alma Paul, 11-13-1878 10-28-1953
SOCKWELL, Florence N., 10-6-1873 12-22-1937
MILLER, Virgil Thomas, 1907-1975
SOCKWELL, Paula SAVAGE, 1-5-1945 7-19-1973
DICKSON, Rubert, 5-25-1907 9-18-1967
DICKSON, Hermie, 11-22-1908 No Date
DICKSON, Mary Lynn, 9-26-1935 8-8-1937
ANDREWS, Cecile STUART, 11-5-1894 7-6-1964
ANDREWS, Rufus Perry, 12-5-1891 1-7-1975
STEVENS, Floy, 1890-1971
ANDREWS, Henrietta, 1871-1941
ANDREWS, Charlie H., 1866-1954
WARREN, William Hackley, 1858-1936
WARREN, Mattie Lee, 1870-1957
WARREN, William Carl, 1891-1963
WARREN, Ray Leon, 1899-1951
WARREN, Bill, 1896-1975
WARREN, Virgil C., 1893-1956
TAGGART, Lucius J., 5-2-1869 3-4-1957
TAGGART, Mattie A., 10-1-1872 3-13-1956
MASON, Ernest L., No Dates
FOUSE, Angela Dawn, 8-28-1961 1-30-1962
MORRIS, Henry L., 9-11-1883 1-6-1962
NORTHCUTT, Ira H., 9-3-1912 7-17-1961
NORTHCUTT, Pearl, 8-14-1917 No Date
MIZE, Robert Carrol, 1-26-1882 2-5-1965
MIZE, Sarah Lou Ella, 7-3-1886 8-23-1962
SALTER, Philip R., No Dates
SALTER, Eula Mae, 12-26-1896 3-13-1972
NELSON, Louise, 9-17-1912 No Date
SPALDING, Margaret Jean, 1939-1945
NELSON, Doll, 5-2-1887 11-4-1947
        married 1-2-1910
NELSON, Betty E., 9-18-1892 No Date
HOWELL, Ruby MOORE, 6-25-1905 10-30-1951

MOORE, Bertie PUCKETT, 3-4-1871 7-21-1955
MOORE, Fred Kenneth, Tex., S-1, U. S. Navy, W. W. II, 12-17-1921 12-7-1941
COKER, J. B., 1859-1955
COKER, Rosa Etta, 1873-1946
TAYLOR, Rose Mary G., 11-13-1910 9-25-1946
BOYD, Charles R., 1882-1966
BOYD, Minnie, 1884-1953
BRADFORD, O. F., 1886-1968
BRADFORD, Mrs. O. F., 1895-1946
GAVEN, Rose Marie, 5-7-1881 2-5-1956
GAVEN, Nelson D., 10-31-1880 12-6-1946
SCOTT, Sharon Ann, 7-14-1946 3-22-1949
LOGAN, William, 1871-1963
LOGAN, Skinner, 1876-1945
BICK, Lolian MC KEE, 1905-1947
ROREX, William H., 10-28-1892 10-14-1963
FLEMING, Martha Louise, 10-14-1927 10-16-1933
FLEMING, John Payne, 3-9-1892 5-23-1967
SMITH, Dorsey E., 8-6-1895 3-2-1963
SMITH, Dorsey C., Tex., 354 Inf., 89 Div., W. W. II.,
                                    11-9-1925 4-11-1945

MORRIS, Jess F., 1888-1945
SWINDELL, Curney Thomas, 7-6-1892 1-17-1959
SWINDELL, Beulah BAKER, 4-27-1893 2-6-1961
TAPP, Doss, 10-7-1898 No Date
TAPP, E. M. "Matt", 4-18-1872 3-26-1962
TAPP, Mollie, 12-30-1875 4-21-1949
BRIDGES, Jack E., 1887-1947
BRIDGES, Bernice, 1893-No Date
CUMMINGS, Robert M., 5-21-1882 12-8-1944
CUMMINGS, Nellie G., 9-10-1890 12-27-1972
DALE, Walter, 7-20-1875 6-26-1945
DALE, Pearl, 5-2-1882 8-14-1973
WALLACE, John Bert, 1890-1954
WALLACE, Ida Hellen, 1894-1954
WALKER, Sarah BOULTON, 1893-1966
BOULTON, Robert L., 1895-1947
DOUGLAS, Melvyn T. "Red", 1-19-1913 9-4-1950
DOUGLAS, Hazel MAYS, No Dates
DOUGLAS, Melvyn T., Tex., S-Sgt. 1103 AAF Base Unit, W. W. II.,
                                    1-19-1913 9-4-1950

AREY, Ova, 5-29-1895 No Date
AREY, Milford, 4-13-1891 9-29-1966
LUTZ, Alex B., 3-5-1874 1-25-1959
LUTZ, Martha E., 2-1-1872 4-15-1955
MACKEY, James L., 1-8-1873 3-8-1962
MACKEY, Viola J., 3-31-1881 12-11-1955
MC BRIDE, Thomas P., 9-9-1871 12-15-1973
MC BRIDE, Rena, 3-8-1879 8-26-1959
LUCKETT, Hurchel G., Tex., Cpl., 28 Marines 5th Marines Div., W. W. II.,
                                    4-25-1921 3-2-1945

WRIGHT, Burch, Tex. SK-2, U. S. Navy, W. W. I., 11-1-1892 6-24-1967
MC WHIRTER, Ira M., 1890-1957
1 Funeral Marker

MC WHIRTER, Nettie R., 9-26-1889 3-28-1951
NEWBY, Iva Lorene, 1905-1945
WALLACE, Mary Emma, 8-3-1905 1-5-1968
BURCH, Lemuel C., 3-25-1870 9-10-1945
BURCH, Emma B., 2-18-1875 No Date
DOUGLAS, Charlie C., 1882-1965
DOUGLAS, Vannah DRAKE, 1885-1949
BURCH, Walker E., Tex., Momm 1, U. S. N. R., W. W. II.,
                              12-12-1899 9-24-1953
BRUNDIDGE, Vera B., 1-22-1901 1-22-1968
LONG, Delbert, S-Sgt, Killed in Belgium, 1915-1945
CHUMLEY, Raymond F., Tex., Pvt., 31st. Inf., 2-10-1898 9-17-1945
CHUMLEY, Lillie Maud, 4-8-1901 8-8-1974
BLOUNT, Ruth ATKISSON, 11-28-1894 7-9-1953
HUGHES, R. B., Jr., 1936-1945
SULLIVAN, Grover C., 6-26-1890 -6-22-1944
SULLIVAN, Cam N., 2-2-1890 11-23-1967
SULLIVAN, John L., 4-6-1883 2-12-1944
SULLIVAN, Elizabeth EVANS, 3-6-1889 12-12-1955
MC KEE, Louis M., Sr., 1880-1952
MC KEE, Lillie B., 1882-1973
MC KEE, Harry L., 1916-1945
BOLTON, T. D., 4-13-1888 1-11-1966
BOLTON, Dora M., 11-6-1890 7-30-1945
NORRIS, A. Orion, 1896-1949
POTEET, Lucious B., 9-17-1873 9-1-1946
POTEET, Mary E., 3-9-1889 No Date
POTEET, Sarah M., wife of L. B., born Lee Co., Va., near Jonesville,
                              12-8-1874 5-9-1907
POTEET, Joe Gleen, 2-23-1911 3-19-1969
SWINDELL, Claud, 11-9-1898 3-31-1956
SWINDELL, Ella, 11-16-1902 9-20-1971
STIMSON, W. E. "Billy", 1894-1968
STIMSON, Ruby, No Dates
NIX, Mrs. Janie, 1871-1920
NIX, Gussie M., 1895-1942
WATERS, Seldon David, 10-13-1923 2-11-1950
PARR, Luther P., 4-2-1885 8-8-1944
PARR, Chlora A., 11-8-1880 9-15-1943
BENNETT, Jesse A., 1909-1941
CLAIBORNE, Fleetwood A., 1882-1958
CLAIBORNE, Montra M., 1887-1952
SHOFNER, Craddock L., 1896-No Date
SHOFNER, Vertis COOK, 1909-1944
SHOFNER, Hugh, 1898-1949
SHOFNER, Evelyn, 1909-No Date
LAWRENCE, Harding L., Jr., 4-15-1944 7-8-1945
HERNDON, Thomas Taylor, 1878-1943
HERNDON, Evelyn HYDE, 1881-1966
OLD, Gordon M., 1925-1943
POTEET, Linda Ann, 12-15-1942 1-28-1944
LYBRAND, Afton, 5-26-1890 2-3-1945
LYBRAND, Ethel, 7-27-1893 11-14-1962
NOLAND, Ruby D., 1894-1948

MILLER, Jesse Lee, 6-5-1914 12-22-1968
REYNOLDS, Stella HUDSON, 6-23-1899 2-19-1973
REYNOLDS, S. W., Husband of Stella, buried in Dyersbury, Tenn., No Dates
HUDSON, Donna Pearl, 6-2-1881 12-21-1944
HUDSON, Linton, 3-10-1877 4-2-1966
HUDSON, Thomas Woodrow, 12-26-1912 7-6-1913
OLD, Idella NELSON, 4-18-1890 No Date
OLD, Henry Gordon, 8-17-1886 2-26-1966
WILLIAMS, William Murl, 1929-1943
WILLIAMS, William J., 1883-1966
WILLIAMS, Uzzie Purdie, 1891-1945
CAPLINGER, E. Bryan, 1897-1959
CAPLINGER, Connie, 1901-1964
TREDWAY, George E., 1886-1964
TREDWAY, Viola C., 1896-1972
TREDWAY, George E., Tex., Cpl., Co. C., 144 Inf., .W.W. I.,
                                    1-30-1886 4-26-1964

HARTLEY, O. M., 1882-No Date
HARTLEY, Nettie, 1881-1964
KENNEDY, Mack M., 1896-1961
KENNEDY, Viola K., 1900-No Date

CONFEDERATE MONUMENT
        " IN MEMORIAM CONFEDERATE VETERANS
                1861-1865
             LOVINGLY DEDICATED BY GREENVILLE
             CHAPTER # 1236, UNITED DAUGHTERS
             OF THE CONFEDERACY, 1941   "

                        SECTION "C"

BROWN, George, 1882-1921
BROWN, Lloyd, 1884-1919
PARTAIN, S., 8-22-1872 5-5-1924
PARTAIN, Vela F., 3-27-1882 No Date
GRAHAM, T. E., Jr., Tex., S-2, U.S.N.R.F., W. W. I., 5-18-1897 9-1-1928
GRAHAM, T. E., Sr., 9-18-1866 1-29-1925
MC MILLAN, Claud, 1879-1967
MC MILLAN, Edna, 1886-No Date
PATTERSON, Lillan E., 7-29-1890 7-25-1924
MC MILLAN, Richard L., son of A. C. & E. M., 5-30-1908 5-9-1917
MC MILLAN, Lee, 1846-1922
MC MILLAN, Alice, his wife, 1851-No Date
HUNT, Lena, wife of W. T., 1893-1919
JONES, Herbert I., 12-27-1875 11-24-1960
JONES, Mattie J., 7-21-1881 7-19-1924
HUMPHREYS, Vera, dau. of Rev. & Mrs. W. J., 1908-1924
WEST, W. T., 10-1-1858 1-13-1916
STINSON, James S., 1834-1923
STINSON, Mary E., 1839-1934
THOMPSON, Roy L., 12-13-1887 12-12-1919
DE FEE, Asa W., 1-12-1874 No Date
        married 2-15-1920

DE FEE, Myrtle B., 5-17-1889 No Date
DE FEE, Willie R., 1869-1918
BYERS, Liva H., 1891-1970
BYERS, Lillie A., 1886-1960
LOVINGGOOD, Suda "Toby", 1911-1971
LOVINGGOOD, Laudis N., 7-24-1908 8-18-1922
LOVINGGOOD, David E., 6-28-1882 10-30-1928
LOVINGGOOD, Susie R., 1883-1954
KERR, Infant son of Mr. & Mrs. H. L., died 5-1926
SANDERS, Flora, 1899-1937
SANDERS, Sina C., 1872-1926
1 - ROCK
MABRY, H. G., 1892-1929
PIERCE, Larbu, 1893-No Date
PIERCE, W. Buren, 1894-1935
PIERCE, Lewis, son of W. B. & L. B., 2-2-1919 3-17-1919
ROUTH, Joe Wayne, son of Joe M. & Gisela, 1962-1963
ROUTH, Jaunita, 1925-1927
ROUTH, Ray Kenneth, 1931-1933
ROUTH, Horace O., 1-24-1888 10-14-1951
ROUTH, Annie B., 7-15-1895 1975
WILKERSON, John Morris, Tex., Pfc., U.S.A., W. W. II., 9-2-1897 11-9-1972
BRINEY, Mary, 1844-Date Underground, unreadable
SMITH, Franklin Delbert, son of Mr. & Mrs. H. F., 1911-1919
1 - Stone unreadable
O'HARE, Bessie L., 12-10-1910 8-27-1921
1 - Funeral Marker unreadable
BURROUGHS, Bud J., Tex., Pvt., 143 Inf., W. W. I., PH,
                                    3-15-1897 9-23-1961
MC WILLIAMS, Mae Ellen, 3-19-1927 8-17-1968
DUNLAP, Annie Belle, 1863-1930
DUNLAP, William A., 1866-1943
WALLACE, Effie Mae, 1910-1929
WALLACE, Julia Ann, 1879-1950
WALLACE, Willard L., 1879-1962
WALLACE, Isaac E., Jr., 1927-1929
COOK, Minnie T., dau. of H. C. & E., 10-5-1927 4-24-1928
RODGERS, Nan J., dau. of Rev. & Mrs. J. P., 1893-1918
RODGERS, J. Frances, dau. of Rev. & Mrs. J. P., 1917-1918
ROBEY, Leonard, 1797-1862   (OLDEST DATE OF BIRTH IN CEMETERY)
ROBEY, Nancy, 1806-1889
BARKLEY, H. GUY, 3-11-1902 12-25-1967
BARKLEY, Nell S., 11-7-1902 No Date
HUNTER, Rev. John S., 1872-1930
HUNTER, Mary Emma, 1877-1957
EASLEY, R. Taylor, 1-1-1853 8-14-1928
EASLEY, Sarah E., 8-12-1855 6-14-1943
EASLEY, Onie B., 11-10-1892 7-13-1960
LEE, Mattie M., 1861-1932
1 - Stone Broken Up, unreadable
JOHNSTON, Cora B., 9-20-1884 7-24-1954
JOHNSTON, Thomas E., 12-3-1880 4-10-1953
SWINNEY, Elizabeth Fannie, No Dates
SWINNEY, William Allen, No Dates

CHAMBLIS, Clyde O., Tex., Pvt., 368 Air Base Sq. AAF, W. W. II.,
7-26-1903 8-3-1956

CHAMBLIS, Sarah, 10-19-1874 4-2-1961
CHAMBLIS, J. F., 1881-1963
CHANOS, Peter, died 10-15-1924
CHANOS, Mary, died 1-2-1923
DEMACOS, Jim, No Dates
TAGGETT, Andrew W., 1915-1931
GALBRAITH, A. J., 1830-1921
MOSS, Lou, 1865-1960
MOSS, John T., 1857-1921
HAWKINS, Sarah, 1848-1932
HAWKINS, S. D., Co. E., 15th. Texas Inf., C.S.A., No Dates
WOOTEN, S. B., 1916-1919
WOOTEN, Minnie, 1890-No Date
WOOTEN, Arby L., 1889-1947
DAVIS, Charles W., 1-9-1901 6-4-1957
DAVIS, Marjorie, 3-16-1917 No Date
JACKSON, J. E., Jr., 1908-1918
REYNOLDS, Mrs. Edith, 1888-1975
REYNOLDS, Locke C., 1884-1970
GRAY, William R. "Bob", 12-24-1876 9-30-1967
GRAY, Bertha A., 8-2-1882 11-17-1967
GRAY, Camilla, 1869-1966
SMITH, Ella A., 8-25-1963 7-20-1964
CHAPPELL, Rev. P. E., 7-16-1895 No Date
CHAPPELL, Eva SMITH, 5-19-1901 6-24-1924
HAMBLEN, James M., 11-17-1868 11-24-1935
HAMBLEN, Edward R., Va., Mess Sgt., 2nd. Field Art., died 6-26-1924
BREEDING, Lawrence Nunn, 1882-1955
BREEDING, Vaughn Standifer, 1889-1966
BREEDING, Lawrence Standifer, 1919-1921
MERCER, Georgia Era, 1890-1971
MERCER, George W., 1888-1952
JONES, Dora Elta, 1871-1953
JONES, George T., 1862-1946
JONES, Juda Ann, 1842-1920
JONES, Jessie, dau. of Mr. & Mrs. George Jones, 12-26-1897 10-26-1912
ROUTH, William Oscar, 5-27-1884 11-5-1918
ROUTH, Edna SIMMONS, 1-21-1888 9-27-1954
ROUTH, Infant, 1936-1936
ARMSTRONG, Willie, 6-27-1866 8-12-1959
JACKSON, Solistina M., 1849-1919
POOLE, Preston, 1867-1925
POOLE, Willie M., 1871-No Date
HAWKINS, Arl Q., 1889-1955
HAWKINS, Annie I., 1891-1969
HORTON, Forrest, 1896-1932
HORTON, Allie, 1892-No Date
HORTON, James R., 7-19-1860 12-22-1919
HORTON, Lena HINDMAN, 6-16-1870 7-12-1893
HORTON, James R., died 1861
1 - Stone
HORTON, Charlie, 1868-1870

KNOX, W. S., 11-10-1870 12-6-1922
MAY, Wilburn, Tex., Pfc., Co D, 2nd. Bn., U. S. Guards, W. W. I.,
                                    10-26-1887 12-31-1958
SWINNEY, Hoyt L., 2-11-1908 11-14-1928
SWINNEY, N. L., 10-14-1876 10-11-1928
WARD, James W., M. D., 1879-1956
WARD, Rena STRICKLAND, 1884-1968
WARD, Irvan M., M. D., 1906-1965
SWINNEY, Idora May, Dau. of W. A. & E. F., 5-15-1880 9-10-1880
MOORE, Elizabeth BYERS, 1-21-1916 No Date
        married 3-23-1935
MOORE, Claude Wasson, 12-13-1912 10-29-1964
MC GUFFIN, Myrtle, 1893-1924
ERWIN, W. G., 1885-1952
DUNCAN, Doris Jean, 7-15-1927 9-11-1929
DUNCAN, Mrs. W. A., 1-6-1905 6-3-1964
PIERCE, Jimmie F., 5-22-1914 6-23-1934
PIERCE, Mrs. James S., 7-8-1885 4-28-1943
PIERCE, James S., 1-8-1881 5-7-1945
WILLIS, Fred, 1891-1963
PATTON, James A., Penn., Pfc., 89 Sig. Co., 89 Inf. Div., W. W. I & II.,
                                    1-5-1889 9-16-1961
PATTON, Jimmie, 10-26-1921 10-12-1925
TODD, Christine, died 6-25-1925
TODD, Charles E., died 12-5-1940
CHAVEY, Eugenia M., 1895-1961
CHAVEY, A. Fred, 1894-1925
O'BRIEN, John E., 1867-1936
O'BRIEN, Nellie F., 1874-1961
WARD, Julia S., 1910-1944
WARD, Ota H., Cpl., 3rd. Texas Inf., 2-4-1877 12-11-1944
WARD, Robert Milton, 2-2-1885 8-20-1924
WARD, Martha Mae, 1-8-1913 12-23-1931
CAIN, J. P., 5-21-1869 3-21-1928
CAIN, Nellie A., 3-23-1874 7-11-1923
BOWEN, John P., 1849-1925
BOWEN, Jane H., 1851-1916
BLYTHE, Lucille, 10-11-1915 10-19-1969
WHITE, Margarett Alice, 1880-1974
        married 1897
WHITE, William Thomas, 1877-1950
JONES, Robert C., 1844-1922
JONES, Cordie M., 1860-1935
JONES, Robert Bowen, 1908-1912
DE LOACH, K. S., son of Era KING DE LOACH, 8-20-1912 8-24-1912
DE LOACH, Josephine F., 6-16-1865 10-18-1902
FOSTER, Mary E., 1844-1924
SCOTT, Eugene Douglas, 1911-1931
TODD, Edward L., died 8-4-1926
WILLIS, W. C., 1885-1968
1 - Funeral Marker Unreadable
WILLIS, D. B., 1848-1889
WILLIS, Mattie Y., 1850-1937
KING, Tolbert, son of Mr. & Mrs. Jas. H., 11-23-1893 11-18-1911

KING, Nancy T., 1862-1949
KING, James H., 1857-1930
DE LOACH, Eva KING, 1-31-1884 1-18-1962
BROWNLOW, Willie Mae, 10-18-1889 5-10-1965
KING, Ruth E., 8-31-1903 11-4-1972
          married 6-12-1921
KING, Ray W., 10-10-1902 5-21-1973
HOFF, J. C., 3-31-1855 8-19-1917
HOFF, Zora BELL, 1874-1975
CASTLEBERRY, Felix H., 3-16-1886 5-23-1958
CASTLEBERRY, Mattie L., 10-23-1891 No Date
COOK, J. C., died 11-22-1918
ROPER, Mattie HORNE, 1847-1928
ROPER, G. H., son of O. J. & Mattie, 12-1-1877 9-2-1879
LYONS, Thomas J., son of W. J. & M. E., 2-25-1871 9-17-1874
STROUP, Lillie Mary, 1902-1929
JONES, Anna Grace, 11-17-1892 2-1-1966
          married 2-11-1913
JONES, Troy P., 1-8-1892 10-6-1973
PENNINGTON, D. C., 1882-1930
ERWIN, Laura WINEINGER, 1887-1941
ERWIN, R. G. "Bob", 1887-1948
ERWIN, Twins, 1927-1927
ERWIN, Twins, 1927-1927
LINSTEADT, Myrt, 10-21-1919 9-4-1950
LINSTEADT, Teddy, 10-21-1919 1-13-1952
MC GUFFIN, W. E., Bois D Arc Camp # 3, W. O. W., 11-9-1872 10-20-1909
MC GUFFIN, Lula B., dau. of J. H. & M. M., 8-24-1871 8-26-1871
MC GUFFIN, Geo. Allen, son of J. H. & M. M. , 11-2-1877 11-3-1878
HORN, Isa Dore C., dau. of J. E. & M. E., 4-25-1874 1-23-1875
HORN, Cora, dau. of J. E. & M. E., 3-27-1882 4-5-1882
HORN, Jimmie, dau. of J. E. & M. E., 7-3-1889 11-6-1889
HORN, Mollie Elizabeth, wife of J. E., 7-5-1857 6-14-1892
HORN, J. E., 5-3-1849 5-27-1929
HORN, Ida K., wife of J. E., 2-19-1856 6-8-1910
KING, Larry, No Dates
HORNE, W. A., 11-4-1823 9-19-1885
HORNE, Mrs. N. W., 5-22-1823 1-14-1906
WARREN, Amy N., wife of J. L., 5-12-1855 12-31-1905
WARRENBURG, D. Y., 9-22-1853 12-12-1880
WARRENBURG, Cordelia, dau. of D. Y. & A. N., 2-28-1878 12-17-1879
WARRENBURG, Edna, dau. of D. Y. & A. N., 9-6-1876 8-1-1877
WARREN, J. L., 11-14-1853 2-4-1913
STEELE, David A., 11-21-1883 3-21-1961
STEELE, Hattie B., 3-26-1883 11-3-1941
ERWIN, Barbara Sue, 1935-1953
ERWIN, Leo, 1914-1971
BRANCH, James E., 12-11-1903 12-2-1934
SIMMONS, James Rueben, 1880-1933
SIMMONS, Mattie Lee, 1885-1957
HORNE, G. A., 7-11-1918 3-18-1922
HORNE, Clara, 10-16-1893 2-9-1971
HORNE, Allie, 1-7-1891 No Date
WINEGER, Mrs. L. H. "Mattie", 3-21-1878 2-15-1963

WINEGER, L. H. "Louis", 4-19-1868 7-31-1943
HORNE, George S., 6-11-1853 9-16-1925
HORNE, S. M., 12-2-1857 10-25-1939
HORNE, Mrs. W. A., 1861-1938
HORNE, W. A., 1851-1939
REAGAN, Grover C., 10-23-1888 10-12-1953
OWENS, William, 1815-1895
OWENS, Elizabeth, 1844-1905
WRIGHT, John T., 1867-1926
WOODARD, Aubrey Joe, 5-6-1930 7-3-1930
BUNTON, Charlie E., 1857-1941
BUNTON, Elizabeth, 1848-1925
HARPER, Robert J., 5-4-1850 10-10-1931
HARPER, Loretta E., 8-25-1851 2-22-1923
SPRADLING, Hugh D., Sr., 11-2-1890 11-3-1958
        married 5-10-1934
SPRADLING, Annie M., 8-4-1905 3-22-1972
SPRADLING, Hugh D., Tex., Pfc., Co. H., 359 Inf., W. W. I.,
                            11-2-1890 11-4-1958

SULLIVAN, P., Sr., 1861-1933
SULLIVAN, Alta M., 1885-1928
PATTILLO, George L., 9-4-1864 8-17-1925
PATTILLO, S. Electa, 4-17-1877 No Date
PADEN, Anderson P., 1850-1926
SARGENT, J. W., 12-6-1927 12-29-1928
SARGENT, John, 12-6-1927 1-18-1928
NORRIS, Mrs. J. P., 1875-1927
NORRIS, J. P., 1866-1932
WILDE, Ed L., 4-17-1867 8-1-1938
WILDE, Essie H., 3-22-1875 5-9-1925
WILDE, Maurice H., Tex. Sgt., Co. H., 359 Inf., W. W. I.,
                            11-23-1891 4-1-1963

WRIGHT, William L., 1859-1938
WRIGHT, Dola, 1869-1928
BOLTON, Lucille, 1-8-1908 11-5-1912
BOLTON, Dale, 12-6-1912 6-2-1915
BOLTON, E. D., 1884-1949
BOLTON, Annie M., 8-6-1882 8-30-1963
COLE, Mattie B., 1869-1947
LILLY, Joel R., 1868-1928
LILLY, Jennie R., 1875-No Date
MERRELL, Alma BOLTON, 1909-1928
WICKER, James T., 7-26-1843 4-21-1928
WICKER, Nancy E., 1852-1945
FRASER, Stephen H., 4-20-1890 4-20-1957
CHRISTOPHERSON, James S., 2-7-1881 8-27-1962
CHRISTOPHERSON, Mary Ann, 2-24-1885 1-31-1957
BARKER, Nellie, 1900-1930
FLOYD, Lessley F., 1900-1964
TURNER, Elmer, 4-19-1880 11-1-1937
TURNER, Jimmye A., 9-1-1885 3-8-1964
TURNER, Charles A., 3-19-1909 10-16-1930
WESTON, Milam, 1901-1930
WESTON, Teddlee Naomi, 1901-1963

TAYLOR, J. Wallace, 1874-1928
SHIPP, Raymond Lonzo, 8-4-1879 3-10-1941
SHIPP, Maud Lou, 3-19-1885 5-9-1952
WEBB, Mrs. A. S., 1853-1931
MORROW, Foster, 11-6-1878 9-13-1944
MORROW, Emma, 4-15-1872 11-19-1931
MOYERS, Celesta B., 3-23-1887 7-17-1971
MOYERS, Jacob B., 2-20-1881 6-30-1931
MARTIN, Claude L., 12-8-1897 9-26-1973
MARTIN, Mrs. Claude L., 1907-1959
MARTIN, Bobbie Jack, 7-1931 8-1932
SHIELDS, Johnnie Mae ENGLAND, 2-25-1894 8-22-1931
GUICE, Taylor, 11-16-1889 12-9-1931
GUICE, Jacob H., 3-22-1857 3-5-1932
FREY, Bess GUICE, 10-9-1892 8-26-1965
WARREN, Boyd, 1904-1932
WOLFE, Virginia M., 1891-1975
MILLER, A. P., 3-1-1887 6-1-1939
MILLER, A. Harrell, 1916-1933
WESTON, Palestine W., 5-8-1859 1-18-1941
WESTON, Mary Jane, 11-12-1861 6-30-1939
WRIGHT, Spencer L., 1861-1940
WRIGHT, Minnie M., 1863-1939
TUCKER, William Adam, No Dates
TUCKER, Mary Elizabeth, No Dates
TUCKER, Elizabeth HAUK, No Dates
DUNCAN, Lewis J., 1871-1944
DAUGHENS, Annie HENDERSON, 2-24-1872 12-3-1938
GREGG, Kate HENDERSON, 1883-12-9-1919
NORMAN, Mary O., 1908-1938
NORMAN, William M., 1937-1938
NORMAN, Jarrell E., 12-28-1933 12-30-1933
CAMPBELL, John Edgar, 9-2-1876 8-24-1955
CAMPBELL, Martha TENDER, 9-10-1849 11-18-1937
CAMPBELL, Thomas Jefferson, 9-4-1871 12-29-1959
MURRELL, Eloise CAMPBELL, 11-21-1882 2-11-1966
FITZWATER, Grace CAMPBELL, 5-5-1878 2-2-1964
FITZWATER, John William, 5-12-1876 1-8-1952
ILIFF, Mrs. Carl "May", 8-20-1879 7-17-1973
ILIFF, Carl A., 8-17-1881 1-25-1941
WICKER, Elizabeth G., 1-4-1890 11-12-1936
RAY, Lucy A., 1863-1950
RAY, John S., 1857-1936
RAY, William B., 1899-1933
SHAW, Mattie, 1867-1940
SHAW, T. J., 1861-1922
MC ALLISTER, A. G., 1894-1923
IRBY, Murfee, 1877-1923
ALLEN, Helen F., 1903-1960
BAIRD, Mrs. Hamilton, 1873-1956
HAMILTON, W. R., 1870-1919
HAMILTON, Melva "Hamp", 1-27-1910 1-31-1976
WHATLEY, Vennie S., 1879-1951
SHOFNER, Mrs. Boyd E., 1887-1929

SHOFNER, Boyd E., 1877-1935
HENDERSON, W. E. "Bill", 1884-1950
HENDERSON, Nettie S., 1890-1923
CANTRELL, John M., 1894-1968
CANTRELL, Dr. Charles E., 1859-1919
CANTRELL, Perrilda E., 1862-1934
CANTRELL, Hugh D., 1884-1920
CANTRELL, D. F., 1880-1949
CANTRELL, Martha J. REIMERS, 3-6-1893 12-16-1931
PRATT, James W., 1882-1964
PRATT, Verna, 1884-1932
THOMASON, John Robert, 1865-1933
THOMASON, Rosa Belle, 1871-1938
DUFF, Gordon C., 7-23-1897 10-25-1941
DUFF, Sam C., 12-11-1864 11-17-1928
DUFF, Eolia D., wife of Sam C., 1865-1919
DUFF, Margaret, 1-8-1906 3-1-1923
LEE, Glenna D., 12-17-1891 4-5-1944
DOLL, Frederick W., 1869-1937
MC CLAIN, Ray C., 1898-1934
SMITH, Hassie B., 1885-1926
SMITH, Sperry A., 11-1-1851 3-14-1919
SMITH, Sallie D., 9-13-1861 5-14-1937
SMITH, John Will, 1883-1954
DEES, Nannie P., 1867-1943
DEES, Robert E., 1862-1919
DEES, Hulbert G., 1911-1937
DITZLER, Elzada C., 1879-1960
DITZLER, William C., 1868-1924
NEAL, James Ray, Corpl., 90 M. P. Co., died 4-1-1930
NEAL, J. R., 8-30-1893 4-1-1930
ELLIS, L. H., 1-21-1861 12-27-1928
ELLIS, Mrs. L. H., 6-1-1869 6-7-1965
ORR, Ben E., 1875-1929
SMITH, W. Andy, 1859-1933
SMITH, Mary A., 1866-No Date
ALLEN, James W., 1883-1966
        married 5-7-1905
ALLEN, Hattie A., 1887-No Date
WRIGHT, Homer G., 11-14-1888 10-16-1930
MOORE, Thomas Nall, 1889-1939
JOHNSON, Benjamin Franklin, 1883-1932
CLARK, James G., 11-17-1871 4-9-1948
CLARK, Mary Lee, 4-21-1874 12-30-1934
MC GREGOR, Hattie M., 1875-1956
MC GREGOR, Charles D., 1875-1935
DAVENPORT, Maria S., 1856 12-20-1915
JOHNSON, Sarah Jennie Lynn, 1863-1955
JOHNSON, James Washington, 1858-1937
TERRY, Billy Carl, Tex., Avn. Cadet A. A. F., W. W. II.,
                                8-26-1924 5-29-1966
TERRY, Mary Anne, 12-27-1929 5-14-1932
DICKEY, Flora Alma TERRY, 4-8-1896 6-14-1946
TERRY, Wm. Carl, Tex., Sgt., 312 Repair Unit, M.T.C., died 4-3-1937

GLASSCOE, Martha Marie, 7-24-1947 7-27-1947
MOLEN, Claude E., 2-15-1887 5-13-1961
SHAW, Jason C., 12-23-1873 11-22-1948
SHAW, Katie F., 12-14-1881 12-11-1969
ELLIOTT, George W., 1870-1945
ELLIOTT, Martha E., 1868-1949
DUKE, Myrtle R., 11-8-1899 7-4-1920
DUKE, Myrtle Lara, 7-22-1917 7-4-1920
BARLOW, Louise, 1867-1918
BARLOW, Rosalie, 1845-1922
BARLOW, Charra E., 1878-1960
BARLOW, Valeria E., 1880-1961
BARLOW, Dora B., 1876-1914
BARLOW, Edwin D., 1873-1943
LA ROE, J. F., Jr., 1884-1919
LA ROE, Rose L., 1876-1966
LA ROE, Emma Frances, 1856-1946
LA ROE, John Franklin, 1853-1921
WILLIAMS, Grace, 1887-1957
WILLIAMS, Joe D., 1887-1941
LOCKHART, Thomas Ellis, 1885-1946
LOCKHART, Ethleen DOBBS, 1887-1921
BROOKS, Winnie, died 1-18-1927
BROOKS, Samuel B., 1877-1930
CAMP, Hugh B., Tex., 1st. Lt., 166 Depot Brig., W. W. I
                              10-2-1895 10-4-1948
CAMP, Mrs. W. R. J., 5-30-1862 1-18-1941
CAMP, W. R. J., 3-28-1862 12-11-1929
CAMP, R. P. "Fritz", 1-19-1889 9-29-1944
RABB, James Barney, 1857-1939
RABB, Mattie BELL, 1856-1938
HART, Burtus Rabb, 1903-1918
HART, Bama Adelyne, 1901-1920
HART, Mrs. Patti, 1882-1959
ORAND, Mrs. Idabell, 1876-1953
JONES, Mrs. Bessie WISE, No Dates
JONES, Jeff Cole, No Dates
ADKINSON, James W., 1864-1952
ADKINSON, Florence N., 1870-1919
JENNETT, Jureta Roselle, died 1-4-1925
JENNETT, John William, died 4-10-1927
JENNETT, Norma R., died 2-7-1966
LANGFORD, Mary J. F., 1-8-1838 9-3-1921
DUCK, Mrs. Mildred, 1891-1975
DUCK, Allen Douglas, 8-2-1884 6-3-1926
MC SPADDEN, James Anderson, 1-22-1862 5-25-1961
MC SPADDEN, Ida LANGFORD, 7-13-1874 3-9-1955
JONES, Lois MC SPADDEN, 5-17-1895 9-28-1956
MC LARRY, Herbert I., 4-4-1887 6-8-1962
MC LARRY, Ann, 1918-1918
MC LARRY, Jan, 1918-1918
MC LARRY, Billy Jo, 6-6-1920 1-28-1921
MC LARRY, Herbert I., Jr., 1923-1926
COOPER, Arch, 1856-1928

COOPER, Mary, 1862-1938
COOPER, Mattie Lou, 2-11-1896 1-3-1960
SIMMONS, Linnie Lee, 9-27-1888 7-1-1971
GEAR, Daniel Beecher, 1887-1929
MC LARRY, Virginia, 1859-1937
MC LARRY, John I., 1856-1930
IVY, John F., 1873-1940
IVY, Jessie W., 1877-1973
DOBBS, William O., Tex., 1st. Sgt., 66 Cav. RCN TRP, 66 Inf. Div. W. W. II
                                    6-13-1911 1-4-1945
DOBBS, Cenie Mae, 4-17-1894 2-12-1927
DOBBS, William Christopher, 9-14-1880 3-26-1959
KIZER, Sallie, 1874-1968
KIZER, J. V., 1870-1926
ELLIS, Mary C., 1852-1929
ELLIS, J. W., 1843-1935
DREW, Ruth MC WHIRTER, 9-12-1886 2-22-1973
MC WHIRTER, Rev. Charles Ira, 7-28-1849 3-26-1935
MC WHIRTER, Mary SAMUEL, 3-6-1861 3-19-1924
MC WHIRTER, H. Hugh, 2-10-1893 5-1-1972
MC WHIRTER, Estelle, 5-27-1896 12-16-1960
DUNCAN, Elizabeth, 1867-1946
DUNCAN, Charles, 2-19-1866 7-15-1926
YORK, Hazel ALLISON, 1893-1945
LANCASTER, Sarah Belle, 1866-1935
LANCASTER, Harvey F., 1865-1931
LANCASTER, Henry Curtis, 1887-1925
HOOKER, A. E., 5-3-1835 6-8-1924
MC BRIDE, Mollie M., 1871-1961
MC BRIDE, Ollie, 1904-1962
STRICKLAND, Eleanor Jean C., 1910-1942
CRABB, Eula MC BRIDE, 1891-1961
CRABB, Martha Lois, 1914-1921
NEYLAND, Mayo Williams, 1861-1949
NEYLAND, Mrs. Emily W., 1838-1924
NEYLAND, Pauline LEWIS, 1861-1932
NEYLAND, Robert Reese, 1858-1935
FITZPATRICK, Jennie, wife of J. C., 12-28-1850 12-7-1923
DIAL, Alma HARGETT, 9-12-1867 3-30-1926
HARGETT, William B., 6-15-1838 1-29-1924
DIAL, Joseph G., 4-29-1859 1-5-1924
DIAL, Oscar Hargett, 10-25-1900 7-27-1930
CRAIN, Elizabeth DIAL, 8-24-1893 9-5-1954
WHITE, Susan RILEY, 8-31-1870 11-7-1946
WHITE, W. B., 1-24-1866 11-24-1931
WHITE, R. Clyde, 1-23-1894 4-5-1964
WHITE, William Archie, 1889-1973
WHITE, Viola B., 1894-1966
POWELL, Mrs. G. Veston, 1887-1934
POWELL, Galveston V., Tex., Pvt., Co. C., 3 Rgt. Tex. Inf., S. M. War
                                    3-3-1881 5-10-1966
WHITE, J. C., 1858-1923
WHITE, Nancy J., 1868-1947
WHITE, Elizabeth, 1894-1936

ADAIR, Albert G., 1855-1919
MC CLINTOCK, Alfred Adair, 1917-1948
KENNEDY, Charles T., 1868-1923
KENNEDY, Ann B., 1871-1954
HANEY, Helen P., 8-8-1927 3-15-1931
COOK, Dr. S. C., 1883-1968
COOK, Willie Elizabeth, 1885-1958
COOK, Cora Lee, 1889-1920
BOSWELL, Virginia Lee, 1916-1969
PEELER, George L., 1847-1918
PEELER, Josie DUNBAR, 1855-1936
CARAWAY, A. S., 1846-1933
CARAWAY, Mary J., 1868-1942
CARAWAY, Lucy A., wife of A. S., 1847-1920
LITTLE, Nathaniel C., 12-4-1861 9-24-1931
LITTLE, Lillie H., 11-26-1969 5-17-1948
SMITH, Alice PEELER, 1879-1943
WALLACE, Isaac E., 3-12-1900 10-19-1956
WALLACE, Jessie Lee, 11-1-1896 No Date
WILBANKS, Lenora B., 1875-1903
WILBANKS, Dr. M. L., 1874-1941
WILBANKS, Mrs. M. L., 1878-1965
WILBANKS, Aelda V., 1899-1918
WILBANKS, Jacob B., 1847-1931
WILBANKS Ophelia, 1846-1931
TOLBERT, Jay T., Tex., Tec-4, 95 Gen. Hospt., W. W. II
                                        9-4-1916 1-5-1961

SUDDUTH, Harriett Ann, 1866-1947
SUDDUTH, Tom, died 9-17-1920
TOLBERT, Della S., 7-1886 11-1954
TOLBERT, J. D., 1876-1937
CONE, Mary J., 1873-1942
CONE, F. H., 1874-1950
CONE, W. E., 1899-1918
ALSOBROOK, W. W., 11-12-1850 7-31-1925
PAYNE, Ella SCOTT, 1-8-1855 5-26-1927
PAYNE, Lewis, 11-4-1852 1-15-1930
EAST, Thomas H., 4-26-1892 10-28-1918
EAST, Ella Maebelle, 4-26-1892 10-27-1918
CHEEK, C. Spurgen, 3-19-1893 2-11-1921
CHEEK, James N., 5-26-1887 11-19-1958
CHEEK, C. E., 6-20-1858 1-13-1919
CHEEK, Sarah, 7-11-1861 4-14-1929
CHEEK, Layton, son of C. E. & S. L., 9-4-1903 9-21-1906
CHEEK, John M., 1875-1955
CHEEK, Ella K., 1881-1974
CHEEK, Edna L., 5-22-1890 1-19-1936
CORLEY, Douglas, 1924-1932
WATSON, Homer, 1880-1946
GREENWADE, Paul V. "Pevy", 1893-1959
GREENWADE, Nora M., 1897-1968
HOWELL, Willie, 1878-1964
HOWELL, James, 1868-1922
HOSKINS, Ernestine N., 11-27-1897 No Date

HOSKINS, Colonel Otis, 11-16-1884 12-24-1966
HOSKINS, Infant Dau. of Mr. & Mrs. C. O., 5-19-1919 5-19-1919
NORMAN, Irline, 10-22-1899 3-16-1970
NORMAN, O'Neal, 1933-1940
NORMAN, W. Hiram, 1901-1934
NORMAN, William L., 1860-1939
NORMAN, Mary E., 1869-1920
SIMMONS, Mrs. Watt B., 1876-1936
SIMMONS, Watt B., 1871-1936
WHITEHEAD, Dave B., 1896-1957
BOYLE, Stella R., 12-19-1878 1-9-1929
BOYLE, John O., 8-29-1868 4-26-1941
SMITH, Mile Allen, 1885-1944
SMITH, Quie E., 1874-1954
SMITH, Ben T., 1873-1938
MONROE, Mrs. J. H., 10-29-1876 8-18-1968
MONROE, J. H., 12-4-1866 3-12-1933
MONROE, Ed Balthrop, 8-8-1908 9-6-1915
MILLER, Wesley M., 1-1-1868 6-24-1931
MILLER, Fannie L., 1-11-1869 7-16-1940
BUTLER, W. A., 10-9-1892 6-13-1974
BUTLER, Bessie, wife of J. J., 11-5-1858 12-9-1943
BUTLER, J. J., 11-21-1853 12-5-1928
MAYS, J. B. "Bac", 2-21-1901 11-26-1974
MAYS, Johnnie M., 7-1-1916 No Date
MC BRIDE, Bertha CASTLEBERRY, 1881-1949
MC BRIDE, Albert Sidney, 1872-1932
WEEDEN, Haidee May, 1879-1949
WEEDEN, William Clinton, 1869-1931
CASTLEBERRY, James Watkins, 1849-1936
CASTLEBERRY, Martha Jo Anna, 1860-1933
WHATLEY, Lucy Elizabeth, 5-27-1869 2-19-1946
WHATLEY, Jack, 7-7-1903 8-22-1931
WHATLEY, Seaborn Jones, 3-26-1858 1-10-1940
WISE, Vida SWIFT, 1878-1966
WISE, W. B., 1866-1938
BERRY, W. R. "Bill", 1899-1968
WISE, Arthur O., 1893-1956
WISE, Rogers C., 11-9-1895 11-17-1964
SULLIVAN, Otus U., 4-7-1888 1-26-1949
ROBERTS, Mary E., 12-13-1872 12-20-1971
FISHER, Edith IVY, 1910-1955
KERR, Kizzie R., 1871-1948
BABCOCK, Charles H., 1862-1948
BABCOCK, Abram D., 1896-1924
BABCOCK, Carrie Louise, 1872-1944
VAUGHN, Benjamin Franklin, 1871-1957
VAUGHN, Amelia UP-THE-GROVE, 1875-1931
HAGAN, Burgess M., Pfc., U. S. Army, W. W. I., 6-10-1896 11-10-1971
MC LAIN, Clarence E., 11-18-1872 9-24-1927
MC LAIN, Susie M,. 7-22-1875 7-27-1963
MC LAIN, A. L., Tex., Pvt., Cen. Inf., Off., TNC SCH., W. W. I.,
                            6-4-1899 10-23-1938
MC LAIN, Clarence E., Jr., Tex., Sgt., 556 Bomb Sq., AAF, W. W. II.,

11-11-1904 9-30-1957

MURPHY, Elizabeth L., 8-18-1848 7-3-1937
THOMPSON, Lamar, 1-19-1873 11-11-1962
THOMPSON, Sarah Esther, 4-5-1877 8-8-1953
GREEN, Johnnie May, 1905-1932
GREEN, Margaret ELLIS, 1877-1954
GREEN, Marvin Elmer, 1877-1959
TISCHMACHER, Jack, 1876-1933
WINEINGER, Mrs. W. M., 10-10-1867 9-24-1962
WINEINGER, M. W., 2-7-1856 11-4-1946
NORRIS, William Walter, 5-28-1880 9-2-1951
LEINART, Velma FISHER, 7-26-1916 7-14-1973
FISHER, Herman H., 3-20-1914 5-5-1965
TURNER, Billie, 1906-No Date
TURNER, William G., 1899-1951
ROBERTS, Washington D., Tex., Mus., 1st. Cl., U. S. Army, W. W. I.,
                                    2-22-1895 3-17-1973
SHARP, Frances Ann, 2-16-1946 11-17-1963
KALE, Ada M., 1890-1963
KALE, Doss M., 1881-1949
FLETCHER, Lela J., 1-31-1897 2-13-1961
FLETCHER, James R., Tex., Pfc., 37 Inf., W. W. I., 1-24-1891 3-18-1949
GREAVES, Robert Wesley, 11-13-1889 No Date
GREAVES, Mattie FRANK, 3-16-1889 4-14-1975
TAYLOR, Mary C., 1876-1950
FACTOR, Verue D., 10-22-1898 No Date
FACTOR, Weldon E., 7-6-1888 11-5-1959
GEORGE, Jesse F., 9-15-1884 2-22-1949
GEORGE, Mrs. Jesse F., died 12-6-1960
FAIN, Dr. John N., 1868-1930
COOK, Mrs. J. N., 3-28-1862 2-8-1937
COOK, Ray, son of Mr. & Mrs. J. N., 1911-1927
COOK, Jack, son of Mr. & Mrs. J. N., 1929-1970
COOK, John H., 1884-1975
SWEETON, Clyde A., 12-7-1876 8-22-1935
SWEETON, Rowena EASTMAN, 1-31-1880 9-5-1928
PHIPPS, Emmett, 1879-1951
PHIPPS, Mrs. Alpha A., 1882-1973
PHIPPS, Alpha A., 1883-No Date
PHIPPS, Curtis, 1916-1946
KILLOUGH, W. G., 1912-1969
JARED, Eunice J., 1894-1946
JARED, J. Preston, 1892-1967
LAING, Lula R., 3-25-1887 5-9-1970
LAING, Thomas D., 4-24-1886 1-13-1971
HODGES, Carrie BURNS, 8-24-1886 No Date
HODGES, Gus Macey, 8-24-1883 6-4-1961
GILLHAM, James D., 1903-1971
KLOXIN, Thelma L., 12-2-1900 No Date
KLOXIN, Arnold E., 4-5-1905 No Date
ROBERTS, V. Darr, 2-22-1855 3-17-1973
LANE, Mary L., 8-5-1878 2-3-1949
LANE, Charles L., 3-11-1870 No Date
OWENS, Oscar C., 1-11-1894 1-10-1969

OWENS, Carrie E., 3-30-1900 No Date
OWENS, Ira Tom, 4-8-1873 3-26-1942
OWENS, Myrtle Ann, 12-30-1876 6-17-1931
KELLY, William M., Jr., 1908-1966
KELLY, William M., Sr., 1872-1951
KELLY, Mary Lou, 1872-1951
KELLY, Mamie Lou, 1877-1949
HALL, George B., 2-16-1861 11-27-1924
HALL, Minnie, 9-19-1874 3-13-1971
HALL, Mary L., Dau., of G. B. & M., 10-30-1895 10-31-1895
HUFFMAN, Velma HAYTER, 1891-1962
HUFFMAN, William G., Jr., 1890-1930
MC KINNEY, Alpha Omega, 1869-1960
MC KINNEY, John Thomas, 1869-1931
ALLEN, John Thomas, 1-13-1838 11-17-1919
ALLEN, Morning M., 4-8-1859 12-22-1935
ALLEN, George W., 9-17-1888 9-22-1920
HALE, Joan, dau. of Mr. & Mrs. J. F., died 12-14-1941
WINANS, Lewis H., 8-23-1891 1-15-1969
WINANS, Mary, wife of L. H., 5-21-1897 3-25-1928
WINANS, Effie L., 11-6-1870 12-4-1943
WINANS, Henry S., 9-11-1860 6-1-1940
MEEKS, J. W., 1869-1946
MEEKS, Mrs. J. W., 1874-1932
HAMILTON, Ray B., 10-22-1902 No Date
HAMILTON, Gladys E., 4-20-1903 No Date
SMITH, Guy, 7-4-1876 4-23-1954
SMITH, Bessie M., 3-8-1876 10-2-1964
PERDUE, James Edwin, 2-28-1931 11-12-1933
HANEY, Infant, died 1937
PATZOLT, Fritz, 1884-1942
SADLER, Grover C., 8-6-1885 11-20-1959
SADLER, Lena E., 6-9-1885 No Date
BOWEN, Eula V., 1889-1973
BOWEN, George T., 1889-1971
PORTER, James B., 1876-1956
PORTER, Eva M., 1875-1948
ROSS, Joel W., 1883-1952
ROSS, Pearl B., 1886-1957
WILLIAMS, Granville E., 4-6-1903 1-2-1973
WILLIAMS, Virgie L., 11-23-1906 No Date
WILLIAMS, Infant son of G. F. & Virgie L., died 3-17-1935
TROY, Mike, 2-20-1925 3-8-1938
JACKSON, Lyda R., 1857-1938
WEEMS, Andrew J., 1872-1951
WEEMS, Maude M., 1879-1954
CHARLES, Ben N., 1883-1951
CHARLES, Arthur G., 4-23-1909 10-29-1965
CHARLES, Mertle M., 1885-1950
HARPER, James Elsie, 1880-1941
HARPER, Delia ROSS, 1885-No Date
HARPER, Lawson H., Tex., s-1, U. S. N. R., W. W. II., 5-13-1908 2-15-1962
MC KINNEY, W. R., 7-26-1886 10-17-1960
MC KINNEY, Mrs. W. R., 2-20-1887 4-10-1965

MC KINNEY, Thomas Young, 6-21-1906 2-19-1945
WILKINSON, Nellie J., 12-30-1870 5-7-1954
POTTS, H. C., 1873-1946
POTTS, Alice V. "Birdie", 1897-1971
PATTILLO, H. C. "Pat", 10-13-1925 12-19-1970
TURNER, Sam D., 1893-1962
TURNER, Nancy S., 1895-No Date
TURNER, Arthur, 1914-1950
WEBB, John W., 1879-1961
WEBB, Mrs. Mary S., 1888-1976
NICHOLSON, E. M., 5-28-1870 11-26-1956
SKAGGS, Noah Adolphus, 5-20-1889 6-24-1956
WOODSON, Willie W., 3-8-1892 10-22-1957
BARKLEY, Thomas A., 2-5-1876 4-27-1950
ABELL, Mary Siney, 6-1-1871 9-11-1955
SHIRRA, Pette, 1875-1952
MIRACLE, O. O. "Fussie", 11-28-1900 5-11-1958
FOWLER, James H., 1927-1966
FOWLER, Willie D., 2-1-1894 3-8-1974
FOWLER, Herman, 12-25-1886 2-21-1931
HUTCHINGS, Bobby D., 1957-1965
HUTCHINGS, Bernei Ray, Tex., Cpl., U. S. Army, 2-15-1932 10-30-1965
MC CONN, James Clifton, 3-27-1903 11-6-1948
HUTCHINGS, James R., 1954-1965
TURNER, Marvin L., Tex., Pvt., 4th. Tex. Inf., N. G., died 7-11-1937
HARBUCK, Lillian, 1887-1973
HARBUCK, A. L., 1875-1951
FULCHUM, Fannie E., 8-30-1894 9-1-1896
SWINNEY, Curtis L., 1906-1940
TURNER, Chandler, 1893-1921
TURNER, Ida F., 1867-1955
TURNER, Harvey, 1867-1935
THOMPSON, Charlie F., 1911-1966
1 - Funeral Marker Unreadable
FRYER, Lt. William T., Co. A., 5th. Ky. Mtd. Inf., C.S.A., 1838-1883
SWINNEY, Idora May, dau. of W. A. & E. F., 5-15-1880 9-10-1880
SWINNEY, Hoyt L., 2-11-1908 11-14-1928
SWINNEY, N. L., 10-14-1876 10-11-1928
WARD, Jas. W., M. D., 1879-1956
WARD, Rena STRICKLAND, 1884-1968
WARD, Irvan M., M. D., 1906-1965
PENNINGTON, D. G., 1882-1930
JONES, Anna Grace, 11-17-1892 2-1-1966
          married 2-11-1913
JONES, Troy P., 1-8-1892 10-6-1973
STROUP, Lillie May, 1902-1929
THOMASSON, Frank V., 9-19-1926 12-24-1960
BRIGHAM, J. A., 1888-1931
CORLEY, Nellie B. VESTAL, 1905-1965
CORLEY, Ennus C., 1874-1955
CORLEY, Rosa B., 1880-1929
TURNER, Mrs. Mina, 9-19-1882 8-22-1928
SNELL, Harriett Elphine, 1858-1928
SNELL, James Rogers, 1858-1931

PALUCH, Delsie THOMASSON, 3-9-1908   12-23-1960
LUPFORD, Hattie, 1902-1929
FOWLER, Willie D., 2-1-1894   3-8-1974
        married 8-20-1911
FOWLER, Herman, 12-25-1886   2-21-1931
FOWLER, James H., 1927-1966
MIRACLE, A. O. "Fussie", 11-28-1900   5-11-1958
BUNCH, L. Kermit, Tex. Cem., U. S. N. R., W. W. II., 12-28-1908   2-3-1961
DUCK, Elizabeth CANDLER, 1891-1976
CANDLER, George N., 1873-1931
CANDLER, Izola Marie, 10-3-1914   6-26-1924
CANDLER, Olga Daze, died age 3 yrs.
HAMILTON, Sanford, Co. B., 22nd. Ohio Inf., No Dates
BLAIR, Mrs. Kittie, 1899-1970
HARWELL, Samuel E., 1867-1929
HARWELL, Sarah B., 1867-1951
2 - Stones Unreadable
COOK, John C., 11-9-1859   12-22-1933
COOK, Camiller I., 2-7-1859   12-30-1933
ERWIN, Laura WINEINGER, 1887-1941
ERWIN, R. G. "Bob", 1887-1948
ERWIN, Twins, 1927-1927
LINSTEART, Myrt, 10-21-1919   1-13-1952
LINSTEART, Teddie, 9-4-1950   1-13-1952
ERWIN, Leo, 1914-1971
ERWIN, Barbara Sue, 1935-1953
WARD, William B., 1876-1934
WARD, Sallie B., 1878-1952
WILSON, Pinkney, 1858-1929
WILSON, Arrie, 1870-1954
KELLY, A. E., 1871-1929
WELLS, Mrs. T. A., 5-31-1856   9-26-1929
WELLS, T. A., 11-16-1856   1-7-1929
ROGERS, Sarah Ida, 10-10-1862   6-9-1945
ROGERS, O. B., 4-19-1858   11-21-1928
MC KINNEY, William Lee, 1885-1963
        married 3-25-1906
MC KINNEY, Bessie REESE, 1888-1970
REESE, Hazel J., dau. of J. T. & Annie, 1901-1902
REESE, M. E., (Brother), 1866-1903
REESE, W. C., (Father), 1841-1911
REESE, E. J., (Mother), 1844-1913
LEWIS, C. W., 1859-1934
DUCK, Walter E., Tex., Pvt., Co. F., 12 Eng., W. W. I., 12-4-1891   6-23-1964
GRANFILL, Thelma KENDALL, 3-11-1902   3-21-1965
WARD, Maud E., 1887-1964
        married 10-25-1908
WARD, J. Rawyer, 1877-1971
VOUGHT, Loreda WARD, 10-25-1909   2-27-1932
WARD, W. B. "Bill", Jr., 1906-1962
PETTERS, Inf. son of Rev. & Mrs. W., died 5-4-1939
HALL, Rosalie "Totsie", 1900-1938
BRANCH, James E., 12-11-1903   12-2-1934
MILLER, A. Harrell, 1916-1933

MILLER, A. P., 3-1-1887 6-1-1939
WOLFE, Virginia M., 1891-1975
BARRETT, A. C., 1919-1967
BENTON, Frank M., 1887-1954
BENTON, Georgia, 1890-1961
BENTON, Frank M., Jr., 1919-1932
BOWEN, Eula V., 1889-1973
BOWEN, George T., 1889-1971
HANEY, Infant, died 1937
PERDUE, James Edwin, 2-28-1933 11-12-1933
MORROW, Foster, 11-6-1878 9-18-1944
MORROW, Emma, 4-15-1872 11-19-1931
SHIELDS, Johnnie Mae ENGLAND, 2-25-1894 8-22-1931
GUICE, Taylor, 11-16-1889 12-9-1931
FREY, Bess GUICE, 10-9-1892 8-26-1965
GUICE, Jacob H., 3-22-1857 3-5-1932
WARREN, Boyd, 1904-1932
SPRADLING, James Christopher, born & died 6-2-1947
SPRADLING, John Lewis, Jr., 7-5-1944 7-8-1944
GREEN, Claud Houston, 5-28-1899 10-11-1954
GREEN, Vivian LAWRENCE, 4-5-1921 4-1-1946
PERRY, Myrtle E., 6-25-1894 3-9-1969
JOHNSON, Therman L., Tex., Pvt., Med. Dept., W. W. I.,
                                    5-28-1899 7-13-1971
JOHNSON, Myrtle C., No Dates
CALDWELL, Ida Lou Vee, 1921-1970
          married 1-23-1942
CALDWELL, T. A., 1918-No Date
PETTY, Cass D., 9-25-1906 7-14-1944
MILLER, Jas. P., No Dates
MILLER, James Tolbert, 12-11-1949 12-12-1949
MILLER, Juadeen D., No Dates
MILLER, E. Cecil, No Dates
MILLER, Alarine D., No Dates
DAMRON, Lorine A., 1891-1972
DAMRON, John W., 1887-1949
BARKER, Sandra, 6-27-1943 4-18-1948
ORR, Robert R., 1894-1975
ORR, Alpha Gladys, 1898-1949
BURNETT, Lena MC BRIDE, 12-19-1882 10-18-1971
BURNETT, William Berry, 8-10-1873 12-3-1948
SHEPPEARD, Gabe, 7-18-1887 8-31-1948
WILLIAMS, J. Herman, 3-11-1904 8-14-1959
WILLIAMS, O. R. "Ott", 6-15-1897 12-9-1969
JENKINS, John W., 5-26-1875 12-9-1954
JENKINS, Nora, 10-1-1879 6-10-1962
KITCHING, J. B., 1874-1953
KITCHING, Alpha G., 1883-1962
HANSON, Nellie Hortense, 2-3-1899 1-22-1951
SHIRRA, Pete, 1875-1952
ABELL, Mary Siney, 6-1-1871 9-11-1955
BARKLEY, Thomas A., 2-5-1876 4-27-1950
YOUNG, Samuel M. "Sammy", 1913-1947
BETHELL, Leon W., 1877-1947

BETHELL, Katherine M., 1881-1959
FAGG, Cary A., 5-11-1880 10-28-1961
FAGG, Edna ROUSE, died 10-15-1946
MONROE, Allie, 1-10-1886 11-16-1956
SIGLER, Mattie, 2-17-1860 12-16-1946
SIGLER, George W., 12-3-1880 4-14-1966
WALKER, Bert J., 1893-1944
HUDSPETH, Lt. Col., John H., 9-10-1908 2-14-1974
HUDSPETH, R. O., 1878-1959
HUDSPETH, Murphy, 1877-1964
CREEL, William R., 1875-1955
CREEL, Mrs. W. R., 1871-1967
CREEL, James E., 11-18-1933 10-10-1948
CREEL, Ione RIGNEY, 1903-1975
PRESLAR, Verbena H., 1881-1960
BUSBY, Delbert G., 1913-1971
HOLLEMAN, Aythchiee, 5-13-1895 7-10-1968
DUNLAP, Jesse Roger, Pfc., U. S. Army, 4-1-1935 7-20-1967
THOMPSON, Cecil F., Tex., Pfc., U. S. Army, W. W. II.,
                              11-24-1904 10-22-1971

HARWELL, Allie, 1895-1970
ACREY, William D., 1879-1950
ACREY, Mary L., 1888-1974
LONG, Exa MOSS, 11-3-1888 1-8-1968
DAWSON, Clyde Eldon, Tex. Sea., U. S. Navy, W. W. I., 1897-1950
LEWIS, Pearl E., 1-8-1904 9-1-1953
WILKES, Rebia, 5-29-1882 4-2-1958
PEARSON, William Robert, 8-31-1919 8-12-1975
          married 12-16-1936
PEARSON, Georgia S., 6-30-1922 No Date
TEDDLIE, Edna P., 4-3-1880 2-22-1959
TEDDLIE, Tillit S., 6-3-1885 No Date
CORBET, Z. X., Sr., 1885-1965
BEAUCHAMP, Tommye, 1902-1968
AUSTIN, Walter, 1898-1952
BERNARD, Lela C., 11-14-1891 5-6-1973
BERNARD, Ed., Sgt., U. S. Army, 3-13-1894 2-25-1975
BENNETT, James T., Sgt, 2nd. Tex. Field Arty, N.G., 6-18-1898 8-13-1944
BENNETT, Inez C., 8-20-1899 4-13-1971
OMOHUNDRO, Samuel, Tex., Sgt., 60 Const. Arty., 1-13-1898 6-5-1946
BADEN, Myrtle, 6-19-1891 8-18-1970
BADEN, William Roy, 5-21-1893 4-20-1960
YOUNGER, W. H. H., 11-17-1858 2-14-1949
YOUNGER, Minnie R., 6-4-1872 11-28-1947
WILLIAMS, Jesse R., 10-27-1868 10-24-1947
WILLIAMS, Martha J., 7-12-1874 6-6-1961
WILLIAMS, George D., 1874-1958
WILLIAMS, Ida C., 1873-1949
RUSSELL, Willie Lee, 1899-1942
GIPSON, Dewey, died 1974
GLASSCOCK, Henry Arthur, 3-3-1884 10-2-1948
GLASSCOCK, Anna Mae, 4-4-1883 No Date
LYDAY, Lewis Ivan, 1886-1931
LYDAY, Nannie Flora, 1887-1963

SHARPLEY, Virginia Jane, 1-17-1917 10-24-1925
SHARPLEY, Carrie Elizabeth USLETON, wife of A. L. SHARPLEY, married 1-30-1916
                                   mother of Virginia Jane, Kathryn Elizabeth,
                                   James Lyttleton SHARPLEY
                                      10-17-1894   1-10-1934
SHARPLEY, Arthur Lyttleton, 10-12-1894 6-23-1968
          married 7-5-1936
SHARPLEY, Locke BALLARD FUGATE, 8-6-1899 12-2-1968
                            Mother of Ken Fugate
SKAGGS, Mathew L., 1-22-1875 2-23-1950
SKAGGS, Bonnie WELLS, 6-5-1903 11-11-1946
DORSETT, Cotton, 3-23-1902 4-17-1950
AVERY, Louisa O., 1880-1955
AVERY, Asa R., 1874-1948
RUSSELL, Roy Logan, 1893-1967
CORLEY, Clotile, 1902-1970
BROWN, Bertha C., 1893-No Date
BROWN, Harvey E., 1892-No Date
PEARSON, Lillian S., 8-17-1894 8-23-1965
PEARSON, William W., Tex., Capt., U. S. A., W. W. I.,
                              6-10-1883 2-13-1949

MC CORMICK, Walter B., 1872-1950
BARR, Alice THURMAN, 1888-1954
THURMAN, Allen G., 1878-1930
GRAY, Morgan, 1879-1894
GRAY, William R., 1850-1916
GRAY, Mollie E., 1852-1926
GRAY, Burke, 1881-No Date
GRAY, Grace O'CONNER, 1885-1932
GRAY, Robert G., 1890-No Date
LEWIS, Pearl E., 1-8-1904 9-1-1953
ARNOLD, Karl O., son of W. M. & M., 7-30-1875 9-25-1876
FAULKNER, A. E., 12-2-1878 6-4-1907
MC NAMEE, Lavina Leander, 1874-1912
MC NAMEE, David Franklin, 1865-1930
MC NAMEE, Julia A., wife of D. F., 1880-1952
HUNT, James S., 7-30-1859 8-17-1908
HUNT, William W., 5-29-1886 8-14-1907
HUNT, Hannah D., 3-16-1823 3-31-1907
HUNT, Richard V., 9-21-1881 9-17-1905
HUNT, Mertlette, 3-24-1859 4-30-1919
HUNT, James L., 12-3-1883 10-12-1958
HUNT, Ollie Otto, Tex., Pfc., U. S. A., W. W. I, PH.,
                              7-29-1891 12-29-1961
HUNT, Mary E., 9-9-1887 8-14-1954
HALE, A. M., 2-8-1822 10-7-1882
HALE, Sarah, wife of A. M., 12-4-1825 11-20-1897
HALE, Doray, 1-7-1883 7-21-1883
WRIGHT, J. W., 5-14-1872 2-21-1902
NIX, Francis M., son of Jim & Renie, 1-7-1904 5-14-1907
HALEY, Thomas W., 1848-1912
HALEY, Mary H., wife of T. W., 1851-1895
WISE, Lula, 1874-No Date
WISE, J. R., 1870-1941

HALEY, Ola COMER, 1873-1936
HALEY, David T., 1870-1939
INGRAM, Della F., wife of W. B., 9-28-1866 8-30-1901
                    Erected by Greenville Grove # 2, W. O. W.
BRAKEBILL, Neppie J., dau. of L. B. & A. M., 11-7-1882 12-20-1889
1 - Stone Broken, Unreadable
MC DONALD, Unreadable   , died 5-24-1878, age 83 yrs., 9 mos., 19 dys.
RYAN, G. W., Sr., 1857-1931
RYAN, Jennie, 1870-1944
RYAN, Kate, 1895-No Date
HALE, Hugh C., 3-15-1829 3-11-1874
HALE, Cordelia, wife of H. C., 1-17-1824 4-26-1871
PREBLE, La Velle Henry, Kansas, Pvt., STU Army TG Corps, W. W. I.,
                    4-5-1900 6-24-1951

DECKER, Owen H., 1889-1966
DECKER, Birdie J., 1885-1947
HOLLOWAY, Talford G., 1886-1946
HOLLOWAY, Sallie B., 1889-1972
MARTIN, Jerry R., 3-3-1912 5-5-1946
MARTIN, Tommie D., 1-31-1916 No Date
GREVE, William W., 1892-1955
GREVE, Nannie Mae, 1893-1945
CHAMBLISS, Benny Ray, 2-17-1940 7-20-1970
ASBERRY, Mrs. Della, 1872-1967
GRAHAM, Victoria HACKNEY, 9-5-1888 No Date
GRAHAM, R. A., 7-6-1888 9-11-1968
KEES, Benton O., 4-16-1904 3-8-1946
SAMFORD, Mrs. Cora, 1888-1962
SAMFORD, William E., 6-28-1882 9-24-1946
WARD, Robert G., Texas, Capt., 191 Tank BN, 45 Inf. Div., W. W. II.,
                    5-18-1916 5-23-1945

MARTIN, George J., 1-29-1887 1-17-1949
MARTIN, Lala B., 4-28-1890 2-27-1964
GREEN, Arthur P., 6-10-1882 1-8-1965
GREEN, Lula BILLINGTON, 10-28-1887 6-30-1960
PERRY, M. F. "Fill", 1856-1948
PERRY, Alice, 1870-1967
HOLLOWAY, Henry E., 1874-1948
HOLLOWAY, Annie S., 1894-1975
THOMPSON, Mrs. W. E., 12-27-1885 5-16-1967
THOMPSON, William E., 12-25-1874 2-22-1949
ENGLAND, Mrs. Nick, Sr., 1902-1971
ENGLAND, Nick M., Sr., 8-6-1887 4-23-1952
NYFELER, Dwight Nicholas, died 10-26-1948
ROWELL, R. L., 1928-1948
AKINS, Y. B., Tex., Pvt., U. S. A., W. W. I., 1-1-1898 11-16-1960
DRAKE, Ollie V., 7-10-1908 2-26-1948
HEAD, Eula Mae, 5-13-1896 2-5-1972
HEAD, L. D. "Dee", 1891-1947
MILTON, Pauline, 8-10-1894 3-1-1947
KERR, W. C., 1856-1941
HOCKETT, David Howard, Tex., Sgt., 9 Regt., U.S.M.C., 3 Div., W. W. II
                    9-21-1925 3-7-1943
TURNER, Ollie G., 11-20-1887 2-4-1966

TURNER, No Names or Dates (CRIPS)
TURNER, NO Names or Dates (CRIPS)
MOSER, Wilma Fay, 2-20-1927 4-13-1948
PEERSON, Thomas Sherwood, 10-4-1868 1-13-1958
PEERSON, Pearl DARNALL, 8-26-1875 10-10-1948
MC CLAIN, Jas. E., 1889-1948
BROTHERTON, Ruby G., 1892-No Date
BROTHERTON, Jas. L., 1883-1953
LUCKETT, Clarence B., 1889-1966
LUCKETT, Annie M., 1895-1962
CAUSEY, Wayne Ray, 6-15-1953 8-13-1953
WADE, Joseph E., 3-31-1891 5-8-1949
GILES, Mary Frances, 11-16-1945 12-3-1948
GILES, V. J., 10-2-1919 12-6-1949
LAINART, Lizzie B., 4-3-1887 4-6-1973
LAINART, Samuel D., 6-25-1881 1-14-1937
HARRIS, L. T. "Buster", 7-4-1911 1-13-1961
STARNES, Rena BLADES, 1876-1954
STARNES, Thomas Dupree, 1876-1954
KERR, Caleb, 1900-1919
KERR, Tina, wife of W. C,, 1870-1920
PRICE, Rufus L., 3-6-1881 10-17-1951
PRICE, Janis A., 5-1-1876 5-17-1959
PRICE, Thomas D., Tex., Pvt., 36 Co., 165 Depot Brig., W. W. I.,
                                6-17-1895 4-10-1960

MAYS, Samuel N., 7-12-1884 4-5-1937
MAYS, Emma STARKEY, 12-14-1889 11-13-1949
MAYS, F. Erdman, 1-22-1916 4-11-1973
WHITE, Mary Magdalene, 1879-1954
WILLIAMS, W. Ernest, 2-10-1877 2-7-1950
WILLIAMS, Sibyl M., 1-31-1911 No Date
MC CAIN, Billy R., Tex., Avn. Cadet, 3024 AAF Base Unit, W. W. II.,
                                12-18-1918 2-24-1951
HALE, James Henley, 9-23-1886 3-25-1953
        married 1-12-1908
HALE, Mattie Lou, 11-17-1887 8-19-1973
JONES, Rufus Calvin, 5-26-1878 6-23-1958
SPRADLING, Nettie, 1888-1975
SPRADLING, Arthur B., 1881-1975
BENNETT, M. Lorena, 10-9-1895 5-8-1968
        married 8-9-1912
BENNETT, Wade L., 7-5-1892 No Date
BENNETT, Lanell & Daughter, 1922-1949
JONES, Jennye V., 1888-1963
JONES, Mona Louise, dau. of Jennie V. & Marvin S., 1913-1925
PATTEN, Bettie, 1885-1949
PATTEN, Loyd H., 1883-1971
MC DONALD, W. C., 1887-1955
MC DONALD, Ollie, 1889-1960
MC DONALD, B. G., 1929-1947
SIMS, D. G., 1931-1947
PRICE, H. Emmett, 1891-1958
DUNKIN, Mitchiner M., 1-4-1895 7-11-1947
TOOLEY, Florence, 1879-1970

LAMBE, Lena, 1909-1937
PICKETT, Bert, 6-30-1909 10-9-1975
PICKETT, Lidy, wife of Bert, 6-26-1915 3-26-1957
COPELAND, Finis T., 10-27-1901 10-21-1975
TYLER, Randy Randall Edward, 1-8-1956 6-26-1963
BAKER, Josephine, 12-11-1871 9-17-1948
COLLINS, Lizzie, 1890-No Date
COLLINS, Cleve C., 1885-1950
BRADLEY, E. Raymond, 1896-1950
CLARK, Charlie, 1882-1949
CLARK, Eula F., 1886-1969
MEREDITH, Harry, 1879-1948
FRAZIER, Mary Ann, 1882-1973
MOORE, Ethel, 5-14-1882 10-4-1947
MOORE, G. F., 12-4-1882 6-25-1965
COPELAND, Forest L., 9-20-1906 2-13-1970
COPELAND, Lorine S., 12-15-1907 No Date
BALL, Mrs. J. F., 1881-1947
BALL, John F., 1876-1958
SMITH, Mary, 1865-No Date
SMITH, B. F., 1857-1947
MC CORMICK, Leona PICKETT, 8-24-1912 8-13-1944
PICKETT, Mary Elizabeth, 2-12-1919 5-15-1938
BACK, Susan E., 9-27-1866 7-25-1946
BACK, Granville B., 3-4-1870 6-21-1940
MORGAN, Mark, 2-24-1870 11-6-1937
MORGAN, Nannie L., 11-4-1874 9-5-1956
OLER, J. K. "King", 1891-1957
OLER, Gladys PORTER, wife of J. K., 1895-1972
PEARCE, A. H. "Lon", 5-8-1884 1-5-1953
ISHMAEL, Malcolm Ray, 1-21-1950 11-6-1952
DUNLAP, Walter D., 1890-1952
BALDWIN, Guy Alton, 10-18-1904 5-15-1957
BALDWIN, Sue P., wife of G. A., 11-24-1905 11-11-1973
CUSHING, Marion Springer, 7-16-1900 3-18-1959
CUSHING, Frank W., Minn., Sgt., 151 FA, 42 R. Div., W. W. II.,
                                    12-29-1898 2-25-1956

BALL, Stanley C., 6-7-1901 11-7-1956
MAUST, Harry Luis, Jr., 1901-1906
MAUST, Mary Lou BANNER, 1877-1970
MAUST, Harry, 1870-1935
WRIGHT, GUs W., 2-24-1885 9-27-1938
WRIGHT, Myrtle, 11-14-1894 12-9-1973
        married 2-11-1912: Children: Mary, Essie, Johnnie, Daphine, Jewel,
                                Wilburn, Dot., and Wanda WRIGHT
HORROCKS, Emma L., 6-26-1876 4-23-1951
HARPER, Cora Lee, 4-5-1879 1-12-1954
HARPER, Louis Elmer, 3-6-1877 5-24-1957
JOHNSON, Christy Ann, 2-28-1962 1-27-1963
MORGAN, Patricia J., 1958-1963
DUGGER, Mary Frances, 1866-1963
SHUFFIELD, Infant, 1967-1967
ROBINSON, Michael L., 1965-1965
BRAND, Sherry Ann, 1-2-1964 1-6-1964

FITCH, Infant Twins, 1967-1967
MULLINS, John, 1963-1963
FITCH, Steven Wayne, 1965-1965
ONLEY, Tony, died 7-4-1965
ONLEY, Joey, died 7-4-1965
TUCKER, Grady O., 1965-1965
BAKER, Jack W., Jr., 1966-1966
GLASSCOE, Guy, 1921-1975
GLASSCOE, William L., 1952-1954
WRIGHT, Addie May, 1894-1948
HIGHSMITH, Lewis W., 1861-1936
HENDERSON, Nora, 1878-1950
HENDERSON, Robert H., 1872-1936
BRECHEEN, Essie M., 1900-1938
BRECHEEN, Dewey R., Tex., Pvt., U.S.A., W. W. II.,
                              5-27-1889 10-24-1950
GASTON, William Boyd, 10-7-1904 7-23-1936
GASTON, Bettie LOWRY, 1880-1945
GASTON, David R., 1871-1943
HUNTLEY, Mrs. L. B. "Inez", 1883-1952
HUNTLEY, L. B. "Bob", 1874-1944
LEGGETT, Harley Tom, 1906-1968
LEGGETT, Florence WOOD, 1872-1946
LEGGETT, Henry T., 1869-1944
MC WHORTER, Mrs. Marvin, 1887-1947
MC WHORTER, Marvin, 1888-1950
MC WHORTER, Ted B., 1926-1967
MC WHORTER, Melvin, 1920-1969
LEGGETT, Jessie L., 1904-1973
LEGGETT, Frank, 1898-1975
MC ALLISTER, Hansel, 10-23-19_2, 10-20-1944
MC WHORTER, Charles, 1910-1973
SMITH, Loula Mae, 10-11-1903 6-28-1975
SMITH, James Gaston, 7-27-1887 12-2-1944
SMITH, James G., Jr., Tex., Pvt., U.S.A., W. W. II., 5-29-1923 10-15-1973
WHITE, Caldonia Isabelle, 7-31-1860 8-16-1944
WHITE, William Taylor, 11-18-1856 5-12-1949
MC ADAMS, Mrs. Ruth MARCHAM, 1874-1944
MC ADAMS, Alex Lee, 1865-1957
CAGLE, Ruby Ree MC ADAMS, 3-8-1903 5-26-1970
WEBB, Howard C., 1875-1946
RAGSDALE, Jennie CARAWAY, 12-12-1874 10-18-1968
RAGSDALE, Cyrus W., 9-6-1871 6-15-1959
PITTS, Gertrude, 8-11-1875 10-8-1965
PITTS, Alexander C., 3-14-1863 8-16-1943
LAMBERT, Roy D., 3-7-1909 4-22-1958
LAMBERT, Ina L., 9-13-1904 8-16-1944
LEWIS, Andrew, 1869-1966
LEWIS, Ida, 1876-1946
ORR, Ocie C., 1884-1968
ORR, Cora D., 1888-1947
TURNER, R. Marvin, Sgt., U. S. A., W. W. I., 1892-1975
BRUCE, Noble C., 1-14-1880 3-28-1949
BARLEY, Zonna, 1905-No Date

SPRADLING, Winnie, 1903-1964
RICE, M. Ola, 1881-1960
RICE, J. Frank, 1874-1944
HOLLEY, Linda Fay, 1944-1949
DOUGLAS, Billy R., 1927-1949
SCHOTT, P. L. ,10-20-1870 2-2-1949
SCHOTT, Mrs. P. L., 2-26-1877 10-28-1960
SCHOTT, Leslie A., 9-27-1896 10-18-1973
SCHOTT, Mrs. Leslie A., 1-25-1915 9-9-1973
SCHOTT, James Earl, 10-11-1898 12-24-1968
COOPER, Emma, 1893-1949
COOPER, Frank J., 1892-1968
WILLIAMS, Tom L., 5-11-1895 10-23-1959
LEE, Warner, 11-1-1885 4-28-1968
LEE, Julia, 9-20-1885 11-14-1969
RILEY, Alfred Mosse, 10-1878 7-1949
WHATLEY, Bob, 1-2-1888 12-27-1970
WHATLEY, Mae, 10-2-1904 No Date
EASON, Frances HUMMELL, 8-31-1913 2-16-1974
EASON, Louise EPPES, 2-5-1887 1-22-1951
MC CLENDON, J. W., Tex., Pfc., 363 Inf., W. W. II., 12-15-1920 12-26-1944
PAGE, Mattie Mae, 1893-1947
1 - FUNERAL MARKER
DYER, Charles J., 1869-1946
LONG, Cordelia "Ma", 8-5-1869 5-10-1946
PRICE, J. W., 2-28-1893 3-31-1960
PRICE, Belle, wife of J. H., 1858-1924
PRICE, Walter R., 12-8-1883 8-19-1919
LANDRUM, Beulah B., 1869-1943
LANDRUM, Z. B., 1870-1941
LANDRUM, Edward E., 1896-1951
MATHEWS, Mrs. Angie, 1871-1944
PIPPIN, Mrs. J. H., 1880-1942
PIPPIN, J. H., 1876-1969
FORD, Johnnie Ruth, 1918-1945
FORD, Maggie, 5-11-1883 1-2-1947
MILLER, Belle, 1871-1954
MILLER, John, 1864-1953
JULIEN, Richard W., 11-1-1914 7-18-1942
WHITWORTH, Frances E., 11-18-1880 2-17-1966
WHITWORTH, William F., 5-10-1875 1-27-1943
WILLIAMS, Ada, 10-11-1886 10-23-1954
CUNNINGHAM, Gracie, 1897-1965
CUNNINGHAM, Rev. W. J., 1883-1943
NATION, Charlie Elvin, 1891-1944
NATION, Effie Mae, 1894-No Date
STOVER, Nancy Jane, 12-24-1865 1-20-1944
MC GUIRE, Miranda E., 1863-1944
MC GUIRE, Charles A., 1858-1946
RIGGINS, Mrs. Howard, 1899-1964
COLEY, Lavesta WATERS, 11-1-1908 4-17-1943
WATERS, Iva, 1877-1950
WATERS, Jim, 1876-1952
GLOSSUP, Gladine, 1917-1943

PARISH, Berry, 10-8-1863 6-28-1944
PEATON, James P., 3-28-1889 11-5-1959
GLOSSUP, Leon, 1922-1943
GLOSSUP, Cassie, 1893-1975
GLOSSUP, J. B., 1891-1961
GLOSSUP, Fay, 1927-1935
GRAHAM, Dora G., 1884-1966
GRAHAM, Frank F., 1875-1943
DELEZ, Alfred J., 1872-1943
STRICKLAND, Emma, 11-10-1876 5-1-1957
STRICKLAND, A. L., 10-19-1883 1-18-1944
CASEY, Mrs. Volley, 6-18-1918 8-7-1947
BELLAH, Robert L., 1882-1952
BELLAH, Lula Ann, 1884-1939
POLK, Wilmuth J., 1867-1953
POLK, James K., 1860-1939
WEST, William Joseph, 1891-1939
MILLER, Flora ATKINS, died 1962
TERRY, Robert M., 10-31-1891 10-26-1941
          married 9-2-1915
TERRY, Macel L., 2-24-1898 3-16-1975
TERRY, Edna Loise, died 11-16-1921
FOWLER, Anna Bell KING, 4-26-1872 11-17-1939
ALEXANDER, Carrie Lenora, 7-2-1858 7-9-1940
ALEXANDER, John Wesley, 2-6-1856 7-5-1940
MC BROOME, Henry Lee, Tex. Pvt., U. S. A., W. W. I.,
                              8-30-1893 3-22-1967

HOLLIDAY, Dainty PRICE, 1888-1976
HOLLIDAY, Malcom Ed, 1884-1961
GARLAND, Hester, 1898-1976
GARLAND, Carl D., 1894-1954
NEELY, Iona R., 1868-1952
NEELY, Thomas, 1862-1938
CAGLE, John A., 1863-1940
CAGLE, Lillian M., 1873-1957
HENDERSON, W. Harold, Tex., Pvt., U. S. M.C., died 2-18-1940
HENDERSON, Finis, 1918-1953
MAPLES, Lawrence Douglas, 11-21-1938 2-28-1939
HANEY, Ernest, 1883-1972
HANEY, Maltye Lou JOHNSON, 10-20-1884 12-4-1937
LANDRUM, Ruby P., 8-19-1900 9-11-1975
LANDRUM, William P., 1893-1940
BRANCH, J. C., 1915-1936
BRANCH, C. J., 1884-1966
BRANCH, Lera, 6-7-1893 6-22-1972
CHILDRESS, Samuel F., 1889-1949
CHILDRESS, Annie Lee, 1896-1946
BULBROOK, Anna MARSHALL, 7-26-1871 4-17-1921
BULBROOK, Harry, 10-16-1861 6-28-1941
BULBROOK, Anna Virginia, 5-19-1911 11-17-1938
MARSHALL, Andrew Soule, 8-21-1845 10-19-1926
MARSHALL, Mary MARTIN, 12-15-1848 6-13-1935
MARSHALL, Mary, 3-8-1878 4-20-1950
MARSHALL, Ellen, 4-4-1881 10-4-1972

DAVIS, Maggie M., 1878-1936
DAVIS, Walter C., 1873-1939
TURNER, Lella Pearl, 6-24-1893 9-14-1976
TURNER, Martin Luther, 3-11-1888 4-30-1955
DICKENS, Virginia D., 1-28-1863 5-1-1945
DICKENS, Samuel M., 2-20-1857 12-13-1936
BROWN, Constance REDMOND, 1851-1938
HUDDLESTON, Betty, 1868-1940
HUDDLESTON, Gene, 1902-1959
ALEXANDER, Rubye RIKE, wife of Ray H., 1894-1938
ALEXANDER, Ray H., 1884-1955
MC ALLISTER, Maggie, 7-2-1875 9-18-1943
MC ALLISTER, A. C. "Neal", 6-27-1873 11-13-1938
PORTWOOD, Madaline RUSSELL, 1870-1958
PORTWOOD, Charles Madison, 1868-1938
BALL, Thomas A., 11-25-1856 5-10-1937
BALL, Caladonia, 6-30-1861 2-11-1943
BARBER, Walton I., 10-1-1887 5-15-1964
BARBER, Wallace, 1911-1934
HOLCOMB, J. C., 1867-1935
HOLCOMB, Mrs. J. C., 1868-1957
HOLCOMB, Mark Hanna, Tex., Gunners Mate, 3 CL, U.S.N.R.F.,
                                    12-16-1896 7-1-1939
HOLCOMB, Eugene "Buck", 1903-1973
LAMBE, Emma F., 1883-1974
LAMBE, Charlie W., 1868-1936
VAN HUSS, Esther, 1898-1936
MAYHALL, Anna Alice, 6-20-1885 3-27-1935
MAYHALL, William Albert, 4-21-1882 9-1-1967
WALLACE, A. A., 3-7-1860 4-3-1935
WALLACE, Mrs. A. A., 7-5-1864 7-20-1936
JONES, Sarah Ann, 1884-1950
JONES, Ray Bert, 1885-1935
DUNKIN, Molly, 1869-1935
DEATON, Jennie B., 5-22-1868 7-7-1956
DEATON, J. H., 7-18-1869 12-16-1937
WILLMON, Emmie Lucile, 1892-1936
GILL, Ada FRENCH, 11-8-1879 8-6-1936
KININGHAM, T. S., 1883-1940
1 - STONE
CASTLEBERRY, S. H., 1852-1936
CASTLEBERRY, Mattie O., 1867-1948
BROOKS, Ethel S., 1888-1958
LIVINGSTON, Mack, 1888-1952
LIVINGSTON, Adelyn S., No Dates
LAXTON, Emma, 1855-1936
LAXTON, William L., 1853-1937
LAXTON, Thomas J., 1897-1948
LAXTON, Elizabeth SWALLOW, 1889-1953
GABLE, Jo Jean, died 5-7-1944
LAZO, Joseph Oscar, Jr., 12-10-1944 12-21-1944
BOOTH, J. B., III, died 9-18-1943
MARSHALL, Joyce Elaine, died 1943
HATHAWAY, Martha J., 10-9-1942 10-11-1942

HERLOCKER, James H., Missouri, 2nd. Lt., 5th. Field Arty., W. W. I.,
9-21-1897 5-20-1969

RODRIGUEZ, Joel A., 1967-1967
1 - FUNERAL MARKER, UNREADABLE
BENNETT, Kathleen, 1967-1967
WALDROOP, James C., 1964-1964
WILLIAMS, Edward Scott, died 1-13-1960

MEMORY LAND CEMETERY

Section "A"

FOUST, Ira E., 1909-1971
FOUST, Oleta M., 1919-1978
ROBINSON, Pete E., 1885-No Dates
ROBINSON, Jennie Y., 1890-1974
BRADBERRY, Earl H., 1898-1966
AYERS, Kenneth E., 1932-No Dates
AYERS, Peggy M., 1936-No Dates
DARDEN, Thomas D., 1891-1967
DARDEN, Mamie M., 1897-No Dates
BILLINGTON, Ben., 1894-1979
HINES, Clyde L., 1899-No Dates
HINES, Ila B., 1903-1972
CUPP, O. A. (Bud), 1901-No Dates
CUPP, Permelia, 1914-No Dates
HAMILTON, C. A. (Pat), 1908-1973
HAMILTON, Marie, 1924-No Dates
MERRICK, Charles Clark, 1899-1971
MERRICK, Aubrey HAYTER, 1899-No Dates
MORRIS, Vander D., 1912-1974
MORRIS, Lois J., 1915-No Dates
WRIGHT, Wm. H., 1931-No Dates
WRIGHT, Marcella E., 1937-No Dates
SMITH, Homer Leon, Tex. Cpl. Co. A., 51 Armd. Engr. BN 6 Armd. Div.,
8-14-1927 10-5-1964

SAMUEL, John H., 1906-1971
TURNS, Jay Ernest, 1894-1969
TURNS, Tula L., 1911-No Dates
HARRIS, James Ray, 1891-1963
HARRIS, Gracie Oneta, 1902-No Dates
BROOKS, M. Madison, 1902-1971
BROOKS, Juliette, 1905-No Dates
AMONETTE, Wilma, 1903-No Dates
PALMORE, Dencie B., 1905-1970
PALMORE, Mattie L., 1916-No Dates
PERRY, Walter, 1893-1963
PERRY, Ella L., 1896-1971
LINDLEY, Sidney L., 11-28-1956 8-1-1960
GIBSON, Jos. E., SP-5 U.S. Army, 10-4-1937 4-1-1977
KEY, Broadus A., 1912-1965
KEY, Ethel Lee, 1907-No Dates
SMITH, Otis B., 1911-No Dates

SMITH, Mildred, 1908-No Dates
ALEXANDER, M. A., 1884-1973
ALEXANDER, Mattie T., 1903-No Dates
PORTER, Milton Schley, 8-14-1898 12-9-1968
BROWN, Ray L., 1908-No Dates
BROWN, Louise L., 1918-No Dates
MC MACKLIN, Johnnie W., Tex. T-Sgt. U.S.A.F., W.W. II, Korea, Vietnam,
                        7-27-1923 1-28-1974

REYNOLDS, Luther B., 1901-1968
REYNOLDS, Ada L., 1910-No Dates
SCHMOLT, Lucille H., 1905-1970
JACOBS, Loyd W., 1912-No Dates
JACOBS, Mozelle MAYO, 1914-1976
ROBINSON, Vernon Leon, 9-10-1913 12-23-1973
HOWELL, W. Marvin, 1909-No Dates
HOWELL, Olevia M., 1919-No Dates
BIRDWELL, Lynn T., 1939-No Dates
BIRDWELL, Barbara J., 1943-No Dates
MILLS, J. Roger, 1915-No Dates
MILLS, Ruby Opal, 1921-1977
MILLS, Roger Q., 1892-No Dates
MILLS, Floy T., 1894-No Dates
DODD, R. Leonard, 1904-1975
DODD, Betty, 1905-No Dates
WALLACE, Jerry Lee, 1950-1968
LANKFORD, Bud, 1908-No Dates
LANKFORD, Ruby E., 1905-1968
GILMER, Vera FOX, 1902-1975
LOPEZ, Frank, 1937-1974
LOPEZ, La Verne, 1933-1976
LOPEZ, John, 1902-No Dates
LOPEZ, Nell, 1917-No Dates
AVEN, Fred L., 1910-1967
AVEN, Opal (Billie), 1907-No Dates
WILLIAMS, Clyde Earl, 1910-1975
WILLIAMS, El Vette, 1912-No Dates
BROOKS, Raymond C., 1910-1968
BROOKS, Lola Faye, 1913-No Dates
GREEN, J. T., (Tom), 1892-1969
GREEN, Bessie A., 1897-No Dates
MC CLAIN, Sidney W., 1891-1961
MC CLAIN, Nettie V., 1892-1976
LOVE, Oliver W., Tex. Pvt. U. S. Army, W. W. II., 12-13-1907 .10-23-1960
PALMORE, Ray Lee, 1907-1978
PALMORE, Goldie M., 1910-No Dates
HENDRY, Auburn C., Tex. Pvt. 1973 SVC Comd. Unit, W. W. II.,
                        3-28-1914 12-23-1961
BRADFORD, Jas. R., 3-6-1934 8-23-1971
PETTY, Elijah, 1889-1973
PETTY, Ora, 1899-No Dates
POTTS, Walter,L., 1895-No Dates
POTTS, Pearl E., 1902-No Dates
MC BROOM, Grover C., 1882-1976
MC BROOM, Victoria R., 1883-1960
ELMORE, Sherfey A., 1889-1978

ELMORE, Gladys V., 1907-No Dates
PARKER, Walker H., 1904-1976
PARKER, Willie Belle, 1910-No Dates
COOK, Delmas Darrell, Tex. BT-3, U. S. Navy, Korea, 4-3-1934 7-11-1963
ATCHISON, Fred, 1893-1966
ATCHISON, Minnie LOCKE, No Dates
RANDOLPH, Jesse C., 1908-No Dates
RANDOLPH, Esther Mae, 1911-No Dates
HARTLEY, S. L., 1897-1971
HARTLEY, Allie, 1896-1968
HATHAWAY, W. A. (Peaty), 1908-No Dates
HATHAWAY, Thelmae, 1912-No Dates
GREEN, Jas. L., 12-29-1919   No Dates
GREEN, Billie Faye, 3-26-1921 5-3-1969
BAKER, Daniel W., 1887-1964
BAKER, Katherine E., 1891-1975
BAKER, Jessie CLARK, 1913-1961
GRAY, Jas. C., 1921-No Dates
GRAY, Willie Jo, 1923-No Dates
ELLIS, E. Wallace, 1923-No Dates
ELLIS, Mary Geneva, 1924-1975
FULTON, George H., 1909-1969
FULTON, Louetta, 1903-No Dates
BRADSHAW, E. N. (Newt), 1884-1975
BRADSHAW, Lillie Mae, 1884-No Dates
RACKLEY, Wm. S., 1914-No Dates
RACKLEY, Claudie , 1911-1970
WACASEY, Homer B., Sr., 1901-1977
WACASEY, Lavina, 1904-No Dates
WILBURN, Jackie Ray, 1941-1974
WILBURN, M. F. (Pete), 1916-No Dates
WILBURN, Jaunita D., 1917-1975
MARTIN, Romy Lee, 10-27-1895 11-4-1968
LOWE, Harold Ward, 1921-1968
LOWE, Lynette C., 1924-No Dates
DARNELL, Jas. Rayburn, Pvt. U.S.Army, W.W. II, 5-17-1905 2-25-1977
DARNELL, Ouida, 12-30-1904   No Dates
THOMASON, Edw., 1898-1968
THOMASON, Lou Ella, 1910-No Dates
GRAHAM, Eli, 1897-1976
GRAHAM, Fay, 1901-1975
LYDAY, Bobby C., 1936-No Dates
LYDAY, Barbara A., 1938-No Dates
TREDWAY, Ira W., 1906-1959
TREDWAY, E. Jewell, 1923-No Dates
EVANS, Cecil B., 1905-1960
EVANS, Vada E., 1905-No Dates
HENLEY, Dial, 1914-1960
HENLEY, Mattie, 1918-No Dates
DAVIS, Aaron B., 1909-No Dates
DAVIS, Claudene, 1917-1978
RANDOLPH, Jesse J., 12-11-1934 6-23-1963
WILLIAMS, Elmo B., 1913-No Dates
WILLIAMS, Idell, 1914-No Dates
WILLIAMS, O. D., 1915-No Dates

WILLIAMS, Billie, 1921-No Dates
KNOX, Thomas Booth, 1888-1966
KNOX, Zana (NEIGHBORS), 1892-1978
CLARK, Grover, 6-7-1890 11-22-1968
CLARK, Myrtle M., 2-7-1891 No Dates
EWING, J. B., 1907-1965
EWING, Louise, 1915-No Dates
MASSEY, Charley, 1889-1962
MASSEY, Sarah, 1888-1961
SWEET, Ray A., 1920-No Dates
SWEET, Jeri H., 1934-No Dates
ROBBINS, Elbert Brice, Tex. Pvt., HQ Co 358 Inf., W. W. II, 12-19-1906
                                                        4-10-1961
COTNER, Clyde E., 1924-No Dates
COTNER, Flossie B., 1922-No Dates
ROBERTSON, Wm. H., 1904-1969
ROBERTSON, Bessie, 1906-No Dates
GREATHOUSE, Tomie, 1894-No Dates
GREATHOUSE, Ethel, 1901-1975
JONES, Jimmie A., 5-19-1910 5-13-1973
JONES, Catharine, 4-19-1912 4-14-1967
EVANS, Marion K., 1875-1961
EVANS, Mollie G., 1885-1976
BURGESS, Merritt R., Sr., 11-8-1902 1-17-1970
BURGESS, Alberta, No Dates
COYLE, Leo Marvin, 1916-No Dates
COYLE, Geneva R., 1919-No Dates
NATION, Gloria BROWN, 1935-1977
CUPP, John A., 1906-No Dates
CUPP, Winnie, 1912-No Dates
MORGAN, Billy W., 1929-No Dates
MORGAN, Betty M., 1931-No Dates
OTTWELL, Bobby A., 1912-No Dates
OTTWELL, Dorothy F., 1923-No Dates
COATS, J. Frank, 1909-1976
COATS, Daphena R., 1909-1974
WILSON, W. E. (Erb), 1885-1878
WILSON, Ethel G., 1890-1978
GARZA, David, 3-3-11972 8-23-1972
POE, Donnie Ray, 1956-1974
TAYLOR, Betty Jean, 2-22-1930 11-22-1976
MONTGOMERY, Wilson L., 1916-No Dates
MONTGOMERY, Delilah M., 1925-No Dates
OLER, Jas. K., Tex. Pfc. H.Q. Sq. Pac. Air SVC Comd, W. W. II.,
                        6-10-1927 2-2-1967
HALE, Claude H. (Shug), 11-29-1907 8-14-1967
HALE, Ruth Opal, 2-9-1908 No Dates
JOHNSTON, Irene GASS, 1891-1961
PEAK, Ruby WOLFERT, 1899-1966
PETLEY, Mary Olive, 1888-1962
WALLACE, John W., 1902-No Dates
WALLACE, Bertha M., 1902-No Dates
CLARK, Benjamin L., 1894-1967
CLARK, Gertie Mae, 1899-No Dates

COLBERT, T. R., 1905-1967
COLBERT, Cherry, 1905-No Dates
FLEMING, Willie, 1898-1965
FLEMING, Pearl, 1907-1974
WEAVER, G. B., 1913-No Dates
WEAVER, Verna Lou, 1915-NO Dates
APPLING, Ernest, 1922-No Dates
APPLING, Mae Jean, 1923-1975
APPLING, Jas. Edwin, 3-30-1955 3-20-1965
HARDIN, Mrs. H. H., 1884-1966
SISK, Ronald Joe, Tex. AlC, U.S.A.F., 8-2-1947 11-12-1968
DANIEL, Arthur C., 1910-No Dates
DANIEL, Laura V., 1908-No Dates
WILLIAMS, E. Garlon, 1914-1965
WILLIAMS, Faye, 1915-No Dates
CHEEK, W. Homer, 1891-1969
CHEEK, Olivet H., 1895-No Dates
HUDSON, N. S. (Preach), 1918-No Dates
HUDSON, Ima Lee, 1918-No Dates
CORLEY, Gordon V., 1923-No Dates
CORLEY, Billie Jean, 1929-No Dates
HALE, Albert, 1899-1976
HALE, Winnie, 1894-1970
MC NALLY, Paul R., 1885-1975
MC NALLY, Ruth I., 1905-1977
SMITH, J. Marvin, 1899-1932
SMITH, Emma M., 1900-No Dates
KURFFEES, Wm. W., 1907-1972
KURFFEES, Mollie, 1880-1973
KURFFEES, C. L., 1910-1976
SANDFORD, Jacob, New Jersey, PFC, U.S.A., W.W. II, 2-12-1912 5-5-1974
SANDFORD, Grace R., 7-22-1909- No Dates
TRIBLE, H. Burt, Jr., 7-28-1948 1-28-1969
PERRY, Engle E., Tex. SSgt. Co M, 158 Inf., W. W. II, 9-19-1915 8-15-1971
PERRY, Vera, 9-8-1910 9-9-1976
SHORT, Homer C., Tex. Cpl., U. S. Army, W. W. II., 6-29-1919 5-14-1971
GOEN, Trent Wayne, 2-10-1961 8-31-1977
LEMONS, Jessie Lee, 1915-No Dates
LEMONS, Mabel A., 1917-No Dates
ADAY, Jesse T., 1900-1976
ADAY, Winnie E., 1903-No Dates
GOEN, Frank W., 11-1-1909 8-17-1977
FOX, Carl, 1898-1965
FOX, Tressa, 1898-1974
HASSELL, Wm. Lee, 1926-No Dates
HASSELL, Billie Jo, 1926-No Dates
BOWEN, Leroy (Hap), 1912-No Dates
BOWEN, Pauline, 1914-No Dates
FITZGERALD, Catharine, 1923-No Dates
KIRBY, Frank, 1903-1972
GODSEY, Ornie E., 1902-No Dates
GODSEY, Annie KIRBY, 1905-No Dates
LANGFORD, Jesse R., 1912-No Dates
LANGFORD, Audrey L., 1921-No Dates

GIDEON, Hollis H., 1911-No Dates
GIDEON, Ruby V., 1911-No Dates
PEARCE, Jewell, 1915-No Dates
CRUMP, Charles Alvin, Tex. Cpl. U.S.M.C., Vietnam, PH&GS, 8-26-1946 5-26-1967
GEORGE, Columbus E., Pfc. U. S. Army, 5-22-1912 7-22-1975
JACKSON, Jas. C., 2-17-1907 10-22-1968
ELLIOTT, Jas. H., 1898-1977
ELLIOTT, Cora Lee, 1902-No Dates
BUMGARDNER, Wm. B., 1916-No Dates
BUMGARDNER, Agnes F., 1914-No Dates
DOOLEY, O. T., 1903-1973
DOOLEY, Opal A., 1908-No Dates
NORRIS, Lillian C., 5-19-1899 3-11-1973
NORRIS, Emmit W., 7-28-1901 No Dates
NORRIS, Ethel Lee, 7-4-1912 8-3-1972
WHITLEY, Marbury H., 1895-1967
WHITLEY, Captolia O., 1896-No Dates
EATON, Rex B., 1918-No Dates
EATON, Mildred, 1920-No Dates
TAYLOR, Nell, 6-23-1928 1-24-1976
TRENTHAM, J. C., Ga. Pvt. U. S. Army, W. W. I., 10-16-1891 7-19-1965
BROWN, B. Neal, 1919-1967
BROWN, Eula Mae, 1921-No Dates
LEE, Marion H., 1919-No Dates
LEE, Gladys N., 1920-No Dates
VAUGHN, Jimmy F., Sr., 1944-1974
VAUGHN, Lorain MC GARY, 1944-1977
RAY, Vernon Eugene, 11-8-1939 5-13-1968
AREY, Cecil, 1909-No Dates
AREY, Ida H., 1906-No Dates
TRIMBLE, Rob N., 1890-1974
TRIMBLE, Winnie C., No Dates
TRIMBLE, Rob D., 1917-No Dates
TRIMBLE, Elayne S., 1919-No Dates
GASWAY, Narvel L., 1923-No Dates
GASWAY, Theda L., 1925-No Dates
GASWAY, C. Walter, 1891-1974
GASWAY, Maud F., 1900-1979
TREADWAY, Logan E., 1905-1978
CARUTHERS, Joe R., 1909-1977
CARUTHERS, Bessie H., 1916-No Dates
RAY, O. A., Tex., Cpl. U.S.M.C., W. W. II, 8-9-1920 12-9-1966
RAY, Oscar Allen, 1887-No Dates
RAY, Edna Pearl, 1891-1973
LEWIS, Winifred G., 1912-No Dates
LEWIS, Dorothy G., 1927-No Dates
LEWIS, Lula M., 1880-1970
LEWIS, Ricky Lynn, 11-10-1958 8-4-1971
HUDNALL, Grace T., 1893-1973
WALL, Jas. D., 1931-No Dates
WALL, Anita R., 1934-No Dates
SLAYDEN, Jas. C., 1899-1975
SLAYDEN, Angie Lou, 1908-No Dates

WRIGHT, Lawrence B., 1904-1969
WRIGHT, Jewell P., 1909-No Dates
KEARNEY, Morris C., 1898-1966
KEARNEY, Ermine W., 1898-No Dates
FLINN, Ray H., 1904-1972
FLINN, Clela C., 1906-No Dates
INGRAM, Eva Mae, 9-21-1933 10-19-1968
MC CLENDON, Katrina, died 7-23-1962
MC CLENDON, Alta Ann., 3-24-1929 4-29-1963
SULLIVAN, Nelson W., 1911-No Dates
SULLIVAN, Nadine I., 1916-No Dates
SULLIVAN, Walter W., 1888-1966
SULLIVAN, Martha A., 1885-1969
CRELIA, Wallace L., 1897-1974
CRELIA, Lillian Maye, 1901-No Dates
DEATON, Charlie L., 1910-No Dates
DEATON, Della Fannie, 1915-No Dates
BLALOCK, Charles P., 4-2-1902 1-3-1964
DUNN, Oscar L., 1888-1974
DUNN, Sina A., 1892-1969
WEATHERFORD, Glen Artis, 1912-No Dates
WEATHERFORD, Dessie Lee, 1903-1973
WILKINS, E. T., "Pat", No Dates
WILKINS, Jewell, No Dates
MORROW, Jas. A., 1921-No Dates
MORROW, Emma L., 1926-No Dates
WILSON, A. A.,"Buster", 1912-No Dates
WILSON, Anna Pearl, 1915-No Dates
HALL, Herbert, 1900-No Dates
HALL, Birdie W., 1907-No Dates
LACY, R. E. "Bob", 1928-1979
LACY, Anna L., 1933-No Dates
DICKENS, Joe, 1917-No Dates
DICKENS, Mary Lee, 1906-1978
SUMMERLIN, Thomas H., 1918-1976
SUMMERLIN, Billie L., 1918-No Dates
LILLEY, Annie Laura, 9-26-1926 No Dates
SUMMERS, Wm. R., 1908-No Dates
SUMMERS, Ruth, 1904-No Dates
LILLEY, Bethel Faye, 12-24-1929 No Dates
BLOYED, Curtis L., 1916-No Dates
BLOYED, Wynona F., 1923-1979
BLOYED, Frank V., 4-19-1920 6-1-1964
BLOYED, Helen J., 5-27-1921 No Dates
MERCER, Charlie, 1903-No Dates
MERCER, Thelma, 1906-1978
SMITH, Earl L., 1896-No Dates
SMITH, Myrtis H., 1901-No Dates
ELMORE, Frank D., 1899-1973
ELMORE, Ethel A., 1903-No Dates
SMITH, George V., Tex. CM-1, U.S.N., W. W. II, 3-24-1919 8-9-1971
JOHNSON, Louis L., 1928-No Dates
JOHNSON, Tommie J., 1932-No Dates
JOHNSON, Ollie, 1903-No Dates

JOHNSON, Viola E., 1913-No Dates
JONES, John Burton, 1900-No Dates
JONES, Hattie Lee, 1904-No Dates
STINEBAUGH, John Allen, 1921-No Dates
STINEBAUGH, Lena, 1937-No Dates
SHIELDS, Charles A. Jr., 6-27-1932 11-19-1978
ALLEN, Marie Ethel, 12-25-1928 4-29-1975
MULLANEY, Edwin P., 1900-1973
MULLANEY, Kathryn L., 1908-No Dates
BOWEN, Jas. W., 1930-1973
BOWEN, Virginia F., 1933-1967
LANDRETH, Jack, 1905-1969
LANDRETH, Alba, 1905-No Dates
MARTIN, Wesley N., 1914-No Dates
MARTIN, Minnie Ruth, 1917-1962
HICKMAN, Jesse H., Sgt. U.S.A.F., W. W. II, 7-7-1914 4-16-1976
BRIGGS, Bryan J., 1898-1966
BRIGGS, Cloyce A., 1911-No Dates
SMITH, Alfred, 1902-1970
SMITH, Nora Blanch, 1907-No Dates
PARKER, Robert L., 1916-No Dates
PARKER, Alene R., 1909-No Dates
HENDERSON, Arthur, 1899-1979
HENDERSON, Zelma, 1906-1972
PICKARD, John Lee, 1913-No Dates
PICKARD, Bernice C., 1919-No Dates
DURR, Edith L., 1902-1975
LOHMANN, Inf. son of Ann Louise and John Mitchell, died 9-12-1975
GORDY, Victor G., 1892-1966
GORDY, Louise M., 1892-1966
LASSITER, H. Jack, 1917-1974
LASSITER, Zelda R., 1925-No Dates
WALKER, J. C. "Mickey", 1915-1979
WALKER, Orlean, 1918-No Dates
SMITH, Warren R., 1916-1979
SMITH, Louise B., 1915-No Dates
HAMILTON, J. W., 2-6-1881 2-7-1962
HAMILTON, Mabel C., 9-16-1895 2-14-1966
MONTGOMERY, Ellen Grace, 1883-1968
VALLANCEY, Nan, No Dates
VALLANCEY, Dr. John H., 1881-1969
VALLANCEY, Lillian C., 1885-1968
WINKLE, Luther Carl, 1901-No Dates
WINKLE, Ruth E., 1917-No Dates
BLUNT, Nora V., 1898-No Dates
AMES, Dudley, 1893-1965
AMES, Maud, No Dates
KING, Jack E., 1895-1970
KING, Laura B., 1894-1967
HALLORAN, Jos. E., 1889-1972
HALLORAN, Eva M., 1893-1966
HANSARD, Grady G., 1913-No Dates
HANSARD, Arvretha, 1913-No Dates
TUCKER, Theo R., 1904-1972

TUCKER, Julia R., 1904-No Dates
TUCKER, Wm. George, 1928-No Dates
TUCKER, Billie G., 1931-No Dates
STOCKHOFF, John Alvin, 1948-1968
HOWARD, Ike, Tex. M-Sgt. U.S.Army, W. W. II, 10-16-1913 3-5-1972
BRAMBLETT, Billy Joe, 1916-No Dates
BRAMBLETT, Pauline L., 1915-No Dates
COATS, Henry L., 1912-1970
COATS, Tenah M., 1905-No Dates
SHELTON, Henry Edw., 1904-No Dates
SHELTON, Clara Loretta, 1903-No Dates
BAILEY, Jas. B., 1918-No Dates
BAILEY, Loleta L., 1915-1971
JONES, Jos. L., 1909-No Dates
JONES, Camie Mae, 1913-No Dates
THOMPSON, John Oliver, 1917-1971
THOMPSON, Ernestine Charlotte, 1924-1966
NORRIS, Gerald R., 1935-No Dates
NORRIS, Gloria A., 1938-No Dates
FELTS, Fermon, No Dates
FELTS, Anita, 12-7-1920 2-24-1964
WILSON, Holley C., 7-17-1891 7-18-1977
WILSON, Relter M., 1-28-1902 No Dates
PHELPS, Manuel E., 1918-No Dates
PHELPS, Imogene M., 1924-No Dates
DAVIS, M. D., 1911-1970
DAVIS, Vada, 1911-No Dates
MOSELEY, Wm. H., 1902-1968
MOSELEY, Eunice L., 1906-No Dates
HOUSER, Grover C., 1897-1970
HOUSER, Carrie B., 1909-1979
WRIGHT, Scott S., 12-11-1888 1-25-1975
WRIGHT, Mary H., 12-29-1892 7-22-1977
SAVAGE, Carroll D., M. D., 1921-1960
DENNIS, Irene, 2-24-1925 4-25-1973
ARANT, Charles E., Jr., 1909-No Dates
ARANT, Winnie A., 1906-No Dates
BENSON, Fletcher Earle, Jr., 1903-No Dates
BENSON, Edna Faye, 1898-No Dates
HOOD, Robert Frank, 1893-1970
HOOD, Eliza Neoma, 1898-1974
HOLMES, Jas. Travis, 1914-1976
HOLMES, Margie Estell, 1922-No Dates
MC ELROY, Denmon E., 1921-No Dates
MC ELROY, Mildred L., 1925-No Dates
DOWNS, Jas. Losh, 3-26-1895 8-9-1964
DOWNS, Arizona E., 9-4-1893 8-18-1971
TURNER, August F., 10-4-1911 1-8-1968
COWSER, Grady, Tex. Tec 5 Co B., 255 Inf., W. W. II, BSM, 5-6-1912 1-18-1962
COWSER, Jaunita, 7-28-1921 No Dates
MC DOWELL, Harvey A., 11-12-1901 10-29-1969
BAKER, Fred, 1895-1968
BAKER, Verna M., 1906-No Dates
RUDD, Marvin, 1902-1972

RUDD, Trudy, 1900-No Dates
SADLER, Ernest J., Pfc. U.S.M.C., W. W. II, 9-3-1920 12-8-1978
SADLER, Alma Frances, 10-9-1922 2-25-1979'
SCOTT, Floyd H., 1910-No Dates
SCOTT, Lillie Mae, 1917-No Dates
DIGGS, Larry Jack, Jr., 8-4-1969 12-21-1974
MOTLEY, David H., 1900-No Dates
MOTLEY, Mabel E., 1906-1971
MOTLEY, Charles C., 1927-1978
POYNOR, Laura L., 1903-1969
CAMP, Nancy Neel, 1936-1976
CAMP, Billie E., 1930-1978
SMITH, Bobby Joe, 1934-1974
SMITH, Helen, 1935-No Dates
DIGGS, Euell K., 1911-1978
DIGGS, Rosaleen, 1915-No Dates
BELL, Richard O., 1906-1967
BELL, Pearlie E., 1913-No Dates
KIRK, Travis E., 1932-NO Dates
KIRK, Bettye L., 1936-No Dates
RAY, Joe Samuel, Tex. Pvt., U. S. Army, W. W. I., 6-26-1889 7-2-1973
GOODE, Marion R., Sr., 1894-No Dates
GOODE, Katie Lee, 1902-No Dates
PORTER, Oscar, 1892-1972
PORTER, Verda, 1899-No Dates
ROY, Ernest E., 1915-1972
ROY, Dorothy, 1923-No Dates
PHILLIPS, Barney, 1894-1974
PHILLIPS, Rena, 1897-No Dates
THORNTON, Shirley Ann (Judge), 1965-1978 (?)
BARRETT, Oscar L., 1919-No Dates
BARRETT, Ocie Mae, 1916-No Dates
BLUNT, Ricky Glen, 10-27-1969 1-16-1970
WINSETT, Berma E., 10-1911 No Dates
ASHLEY, Johnnie L., 1912-1978
ASHLEY, Eva Lorine, 1915-No Dates
HILLMER, Betty V., 7-8-1898 1-25-1972
HILLMER, Lewis W., Mich., Pvt., Co. B., 50 Inf., W. W. I., 1-3-1888 5-1-1962
GREEN, H. D. "Skipper", 8-17-1951 5-11-1969
ROSENBALM, Wm. J., 1903-No Dates
ROSENBALM, Myrtle A., 1901-No Dates
SCOTT, Herman, E., 1905-1967
SCOTT, Melva H., 1905-No Dates
WALKER, Birdecia E., 1886-1978
WALKER, Lela Fay, 1904-1975
POWELL, Jake C., 1902-No Dates
POWELL, Opal Dale, 1904-1969
BYRUM, Jack C., 1885-1976
GIBSON, Ralph F., 1920-No Dates
GIBSON, Helen R., 1925-No Dates
WHITE, Herman L., 1905-1966
WHITE, Ruby S., 1911-No Dates
TERRY, E. Becton, 1910-1964
TERRY, Elaine M., 1915-1977

HARPER, Lena, 1892-1972
HORDIN, Newton C., 1893-1979
HORDIN, Clara Y., 1883-1973
COMER, Bernard O., 1902-1978
COMER, Gladys M., 1903-No Dates
ROSENBALM, Ross Lee, 1900-1978
ROSENBALM, Beauna, 1900-1972
CURREY, Ashley Scott, 12-22-1972   12-24-1972
SMITH, Robert W., 1928-No Dates
SMITH, Nasa P., 1933-No Dates
SMITH, Little Wright, 1897-1971
SMITH, Mae Dell, 1902-No Dates
MC MILLAN, Angus Wyatt, 11-16-1887   7-8-1969
MC MILLAN, Evie Lee, 10-22-1893 No Dates
MC MILLAN, Talmadge O., 1925-No Dates
ASHMORE, Jas. David, 9-4-1950   1-26-1971
REECE, Jesse T., No Dates
REECE, Maggie S., No Dates
BURSON, Hellon (REECE), 1920-1973
PHILLIPS, Harrison A., 1907-1974
PHILLIPS, Alleta F., 1912-No Dates
LITTLE, Gerald W., 1931-No Dates
LITTLE, Barbara J., 1934-No Dates
STANFORD, J. W., 1913-1975
STANFORD, Ida Mae, 1913-No Dates
WADDLE, Lewis C., 4-21-1904   2-8-1972
WADDLE, Vada I., 10-19-1904   No Dates
RICHARDS, Johnny F., Sr., 1918-No Dates
VANDERWILT, Ronald G., 5-30-1960   1-10-1973
HORTON, Fred W., 1906-1969
HORTON, Ovelia E., 1908-No Dates
CROWSON, Athel, 1903-1966
CORNELIUS, Clyde P., 1897-1970
CORNELIUS, Velma B., 1909-No Dates
MC ANN, Thomas V., Tex. T-Sgt. Co. 1, 182 Inf., W. W. II, 10-10-1923
                                                              4-26-1968

MIXSON, Dauthard W., 1920-No Dates
MIXSON, Dean R., 1920-1971
WILLIS, Bennie R., 1930-1971
WILLIS, Jane J., 1931-No Dates
WILLIS, Raye Annette, 1960-1971
KNOX, Porter W., 1914-1976
ASHMORE, William B., 1901-1973
ASHMORE, Nancy Sarah, 1916-No Dates
MITCHELL, George W., 1906-No Dates
MITCHELL, Armenda, 1906-No Dates
HINTON, David A., 1926-No Dates
HINTON, Nadene J., 1930-1971
MC DANIEL, Lucy May, 1905-No Dates
HERVEY, Henry P., 1880-1966
HERVEY, Eulela K., 1887-1975
MC CLURE, Dan, 1892-1974
MC CLURE, Pearl, 1888-No Dates
HAWKINS, H. Robert, 1916-No Dates

HAWKINS, Genevieve, 1922-No Dates
JARVIS, Harrison, 1913-No Dates
JARVIS, Mollie Lou, 1916-1974
CROUCH, Tom L., 1893-1964
CROUCH, Grace H., 1897-No Dates
MC AULEY, Dan Bolin, 1899-1974
MC AULEY, Maureta Ray, 1909-No Dates
LOGAN, Minnie, 9-27-1921 5-21-1975
MILLER, Hazel Tennell, 1926-1976
FREEMAN, Jas. Philip, 3-30-1970 11-28-1975
WINTERS, Theda June, 7-21-1928 4-26-1965
NALLS, Claud B., 5-1-1894 12-31-1974
NALLS, Mary V., 3-4-1898 No Date
WILLIAMS, W. Glynn, 1916-No Dates
WILLIAMS, Aretha L., 1917-No Dates
SMITH, Rayford E., 1920-1974
SMITH, Dorothy M., 1921-No Dates
TERRY, Frank A., 1893-1977
TERRY, Valera WILLIAMS, 1893-1978
TERRY, Jesse B., 1897-1964
TERRY, Lillian BURTON, 1897-1978
JONES, John Paul, Tex. Maj. Ord-Corps, U.S.A.F., W. W. II, BSM, 3-17-1905
                                                                8-7-1960
MELTON, Ernest E., 1893-1973
MELTON, Ida M., 1894-1963
MUSE, Clyde S., 1905-1978
MUSE, Reatha, 1914-No Dates
RUSSELL, Jas. R., 1915-No Dates
RUSSELL, Faye H., 1915-No Dates
MOSELEY, G. S., 1898-No Dates
MOSELEY, Rachel E., 1900-No Dates
MACK, Jos. G. "Fred", 1908-No Dates
MACK, R. O'Dell, 1911-No Dates
WEST, J. L., 1888-1967
WEST, Leta L., 1879-1971
WEST, John L., Jr., 12-4-1921 No Dates
WEST, Margie, 9-13-1928 No Dates
PIERCE, Leland D., A1C, U. S. A. F., Korea, 9-29-1928 1-21-1971
PIERCE, Betty H., 11-8-1930 No Dates
CANAVAN, Alfred R., 1900-1969
CANAVAN, Stella M., 1908-No Dates
ROSENBERG, Jas. E., 1899-1975
ROSENBERG, Mildred S., 1903-No Dates
GREER, G. D., 1910-No Dates
DE GARSO, John, 1910-No Dates
DE GARSO, Ricarda, 1911-1970
WILLIAMS, Jas. L., Tex. T-Sgt, U.S.A.F., W.W. II, Korea, Vietnam,
                    10-7-1922 11-22-1970
NICHOLSON, Ira Osbin, 1895-1978
NICHOLSON, Martha Ellen, 1896-1971
REA, Wilford P., 1910-No Dates
REA, Ruth I., 1920-No Dates
MOORE, Jack H., 1924-No Dates
MOORE, Anita L., 1930-No Dates

MOORE, Gwendolyn, 1950-1969
WILDER, William D., 1899-No Date
WILDER, Minnie A., 1895-No Date
WHITE, Hollis W., 1922-No Date
WHITE, Alice, 1927-No Date
KILGORE, G. L., 1920-No Date
KILGORE, Janie., 1924-No Date
FORD, Mrs. James R., 1891-1964
WINSETT, Henry N., 1899-1974
WINSETT, E. Corene, 1906-No Date
HARRELL, Arthur P., 1892-1968
HARRELL, Mary Lou, 1894-No Date
RANDALL, Samuel K., 1918-1973
RANDALL, Martha, 1920-1976
MC LAUGHLIN, Robert C., 1902-1978
MC LAUGHLIN, Allie T., 1927-No Date
CANNON, D. C. "Dip", 1913-No Date
CANNON, Lillian S., 1917-No Date
PARKER, Elmer C., 1911-1972
PARKER, Hazel W., 1915-No Date
WHITTINGTON, Jimmie E., 1910-No Date
EVANS, Welch, 1887-1975
EVANS, Bessie, 1886-1978
NICHOLSON, C. B., 1923-1978
FLEIG, Marie ECKER, 1911-1973
BILLARREAL, Regino, 5-6-1892 1-12-1975
SIKES, B. J., 1922-No Date
SIKES, Opal, 1936-No Date
MYSINGER, John Ed., 1902-1966
MYSINGER, Celestin Olive, 1907-No Date
LEE, Karen OSTENSON, 2-15-1945 3-11-1968
CLARKSON, Francis M., 1902-No Date
CLARKSON, Annie Mae, 1900-No Date
ALEXANDER, Sam Reeves, 1916-1975
ALEXANDER, Mary Sue, 1918-No Date
JOHNSON, Noah R., 1885-1972
JOHNSON, Ellen M., 1894-1965
MC FARLIN, Joyd L., 1929-1965
MC FARLIN, Faye, 1934-No Date
BELL, Mitchell Lee, 11-25-1960 12-23-1973
MURPHY, Roy S., 9-19-1895 No Date
MURPHY, Lela Mae, 6-12-1899 No Date
TEMPLE, Ben F., 1901-No Date
TEMPLE, Irene S., 1907-No Date
MC MILLON, Hollis C., 1912-No Date
MC MILLON, Cleo, 1912-No Date
HIPPE, Leonard Neil, Va. LCDR U.S.N., W.W. II, Korea, 5-10-1912 6-2-1973
HIPPE, Dorothy M., Tex. AMMZ, U.S.N., W.W. II, 2-12-1912 12-23-1971
LEE, James L., 1925-1974
LEE, Katherine, 1923-No Date
FOWLER, George T., Tex., SACR., U.S.Navy, 10-11-1929 3-7-1970
FOWLER, Rittie G., 4-25-1894 4-21-1975
FELTS, Michael Dean, 1953-1979
FISHER, T. Hunter, 1900-No Date
FISHER, Laclede S., 1911-No Date

NELSON, Rita Helen, 1949-1977
COYLE, Myrtle Irene, 1911-1976
OVERALL, Earl C., 1895-No Date
OVERALL, Mamye E., 1897-No Date
STOVER, Alvin E., 1-16-1900 8-24-1971
STOVER, Hattie C., 5-20-1902 10-30-1967
TRIMBLE, H. Fred, 1919-No Date
TRIMBLE, Dorothy Nell, 1917-No Date

SECTION "B"

FOLLIS, Jay Connior, 3-8-1909 12-18-1968
EDMONDSON, Morton H., 1888-1974
EDMONDSON, Minnie M., 1891-No Date
CARSON, Alfred L., 12-19-1896 1-12-1973
                    married 9-24-1932
CARSON, Maggie S., 12-20-1901 8-11-1977
ASHLEY, Robert P., 1911-1969
                    married 11-2-1929
ASHLEY, Ruby L., 1912-No Date
WHITENER, Donald W., 1943-1969
WHITENER, Charlotte D., 1945-No Date
REEVES, Avon D., 3-23-1920 12-27-1971
REEVES, Beulah F., 2-21-1921 4-12-1976
ALLEN, J. Tillman, 10-21-1915 3-15-1964
ANDERSON, Harvey B., 8-22-1916 3-6-1964
ANDERSON, Dorothy K., 5-20-1912 No Date
ANDERSON, Melvin J., 2-2-1892 No Date
ANDERSON, Janie M., 8-19-1895 No Date
STONE, Roy R., 6-17-1893 7-17-1974
STONE, Margaret, 10-19-1896 6-26-1973
SPEED, Floyd J., 1899-1972
SPEED, Lela O., 1900-No Date
CAGLE, Collins, 6-26-1917 No Date
CAGLE, Betty Lois, 5-26-1926 No Date
SMITH, Dock Joe, 10-8-1889 11-10-1973
SMITH, Myrtle, 3-22-1907 3-28-1978
COTTEN, Herbert Z., 11-30-1900 No Date
COTTEN, Nancy Beatrice, 1-1-1897 2-4-1967
LAKE, Pleasant S., 1876-1961
LAKE, Elizabeth H., 1877-1973
MORGAN, C. Leon, 1918-No Date
MORGAN, Nina Chloe, 1922-No Date
SANDLIN, Col. James Lee, D.D., 4-18-1902 No Date
SANDLIN, Marie JOHNSON, 3-17-1900 No Date
WEST, William E., S-Sgt., U.S.A.F., 9-20-1946 8-28-1974
WEST, Annie Mae, 3-18-1923 No Date
WEST, Henry A. "Buster", 11-5-1918 No Date
NARRAMORE, William Oscar, 8-7-1894 12-9-1966
COZART, Charles Lester, 5-12-1897 9-8-1973
COZART, Lona Kate, 9-3-1904 No Date
WARD, Charles W., 1979-1979
SPENCER, Mary Rita, U.S. Navy, W. W. II., 1923-1976

MARION, Frank H., Tex., M.M 1, U.S. Navy, W. W. I, 5-3-1895 4-8-1966
MARION, Althea PEARSON, 2-24-1905 No Date
WILEMON, E. A. "Ted", 2-25-1909 3-3-1977
WILEMON, Lannie E., 3-31-1917 No Date
WILEMON, Jett U., 11-15-1936 12-15-1975
WILEMON, Claudia J., 11-17-1938 No Date
CLEM, Verona COCHRANE, 1910-1973
CLEM, Fred Clarance, 1906-1978
RICHARDSON, Wiley, 1888-1974
RICHARDSON, Opal, 1892-No Date
KING, Maurine, 1926-No Date
KING, Thomas H., 1930-No Date
KING, Thomas Keith, Tex. Pfc., Co. E., 9 Mar., 3 Mar. Div., Vietnam, PH.,
                    8-14-1946 3-26-1966
BURCHETT, Willie, 4-5-1900 No Date
BURCHETT, Bertha, 3-2-1904 No Date
JOHNSON, Robert J., 1886 No Date
                    Married 1-10-1911
JOHNSON, Josie Ebnar, 1887-1973
NATION, John H., 1903-No Date
NATION, Viola, 1904-No Date
ROBINS, Claud, 1895-No Date
ROBINS, Cora B., 1897-1975
LONG, Luther C., 10-5-1908 4-2-1968
            married 9-2-1927
LONG, Mae Bell, 12-14-1912 No Date
BLAKE, P. M., 1893-1975
BLAKE, Novella M., 1894-No Date
CALLAHAN, Edgar C., 1909-1979
BURK, Willard B., 1895-1971
BURK, Johnnie J., 1894-1977
WALKER, James L., 1889-1960
WALKER, Myrtle A., 1894-1973
ROWELL, E. Quillie, 1888-1968
ROWELL, Tommie Grace, 1897-No Date
BRIDGEWATER, Robert T., 1892-1974
BRIDGEWATER, Bertha A., 1895-No Date
PHILLIPS, Jack L., 11-23-1898 2-21-1968
ROGERS, G. C., Tec.5, U.S.Army, W. W. II, 1922-1975
ROGERS, Laurene V., 10-21-1922 No Date
HINTON, Wm. F., 7-9-1911 No Date
HINTON, Mary Louise, 3-3-1921 No Date
LOWE, Dora Elizabeth, 11-5-1929 12-7-1969
MOORE, Jessie Earl, 1-24-1907 9-30-1972
MOORE, Ella A., 4-12-1904 10-21-1974
SHAW, Daniel Scott, 6-14-1967 1-17-1968
HACKNEY, B. Frank, 12-13-1889 4-13-1979
HACKNEY, Ella ALLISON, 8-16-1898 No Date
MC CURDY, Leucious L., 8-15-1898 4-30-1976
            married 10-23-1931
MC CURDY, Purnie A., 10-4-1911 No Date
KNOX, Richard Evert, 8-17-1917 No Date
KNOX, Norma Mildred PIGG, 2-13-1920 2-27-1975
DAVIDSON, Joseph R., 7-21-1909 7-11-1967

DAVIDSON, Helen M., 12-15-1915 No Date
LEINART, Osie, 10-19-1909 No Date
LEINART, Hazel, 6-20-1908 No Date
BARKER, H. E. "Sonny", 1925-1978
BARKER, Virgie TERRY, 1903-No Date
BRUNER, Mary E., 1899-No Date
BRUNER, Ivory I., 1897-1973
EWELL, Lankford, 1917-1972
EWELL, Virginia, 1920-No Date
STEWART, John P., 1894-No Date
STEWART, Lizzie B., 1897-No Date
WILEMON, W. M. "Bill", 1912-No Date
WILEMON, Opal Ivalee, 1923-1978
WADE, Jack E., BT-2, U. S. Navy, Korea, 5-9-1930 2-13-1978
WADE, Esta L., 12-7-1938 No Date
MONTGOMERY, Ben A., 1904-1977
MONTGOMERY, Leola K., 1913-No Date
NEWHOUSE, Edw. C., 6-30-1901 No Date
NEWHOUSE, Thelma M., 2-12-1909 2-18-1974
BAUM, Annie L., 8-3-1917 7-21-1978
LOVE, Jeff. Ray, Sr., 12-10-1902 8-21-1974
LOVE, Benita Viola, 10-31-1908 No Date
            son of Philip Hodge LOVE and Clarissa B. BOZEMAN
          daughter of Vernon W. HARTHCOCK and Lillie Zelene MOORE
GOLDEN, Nelda Gay, 9-22-1942 10-3-1977
JONES, E. W., 11-21-1939 9-4-1978
JONES, Opal, 12-21-1913 6-2-1976
JONES, Elmer W., 10-9-1909 9-20-1974
MC GAUGHEY, Annie Marie, 5-9-1919 7-21-1966
CRUMP, George, 1926-1977
            married 1-12-1950
CRUMP, Elisie, 1934-No Date
PENNINGTON, George H., 3-11-1920 No Date
            married 12-12-1941
PENNINGTON, Rosalie B., 2-7-1925 6-15-1974
BOLEN, Derrell, 1916-No Date
BOLEN, Louise, 1915-1978
REIGER, Marvin J., 1904-1971
REIGER, Grace A., 1906-No Date
YOUNGBLOOD, Marie MATTHEWS, 10-4-1900 12-15-1974
COPPINGER, Lennis D., 1913-1979
COPPINGER, Clara M., 1916-No Date
CLARK, John Baird, Sr., 11-6-1908 No Date
CLARK, Mary Alice, 5-28-1909 No Date
CLARK, John Baird, Jr., 1-13-1931 2-14-1978
HART, Kit Carson, 11-17-1889 7-15-1975
HART, Frankie BAIRD, 12-4-1897 7-1-1969
SEAMAN, Harriet PATTY, 8-7-1886 7-4-1972   (Mother)
PATTY, Nell Margaret, 12-10-1916 3-18-1966   (Daughter)
FITZGERALD, Richard L., Sr., 1903-1976
FITZGERALD, Maurine BAIRD, 1902-No Date
FITZGERALD, Richard L., Jr., 1934-1973
BAIRD, Ulys C., 3-12-1902 No Date
BAIRD, Beno H., 9-6-1900 6-19-1977

MARTIN, Jas. Alfred, Sr., 10-9-1906 No Date
MARTIN, Elsie CLICK, 10-31-1908 No Date
BERRY, Emmitt W., 7-17-1910 5-15-1978
BERRY, Frances B., 11-8-1915 11-21-1977
GOODMAN, L. W. "Bill", 1916-1968
GOODMAN, Mildred L., 1920-1977
RUSSELL, Robert, 1878-1968
RUSSELL, Naomi, 1887-1976
SOMERS, Dwane, 1926-1975
SOMERS, Corene, 1914-No Date

SECTION "C"

GILBERT, Susan Patricia, 8-30-1961 12-13-1966
WARREN, Earl E., 1-16-1921 12-14-1959
WARREN, Mary V., 11-15-1921 No Date
WARRICK, William Ray, Tex. S-2, U.S.N., W. W. II, 8-13-1925 9-9-1973
WARRICK, Mary Jo, 12-7-1925 No Date
LANGLEY, Everett A., Cpl. U. S. Army, 2-2-1908 6-21-1975
SPRING, John, Jr., 1889-1966
LA FAVERS, Debra Jane, 1-13-1956 3-17-1956
BANKS, William W., La., Band, Cpl., Hdq. Co., 141 FA., W. W. I.,
                                        1-3-1897 12-23-1964
BURKHART, Jacqueline AGEE, 1926-1978
NORMAN, Donald Scott, 1971-1973
FANT, Billy L., 1923-1978
FANT, Ruth W., 1927-No Date
WOOD, Henry O., 1908-No Date
WOOD, Ione E., 1914-NO Date
ARDREY, Ruth WRIGHT, 5-9-1903 12-11-1961
WRIGHT, Raleigh, 6-7-1870 4-18-1971
WRIGHT, Nina PARKER, 5-10-1876 4-7-1966
BRACK, Gilbert Herman, Tex. S-1, U.S.N.R., W. W. II, 3-29-1907 1-20-1960
BRACK, Ruby Pearl, 2-19-1911 2-15-1960
NELSON, Oney E., 1904-1977
NELSON, Josie O., 1912-No Date
PEYTON, Jim H., 1901-1961
CALLAWAY, Jas. W., 1880-1968
CALLAWAY, A. Della, 1889-No Date
CALLAWAY, Everett H., 1905-No Date
CALLAWAY, Alice, 1907-No Date
SPRINKLE, Ettie May, 1903-1956
AGEE, Herman H., 1902-1960
AGEE, Mary Grace, 1904-No Date
SPRINKLE, Larry Dow, died 11-18-1956
RASCOE, Fred A., 1896-1966
DENNIS, John S., 11-9-1947 4-11-1966
BROWN, William Price, Tex. Hq. Co., 161 Inf., Pvt.- W. W. I., 10-7-1895 7-14-1958
BROWN, Willie Inez, 10-31-1907 11-17-1962
ARBUCKLE, C. L., 1922-1966
ARBUCKLE, Evelyn KEITH, 1925-No Date
MORGAN, Diane, 1940-1977
PATTERSON, Byron, 1913-1978

OWENS, Agnes V., 8-22-1888 3-22-1978
DORMAN, Kirtley W., 3-17-1916 4-5-1965
LOCKMILLER, J. F., 1882-1959
PICKLE, Athalene, 1931-1974
WATSON, Curtis B., 1914-1966
WATSON, Bertha Ann, 1894-1975
CLICK, Albert F., Pvt., W. W. I, U. S. Army
            Chaplin, W. W. II, & Korea, 8-18-1898 No Date
CLICK, Margaret W., Registered Nurse, 10-4-1902 12-6-1971
CLICK, Albert Wayne, 1st. Lt., 65th AABn., "B" Batry., 3-14-1929 7-13-1970
WHITE, William M., 1889-1959
WHITE, Margaret C., 1893-1973
WHITE, R. T. "TODD", 1906-No Date
WHITE, Odette F., 1905-No Date
WHITE, James E., 1900-No Date
WHITE, Sarah E., 1900-No Date
WHITE, Charlcie Lou, 1921-No Date
WHITE, Argie B., 1893-1966
WHITE, Dellar May, 1905-No Date
HICKS, Homer P., 1879-1959
HICKS, Pearl V., 1894-1964
MC KEE, A. F. "Bud", 1891-1972
MC KEE, Willie M., 1888-1963
RODDY, Marion S., 1-18-1940 4-17-1970
JONES, R. Amber, 1899-1960
JONES, Alta Mae, 1903-1976
THULIS, Bessie, 1922-1962
THULIS, Gary, 1956-1962
PURKEY, Betty Jean, 9-19-1948 11-22-1962
DICKERSON, Charlie L., 1902-no Date
DICKERSON, Annie Lue, 1909-No Date
LUCKETT, George A., 1929-No Date
LUCKETT, Charlene, 1931-1972
DEWEESE, Luther A., 1902-No Date
DEWEESE, Bertha A., 1912-No Date
KIRK, Emmett M., 1881-1959
KIRK, Elizabeth B., 1886-1972
COVINGTON, Raymond J., 1913-1969
COVINGTON, Eula COATS, 1918-No Date
CUMMINGS, Earl L., 1893-1959
CUMMINGS, Alta C., 1889-1976
SNELL, Charles D., 1894-1978
DYER, Tom B., 1889-1977
DYER, Monnie E., 1893-No Date
ANDREWS, Alluwee C., 1890-1970
ANDREWS, Ella Mae, 1894-1978
CAMPBELL, Charles L., 1899-No Date
CAMPBELL, Myrtle M., 1903-1978
JOHNSON, Billy R., 8-15-1918 No Date
JOHNSON, Geraldyne S., 5-9-1918 No Date
JOHNSON, Sharon Faye, 5-11-1945 10-5-1965
NICHOLSON, May M., 1895-No Date
NICHOLSON, Novice L., 1892-1976
NICHOLSON, Jackie Lee, 9-15-1951 6-12-1971

HEIDMANN, Walter, 5-14-1907 7-30-1958
SMITH, J. Boyd, 10-25-1890 11-26-1965
SMITH, Eula B., 8-30-1890 10-10-1964
SMITH, Noel B., 8-15-1916 12-31-1963
LUCKETT, Odie E., 1900-No Date
LUCKETT, Esther, 1900-1973
CUPP, Jesse B., 1909-NO Date
CUPP, Pauline, 1915-No Date
KING, Tula, 1888-1966
PRATT, Louie A., 1924-1967
WALLACE, L. W. "Fayette", 1890-1977
WALLACE, Fannie Lou, 1892-No Date
LATIMER, Charles Leon, 1920-No Date
LATIMER, Lida Fay, 1920-No Date
CUPP, James B., 1908-1975
WINTERS, James M., died 5-12-1967
WINTERS, Ronald K., 4-4-1970 4-6-1970
WINTERS, Jerry K., 4-4-1970 4-5-1970
ARUNDALE, Alfred Garner, 1917-1967
ARMSTRONG, E. Gordon, 1890-1977
ARMSTRONG, Nellie B., 1905-1978
LEEMAN, Mack, 1879-1975
LEEMAN, Hattie, 1881-No Date
SUMROW, Hubert, 1899-1978
SUMROW, Bonnie P., 1900-No Date
BACKUS, Percy D., 1897-1972
BACKUS, Lydia K., 1906-No Date
RAMIREZ, Martin, 1914-1978
FLETCHER, Herbert H., 1889-1960
FLETCHER, Esta M., 1893-1966
THOMASON, Garland, 1898-1968
THOMASON, Maurine, 1904-1975
EVANS, James C. "Jack", 1912-1966
CROWELL, Howard H., 1924-No Date
CROWELL, Janice G., 1915-No Date
POTEET, Kenneth L., 1922-No Date
POTEET, Jo Ann, 1930-No Date
LOWERY, Grady, 1907-1976
LOWERY, Ruth, 1910-NO Date
COOPER, Ruth, died 2-14-1958
BRIGNON, Louis, 11-22-1891 7-4-1958
BRIGNON, Stella, 11-17-1896 10-5-1970
DUNCAN, Roy Leon, 1910-1973
DUNCAN, Faye Adrine, 1914-No Date
FLETCHER, William m., 1925-No Date
FLETCHER, Maurace M., 1930-No Date
CODY, W. C., U.S. Navy Ret., 1900-No Date
WELLS, Roy C., 1921-1972
WELLS, Corine, 1923-No Date
COLE, Alice FLOYD, 1913-1968
GOODE, Dr. Emmette P., 1890-1970
GOODE, Alpha M., 1891-No Date
MAYNARD, J. C., 1867-1960
MAYNARD, Minnie B., 1877-1964

BARKER, Fred L., 1901-No Date
BARKER, Maggie D., 1901-No Date
SPRINKLE, W. Chandler, 1911-No Date
SPRINKLE, Mildred L., 1918-No Date
HOUSTON, Otto Clyde, 1911-1963
THOMAS, C. Stanley, 1931-No Date
                    married 2-16-1952
THOMAS, Sallye J., 1932-No Date
SPARKS, J. Alexander, 1887-1908
SPARKS, Martha V., 1862-1958
SPARKS, Abner E., 1843-1921
BREWER, William J., Jr., 1910-No Date
BREWER, Anita Nell, 1913-No Date
HOUSTON, Royal V., 1888-1962
HOUSTON, Maude, 1892-1962
HUTCHINS, James F., 1915-No Date
HUTCHINS, Dorothy M., 1921-No Date
JOHNSON, Cleo MOSELEY, 1911-1975
MOSELEY, Truman C., 1906-1958
BRIGNON, William V., 1922-1975
BRIGNON, Jaunita S., 1926-No Date
DRIGGERS, Betty Jean, 4-15-1933 5-12-1968
BOWEN, Elijah A., 1882-1966
BOWEN, Nannie L., 1879-1958
BOWEN, E. A., Jr., 1914-No Date
HARRIS, Duke I., 11-2-1900 2-19-1970
DENTON, William Glen, 1911-No Date
DENTON, Evelyn R., 1922-No Date
MICKLER, Grady J., 3-25-1890 1-16-1975
MICKLER, Meda A., 4-30-1894 5-22-1971
MICKLER, Pat, 1-16-1920 1-12-1965
MAXWELL, Bethel Ray, 1-12-1920 8-19-1969
                    Tex. Pfc., U. S. A., W. W. II, Ph
OWNBY, Arvis L., 1907-No Date
OWNBY, Florence L., 1914-No Date
OWNBY, J. B., 1884-1964
OWNBY, Lula, 1884-1958
STOCKS, Margie OWNBY, 6-18-1910 3-17-1976
MC VAY, Lester, 1893-1958
MC VAY, Ioda, 1898-1975
HAMILTON, Hayden M., 1894-1976
HAMILTON, Lucille H., 1902-No Date
DAVIS, Clyde, 1898-1973
DAVIS, Lerah FARRIS, 1902-No Date
SPRINKLE, Albert M., 1886-1979
SPRINKLE, Jennie, 1893-1972
HOOVER, Horace, 1896-1974
HOOVER, Louise, 1896-No Date
SOCKWELL, Frank, 1891-1975
SOCKWELL, Alene, 1900-No Date
BIGGS, W. E., Sr., 1898-1976
BIGGS, Grace A., 1895-1970
HUNNICUTT, Thomas L., 1892-1964
HUNNICUTT, Stella L., 1903-No Date

NORRIS, Mary M., 1883-1975
KELLY, Marvin Paul, 5-28-1911 No Date
KELLY, Millie Opal, 2-22-1920 No Date
INGRAM, Emmaline R., 1890-1975
WESTON, Nannie Lou, 1911-1976
WINTERS, Maurice E., 1884-No Date
WINTERS, Ollie D., 1889-No Date
TILLERY, Charles Tyson, 3-3-1963   11-19-1963
QUINN, Bennie F., 1909-No Date
QUINN, Wilma Jean, 1916-1969
CANADA, Cecil C., 1917-1974
CANADA, Frances L., 1918-No Date
BACON, Francis Marion, 7-4-1874   5-15-1968
BACON, Mary Adline, 8-2-1884   9-8-1974
DAVENPORT, George E., 1896-1965
DAVENPORT, Lillian B., 1903-NO Date
TROTTER, Garland, 1902-1876
TROTTER, Gladys, 1907-No Date
WALLACE, Malcolm, Tex., 1st. Lt., TC, 3-3-1933   6-5-1959
FLETCHER, W. C. "Buck", 1903-No Date
FLETCHER, Lillie Mae, 1908-No Date
SPRINKLE, Daniel E., 1877-1960
SPRINKLE, Retha D., 1883-1968
WOODRUFF, W. W. "Bill", 1911-1875
WOODRUFF, Allene, 1915-No Date
CALDWELL, Dow H., 1895-1976
CALDWELL, Dollie M., 1890-No Date
LOCKE, Harold L., 10-22-1916   6-5-1957
AIKMAN, James Stephen, Tex. S-Sgt., Hq. Del., 524 M.P. B.N., W. W. II.,
                        1-27-1907 6-16-1959
AIKMAN, Grace Virginia, 8-6-1908   No Date
MELVILLE, James C., 1893-1973
MELVILLE, Nannie L., 1898-No Date
ELDRIDGE, Freeman, 1906-1977
ELDRIDGE, Jettie, 1900-1971
SPIGNER, Ernest, 1882-1965
SPIGNER, Sally C., 1888-1964
SPIGNER, John H., 1896-1967
SPIGNER, Allcie J., 1898-No Date
BURGIN, Ernest W., 1898-No Date
BURGIN, Leatha J., 1899-1971
BURGIN, Mary Jo, 2-18-1925 No Date
HARRIS, Fount L., 1908-1976
HARRIS, Doris A., 1912-No Date
SMITH, Walter W., 1896-No Date
SMITH, Ruby Lee, 1901-1970
BOYD, Willard, 1903-1965
BOYD, Gladys Lorene, 1901-1976
LAMB, Dusti Lynn, 4-3-1967   6-30-1967
HARRIS, Delmar R., 1922-1959
HARRIS, Christine B., 1922-No Date
CARTER, Rev. W. A., D. D., 1895-1959
GREER, Mabel, 1888-1969
GREER, Morris, 1885-1965

SPRINKLE, Mack C., U. S. Army, W. W. I., 1892-1977
SPRINKLE, Lela B., 10-11-1883 10-15-1976
GOVER, A. C. "Curt", 1915-1972   (Father)
GOVER, Michael L., 1946-1972   (Son)
TROTTER, Mrs. G. G., 1882-1956
TROTTER, Charles E., 1921-No Date
TROTTER, Betty D., 1932-No Date
SPEIGHT, Ralph T., 1912-1965
SPEIGHT, Ola B., 1914-No Date
DUNCAN, Madge COWAN, 9-7-1882 6-2-1965
COWAN, William Edward, Tex. CY- U. S. N. R., W. W. II., 1-13-1909 6-20-1955
JONES, Houston L., 1909-1978
JONES, Alma L., 1917-No Date
BIFFLE, Herman, 1908-No Date
BIFFLE, Mabel L., 1910-No Date
HARRISON, Opal O., 4-9-1918 11-19-1969
TUCKER, Martha, 1907-1962
BALLARD, James Arthur, 1897-1974
BALLARD, Stel KIRBY, 1898-No Date
FRYE, John W., 1878-1967
FRYE, Minnie F., 1888-No Date
PEMBERTON, William Jap, 1910-1976
PEMBERTON, Thelma Bell, 1919-No Date
BROWN, Annie, 1872-1957
BREWER, Herbert F., 1901-1966
BREWER, Royetta, 1901-1976
WARREN, Tom W., Pfc., Med. Dept., 359 Inf., W. W. I., 10-24-1891 3-14-1970
MASON, Dewitt C., 1893-1975
MASON, Zela E., 1898-No Date
MC DONALD, Davis, 1920-1970
TATE, Joe Willard, 1916-1967
TATE, Velma Odessa, 1918-No Date
TATE, L. H., 1889-1975
TATE, Dovie, 1894-1975
DENTON, William C., 10-7-1879 10-13-1958
DENTON, Samantha J., 10-30-1879 1-21-1956
YOUNG, Valton H., Tex. M-Sgt., 18 Field Arty Brig., W. W. II.,
                          6-10-1915 6-3-1972
YOUNG, Vera V., 11-8-1913 No Date
NIXON, Albert W., 1889-1962
NIXON, Amanda L., 1893-1966
WALLACE, Morris L., 1908-No Date
WALLACE, Elizabeth M., 1900-1979
POWELL, O. C., 1897-1976
HARRISON, R. E., 2-22-1892 11-22-1971
HARRISON, Pauline E., 3-12-1901 12-21-1963
CARTER, George M., 11-28-1875 4-14-1955
CARTER, Rosa C., 3-22-1889 10-23-1967
GRAHAM, Charlie S., 1892-1964
GRAHAM, Julia D., 1894-1974
COWAN, Margarie C., 1914-No Date
COWAN, Thomas P., 1906-1961
RODDY, Pauline, 1905-1972
ELLIS, Ida SEBLEY, 4-25-1897 12-15-1962

SPEIGHT, Jimmy, 1933-1979
SPEIGHT, Lilbern, 7-23-1910 4-11-1960
CHANDLER, Fannie WEST, 189_-1958
LOWERY, James W., 5-26-1888 5-12-1962
LOWERY, Maggie L., 4-14-1888 3-6-1970
MULLINIX, Sam O., 1898-1961
MULLINIX, Cecil Fay, 1905-No Date
HUDSON, Alma W., Tex. Cpl., Demoilization Gp., W. W. I., 8-23-1896 12-26-1956
CRABB, Jesse P., 1892-1968
CRABB, Grace B., 1897-1953
CRAIGO, Robert A., Tex., Pfc., 36 Mil. Police Co., W. W. I.,
                               8-6-1896 9-15-1955

MILLS, Raymon C., 1912-No Date
MILLS, Christine O., 1921-No Date
GOVER, Dorothy L., 1911-1979
SOCKWELL, James G., 1906-1966
SOCKWELL, Oney C., 1905-No Date
SOCKWELL, Leon "Tuck", 2-21-1903 12-1-1966
SOCKWELL, Goergia O., 11-25-1905 8-31-1972
MAJORS, Rev. W. O., 8-15-1891 No Date
MAJORS, Ethel May, 4-25-1896 3-24-1971
HULSEY, John W., 1891-1959
HULSEY, Lora R., 1906-No Date
CALDWELL, Sidney, 1890-1976
CALDWELL, Nancy, 1892-NO Date
TERRY, Robert J., 1912-1972
TERRY, Opal E., 1909-No Date
TERRY, Charoltte A., 1950-No Date
JACKSON, George B., 1877-1963
JACKSON, Ruth B., 1883-1963
LANDRUM, Oscar B., 1894-1961
LANDRUM, Bessie L., 1896-No Date
MC CLURE, June, 1946-1963
GRAHAM, George L., 1887-1969
GRAHAM, May, 1893-No Date
WALDEN, Oliver J., 1910-No Date
WALDEN, Kate, 1910-No Date

SECTION "D"

LEE, Edward S., 1916-No Date
LEE, Ella Faye, 1924-No Date
HAMILTON, Raymond I, "Red", 1906-NO Date
HAMILTON, Mary Alice, 1904-No Date
SIDES, Charles W., 1905-No Date
SIDES, Opal J., 1910-No Date
HABLUETZEL, Charles Leon, 1912-No Date
HABLUETZEL, Hazel H., 1917-No Date
DUVALL, Erby, 1906-1979
DUVALL, Claudia, 1908-No Date
BOLLES, Charles R., 2-16-1913 6-21-1976
PAYNE, Walter L., 1915-1974
PAYNE, Clyde C., 1908-1975

LIPSEY, Jimmy Leon, 1936-No Date
LIPSEY, Oleta Joyce, 1938-No Date
WILLIAMS, Elmon, 1916-No Date
WILLIAMS, Lorene, 1920-1979
GRANTHAM, Mrs. Emma, 1889-1978
MC CLURE, Jerry Wayne, 10-30-1951 7-8-1978
HENRY, J. B., 1905-1974
HENRY, Thelma, 1910-No Date
TAACK, Grace GILES, 1898-No Date
GLAZE, Millard E., 1908-No Date
GLAZE, Ethel Leona, 1903-1978
KANAZAWA, Masaru, U.S. Army, 10-1-1924 3-18-1978
WENDT, Wanda Jean, 1962-1979
HANNER, Doris, 1921-1978
MILLER, Guy M., 1916-No Date
MILLER, Willie Jo, 1920-No Date
KINSLOW, Jo Ann, 1930-1976
PAYNE, Don A., 1909-No Date
PAYNE, Charlie Jo, 1911-No Date
HARWELL, R. R. "Bob", 1924-No Date
HARWELL, Mary E., 1925-No Date
ROW, Luther C., 1914-No Date
ROW, Lorene G., 1918-No Date
TIPTON, Roy C., 1907-1975
TIPTON, Leta B., 1911-No Date
LURIE, Beulah M. "Aunt Boots", 1905-1978
BURROUGHS, Johnnie E., 1913-No Date
BURROUGHS, Bonnie B., 1913-No Date
ELLIOTT, Timothy S., 10-8-1961 9-29-1977
ROSELL, Marion M., 1905-1978
TRAD, George K., Capt. U. S. Army, W. W. II, 9-5-1910 1-9-1977
LOWERY, Henry M., 1919-1978
LOWERY, Wanda Jo, 1919-No Date
COLLINS, William W., 1921-No Date
COLLINS, Geneva L., 1919-No Date
HEARN, Titus L., 1899-1976
HEARN, Jewel E., 1906-No Date
SANDLIN, Frank M., 1903-1977
SANDLIN, Annie M., 1909-No Date
CATHEY, Hollis, 1907-1977
CATHEY, Melba, 1912-No Date
MILES, James Weldon, 1923-No Date
MILES, Marie Caroline, 1925-No Date
RICHTERS, Ennis, 1925-1977
RICHTERS, Jaynie, 1928-No Date
MERIWETHER, Larry E., 1943-1975
PEARCE, Clarence C., 1911-No Date
PEARCE, Mildred, 1912-1978
LYBRAND, Afton "Sammy", 11-22-1914 4-23-1976
LYBRAND, Margaret S., 5-25-1920 No Date
MC CASKILL, Bobby D., 1932-1976
MC CASKILL, Elizabeth E., 1937-No Date
MILLER, Joe A., 1916-No Date
MILLER, Winnie D., 1913-No Date

CASEY, Ellen Nicole, 5-20-1974 11-30-1974
EICHNER, George L., 1909-No Date
EICHNER, Audrey K., 1913-No Date
REGAN, James O., 1909-No Date
REGAN, Geneva, 1921-No Date
HILL, Artie D., 1906-1976
HILL, Julia D., 1909-No Date
SPAINHOUR, C. W., 1916-No Date
SPAINHOUR, Lois V., 1918-No Date
VAUGHN, William m., 12-14-1887 8-5-1977
GOODMAN, Robert A., 1955-1977
MARTIN, L. M., 1927-No Date
MARTIN, Marguriete, 1924-No Date
HORNE, Robert E., 1926-No Date
HORNE, Mary M., 1932-No Date
JENKINS, Woodrow W., 1917-1975
JENKINS, Eula Faye, 1918-No Date
HICKS, James E., 1911-1976
HICKS, Reubene, 1915-No Date
HIBBETTS, C. William, 1901-1975
HIBBETTS, Mary H., 1911-No Date
POWNELL, Lula K., 1907-No Date
EDDLEMON, James H., Pvt., U. S. Army, W. W. I., 11-22-1888 9-27-1975
EDDLEMON, Iva Ruth, 11-13-1898 8-27-1977
JONES, Laura G., 7-11-1887 3-25-1977
CARTER, Melvin L., 1897-1978
CARTER, Ida Mae, 1914-No Date
BOULTON, Leon B., 1917-No Date
BOULTON, Geraldine, 1917-No Date
GLASSCOCK, James, 1928-1978
FOWLER, John Roy, No Dates
FOWLER, Ethel J., 10-22-1909 6-19-1979
TAYLOR, Brice L., 1924-No Date
TAYLOR, Verline, 1922-No Date
COLE, S. B., 1896-1975
BEALL, Weldon T., 1915-No Date
BEALL, Lois H., 1917-No Date
BROWN, J. Ross, 1901-No Date
BROWN, Willabelle, 1913-No Date
DYER, Charles R., 1896-1975
DYER, Annie R., 1899-No Date
PRICE, Joyce, 1919-1976
PRICE, Ray, 1918-No Date
COOK, Sam, 1908-1975
COOK, Margaret, 1909-No Date
MALONE, Betty, 1918-1978
SMITH, Christieon Nicole, 12-14-1976 2-2-1977
ALSOBROOK, John B., 1894-No Date
ALSOBROOK, Neader E., 1902-1979
HOCKETT, C. R. "Joe", 1907-No Date
HOCKETT, Melba Lee, 1909-No Date
LOCKWOOD, David D., 1931-1978
LOCKWOOD, Betty F., 1946-No Date
MARTIN, Dewey Reados, 1911-No Date

MARTIN, Wilma Mae, 1911-No Date
MC CORMACK, Carl Don, 1938-No Date
MC CORMACK, Linnie May, 1940-No Date
HYATT, M. J. "Jack", 1914-1979
HYATT, Leta R., 1913-No Date
OLER, Helen Grace, 1917-1979
NEWSOM, Clarence M., YNC, U. S. Army, W. W. II., 1918-1977
DOMINGUEZ, Manuel, 1899-1978
DONINGUEZ, Emilia C., 1907-No Date
WATTS, James V., 1928-1976
WATTS, Janice, 1933-No Date
HALL, Eunice Norma, 1925-1979
PORTER, Dayton M., 1901-No Date
PORTER, Bessie L., 1903-1977
VANCE, J. C. "Jack", 1914-No Date
VANCE, Patsy, 1914-No Date
GRAHAM, Mary Alice "Muddie", 1894-No Date
GRAHAM, James A., Pvt., U. S. Army, W. W. II., 1917-1975
GRAHAM, William Albert, 1885-No Date
HAWK, Paul C., 1910-1977
SCARBOUGH, R. E., 1917-No Date
SCARBOUGH, Katherleen, 1920-No Date
GRIMES, Wallace A., PHM, 3 U. S. NAVY, W. W. II., 5-29-1914   2-13-1977
GRIMES, Connie M., 9-25-1915 No Date
CASTLE, Bennie R., 1892-No Date
CASTLE, Lenice M., 1905-No Date
VICKERS, Jimmy, 1949-1977
GLASSCOCK, Clyde B., 1911-No Date
GLASSCOCK, Leta K., 1920-No Date
WHITE, Derrell F., 1938-No Date
WHITE, Patsy J., 1939-No Date
PARMELY, J. Ray, 1905-NO Date
PARMELY, I. Jewell, 1908-No Date
BENNETT, James M., 1927-No Date
BENNETT, Lois L., 1921-No Date
BYRNE, Ethel R., 1926-1978
RAMSEY, Foster L., Sr., 1910-No Date
RAMSEY, Edna K. , 1913-No Date
MALONE, J. D., 1921-No Date
MALONE, Sylvia A., 1937-No Date
SHIELDS, George Wallace, 1918-1977
SHIELDS, Juaneace J., 1920-NO Date
LYTLE, Hubert H., 1909-No Date
LYTLE, Marjorie K., 1914-No Date
NORFLEET, John W., 12-21-1893 6-29-1975
NORFLEET, Lillie M., 1-11-1907 No Date
ROBINSON, Burdette A., 1924-1976
ROBINSON, Clare M., 1918-No Date
WALLACE, Billy Clark, 1930-1976
WALLACE, Bobbie Faye, 1932-No Date
MC CAIN, Eddie, Jr., 1925-No Date
MC CAIN, Mary Helen, 1929-No Date

ROY, Fred M., 1911-No Date
ROY, Beatrice E., 1916-No Date
ROY, Marvin M., 4-29-1920 1-25-1964
PEYTON, Ruth HORTON, 1904-1971
WILLINGHAM, Bailey J., 1891-No Date
WILLINGHAM, Ella D., 1897-1970
HENDRICKS, W. H. "Bill", 1903-1962
BOOSE, Claude L., 1905-No Date
BOOSE, Ruth P., 1913-No Date
BURKS, Carl W., 1912-No Date
BURKS, Bernice E., 1917-No Date
COVEY, Claude A., 1895-1977
COVEY, Rubye O., 1902-No Date
LUTTRELL, Clarence E., 5-3-1886 5-5-1975
LUTTRELL, Bettie, 11-9-1886 6-14-1963
JONES, Fred L., 4-15-1895 4-16-1969
JONES, Cordie, 8-5-1899 9-5-1975
LUTTRELL, Maggie Z., 9-14-1877 12-20-1957
KING, Trudy B., 8-22-1901 8-14-1964
CRAIG, R. Bruce, 1890-1960
CRAIG, Emma E., 1897-1967
BUTLER, Paul E., Sr., 1911-1974
TURNER, Azelle BUTLER, 1929-1971
RUSSELL, Cora, 1874-1958
STEWART, George S., 6-13-1887 4-4-1966
STEWART, Hattie B., 12-28-1894 5-5-1960
PIPPIN, Howard E., 3-7-1926 3-30-1973
SPURLOCK, Byron J., 8-23-1897 10-6-1974
SPURLOCK, Madge E., 7-30-1897 No Date
COBBS, Lewis H., 1908-1973
COBBS, Lettie, 1907-No Date
DUNLAP, Amos L., 1904-1946
DUNLAP, Lois M., 1913-No Date
INABINETTE, James O., 1902-1971
INABINETTE, Ollie K., 1904-No Date
MORGAN, Rayburn E., A.V.N. Cadet, U. S. Navy, 6-13-1927 1-5-1975
MORGAN, Reuben E., 3-7-1902 2-11-1975
MORGAN, Beatrice B., 1-15-1905 No Date
BOLTON, James C., 1903-1964
BOLTON, Eva Ruby, 1902-1970
DEATON, Lloyd Gene, 12-22-1921 9-7-1974
SWANN, George E., 1894-1971
SWANN, Flora Mae, 1903-No Date
CRUMPTON, Murray A., 1932-No Date
CRUMPTON, Freeda M., 1934-No Date
ALLEN, John B., 1887-1975
ALLEN, Daisy WALL, 1894-No Date
REED, Joe, 4-3-1903 No Date
REED, Mabel, 10-7-1903 No Date
CASSELL, Kelly, 1917-1977
CASSELL, Mary E., 1931-No Date
LINDSEY, William O., 1907-1968

LINDSEY, Loucille N., 1920-No Date
CARDWELL, Edgar L., 9-5-1891 8-13-1969
CARDWELL, Nora L., 7-4-1893 8-20-1969
CARDWELL, Oscar C., 1893-1955
CARDWELL, Jennie B., 1892-No Date
CARDWELL, B. Leon, 8-27-1911 10-22-1959
KING, Bernice, 1946-1974
BAKER, Harold J., 1923-1976
LANDRUM, Walter Gerald, 1938-1978
MILLSAP, Arlin, 1905-1977
MILLSAP, Melba, 1914-No Date
CURRIN, A. V., 1921-1957
MILLSAP, Patsy L., 1936-No Date
TURNBOW, Martha Jean, 1937-1974
FLETCHER, Mary E., 7-3-1892 5-13-1975
FLETCHER, Willie C., 5-17-1895 7-16-1963
BUCK, Opal Louise, 1928-No Date
SHIELDS, James A., 1892-1976
SHIELDS, Sarah E., 1894-1978
LINCYCOMB, Robert E. Lee, 1892-No Date
LINCYCOMB, Matilda Irene, 1897-1977
STAPLETON, Willard, 10-3-1892 9-20-1954
STAPLETON, Ethel, 8-31-1904 No Date
MARTIN, Eva I., 10-13-1886 1-14-1970
MARTIN, Charlie M., 4-1-1883 9-6-1963
HACKNEY, Margaret C., 12-12-1877 2-28-1961
HACKNEY, George W., 8-8-1874 10-31-1965
CAWTHON, John Harvey, 1900-1969
CAWTHON, Willie Irene, 1903-No Date
WOOD, A. J. "Jack", 1911-1968
WOOD, Bessie, 1911-No Date
NEEDHAM, Charles A., Tex., S-Sgt., 20 TAC FTR WG AF W. W. II, Korea.,
                         12-20-1924 10-29-1959

HARPER, Byron Ross, 1904-1969
HARPER, Mary E., 1913-No Date
HARPER, David Ray, 11-27-1955 11-28-1955
HUDSON, Bennett A., 1905-No Date
HUDSON, Opal W., 1910-1979
BRINGLE, Dave Lawrence, 1898-No Date
CALLAWAY, S. Ray, 1904-1966
CALLAWAY, Ina B., 1911-1972
CALLAWAY, Bobby Ray, 1928-1970
LINGO, Ernest, 1900-1978
LINGO, Pearl B., 1907-No Date
STASTNY, Clement S., 1907-1958
STASTNY, Mamie F., 1910-No Date
BETHELL, Lynn L., 1900-1971
BETHELL, Agnes W., 1907-No Date
SMITH, Charles A., 1898-1968
SMITH, Beulah A., 1900-No Date
NORTHCUTT, Earl T., 1-18-1907 7-23-1969
MARTIN, Leonard G., 1910-No Date
MARTIN, Janie R., 1919-No Date
FRAZIER, Weldon I., 1907-No Date

FRAZIER, Bessie W., 1911-No Date
NEEL, Edd, 1875-1960
NEEL, Roxie, 1899-No Date
NEEL, Jessie Don, 1913-1964
NEEL, Clifford M., 1910-1972
WARD, Wesley W., 6-29-1958   11-16-1973
BENCH, Wallace A., 1915-No Date
BENCH, Mildred L., 1916-No Date
BRIGMAN, Norman O., 1935-1959
BRIGMAN, Susie L., 1908-No Date
BATY, Randy W., 1955-1976
HOBBS, Myre Faye, 1-18-1919 3-4-1975
HART, Hester Paralee, 1870-1958
GREER, Edna V., 1910-1976
BLACKSHEAR, J. K., 1915-No Date
BLACKSHEAR, Ettie Orene, 1915-No Date
SHARP, William Glen, 1919-1975
SHARP, Virginia H., 1923-No Date
LUCAS, R. Wayne, 11-3-1927 7-18-1975
LILLY, James Walter, Tex., Pvt., HQ Co., 359 Inf., W. W. I.,
                              8-24-1894 11-17-1970
BANKS, Johnnie Mae, 9-16-1922 1-13-1968
MILNER, Thomas L., 1898-1955
MILNER, Frank, 1907-1976
LONG, Willis M., Tex., Pvt., U. S. Army, W. W. II, 4-18-1909 8-19-1972
TIPPITT, Jennie Lee HARRIS, 7-18-1891 7-2-1961
TIPPITT, James E., Tex., Pvt., U. S. Army, W. W. I, 6-22-1893 2-14-1971
SPRINKLE, Raymond F., 1891-1970
SPRINKLE, Alma J., 1893-No Date
MOORE, Dale, 1913-1976
MOORE, Billie Jo, 1916-No Date
PETTY, Allen, 1930-No Date
PETTY, Carole, 1940-No Date
TERRY, Herbert Hendrix, 1920-No Date
TERRY, Jessie M., 10-20-1890 No Date
TERRY, Willis R., 2-8-1888 7-31-1962
RICE, Arthur W., Pvt., U. S. Army, W. W. I., 11-14-1895 8-20-1976
RICE, Exar L., 10-25-1904 No Date
NORRIS, James C., 1902-No Date
NORRIS, Tressie M., 1903-1962
MORRISON, Fletcher T., 1914-1974
MORRISON, Imogene H., 1915-No Date
DEATON, John H., 1904-No Date
DEATON, Ruby L., 1908-1978
MOORE, William H., "Bill", 1914-1977
MOORE, Marie C., 1920-No Date
PHILLIPS, Donna Marie, 1964-1972
BAILEY, L. A. "Albert", 1881-1971
CONE, Andy B., 1878-1957
CONE, Nancy J., 1878-1961
BLACKWELL, N. C. "Lee", 1898-No Date
BLACKWELL, Edith M., 1902-No Date
HARPER, William B., 10-18-1906 No Date
HARPER, Werdna Rose, 1-23-1906 8-6-1972

ALLEN, Arnie L., 1919-No Date
ALLEN, Mildred H., 1920-No Date
DICKERSON, Joseph C., 9-17-1898 No Date
DICKERSON, Lula Mae, 2-19-1902 7-19-1955
DEES, No Name No Dates
COLEMAN, Newton Leroy, 10-28-1906 11-19-1977
COLEMAN, Lizzie Mae, 4-29-1910 No Date
COLEMAN, Martha Lou, 8-14-1928 8-30-1937
COLEMAN, Raymond H. D., 9-15-1927 8-12-1928
BALDRIDGE, Dewey R., 1898-1978
BALDRIDGE, Roxie W., 1898-No Date
SUMMERLIN, William Homer, 1887-1972
SUMMERLIN, Eunice, 1888-1973
DECKER, F. Wayne, 1916-1970
DECKER, M. Lucille, 1917-No Date
MORRIS, Ida M., 1900-1954
WILSON, Roy A., 1898-1978
WILSON, Willie Lou, 1901-1978
ROBBINS, Samuel F., 1894-1968
ROBBINS, Era SMITH, 1903-No Date
SMITH, Deborah Jean, died 4-23-1954
              Inf. Dau. of Beno & Edna Jean SMITH
DECKER, Thomas Hal, 1910-1970
DECKER, Zora P., 1909-No Date
JACKSON, Mildred, 2-2-1924 11-16-1970
HUDSON, Mary JACKSON, 8-9-1937 6-7-1973
MORRIS, Hagood W., 1920-No Date
MORRIS, Marjorie C., 1922-No Date
WADE, Ray Bernard, Pvt., Army Air Force, W. W. II., 4-11-1905 1-31-1974
ADAMS, Doris A., 1930-No Date
ADAMS, James L., 1926-1976
POTEET, Hazel E., 1909-No Date
POTEET, Dova J., 1913-No Date
MACKIE, Leland F., 1902-1958
WEBB, Velvia L., 1894-1974
CLARK, Cecil D., 1918-No Date
CLARK, Maurine, 1928-No Date
RUCKER, Maude, 11-16-1889 5-10-1956
RUCKER, Fernie S., 9-30-1890 2-5-1964
STRICKLAND, Herman H., 1904-No Date
STRICKLAND, Bertie O., 1904-No Date
LOWE, Floyd Henry, Tex. Pvt., Co. G., 9 Inf. 2 Div., W. W. I., PH
              8-26-1896 1-14-1954
DEATON, Raymond H., 1928-No Date
DEATON, Melba M., 1935-No Date
DEATON, Bobby Ernest, 1935-1955
WORTHEN, Robert E., died 1973
WORTHEN, Fairy M., 1896-No Date
TODD, Herbert S., 1884-1966
TODD, Alice M., 1890-No Date
HULSE, Aaron R., 9-4-1892 12-23-1955
HULSE, Rose, 5-6-1886 12-29-1963
CAMP, George Roy, 10-26-1892 12-27-1966
CAMP, Artie J., 10-16-1894 10-18-1977

DAVIS, J. P. "Butch", 1912-1968
DAVIS, Buena "Bill", 1919-No Date
BROYLES, Gladys, 1903-1979
RODDY, Floyd, 1908-No Date
RODDY, Cordy Mae, 1916-No Date
CLARK, Quentine F., 4-23-1919 10-4-1976
CLARK, Margueritte E., 7-19-1924 No Date
HAMPTON, Ross F., 4-24-1902 12-17-1972
HAMPTON, Jewell, 5-5-1903 No Date
SHAW, Weldon H., 1908-1963
SHAW, Etta Mae, 1905-1978
SHAW, James W., 2-14-1935 No Date
STEWART, Lee Keith, 1-27-1954 1-29-1954
GARRETT, Tallie D., 1881-1959
GARRETT, Lela S., 1882-1971
WIGGS, Claud S., 1910-No Date
WIGGS, M. Lavera, 1912-No Date
GAY, J. D., Sr., 2-28-1903 No Date
GAY, Grace Lillian, 3-26-1898 7-9-1972
SMITH, Randall W., 6-20-1922 4-21-1970
CLEVELAND, Oley, 1911-No Date
CLEVELAND, Cecil, 1912-No Date
SCHULZ, John J., 1918-No Date
SCHULZ, Feddie M., 1908-No Date
HISE, Cleo, 1899-No Date
HISE, Nancy, 1898-No Date
FARMER, Randolph W., 1889-1963
FARMER, Bessie Mae, 1894-No Date
BENCH, Marion Arvel, 10-14-1900 9-12-1961
BENCH, Ada Lovera, 4-10-1900 No Date
POE, S. J., 1914-No Date
POE, Oleta, 1915-1978
JACKSON, J. Hilton, 5-16-1918 10-5-1961
MORRISON, Ollie B., 1888-1978
ORR, George B., 1-13-1910 9-5-1968
MC KINNEY, Raymond C., 1908-No Date
MC KINNEY, Georgia Faye, 1915-No Date
BAUGHN, Charles Rives, 1911-1973
PEAK, Clyde L., 1896-1977
PEAK, Anna Mae, 1900-1965
GROVES, Lee, 1914-No Date
GROVES, Oleta, 1924-No Date
HOFF, George W., 5-2-1893 No Date
HOFF, Bartis L., 10-4-1902 No Date
OLIVER, William T., 11-10-1895 No Date
OLIVER, Tammie J., 10-15-1908 9-28-1966
THOMAS, Walter J., 1884-1964
THOMAS, Fannie M., 1896-No Date
NORMAN, Addie, 1885-1975
ROGERS, Debra, died 1954
BECKNELL, David J., 9-8-1887 4-10-1957
BECKNELL, Ada Mae, 1904-No Date
SHIELDS, Arden C., 6-3-1915 12-24-1973
NOXSEL, Herbert L., 8-20-1915 10-23-1967

NOXSEL, Annie Mae, 1-25-1917   No Date
FEAGIN, Ernest L., 1911-No Date
FEAGIN, Anna M., 1917-1978
BIVINGS, Heather Ann, 11-5-1970   4-21-1976
FEAGIN, Charles Albert, 11-7-1934   No Date
FEAGIN, Herbert, 5-21-1886   7-24-1965
FEAGIN, Dollie, 9-3-1885   7-7-1972
FEAGIN, William Herbert, 7-28-1906 12-15-1963
FEAGIN, Doris Katherine 10-25-1924   5-21-1965
ELEY, Jessie Roy, 3-26-1896   12-28-1967
ELEY, Bessie Cleo, 6-10-1908   No Date
HICKOK, Cecil F., 11-14-1921   No Date
HICKOK, Emma M., 9-4-1921   No Date
DAVIS, James E., Jr., 2-18-1953   9-8-1970
SIMMONS, Edgar M., 1901-1964
SIMMONS, Lethe M., 1902-1979
SARE, Max L., 1910-1974
SARE, Harriett E., 1916-No Date
BENTLEY, Carl, 1917-1977
BENTLEY, Margry, 1920-No Date
ELEY, Homer D., 1900-1970
ELEY, Flossie V., 1907-1979
CANDLER, Edward C., 1897-1975
CANDLER, Padie M., No Dates
GOSSETT, Weldon L., 1921-No Date
GOSSETT, Mary, 1919-No Date
LUMPKIN, Lawrence E., Sr., 9-8-1892   2-25-1968
LUMPKIN, Mamie Non, 12-18-1893   11-2-1977
STRICKLAND, Ellie E., 1906-1972
STRICKLAND, Nettie J., 1907-No Date
WALDROP, Beman F., 8-11-1912   12-16-1971
WALDROP, Ruby TRAYLOR, 4-1-1921   12-30-1964
REISOR, Bert T., 1910-No Date
REISOR, Geneva E., 1913-No Date
REISOR, Clarence E., 1911-1973
REISOR, Edna M., 1915-No Date
TREDWAY, Hugh Clark, 1903-1966
TREDWAY, Oral DUKE, 1909-No Date
FERGERSON, Joe C., 1888-1963
FERGERSON, Noya, 1898-No Date
STRAWN, Johnnie E., 1913-No Date
STRAWN, Evelyn R., 1915-1973
TIMBERLAKE, Charles F., 1885-1978
TIMBERLAKE, Myrtle A., 1894-1969
MASSEY, George Henry, Tex. Sgt, U. S. A. F., W. W. II., 2-6-1923 2-4-1960
POPE, Johnny Mac, 6-15-1959   6-15-1975
POPE, James Ray, 9-29-1939   8-16-1965
POPE, Almon T., 9-8-1903   2-1-1977
POPE, Pearl, 12-6-1903   2-5-1977
THOMASON, Aulby W., 1915-1977
THOMASON, Ola Irene, 1917-No Date
HANEY, Granville O., 1893-No Date
HANEY, Oma May, 1894-1963
FARMER, Clyde L., Tex. Tec-5, 46 Engr-Const. BN. W.W. II, 3-15-1912   3-14-1963

SHEPHERD, Inf. Son of George & Betty, b. & d. 1957
SHEPHERD, Charlie, 1903-No Date
SHEPHERD, Kattie Lou, 1903-1977
MASSEY, Jeff D., Sr., 1886-1977
MASSEY, Stella L., 1890-No Date
DOAN, John Leon, 1904-1976
DOAN, Lometa B., 1902-No Date
O'NEIL, Nannie F., 1894-1961
O'NEIL, Edward W., 1897-1957
WOODARD, S. O., 1-20-1892 7-1-1956
WOODARD, Lottie, 10-25-1889 4-13-1976
RICHTERS, Jack, 1910-1978
RICHTERS, Flossie, 1916-No Date
MITCHELL, Fred, Tex. Pvt., U. S. Army, W. W. I, 9-15-1893 8-19-1965
MITCHELL, Bain M., Tex. Cpl., 147 Armd. Inf., B. N. Korea.,
                1-2-1923 8-19-1970
BRANTON, David A., 1884-1963
BRANTON, Dora A., 1882-1973
KERR, Annette, 1961-1974
MINTER, Joseph C., 1877-1962
MINTER, Minnie E., 1896-NO Date
KING, Joe C., 1921-No Date
KING, Jessie Fay, 1926-No Date
MORROW, Verner E., 8-25-1908 NO Date
MORROW, Juanita Mae, 2-13-1911 4-16-1974
HERBERT, Lowery M., Tex. Pvt., Co. C., 752 Tank BN, W. W. II.,
                12-16-1912 2-17-1972
CONRADT, J. C., 1908-NO Date
CONRADT, Letha ASHBY, 1911-No Date
TAPP, Roy M., 1909-No Date
TAPP, Emma M., 1910-No Date
LUMPKIN, No Name No Dates
MC DANIEL, Paul, (Son), 1912-No Date
MC DANIEL, Lady Holder, (Mother), 1885-1973
CHAPMAN, Raymond S., 1923-1972
CHAPMAN, Camille C., No Dates
DICKSON, William K., 1911-No Date
DICKSON, Annie Mae, 1911-No Date
STEGER, Graham, 1911-1977
STEGER, Edith, 1918-No Date
ROGERS, Harry, 1881-1954
ROGERS, Mary, 1892-No Date
WEATHERLY, John I., 8-5-1886 4-5-1974
WEATHERLY, Rosa E., 8-4-1900 No Date
HARBIN, Arthur Lee, Tex., Sgt., 245 Base Unit, AAF, W. W. II.,
                11-6-1912 7-11-1962
HARBIN, Ricky Lee, died 9-4-1954
BREWER, William Carson, Pvt., U. S. Army, W. W. I, 1892-1978
LAMM, Johnnie Earick, Tex. Cpl. Btry C., 46 Art., 3-3-1932 2-24-1957
WEATHERLY, Billy Joe, Tex. Cpl. U. S. Marine Corps, Korea, 5-14-1931 11-30-1956
EVANS, Cordelia A., 2-2-1875 1-19-1972
SEALEY, Olive Buster, 1901-1978
FORD, Arie, 1914-1978
FORD, Frances D., 1922-No Date

BRIDGES, Julius F., Tex. T-Sgt., Army Air Force, W. W. II., SS-AM & 9 OLC-PH,
                    12-22-1915 11-20-1965
PHILLIPS, Sylvester, 1911-1963
PHILLIPS, Grace, 1909-1977
STEPHENS, E. E., 1910-1976
STEPHENS, Ruby, 1910-1955
WHITNEY, Earl D., 1914-1975
CATHEY, Raymond, 12-6-1908 12-4-1978
CATHEY, Rilla, 12-27-1918 No Date
SULLIVAN, Thomas J., 1887-1969
SULLIVAN, Elmer M., 1898-No Date
DOOLY, Daniel Nathan, Pvt., U. S. Army, W. W. I., 11-12-1898 9-25-1969
DOOLY, Sam H., 4-17-1895 5-25-1964
MASSEY, Jeffrey Paul, 5-5-1968 5-10-1968
MASSEY, Jefferson Davis, Jr., 1914-1965
MASSEY, Pauline B., 1918-No Date
HAGAN, John W., 1893-1953
HAGAN, Edna G., 1898-1978
RUSHING, Otis L., 1903-1976
RUSHING, Ethel J., 1903-No Date
IRVIN, George Trice, 1906-No Date
IRVIN, Thelma TERRY, 1912-No Date
HUNT, Herman, Tex. Pvt., 29 Co. 165 Depot Brig., W. W. I, 9-20-1894 12-21-1953
HUNT, Frankie TERRY, 2-20-1896 2-28-1974
DIGGS, Sarah Jewell, 5-2-1903 No Date
DIGGS, James Spencer, Tex. Pvt., U. S. Army, W. W. I., 10-17-1895 1-19-1972
DELNEGRO, Mollie Elizabeth, 7-29-1893 3-10-1957
BIRD, John Wesley, 9-22-1876 5-13-1956
BIRD, Vivian Viola, 12-4-1890 8-2-1956
SWEET, Charles W., 1891-1973
SWEET, Florence L., 1898-1975
HOUSER, Dennis M., 9-29-1942 9-2-1964
WEAVER, Howard R., 1907-No Date
WEAVER, Beatrice, 1910-1964
TOLBERT, Tom, 1893-1970
TOLBERT, Alice M., 1895-No Date
CURRIN, Wallace J., 1908-1975
CURRIN, Rogene, 1910-No Date
SMITH, J. E. "Dick", 1896-1966
SMITH, Hazel M., 1897-No Date
ROGERS, Winford J., 1931-1970
ROGERS, Wanda L., 1933-No Date
WILLCOX, G. W., 1889-1972
WILLCOX, Evie, 1890-1978
MAY, Clyde, 1908-No Date
MAY, Laura E., 1910-No Date
JENNINGS, Elmer, Tex., Pvt., Btry B., 126 Fld. Arty., W. W. I.,
                    2-14-1889 10-5-1962
GLENN, George W., 1891-1958
WORCESTER, Charles A., 7-8-1888 5-21-1954
SMITH, Aaron E., 1899-1978
SMITH, Ruby F., 1901-No Date
RUST, Billy Joe, S-2, U. S. Navy, W. W. II, 5-2-1927 5-9-1978
LOWE, Morgan, 1918-1977

LOWE, Patricia, 1929-No Date
NEWELL, Mildred L., 1923-1969
ARNOLD, James E., 1890-No Date
ARNOLD, Evelyn C., 1903-No Date
PULLEN, Thomas F., 1890-No Date
PULLEN, Cora Mae, 1894-No Date
MACK, Columbus M., 1890-1974
MACK, Lillie D., 1892-No Date
CATHEY, Ronnie Leon (son), 1943-1974
CATHEY, Alene L., 1920-1957
CATHEY, Leon, 1916-1973
CATHEY, Ann, 1930-No Date
SMITH, Andrew, 1877-1966
SMITH, Roberta, 1885-1970
BATTLE, J. Larry, 1946-1967
LONG, William C., Tex., Pfc., 301 SVC., GP. AAF, W. W. II,
                    9-23-1911 6-26-1969
LONG, Ernest Lee, 8-13-1891 4-22-1965
LONG, Frances Hollie, 7-30-1909 11-28-1959
RODES, Mrs. Rosa, 8-6-1875 11-14-1966
FUGITT, Gilbert, 1913-No Date
FUGITT, Exie Lee, 1914-No Date
COOMER, W. J., "Red", 1895-1963
COOMER, Mary R., 1892-1961
DOOLY, Dorcas E., 3-22-1873 4-8-1965
DOOLY, Goerge W., 9-25-1870 6-22-1955
WACASEY, Homer B., Jr., 4-13-1924 No Date
WACASEY, Dorothy F., 11-14-1924 No Date
DOOLY, Roy D., 4-7-1906 5-2-1975
DOOLY, Alice BIGBEE, 8-19-1906 No Date
BIGBEE, Robert Yuless, T-Sgt., U. S. A. F., W. W. II, 3-5-1916 3-31-1978
LYTLE, T. H. "Doc", 1892-1962
LYTLE, Ila D., 1895-1968
LYTLE, Joe, 1922-No Date
LYTLE, Pauline, 1922-No Date
NIX, J. Howard, 1902-1978
NIX, Una Kay, 1904-1967
MITCHELL, Joseph Chester, 1900-1961
MITCHELL, Edith Odell, 1912-No Date
PEAVEY, R. J., 1910-No Date
PEAVEY, Jewell, 1915-No Date
WARREN, Howard Ray, 1919-1964
WARREN, Iliff V., 1921-No Date
WARREN, Tommie R., 1924-No Date
LAMM, Orville C., 1908-1974
LAMM, Edith R., 1911-No Date
PRINCE, Andrew J., 1891-1969
PRINCE, Sarah C., 1901-No Date
SHAW, Travis B., 1911-1970
SHAW, Kitty M., 1913-No Date
COMBEST, Alvin, 1905-No Date
COMBEST, Irene E., 1904-No Date
GRAY, Monroe F., Tex., Pvt., Co. C., 110 Ammo Train, W. W. I,
                    7-8-1894 10-3-1967

MC PHERSON, Coleman J., 8-6-1900 No Date
MC PHERSON, Bertha J., 1-15-1904 No Date
FUNDERBURG, E. D."Jake", 2-19-1892 12-25-1960
FUNDERBURG, Laura MACK, 1-20-1892 6-24-1964
BLAND, Lorena COOPER, 3-5-1916 1-15-1963
TYNES, Willard Lynn, 8-27-1953 8-16-1969
BROOKS, Billy W., 8-21-1930 2-16-1959
LINDSEY, Michael Ray, died 1-11-1956
LINDSEY, Melvin E., 1930-No Date
LINDSEY, Lorene J., 1931-No Date
BENTON, J. Walton, 1894-1973
BENTON, Vera H., 1896-No Date
SELLERS, Guy Edward, died 1967
KRODLE, William S., 1884-1966
KRODLE, Ola J., 1897-1969
INGLISH, Catharine Leona, 3-13-1906 7-11-1967
INGLISH, H. Walter, 9-13-1873 4-20-1963
INGLISH, Eva L., 7-31-1879 11-3-1954
WILSON, Ebb L., 1907-1974
WILSON, Eleanor, 1901-No Date
YOUNG, George C., 1907-No Date
YOUNG, Ausit Willie, 1915-No Date
ATTAWAY, Dalton N., 1912-1954
BURNS, Jas. A., 10-18-1893 12-4-1967
BURNS, Cora A., 9-17-1895 2-19-1962
SHEPHERD, Ben D., 1888-1974
SHEPHERD, Jennie Mae, 1892-1972
SPEARS, David A., 6-19-1896 4-3-1973
SPEARS, Ruth, 9-5-1897 7-10-1972
BOWERS, Ishmeal E., 9-28-1900 9-12-1973
BOWERS, Gracie L., 6-16-1908 1-22-1972
JONES, Charlie J., 1920-1968
JONES, Bobbie J., 1926-No Date
LAXTON, W. S. "Bill", 1893-1975
LAXTON, Laura M., 1893-1978
HOOPER, Walter Mack, 1896-1979
BISHOP, Frank F., 10-3-1901 No Date
BISHOP, Ethel E., 12-8-1901 11-13-1970
SAMPLES, Ira Albert, 1904-1973
SAMPLES, Ruby Lee, 1913-No Date
DAVIS, Leroy B., 4-8-1886 9-11-1954
DAVIS, Lillie J., 9-18-1888 4-1-1963
FOWLER, Winton T., 12-27-1909 11-18-1971
FOWLER, Bessie O., 1915-No Date
JENKINS, Fred M., 1916-1976
JENKINS, Lillian E., 1925-No Date
BOWERS, William l., 1929-1971
BOWERS, Ravenna A., 1933-No Date
STEPHENS, Anna Ellon, 1913-No Date
STEPHENS, Dorothy Jewell, 1926-1957
STEPHENS, Andrew J., 1881-1973
STEPHENS, Bennie, 1890-No Date
WILSON, Jas. W., Sr., 1908-1976
THOMASON, Clay A., 1909-No Date

THOMASON, Avis N., 1909-1979
MORRISON, Jennifer Lea, died 12-6-1965
ROBINSON, William B., 1909-No Date
ROBINSON, Monnie M., 1917-1977
DANEWOOD, I. D. "Danger", 1878-1961
DANEWOOD, Edna P., 1889-1975
DANEWOOD, Johnnie, 1914-1964
BROOKS, Cameron M., Tex. F-1, U.S.N., W. W. I., 12-22-1893 3-10-1956
BROOKS, Callie COX, 1-11-1897 1-12-1979
COX, Altie Blanche, 1890-1970
RAY, Ben F., 2-4-1873 7-4-1955
RAY, Myrtle D., 6-30-1889 3-20-1974
NAILS, W. J. "Jim", 1887-1966
NAILS, Mattie May, 1891-No Date
DAUGHERTY, Roland E., Tex., S-Sgt., 200 Base Unit A.A.F., W. W. II.,
                          3-26-1917 11-19-1953
KETCHAM, Mindi Lynn, 4-30-1970 5-1-1970
WALLACE, Eston Bryne, 1908-No Date
WALLACE, Stella Jane, 1907-No Date
WARNER, Jesse B., 1926-1969
JONES, Vestus S., 1885-1966
JONES, Lela M., 1889-No Date
SWAFFORD, Robert L., 1898-1978
SWAFFORD, Elizabeth m., 1901-No Date
COKER, Truman W., 1905-1962
COKER, Vera N., 1906-No Date
BOLICK, G. C., 1878-1963
BOLICK, Cora L., 1-26-1878 4-5-1954
ASHLEY, Edd D., 1883-1971
ASHLEY, Audrey L., 1889-1958
ASHLEY, H. T. "Bob", 1872-1958
ASHLEY, Elizabeth, 1887-1969
CHEEK, Aaron Odell, died 5-19-1956
CANUP, Sam, 1902-1955
CANUP, Lottie, 1912-No Date
WALLACE, Robert Harold, 1926-1974
WALLACE, Jennie Merle, 1927-No Date
HALES, J. Wayne, 1908-1970
HALES, Donna R., 1909-No Date
COMBS, Lon E., 12-5-1894 3-24-1961
COMBS, Maude E., 3-24-1895 No Date
HAGAN, James Eulus, 1907-1972
HAGAN, Johnie Marie, 1908-No Date
HAGAN, Floyd D., 1908-1973
HAGAN, Lucille M, 1913-No Date
COKER, Merle Douglas, 1929-1966
COKER, Martha O., 1930-No Date
LE ROSEN, W. Haywood, 1906-No Date
LE ROSEN, Mable M., 1905-No Date
PHILPOT, Sidney G., 1876-1963
PHILPOT, Celia Ann, 1873-1959
PHILPOT, Troy N., 1906-No Date
OWENS, W. L. "Bill", 1905-1977
OWENS, William Kent, 1882-1962

DAVIS, Billie Joej 1920-1975
DAVIS, Annie V., 1921-No Date
GREEN, Rolan L., 1900-1974
GREEN, Ethel, 1900-1973
GREEN, R. B. "Bob", 1902-1958
GREEN, Lula E., 1900-1971
BRITT, Willie C., 3-1-1918 No Date
BRITT, Jesse J., 8-19-1910 2-17-1975
ANDERSON, Dewey F., 1898-No Date
ANDERSON, Annette, 1919-No Date
SHRUM, Lee W., 1882-1958
SHRUM, Lois H., 1888-No Date
BROWN, Jim N., 1894-1977
BROWN, Belle K., 1894-No Date
RHUDY, Lisa Annette, died 9-25-1960
TAYLOR, Thomas H., 1909-No Date
TAYLOR, Saleta JARED, 1913-1972
CALDWELL, Claud R., 1906-1966
CALDWELL, Mary Opal, 1911-No Date
FOWLER, Ethel ROGERS, 2-16-1886 3-8-1965
SMITH, Billy Bob, 1-5-1930 7-21-1954
JOHNSON, Cpl. Claude H., 1908-1972
JOHNSON, Louise L., 1893-No Date
MOON, Barto C., 6-19-1882 12-9-1954
MOON, Cora E., 6-22-1883 5-23-1958
1 - Funeral Marker No Name or Dates
KNEGGS, J. R., 1912-No Date
KNEGGS, Ruby, 1915-No Date
JENKINS, Mittie W., 1900-1979
LITCHFIELD, Jesse J., 5-17-1899 7-14-1972
LITCHFIELD, Mary Lou, 11-20-1900 No Date
BOWEN, James Covey, Sr., 1888-1971
BOWEN, Beulah GOODWIN, 1896-No Date
BOWEN, James C., Jr., 1915-1975
MEYER, Alonzo Jackson, 1879-1968
MEYER, Myrta NICHOLS, 1878-1962
COTTON, Ira, 1898-No Date
COTTON, Coralie, 1911-No Date
ROZELL, Clayton C., 1900-1978
ROZELL, Lurena E., 1902-No Date
MIDDLETON, Tom, 1911-1972
MIDDLETON, Lorene, 1923-No Date
MOORE, Cecil E., 1909-No Date
MOORE, Allene S., 1912-1970
JOHNSTON, W. F. "Ted", 1913-1973
JOHNSTON, Oleta, 1909-No Date
HARTMAN, Edward W., 1884-1957
HARTMAN, Nelly, 1890-NO Date
MONROE, Oliver, 1909-1973
MONROE, Frances, 1914-No Date

PETTY, Richard W., died 9-19-1970
ELMORE, Jas. Jessie, 1971-1971
WHITSON, Michael K., died 1971
WHITE, Greg Alan, died 7-20-1971
HICKS, Heath Hugh, 7-21-1970 7-22-1970
HOWIE, William O., 1-21-1970 4-27-1970
HUDEBURGH, Infant, died 1970
SASSER, Jimmy David, died 1970
ELLIS, Deana M., died 1969
FITE, Melinda Ann, died 1969
NEUHAUS, Inf. son of Robert H. & Beth B., died 1969
WRIGHT, Clifford M., died 3-20-1968
HARVEY, Inf. son of John & Shelia, died 11-4-1967
FLEMING, Dana A., died 1967
WESLEY, Penny, died 1966
ELMORE, Olen Glen, died 1966
LANEY, Laura Ann, died 6-24-1962
TRICE, Richard Alan, 7-13-1962 7-14-1962
FLINN, David Brian, died 5-18-1966
MALDONADO, Pamela Sue, 12-12-1959 4-26-1961
SMITH, Dudley,B., 5-24-1972 5-29-1972
YORK, Infant, died 1972
GUAJARDO, Chabila Juanita, died 1974
NUTT, Infant, died 1875
WHITE, Jonathan Hoyit, 6-30-1976 8-8-1976
FOX, Stephen Paul, died 1978
VIRGIN, Infant, died 1978
BLASKE, Amber K., died 1978
LAJVARDI, Hamed, died 1978
MITCHELL, John M., died 1976
MOSHEIM, Thomas A., died 1974
BRANDON, Ami E., died 1973
HARRIS, Windy Michelle, dau. of Lynn & Diana, died 8-9-1973
HADLOCK, Infant son of Eddie & Donna, died 5-19-1972
BARCENAS, Jesus, died 1972
REECE, Twyla Marie, died 7-4-1959
WINN, Cathy Jeannie, died 1959
BEASINGER, Michael Douglas, 1956-1957
O'NEAL, Faith, died 6-27-1956
MC GINNIS, Michael W., 7-14-1976 1-1977

SECTION "F"

GREEN, Frances Denise, 1-3-1957 1-27-1957
HAMILTON, Henry Hulet, 1-30-1904 2-2-1970
HAMILTON, Gladys RAGSDALE, 11-3-1905 No Date
CAIN, Joe Dayton, 2-22-1919 7-21-1954
FREEMAN, Clyde, 1911-1972
FREEMAN, Jaunita, 1912-No Date
DICKENS, Elmer Ray, 12-1-1897 8-16-1964
DICKENS, Anita LOW, 10-25-1901 No Date

BROWN, Joseph "Joe", W., 1908-1971
BROWN, Elizabeth, 1911-No Date
CATHEY, Truman W., 1906-No Date
CATHEY, Marie M., 1906-1955
MULLINS, Neal M., 1899-1978
TREADWAY, Edd, 9-6-1884 11-12-1964
TREADWAY, Ethel, 9-28-1886 No Date
GREEN, H. E. "Jack", 1900-1972
GREEN, Jessie Faye, 1909-No Date
MC DONALD, Ed, 1884-1968
MC DONALD, Susie, 1891-1957
FERGUSON, Edwin B., 1917-1968
FERGUSON, Wilma Lou, 1921-No Date
FERGUSON, B. Homer, 4-2-1891 12-20-1962
FERGUSON, Nora, 1-31-1891 7-22-1962
MEEKS, Ricky Earl, 12-17-1954 2-22-1955
HEFNER, Everett Wayland, 1891-1965
PITTS, William David, 6-13-1878 4-8-1956
PITTS, Gemma, 1-26-1891 6-14-1971
HEFNER, Joe Fern, 3-21-1900 7-19-1974
HEFNER, James E. "Tootie", 2-20-1924 4-20-1955
GILLIS, Stanley, 1913-No Date
GILLIS, Pauline, 1913-No Date
WHETSELL, John Thomas, 1-2-1891 10-27-1962
WHETSELL, Idella Mae, 10-29-1899 5-28-1956
BISHOP, John A., 1906-1969
BISHOP, Mary C., 1907-No Date
THOMPSON, Egbert, 1-15-1886 12-13-1954
THOMPSON, Maude, 7-13-1886 4-5-1971
HUGHES, Jim A., 1888-1958
HUGHES, Maude, 1888-No Date
LANGFORD, Jas. A., 1896-No Date
LANGFORD, Mildred C., 1901-No Date
DEAN, Archie H., 1908-No Date
DEAN, Mary Hazel, 1913-No Date
WILLIAMS, Mildred SPURLOCK, 6-5-1902 8-1-1974
NIX, Thomas S., 1879-1970
NIX, Mahala Kansas, 1881-1954
BOUKNIGHT, Thurman Alex, 1896-1966
BOUKNIGHT, Valaree HOPKINS, 1901-1972
WALKER, J. M. "Short", 1897-1968
WALKER, Estelle Rose, 1907-1968
BAKER, Jason Mike, 1903-1958
BAKER, Johnnie, 1900-No Date
GLAWSON, Homer, 1891-1978
GLAWSON, Ruth, 1894-1973
SMITH, Ila, (Mother), 1894-1970
SMITH, Fred, (Father), 1886-1955
NORRIS, Leon W., 1-11-1901 2-11-1972
NORRIS, Norma Sue, 2-5-1901 No Date
PARR, William L., 1898-1962
PARR, Lula A., 1898-No Date
DIAL, Jon Ellis, son of Robert & Doris, 11-16-1960 5-10-1961
DIAL, Luther E., 1902-1973

DIAL, Bertha L., 1909-No Date
NEAL, Dewey F., 8-17-1898 7-2-1961
DIGGES, Bertha M., 1880-No Date
COLBERT, Mrs. Ida Bell, 1-1-1915 1-1-1979
PICKRELL, S. David, 1912-1971
PICKRELL, P. Dott, 1917-1979
PORTER, Dow D., 12-22-1897 2-25-1969
PORTER, Nelle H., 3-25-1900 No Date
SIMMONS, Verna, 1904-1969
SIMMONS, Ruby A., 1906-No Date
YARBOROUGH, Charles D., Pfc., U. S. Army, W. W. I., 1892-1977
YARBOROUGH, Bertha A., 1901-No Date
YARBOROUGH, Jerry A., 1935-1979
SMITH, Jesse M., 1888-1967
SMITH, Edna L., 1904-1977
BAKER, Lonnie H., 1897-1955
BAKER, Ima Pearl, 1902-No Date
TILTON, Lloyd F., 1916-No Date
TILTON, Inez W., 1931-No Date
TILTON, Inf. Dau., of Lloyd & Inez, died 1939
SKIDMORE, Cora MINICK, 9-3-1893 6-21-1975
WINSETT, Ewell, 10-21-1911 2-9-1977
WINSETT, Beulah, 8-21-1916 No Date
WINSETT, Terrence, 1892-1974
WINSETT, Martha, 1891-1971
SMITH, C. E. "Jack", 1884-1967
SMITH, Eva Lena, 1888-1965
TAFT, William H., 1-24-1869 2-25-1959
TAFT, Clifford Arnold, 1906-No Date
TAFT, Inez Bonnie, 1908-No Date
RAY, Lois Almeta, 8-3-1920 9-24-1963
DUNCAN, H. Ralph, 1903-1975
DUNCAN, L. Jewell, 1907-No Date
BELLAH, James C., 1913-1979
BELLAH, Myrtle A., 1914-No Date
DOBBS, Emmett W., 1911-1967
STATZER, Garry Lynn, died 2-1-1956
PATTERSON, Arlyn E., 1930-1975
PATTERSON, Wanda N., 1934-No Date
MORGAN, G. Virgil, 1902-No Date
MORGAN, Iva B., 1902-No Date
MORGAN, Virgil D., 1-6-1922 3-9-1976
BURTON, Jesse V., 1901-1978
BURTON, Georgie, 1900-1969
JOHNSON, Byron E., 1912-No Date
JOHNSON, Mildred L., 1920-No Date
PRINCE, Jake R., 1902-1962
PRINCE, Lou A., 1907-No Date
CLARK, Catanna, died 4-16-1954
CLARK, Irvin, 1896-1976
CLARK, Genevieve, 1906-No Date
BAKER, Jas. M., 1885-1968
BAKER, Etta D., 1890-1978
WHITWORTH, Jas. R., 12-6-1900 7-28-1975

WHITWORTH, Irene M., 7-25-1903 No Date
SPRADING, Herbert C., 12-14-1891 7-21-1967
SPRADING, A. Lois, 9-13-1897 No Date
DENNEY, Thomas L., 1898-No Date
DENNEY, Ruth V., 1904-No Date
MAYO, La Rue K., 8-24-1910 10-22-1967
MAYO, (Mother), 1880-1955
LEATHERWOOD, Isaac, 1889-1970
EMERSON, Dennis D., 1899-No Date
EMERSON, Leola C., 1900-No Date
SPOONEMORE, S. Leon, 6-3-1908 No Date
SPOONEMORE, Opal L., 6-1-1911 7-20-1977
STEELE, Lee E., 9-29-1924 No Date
STEELE, Bonnie R., 2-13-1927 No Date
DOWNING, R. P. "Jack", 4-11-1906 11-5-1956
STEELE, Clyde E., 1894-1964
STEELE, Stella Mae, 1896-1961
MORROW, Houston E., 1878-1957
MORROW, Dora, 1878-1962
WILLIAMS, John B., 1901-No Date
WILLIAMS, Charlotte J., 1904-1976
PUGH, O. Weldon, 1915-1979
PUGH, Merle, 1916-No Date
WICKER, Cary, 1893-1953
WICKER, Lillie, 1892-1975
CLEM, Infant, died 3-19-1967
COKER, Harby M., (Father of David & Pamela), 1-29-1899 11-28-1959
MOLENO, Paula Carmen, 2-25-1948 3-29-1978
COMER, Clyde, 1902-1966
MC CARLEY, James Art, 1893-1964
MC CARLEY, Jewel H., 1893-1965
ISHAM, S. Roy, 1897-1978
ISHAM, Nannie A., 1901-No Date
SUMMERS, Thomas W., 1901-1972
SUMMERS, Margaret, 1902-No Date
TRENTHAM, Jas. C., 9-22-1931 5-11-1964
TURNER, Charlie D., Tex. Pvt., 93 Balloon Co., Air SVC, W. W. I.,
                    8-1-1894 8-26-1962
TURNER, Ira Eunice, 10-29-1908 No Date
MOSLEY, Wayne L., 1926-No Date
MOSLEY, Sara C., 1928-No Date
BEANE, Jos. Terrell, III, died 6-15-1954
WHITLEY, George K., 9-13-1907 2-15-1971
WHITLEY, Hattie M., 2-4-1908 No Date
KING, A. C., 1904-No Date
KING, Jimmie B., 1908-1977
HILL, Alva Marie, 5-13-1900 1-26-1977
HILL, Balmer, 10-31-1897 2-1-1969
WALL, Willie, 1895-1976
WALL, Lula, 1898-No Date
HOLLOWAY, Cecil D., 1906-1974
HOLLOWAY, Lois A., 1907, No Date
PACE, F. Liscoe, 1915-No Date
PACE, Mattie Jo, 1913-1957

MOSLEY, Jas. R., 1894-No Date
MOSLEY, Vada E., 1898-1974
BELL, Truman E., 1913-No Date
BELL, Bertha B., 1911-No Date
BELL, William C., 1889-1968
BELL, Maggie, 1894-1979
POWELL, Mary Ruth, 4-1-1895 10-11-1971
CARROLL, Ernest P., 1926-No Date
CARROLL, Gladys, 1920-No Date
HAMILTON, Lane, 1893-1967
HAMILTON, Mollie, 1894-1977
WICKER, Cary, Jr., 1911-1965
WICKER, Edna, 1907-No Date
HELM, L. L., 1886-1969
HELM, Bessie, 1888-1977
SMITH, Wilson M., 3-5-1919 1-21-1968
MC GEE, Ernie J., 1917-No Date
MC GEE, Ona Bell, 1925-1968
FELMET, Henry D., 1897-1965
FELMET, Mattie V., 1897-1964
FITZGERALD, Emmett B., Jr., 1923-1969
CAMERON, F. C. "Buddy", Jr., 9-26-1914 9-17-1968
QUATTLEBAUM, John W., Tex., Pvt., Co. C., 328 Inf., 82 Div., W. W. I.,
            3-2-1892 4-10-1966
QUATTLEBAUM, Annie O., 9-15-1913 4-1-1979
MAYS, G. V., 1918-No Date
MAYS, Effie Leah, 1920-No Date
REYNERSON, Don T., 1913-1964
REYNERSON, Martha N., No Dates
DENT, Mack, 1891-No Date
DENT, Denty, 1894-1954
KITCHENS, Lou, 1884-1963
KITCHENS, Mozelle, 1909-No Date
YOUNG, J. Ray, 1905-No Date
YOUNG, Pauline K., 1906-No Date
ISHAM, Robert A., 1913-No Date
ISHAM, Ethel Alene, 1915-No Date
SMITH, Alec L., 1902-No Date
SMITH, Bessie L., 1905-No Date
THOMPSON, M. L. "Bud", 1887-No Date
THOMPSON, Maggie, 1889-No Date
THORNTON, Mary Jane, 1927-No Date
THOMPSON, Jas. Alfred, 1911-1978
EDWARDS, Guy H., 1889-1961
RIDDLE, Ernest J., Jr., 8-22-1929 11-4-1970
         (Father of Ray, Wayne, Wendy and Susan)
RIDDLE, Ernest J., 1910-1957
RIDDLE, Jessie G., 1905-No Date
TURNER, Fred E., 1906-1967
TURNER, Wilma M., 1914-No Date
MC CLELLAND, Hugh C., 1882-1970
MC CLELLAND, Callie, 1882-1957
KELLY, Patrick Jas., Tex., 1st. Lt., 2519 Base Unit, A.A.F., W. W. II.,
         DF-C-AM, 4-7-1916 9-3-1959

KELLY, Mary M., Tex., 1st. Lt., Army Nurse Corps, W. W. II.,
                    6-18-1915 10-16-1960
KELLY, Pliny M., 1892-1962
KELLY, Lon V., 1891-No Date
STONE, Billie ROGERS, 1929-No Date
STONE, A. G., 1916-1977
STONE, Marietta, 1924-1965
WASHBURN, Knox E., 1896-No Date
WASHBURN, Lena Mae, 1898-1953
RASH, Stacey, 1916-1967
RASH, Lera, 1918-No Date
MORRISON, Wilma F., 4-18-1921 10-8-1977
ADAMS, Luther C., 1910-No Date
ADAMS, Sadie Rosie, 1912-No Date
MOREHEAD, Miles M., 7-10-1909 10-10-1971
KELLY, Pliny Mitchell, Tex. Flt. O., 313 Troops, Carr., G. P., A.A.F., W.W.II,
                    8-12-1914 4-17-1960
TARPLEY, Richard E., 1886-1969
TARPLEY, Claribel, 1893-1975
WRIGHT, Monte Lee, 1891-1961
WRIGHT, Gracie Pearl, 1901-1953
ROBERTS, Jill Marsha, 3-16-1968 6-6-1968
ROBERTS, Arvin W., Tex., F-1, U.S.N.R., W.W. II., 10-17-1903 9-29-1963
LIPSEY, Grady Leon, 1902-1962
LIPSEY, Lillie M., 1905-1974
LIPSEY, Edward Marshall, 1877-1953
LIPSEY, Nannie B., 1881-1962
SMITH, Eldred Guy, 1889-1970
SMITH, Nancy Mae, 1906-No Date
DODSON, Dennis Weldon, 9-27-1957 4-22-1960
CONNALLY, Emma L., 12-20-1879 8-4-1958
PEPPER, Martha E., 1876-1973
NUTT, Elmer, 1897-1957
NUTT, Clara Ethel, 1901-1954
DUVALL, Eulan, 1920-No Date
DUVALL, Vernelle, 1924-No Date
LAWHON, Rev. Luther M., 1885-1968
LAWHON, Bertie K., 1889-1975
JONES, Mittie J., 1881-1952
JONES, William R., 1879-1962
BOWDEN, Marilyn MC WHIRTER, 1929-1958
MC WHIRTER, Ethel, 1891-1972
MC WHIRTER, Clint, 1885-1970
FITZGERALD, Emmitt B., 1889-1979
FITZGERALD, Mattie, 1896-1960
SKAGGS, Alfred L., 1897-1966
SKAGGS, Lena B., 1909-No Date
WELBORN, Robert S., 1906-1968
WELBORN, Georgia F., 1908-No Date
STRAWN, John P., 1883-1954
STRAWN, Ida M., 1889-1974
WALLACE, Ray, 3-29-1872 1-15-1957
WALLACE, Mineola, 10-26-1879 4-29-1971
FLEWHARTY, Jesse Harry, 1-14-1902 5-5-1966

CANNON, Charlie V., 11-19-1902 3-10-1955
BROTHERS, Luther R., 5-26-1897 7-7-1964
BROTHERS, Grace M., 9-25-1902 No Date
PIERCE, Charlie E., 1892-1974
PIERCE, Beatrice, 1895-No Date
MANLEY, Lee, 1887-1974
MANLEY, Mamie, 1893-No Date
HABLUETZEL, Grover C., 1888-1966
HABLUETZEL, Lulil K., 1898-1954
LAKE, S. Alton, 1905-1979
LAKE, Virginia L., 1911-No Date
LAKE, Cecil A., 1931-1970
ROBERTSON, J. Morris, 1916-No Date
ROBERTSON, E. Freida, 1919-No Date
MITCHELL, Charley E., 8-4-1876 4-23-1960
MITCHELL, Lucy Jane, 10-26-1875 8-31-1958
CLEM, Vance Evans, 11-1-1933 10-22-1966
CLEM, Lalla ROOKH, 11-16-1904 No Date
MC CASKILL, Carl L., 1896-1970
MC CASKILL, Georgia E., 1896-No Date
LAMB, Bernard S., 1908-1976
LAMB, Ava Lee, 1908-No Date
THOMPSON, Abner L., 1872-1958
RICHARDSON, John W., 1-11-1883 2-18-1961
SPURLOCK, Thomas J., Jr., 1912-No Date
SPURLOCK, Fayree V., 1915-No Date
HARRIS, Jasper, Tex., Cook., 323 Fld. RMT Sq. QMC, W. W. I.,
                          6-18-1894 5-16-1961
HARRIS, Ruby Mae, 11-4-1906 7-3-1966
LIPSCOMB, Wayne A., 1919-No Date
LIPSCOMB, Inez R., 1903-No Date
SPURLOCK, MAttie L., 10-27-1876 11-18-1964
SPURLOCK, T. J., Sr., 10-7-1868 10-9-1954
CHANDLER, Theo A., 5-10-1908 No Date
CHANDLER, Mamie I., 12-24-1907 1-7-1976
HENLEY, Homer W., 8-31-1901 No Date
HENLEY, Mary E., 7-27-1902 No Date
EDWARDS, John, 1870-1961
EDWARDS, Dussie E., 1888-1974
EDWARDS, Ray, 1930-1962
STIPP, Bladen M., 1889-1972
STIPP, Lillie M., 1883-1971
NEWMAN, Hubert Lavon, 2-15-1930 11-18-1960
PICKENS, Aubrey, 1900-1960
PICKENS, Bertha, 1900-No Date
PETTUS, Della M., 1882-1971
PRESS, Jas. F., 1905-1963
WATERS, Melva Jean SMALLEY, 1927-1978
SMALLEY, Nell M., 1908-1956
LEINART, Hazel Marie, 1917-1966
ALEXANDER, Glyn A., 1886-1955
ALEXANDER, Annie REEVES, 1888-1958
HUDSON, D. G. "Pete", 11-10-1902 2-2-1976
HUDSON, Minnie, 10-24-1903 No Date

HUDSON, Cecil, 6-19-1893 No Date
HUDSON, Stella G., 8-3-1894 4-9-1965
OLD, Margie Ruth, 1-10-1936 11-15-1959
ALLEN, J. B. "Burt", 1906-1962
ALLEN, Alta, 1911-No Date
THOMAS, Fonda D., 1917-1958
THOMAS, Ira C., 1883-1962
THOMAS, Winnie L., 1892-No Date
CARTER, Jas. R., 5-4-1887 5-16-1965
CARTER, Fronie E., 12-29-1892 11-16-1962
WEEKS, Rhyad, 1918-1975
WEEKS, Marie, 1921-No Date
COPELAND, A. Parker, 1884-1957
COPELAND, Mae, 1887-No Date
KILGORE, Roy, 9-26-1892 7-3-1962
KILGORE, Nova, 7-29-1894 No Date
SHELTON, Lorena, 1917-No Date
SHELTON, Orville E., 1909-1972
PAYNE, John E., Jr., Tex. Cpl., Tex. Air Force, W. W. II.,
                              2-10-1922 1-20-1958

DICKMAN, Fred, 1887-1960
DICKMAN, Dernye B., 1895-No Date
WATTS, Donald Lee, 1-26-1936 9-7-1953
WATTS, Robert Leon, 1903-1963
WATTS, Geneva L., 1906-No Date
SMITH, Joyce, 1922-1953
DRAKE, Mrs. F. L. "Billie R.", 6-12-1930 4-13-1965
PARTINGTON, J. R., 1891-1955
HESTER, James R. "Bud", 7-16-1920 7-25-1963
HESTER, Mary Margaret, 3-26-1919 No Date
GARRETT, Billy Wayne, 1942-1962
GARRETT, Walter L., 1891-1966
GARRETT, Rosa Mae, 1900-No Date
LOVE, Rufus B., Sr., 1905-1955
LOVE, Myrtle C., 1904-1955
LOVE, Rufus B., Jr., 1939-1955
LOVE, Samuel A., 1942-1955
IRONS, Raymond E., 1906-No Date
IRONS, Ethel M., 1909-No Date
KILGORE, Olen J., 1922-1977
KILGORE, Gladys, 1921-No Date
KILGORE, L. J., 1918-No Date
KILGORE, Thelma W., 1919-No Date

SECTION "A"
(CONT'D.)

STAPLETON, James C., 5-21-1928 5-25-1975
HOLLON, Dan P., 1910-1978
HOLLON, Tommy L., 10-6-1938 8-4-1976
LINCOLN, O. H. "Abe", 1902-1953
LINCOLN, Eunice W., No Dates
JOHNSON, Marvin Wade, 1910-No Date
JOHNSON, Shirley Laurette, 1913-No Date

PRUETT, A. Lee, 1889-1958
PRUETT, Nora E., 1892-1977
TERRY, Marvin B., 1896-1963
TERRY, Henrietta M., 1904-No Date
DIETZ, Oscar L., 1892-NO Date
DIETZ, Bertie J., 1894-1966
FUGETT, Preston, 1916-1979
MILLER, John Henry, Tex., Lt. Col., U. S. Army, W. W. I & II.,
                    1-1-1897 3-26-1957
SULLIVAN, Nancy Elizabeth, 1880-1956
MADDOX, George W., 1st. Lt., U. S. Army, W. W. II., BSM,
                    11-4-1911 3-14-1956
1 - Stone Missing
OLIVER, Laurel PARKS, 2-21-1884 6-22-1966
HAYES, Leo P., 1906-No Date
HAYES, Lyma E., 1905-No Date
HAYES, Jimmie L., 1928-1956
LIPSCOMB, George F., 1872-1964
LIPSCOMB, Dora L., 1887-1965
DUKE, Robert Irl, 1-2-1892 10-7-1954
DUKE, Artilia May, No Dates
STEWARD, Jessie Leona "Mama Bill", 1904-1967
SISCO, Lenora Mae, 1899-1970
JOHNSON, Eula Mae GREEN, 1914-No Date
GREEN, C. B., 1895-1971
GREEN, Dillie SISCO, 1894-No Date
GREEN, Lowell J., 1922- No Dates
HACKNEY, Monroe, 1925-No Date
HACKNEY, Martha Jo, 1926-No Date
HACKNEY, Archibald M., 1883-No Date
HACKNEY, Eva Frances, 1896-1974
GRISSOM, Tommie A., 1908-No Date
GRISSOM, Myrtle M., 1899-1966
KING, Paul P., 2-21-1883 7-12-1955
MITCHELL, Dennis J., 7-16-1953 2-20-1974
BOWMAN, Lucius Linton, Jr., 9-16-1899 1-6-1963
BURNETT, G. Frank, 1884-1966
BURNETT, Emma Dell, 1887-1976
SCOTT, Evert Hagan, Tex. Pvt., Hq. 3 Inf., W. W. II.,
                    2-23-1910 3-4-1967
SCOTT, Donnis A., 7-19-1910 No Dates
NEWMAN, Raymond E., 7-17-1907 No Date
NEWMAN, Ina O., 2-18-1905 No Date
WALLACE, R. Guy, 1891-1967
WALLACE, Poshia M., 1893-No Date
MORRIS, No Name or Dates
MORRIS, James E., 1897-1972
MORRIS, Jewell, 1904-1970
ROBBINS, E. Paul, Sr., 1909-1974
ROBBINS, Janice, 1911-No Date
DIBENHAM, Lowie W., 1897-1975
DIBENHAM, Gladys, 1900-No Date
HOLLERARD, Benjamin Rudd, 1894-1974
HOLLERARD, Ethel Lou, 1889-No Date

STEPHENS, Ernest E., 1899-1971
STEPHENS, Thelma G., 1899-1976
RUDD, John C., 1913-1959
RUDD, Lois, 1913-No Date
SEMENTO, Capt. John A., 1913-1961
DAVIS, Grady C., 1897-1961
SPOONEMORE, Oscar T., Tex., Pfc., Army Air Force, W. W. II.,
                                    11-28-1901 11-16-1971
SPOONEMORE, Sallie W., 3-11-1905 7-25-1977
ALLEN, Samuel W., 1911-No Date
ALLEN, Ollie Mae, 1912-No Date
ROSS, Carl W., 1909-1973
ROSS, Imogene, 1915-No Date
ROSS, Charlie A., 1883-1956
ROSS, Purnia C., 1890-No Date
YARBOROUGH, James R., Tex., Cpl., U. S. Army, 3-4-1933 10-19-1956
YARBOROUGH, Debra Lee, 11-20-1956 11-21-1956
YARBOROUGH, Lee Ann, dau. of Jerry & Sharon, died 1-24-1975
RICKMAN, Warner K., 1892-1974
RICKMAN, Gertie, 1894-No Date
MAYS, W. B. "Dub", 1913-No Date
MAYS, Pauline RICKMAN, 1919-1978
MALONE, Harold J., Conn., Pvt., U. S. Army, W. W. I.,
                                    7-1-1897 7-21-1973
REED, T. P. "Bud" "Pop", 1907-1968
LUHN, Julius R., 11-10-1888 10-16-1966
LUHN, Bettie S., 6-14-1882 6-11-1965
LANGFORD, John Rex, 1910-1970
LANGFORD, Willie C., 1909-No Date
WOODARD, Baxter T., 1901-1978
WOODARD, Faye, 1905-1963
WINDLE, James Edgar, 1894-1965
MC ANN, Alicia Janice, 9-8-1949 5-13-1966
GEORGE, Pearl E., 1883-1974
GEORGE, Halberta, 1915-1972
ASKINS, Robert, 2-3-1894 3-17-1979
ASKINS, Sallie J., 9-30-1897 No Date
ASKINS, Edan, 1920-No Date
ASKINS, Leona Edith, 1918-No Date
BRADLEY, Weldon E., Sr., 1907-1970
BRADLEY, Cornelia T., 1905-No Date
CLARK, Jack, 1904-1959
CLARK, Foy A. "Ninnie", 1911-1957
WATSON, Alvin C., Tex., Pvt., U. S. Army, W. W. I.,
                                    9-11-1902 10-8-1973
WATSON, D. Alene JONES, 1918-1958
HUDSON, David Earl, died 9-5-1955
HUDSON, Knighton P., 3-31-1918 1-12-1972
HUDSON, Maple V., 2-28-1916 No Date
BECTON, Joseph D., 1895-1970
BECTON, Edith R., 1910-No Date
BURNETT, Elliott, 1903-No Date
BURNETT, Lucile, 1904-1978
DAVIS, Lee, 1897-No Date

DAVIS, Alliene, 1902-1961
CALDWELL, Bille H., 11-12-1881 12-23-1963
DAGLEY, W. T. "Tom", 1885-1955
DAGLEY, Lakie M., 1887-1956
WHITE, Floyd, 1914-1967
WHITE, Lucille, 1915-1977
CALLAWAY, A. Burton, 1909-No Date
SAMPLES, Michael De Waine, 1951-1970
MOORE, Guy M., 1885-1966
MOORE, Tassie H., 1907-No Date
DUNN, Raymond, 1909-No Date
DUNN, Era O., 1918-No Date
HOLLINGSWORTH, John Wesley, 5-25-1887 7-18-1969
HOLLINGSWORTH, Willie, 2-24-1886 9-28-1972
VAUGHN, Edward T., 8-5-1917 5-20-1971
VAUGHN, Louise COLE, 5-27-1915 No Date
SHANKS, P. O. "Phineas", 1885-1968
SHANKS, Ella L., 1893-No Date
WELLS, W. Melvin, Tex. Sgt., 226 Base Unit, AAF, W. W. II.,
                    12-5-1905 5-26-1957

GILMORE, Clarence B., 1897-No Dates
GILMORE, Della M., 1902-No Date
ALLEN, Fannie Cornelia KEY, 1-21-1905 1-13-1965
ALLEN, Truman, 1901-1979
KEY, Dora May, 1885-1974
KEY, Tandy Lee, 1881-1962
HOLLINGSWORTH, I. N. "Dick", 1-10-1913 No Date
HOLLINGSWORTH, Frances L., 9-3-1915 7-9-1961
ALLGEIR, Leota O., 1911-1966
ALLGEIR, Otto P., 1904-1974
ALLGEIR, Otto O'Neal, 1st. Lt., 41st. ATS., U. S. A. F.,
                    5-24-1934 10-9-1961

SHEPHERD, Esker, 1902-1971
SHEPHERD, Iva M., 1902-No Date
HOWSE, Aloyce E., 5-12-1907 6-15-1959
CRANFILL, Mary E. HOWSE, 5-22-1907 5-5-1977
HARTSFIELD, Willie H, 1898-No Date
HARTSFIELD, Fannie B., 1899-1973
HARTSFIELD, Ilene E., 1918-No Date
THARP, James Ray, 9-15-1923 5-10-1975
THARP, Marie H., 8-15-1922 No Date
OSBORNE, Samuel M., 6-1-1914 4-7-1977
OSBORNE, Hazel L., 9-13-1915 No Date
SPOONEMORE, Roy, 1895-1978
GLASSCOCK, Belva K., 1-14-1888 2-25-1974
BAGGETT, Coy, 10-7-1889 9-21-1971
BAGGETT, Lola M., 11-13-1894 5-1-1954
REYNOLDS, Henry L., 11-29-1885 2-14-1972
REYNOLDS, Carvie, R., 9-18-1889 2-8-1973
SIKES, William W., 1882-1970
SIKES, Rhoda P., 1889-1972
OLIVER, Eugine P., 1882-1953
OLIVER, Evie C., 1887-1977
COATS, Lorenza Carl, 4-12-1891 4-12-1963

COATS, Mary DELMON, 6-29-1894 4-24-1976
ALLEY, John B., 4-7-1893 No Date
ALLEY, Maude L., 11-25-1897 No Date
SPENCER, Aubrey C., 1891-1976
SPENCER, Bulah O., 1898-No Date
ELLIOTT, T. R., 1919-No Date
FLLIOTT, Alta O., 1919-No Date
SANSING, Hubert L., 1914-1954
GARRETT, Louie R., 11-11-1935 4-16-1967
FULLINGTON, Raymond W., 1901-1957
FULLINGTON, Lina GREEN, 1905-1971
STAPLETON, Worley, 1903-No Date
STAPLETON, Fannie Evelyn, 1922-No Date
RENFRO, R. L., 1922-No Date
RENFRO, Dorothy K., 1921-No Date
WHITE, Gordon W., 1917-1978
WHITE, Mary C., 1920-No Date
GASTON, Henry W., 1913-1971
GASTON, Pauline C., 1914-No Date
COOPER, Robert W., 4-8-1888 8-6-1975
COOPER, Lottie E., 9-15-1892 No Date
GRAVES, Janelle, 9-20-1931 5-21-1967
CHAPMAN, Robert L., 1916-No Date
CHAPMAN, Lola W., 1917-No Date
CORLEY, Hershel, 1908-No Date
CORLEY, Gracie M., 1912-1969
RENFRO, Roy M., Sr., 1919-No Date
RENFRO, Selma, 1917-No Date
RENFRO, J. W. "Pete", 1925-No Date
RENFRO, Audrey PEBBLE, 1930-No Date
STEWART, Will, 4-9-1888 12-8-1960
STEWART, Vera Jane, 7-30-1891 2-21-1972
SANSING, Robert L., 2-23-1884 10-29-1961
TURNER, William Henry, died 11-6-1975
JINKS, C. Homer, 1905-1975
JINKS, Arlie E., 1911-No Date
WALKER, William F., 1882-1965
WALKER, Gussie, 1884-1955
BURTON, J. E. "Bud", 1909-No Date
BURTON, Nettie E., 1913-No Date
LANDINGHAM, _____, 1-31-1898 6-16-1955
STEPHENS, Grace GIST, 1905-1962
SCHIFF, Leon, 7-23-1879 8-19-1967
SCHIFF, Olie KING, 9-7-1880 2-7-1963
NEEL, NO Name or Dates
OVERBY, N. Durwood, 1907-1959
OVERBY, E. Clifford, 1909-No Date
WILLIAMS, No Name or Dates
KELLY, Saundra Joy, 1946-1967
GRAVES, Glen J., 1914-1976
GRAVES, Jimmie, 1913-1978
RUST, S. Renford, 1904-No Date
RUST, Mertie I., 1905-No Date
PINSON, Rease A., 1911-No Date

PINSON, Thelma H., 1918-No Date
AREY, C. G. "Cliff", 1910-1966
AREY, Lois L., 1910-No Date
JENKINS, Neal B., 1903-1973
JENKINS, Janet HARRELL, 1902-No Date
COMPTON, Jewel J., 1900-1978
SANDIN, Jeffrey Paul, 11-18-1972 5-2-1974
HUDGINS, C. M., 1895-1956
HUDGINS, Mae, 1901-No Date
HUDGINS, Billy Howard, 1927-No Date
HEMSELL, Clenon C., 1904-1967
HEMSELL, Helen B., 1906-No Date
HOLLOWAY, James E., 1920-1978
HOLLOWAY, Ruby E., 1926-No Date
ROSSON, Frank, 1888-1977
ROSSON, Minnie, 1898-No Date
BABB, James Robert, 7-2-1882 3-13-1956
MONEY, Marie Ilecne, 10-15-1919 8-2-1955
COX, Mary J. "Mollie", 1876-1958
TAYLOR, William B., 2-12-1887 12-5-1970
TAYLOR, Georgia T., 10-15-1891 1-14-1963
HARTHCOCK, Vernon W., 1880-1957
HARTHCOCK, Lillie MOORE, 1882-1963
MORRIS, Maxie R., 1904-No Date
MORRIS, Flossie L., 1908-No Date
LINDSEY, Horace F., 1909-No Date
LINDSEY, Lucille M., 1915-No Date
ROBINSON, Clark, 1-19-1936 6-16-1965
ASKINS, Bulah Mae, 1892-No Date
PATTERSON, William Marcus, 8-25-1975 3-27-1963
PATTERSON, Bessie CANDUS, 4-10-1882 9-3-1959
POPE, Myra Jean, 12-23-1937 8-31-1973
KELLY, Earl C., 1898-1969
KELLY, Reine, 1900-1976
MULLINS, W. J., 1901-1953
MULLINS, Angie E., 1898-No Date
WARNER, Sarah Ellen, 9-4-1882 12-2-1965
ELLIS, Henry J., Sr., 1907-No Date
ELLIS, Ruth, 1910-no Dates
HALL, Lake, 1897-No Date
HALL, Luanna, 1889-1962
BRUCE, Raymond M., 3-29-1919 2-22-1973
BRUCE, Lola L., 2-26-1919 No Date
STAPLETON, Sam Jones, 1885-1979
WILBURN, William Clarence, 1899-No Date
WILBURN, Elizabeth Mae, 1902-1974
HIGHSMITH, Boyd D., 1896-No Date
HIGHSMITH, Opal F., 1908-No Date
CURRIN, Doyle C., 1930-No Date
CURRIN, Thelma R., 1926-1971
CURRIN, Robert Frank, 1901-No Date
CURRIN, Bessie Leviette, 1905-No Date
STRATTON, Dennis Lee, 10-26-1940 6-25-1964
STRATTON, Monty F., 1912-No Date

STRATTON, Ethel E., 1916-No Date
PANNELL, Quincy, Pvt., Co. B., 112 Inf., 28 Div., W. W. I.,
                                  7-2-1888 12-17-1956

BIRLINE, John M., 1888-1956
WHITE, Raymond R., 1890-1963
WHITE, Josie, 1890-1973
CAGLE, William H., 1884-1969
CAGLE, Maggie M., 1888-1971
CARAWAY, Glenn F., 1909-1975
LONG, Adolphus, 9-8-1882 8-27-1954
LONG, Flora Alice, 4-25-1881 9-8-1963
GENTRY, Lonzy P., 1-24-1889 No Date
GENTRY, Luna Alice, 3-18-1891 No Date
REYNOLDS, Egbert C., 1894-1974
REYNOLDS, Lola E., 1907-No Date
COATS, Leonard O., 1907-1973
COATS, Zula M., 1907-No Date
BLANKENSHIP, Eula Mae, 5-13-1905 No Date
BLANKENSHIP, Ferrell G., Tex., Pvt., Co. C., 87 Recon., B. N.
                                  10-13-1928 6-9-1957

SHEARER, Constance, 8-31-1883 2-16-1963
BELL, Garlen O., 1905-No Date
BELL, Bertha L., 1906-1977
HICKS, Albert B., 1907-No Date
HICKS, Aurelia N., 1912-No Date
ROBARDEY, Russell G., 1912-1961
HARGROVE, Haskell, Tex., TEC-3, U. S. Army, W. W. II.,
                                  7-9-1911 4-8-1974
ROSS, Albert D., 10-22-1897 6-27-1962
ROSS, Bell STEPHENS, 11-3-1884 9-7-1967
GIPSON, Lawrence, 1892-1971
GIPSON, Bessie, 1895-1972
DEVENPORT, Loyd V., 1903-1973
DEVENPORT, Bircha E., 1906-No Date
WILSON, Woodrow C., Okla., S-Sgt., 78 Base Unit, AAF, W. W. II.,
                                  10-8-1916 11-26-1959
ARD, J. D. "Buddy", 1920-1977
ARD, Ola BELL, 1884-1958
ARD, Timothy David, 1876-1919
JINKS, Jesse R., 1897-1961
GOIN, Glen, 1916-1973
GOIN, Della M., 1921-No Date
RAGSDALE, William R., 1904-1961
RAGSDALE, Eunia PEARSON, 1910-No Date
HUNT, Nancy Ann RAGSDALE, 1939-1968
MC CORMAC, J. Will, 1884-1960
MC CORMAC, Lela E., 1891-1964
MC CORMAC, Cyril H., Tex., S-Sgt., 1329 Labor Supv. Co., W. W. II, BSM.
                                9-28-1918 10-7-1966
MC CORMAC, James W. "Mack", 1910-1977
MC CORMAC, Vestal, 1914-No Date
TURNER, William V., 5-7-1905 10-25-1965
TURNER, Lavell, 11-4-1912 No Date
GIBSON, Samuel A., Tex., Pvt., U. S. Army, W. W. I.,. 6-2-1897 12-30-1973

NELSON, James E., 1881-1955
NELSON, Mary F., 1899-1960
MC FARLAND, Virgil, 1899-1976
BELTS, Rev. Bill P., 1926-1962
SANDERS, Hubert C., 1901-1971
HOGUE, Larry B., 1931-1974
HOGUE, Mary Elizabeth, 1927-No Date
GIBBS, Curtis W., 1902-No Date
GIBBS, Frances E., 1908-NO Dates
STARLING, F. E. "Bud", 1907-1973
STARLING, Verna E., 1907-No Date
DURRETT, Joe A., Sr., 9-20-1963 (died)
BURNETT, G. L. "Pat", 1904-1970
BURNETT, Delphia R., 1908-No Date
BURNETT, Pat, 1928-No Date
BURNETT, Bertha M., 1929-1976
SINCLAIR, Shelby J., 1915-1979
SINCLAIR, Nell B., 1916-No Date
TAYLOR, Beverly, 6-17-1930   10-24-1963
MONEY, Rickey L., 5-15-1955   12-17-1955
HARTHCOCK, John Weyman, 1910-1974
HARTHCOCK, Hazel YEARY, 1917-No Date

END OF MEMORY LAND CEMETERY

ROSEMOUNT CEMETERY
(COMMERCE, TEXAS)

SECTION "A"

WYNN, Hugh D., 1876-1941
WYNN, Mary T., 1876-1966
TAYLOR, John M., 1880-1914
TAYLOR, Lillian M., 1882-1963
TAYLOR, Melissa E., 1846-1914
TAYLOR, W. J., 1846-1934
LOWE, Glen, 1906-1907
LOWE, W. H., 1850-1906
LOWE, Willie, 1882-1903
MC CLELLAN, John Herbert, 1899-No Date
                married 2-26-1920
MC CLELLAN, Minnie Jewell, 1890-No Date
NUNN, Mattie E., 1866-1903
NUNN, William D., 1859-1938
SMITH, Kate Olive, 12-21-1897   6-14-1963
HOOD, Grant, 1875-1942
HOOD, Kate Olive, 10-3-1873   5-18-1958
OLIVE, Harry V., 1-8-1869   7-28-1903
RANDLE, Anne, 1876-1954
RANDLE, Walta, 1903-1918
RANKLE, Walter, 1868-1903
TAPP, Martha O, 1847-1903
CONDER, William C., 1868-1943

CONDER, Mary Olive, 1871-1922
CONDER, Hazel, 1902-1903
WATSON, Eunice, 6-29-1915 10-18-1958
WATSON, Brady, 10-3-1904 9-7-1966
LEE, Mark, 2-18-1957 2-18-1957
INGRAM, Earld, 3-28-1902 3-2-1903
GRIFFITTS, T. P., 1866-1928
GRIFFITTS, Laura O., 1871-1949
BELL, C. E., 1847-1927
BELL, Nancy Ann, 1847-1926
CROCKETT, Bertha, 3-29-1885 3-13-1961
CROCKETT, Fred E., 12-29-1873 3-16-1956
MALONEY, James M., 9-14-1839 9-10-1902
MALONEY, Martha A., 4-27-1845 9-10-1902
BELL, R. P., 1866-1940
GRIFFITTS, Margie L., 1-23-1901 12-1-1955
GRIFFITTS, Maurine, died 1903
ADDISON, Verda Mae, died 1956
ADDISON, Charles D., died 1973
BRYANT, Emma Alice, 3-7-1883 12-5-1957
BRYANT, Lemuel L., 8-17-1879 11-10-1959
CONDER, Mary Ann, 1839-1911
CONDER, James W., 1871-1920
DYER, Aline, 1906-No Date
DYER, H. M. "Bill", 1894-1961
CAMMERON, Fannie M., 1899-1979
CAMMERON, Hugh A., 1901-1976
RINGOLD, Richard, 1869-1918
JOHNSON, Viola MC W., 11-26-1899 No Date
            married 6-16-1920
JOHNSON, Beemis A., 8-14-1896 8-15-1969
YOUNG, Tom R., 1-9-1891 6-15-1969
YOUNG, Chloe H., 12-8-1890 No Date
PRICE, Beatrice, died 1907
SIMS, Leila C., dau. of J. W. & V. E., 1-19-1850 12-1901
SELF, Elberta, 6-17-1901 No Date
            married 6-4-1920
SELF, Mike E., Sr., 1-18-1900 10-31-1975
STEDHER, Lucinda, 3-1-1831 9-27-1903
PRICE, Melba Melissa, 1-1908 6-1908
PRICE, Jack Taylor, 1917-1918
PRICE, Fredia Virginia, 1903-1923
STEPHENS, Fannie KING, 1876-1952
BRYANT, Jessie, 4-16-1833 5-14-1914
BRYANT, F. N., 6-28-1839 9-25-1909
THOMAS, Margret M., 1-4-1882 11-5-1966
THOMAS, William Frank, 8-22-1878 1-22-1964
BLANKENSHIP, Evelyn, 11-2-1915 2-27-1976
BLANKENSHIP, Rebecca A., 1891-1962
BLANKENSHIP, J. T., 1889-1969
MALONEY, Lela FARROW, 4-19-1857 2-2-1916
MALONEY, George C., 1-12-1848 10-24-1906
GOFF, W. Y., 12-13-1860 7-4-1909
GOFF, Iva Belle, 9-14-1882 9-13-1964

GOFF, Aubrey H., 10-7-1884 3-25-1932
GREGORY, Julia, 5-25-1826 1-31-1912
SMITH, J. J., 1-24-1875 12-6-1908
FOWLER, Mintie A., 1-31-1860 1-12-1918
FOWLER, Evah C., dau. of G. D., 5-28-1881 6-11-1904
FOWLER, Tommie Lucy, 11-8-1879 No Date
FOWLER, George D., 11-1-1859 11-30-1941
BOSTICK, Catherine TEMPLE, 1821-1904
BOSTICK, John Lucien, 1859-1941
BOSTICK, Mary ROBINSON, 1866-1950
KINSLOW, John P., 1889-1933
KINSLOW, Jennie BOSTICK, 1889-1973
HINBLE (?), Loula, wife of Homer R., 11-18-1880 1-19-1911
TROTMAN, Lucy E., 1864-1942
TROTMAN, James Ramsey, 4-10-1860 10-3-1937
TURNER, _____, wife of E. E., 7-28-1836 11-5-1918
WARD, Myrtle BLEDSOE, 6-18-1897 No Date
WARD, Harry C., 8-1-1893 3-13-1960
NORTHSWORTHY, Alfred Guy, 1878-1911
FREEMAN, Nettie, 6-22-1883 3-10-1967
FREEMAN, Joe D., 9-3-1880 3-15-1961
HARRIS, Osborne N., 2-17-1859 8-19-1934
HARRIS, Anne E., 1-22-1857 6-21-1912
HAYSLIP, Ben, 9-7-1881 12-3-1970
HAYSLIP, Willie, 8-3-1891 No Date
HAYSLIP, Mary, 1843-1925
JAMES, Infant of C. C. & L. M., 11-15-1913 1-8-1914
MADISON, Fannie M., 1850-1933
DELANEY, Frank, 1857-1934
TROLLINGER, Nancy Jane, 1870-1948
HOOTEN, James H., 1860-1902
YOUNG, J. E., 1882-1928
YOUNG, J. E., Jr., 1909-1909
YOUNG, Samuel, 1842-1916
YOUNG, Martha Sue, 1847-1925
SHERRA, Addie YOUNG, 1891-1972
KNIGHT, Dollie WOOD, 1879-1966
KNIGHT, Lemuel Lee, 1874-1968
KNIGHT, Lemuel Lee, Jr., 10-27-1925 8-12-1934
KNIGHT, Alton H., 7-7-1904 8-12-1905
KNIGHT, Robert B., 2-3-1911 10-11-1927
MC CAULEY, Fannie A., 1858-1941
WATSON, Annie Cora, 1873-1923
WATSON, Guy Evans, 1879-1931
VALDEN, George M., son of L. & Gloria, 10-21-1901 12-13-1901
WEAVER, Evans Eugene, 1896-1959
WEAVER, Leone PRATT, 1899-1959
BROWNING, Velma, 9-18-1893 No Date
BROWNING, Dan, 8-2-1886 8-5-1968
GARNER, Billie, 1923-1928
BROWNING, _____, Wife of Dan., 1888-1912
GARNER, William F., 1891-1948
NORSWORTHY, P. W., 1872-1929
NORSWORTHY, (Mother), 1848-1918

NORSWORTHY, (Father), 1848-1912
MC DONALD, James H., Pvt., 2nd. Miss. Inf., C. S. A., died 5-20-1914
MC DONALD, _____, wife of J. H., 9-4-1843 1-8-1913
PRATT, D. T., M. D., 1866-1929
PRATT, Maude, 1871-1912
DEALNEY, T., 1898-1918
PIPPEN, Melbal, 1907-1909
PIPPEN, Lillie M., 1887-1973
PIPPEN, W. L., 1878-1938
WARD, Jimmie, Tex., S-Sgt., Army Air Force, W. W. II, AW-3, 2OLC-PH,
                              7-9-1920 10-11-1944
TRAYLOR, Lora V., 2-28-1880 9-11-1975
TRAYLOR, Otho R., 10-18-1889 8-13-1958
TRAYLOR, Margaret Ann, wife of E. A., 7-13-1880 5-29-1909
MC CARTER, R. Edward Lee, 1866-1934
MC CARTER, Nora Jane, 1867-1940
WHITE, F. G., No Dates
HARRELL, Thelma L., 1913-1937
TERRY, Herbert, 1906-1907
TERRY, Inf. son of H. M., 1918-1919
TERRY, Nina A., 1885-1924
TERRY, Jerry Lynn, 1-15-1939 7-20-1939
TERRY, Margaret GIBSON, 1854-1946
TERRY, Milton H., 1851-1931
TERRY, Una SEALY, 3-13-1893 1-4-1926
MC ADAMS, C. A., 8-5-1850 9-18-1907
GILBERT, Annie L., 7-30-1887 No Date
GILBERT, Henry C., 5-17-1892 8-6-1958
RODGERS, Maurine, 12-16-1915 No Date
RODGERS, Joe Bill, Tex., Pfc., U. S. Army, W. W. II.,
                              7-26-1915 6-9-1963

STRINGER, Sophia A., 1846-1906
STRINGER, Ruben E., 1837-1930
VITTITOW, Marvin Read, 1899-1956
VITTITOW, Cecile TOLBERT, 1903-No Date
MAURINE, Laura, 9-23-1901 1-6-1903
RICHARDS, Virgil H., 12-23-1910 6-17-1958
WHITE, Ruth H., 1893-1970
WHITE, Gus F., 1884-1957
GOODMAN, Joseph P., 12-22-1862 5-6-1936
GOODMAN, Edna R., 12-30-1969 8-26-1901
EVANS, Mary LANE, 10-3-1856 1-6-1936
WINN, Clarence, son of H. W. & Laura, 8-3-1903 6-24-1906
SALMON, Lawrence Waldo, 1902-1971
SALMON, Veda Mae CASSELL, No Dates
SALMON, Mary J., wife of A. J., 9-13-1852 8-15-1903
SALMON, Andrew Jackson, 10-27-1854 12-19-1902
SALMON, R. L. "Bob", 1877-1946
SALMON, Eva, 1879-1950
BUSBY, S. E., 12-19-1883 10-31-1918
BUSBY, Ezra H., 7-17-1892 5-4-1972
BUSBY, Irma, wife of S. E., 1891-1962
BUSBY, Rev. Loraine Ophelia, 3-30-1904 5-30-1971
BUSBY, Rufus P., 6-6-1859 6-21-1959

BUSBY, Ophelia R., 5-10-1866 5-29-1931
JONES, Jessie BUSBY, 4-13-1887 2-11-1911
LOWRY, Ima Esther BUSBY, 1896-1977
BREWSTER, Mary HANES, 1903-1935
HANES, Harvey B., 1908-1940
ROBERTS, J. C., 1835-1913
TURNER, Rev. James W., 1875-1949
TURNER, Mildred Louise, 1912-1956
TURNER, Florence S., 1876-1968
STEPHENS, Voncile, died 1912
STEPHENS, Ada D., 1884-1971
STEPHENS, J. A., 1869-1921
WHITE, Sarah C., 8-9-1834 10-20-1914
WHITE, Mary E., 12-20-1871 5-15-1965
NELSON, Mary E., 7-25-1884 8-9-1978
                    married 1903
NELSON, Tom A., 9-27-1882 12-2-1966
NORFLEET, Zuther F., 12-22-1884 No Date
NORFLEET, Jessie B., 9-9-1912 9-9-1912
BULLS, June, 1898-1961
BULLS, Leta N., 1904-No Date
BULLS, Mamie Patric, wife of June, 1-19-1897 1-25-1924
BULLS, Doris Jean, dau. of C. F. & Alice, 8-4-1921 3-11-1923
BULLS, Clarence F., 1895-1950
BULLS, Alice C., 1899-No Date
BULLS, James H., 10-15-1843 12-18-1912
BULLS, Mrs. J. H., 12-3-1848 5-20-1921
BULLS, John H., 3-5-1867 7-24-1941
BULLS, Mary C., 9-2-1878 8-13-1968
BULLS, Edgar Lee, 8-13-1906 10-1-1964
ABERNATHY, Jewell, wife of D. C., 11-21-1891 2-11-1919
FIELDS, Samuel C. A., 11-10-1835 2-25-1934
FIELDS, Charlotte S., 3-20-1849 3-16-1923
FIELDS, Charles Melvern, 10-31-1883 8-23-1907
HEINER, James Harlzell, died 6-1-1928
HEINER, Annie A. E., No Dates
PRIM, R. .A., 1884-1945
PRIM, Claud A., 11-11-1895 9-1-1979
PRIM, Mrs. E. M., 1841-1935
PRIM, Mrs. R. M., 1867-1934
PRIM, Maude, 1888-1907
PRIM, _____, 1857-1931
HAYSLIP, Henry C., 1849-1910
HAYSLIP, Stella M., 5-27-1905 12-7-1910
HAYSLIP, Mary J., 3-6-1912 3-6-1912
HAYSLIP, J. H., 1843-1931
HAYSLIP, Mary, 1835-1915
HAYSLIP, Lela, 1886-1909
FARREL, Porter Hedrick, 1-27-1885 No Date
FARREL, Lucy Alice, 11-7-1891 2-12-1953
MORELAND, Mary Emma, 3-26-1873 11-26-1911
SANDRIDGE, Nina H., 1892-1941
SANDRIDGE, Henry E., 1890-1942
EVANS, B. O., 1-11-1883 9-17-1963

EVANS, Essie, 2-1-1886 1-22-1973
BARRY, William A., 1873 No Date
BARRY, Alice E., 1881-1942
HAMMOCK, Lueasy, J., 11-16-1852 9-6-1939
HAMMOCK, Frank H., 2-23-1854 5-21-1922
HAMMOCK, Henry, 5-19-1881 8-5-1962
JONES, Myrtle Dan., son of G. E. & N. E., 9-13-1892 3-8-1907
LYON, Clarence W., 2-8-1866 9-4-1906
LYON, Faye HARRIS, 12-1-1900 No Date
LYON, Clarence Herbert, 11-6-1899 9-1-1973
WALKER, Jane, died 7-1-1903
WALKER, Mary Ellen, 2-13-1873 10-16-1948
WALKER, Ross, 3-27-1870 8-14-1927
ROSS, W. D. "Buddy", 8-6-1898 6-14-1964
RUCKER, George F., 1874-1961
RUCKER, Martha D., 1884-No Date
WILLSON, S. Thomas, 1891-1965
WILLSON, Lula F., 1893-1977
HERRON, George Walter, 1889-1954
HERRON, Alma M., 1892-1974
HERRON, Jerry W., Tex., Pfc., U. S. Army, 1-26-1928 6-6-1950
LEACH, Infant, died 1912
LEACH, Infant, died 1911
LEACH, Ruby Lucille, 2-10-1910 9-6-1910
LEACH, Edward L., 1886-1957
LEACH, Maude J., 1892-1961
POLSON, Merle Moreland, 1904-1944
HIX, Bess LONG, 1887-1949
LONG, Brice, 8-19-1885 11-2-1949
LONG, Annie C., wife of R. B., 2-18-1859 12-30-1903
LONG, R. B., 11-18-1852 9-3-1925
LONG, James Dupree, Tex., Pvt., Co. E., 4 Inf., TXNG., W. W. I.,
                         7-29-1901 6-30-1964

SMITH, Jess LONG, 1890-1938
SMITH, Thomas W., 1885-1937
MC KINNEY, Charles E., 1874-1959
MC KINNEY, James H., 1870-1931
MC KINNEY, R. F., 12-7-1836 3-20-1909
SCANTLEN, Ladocia F., 1867-1958
SCANTLEN, T. M., 4-20-1868 3-7-1909
PROFFER, J. M., 1-13-1892 No Date
PROFFER, Media M., 5-1-1892 11-22-1971
SALMON, John, 5-29-1908 8-4-1963
JONES, Mary F., 1-9-1849 10-21-1908
JONES, Henrietta, 1-28-1871 9-21-1972
JOHNSON, Sip S., 1874-1954
JOHNSON, Bessie M., 1878-1963
SILMAN, Laura, 1-23-1877 2-7-1906

SECTION "B"

NEAL, J. Tom, 11-21-1858 3-10-1904
NEAL, Virginia Lee, 5-4-1865 6-27-1944
NEAL, John Albert, Tex. BKR-2, U.S.N., W. W. I., 9-12-1891 11-4-1965

NEAL, Sidney H., 7-1-1893   10-25-1906
LEGATE, Charles P., 1895-1979
PRITCHARD, Annie CRAIG, 11-17-1864   2-2-1947
CRAIG, Knox, 8-12-1858   6-23-1906
THOMAS, Daniel P., 10-14-1883   10-18-1950
THOMAS, Dan Tom, 6-22-1911 2-26-1958
KETRON, Clyde, 1-31-1883   4-16-1933
WADE, Gertrude FINLEY, 1885-1965
FINLEY, J. Edgar, 1883-1952
FINLEY, David M., Jr., 1895-1947
FINLEY, David M., Sr., 5-20-1848   2-22-1917
DORRIS, Elizabeth C., 5-3-1822   1-5-1907
FINLEY, Phebe, 8-26-1858   12-23-1928
HODGES, W. B., 3-10-1831   2-1-1916
JOHNSON, R. N., 11-3-1843   4-11-1908
JOHNSON, Robert Neely, 1872-1957
JOHNSON, Sarah Emma, 1875-1923
HEWITT, Helen, died 1908
HEWITT, Jack E., 1901-1962
HEWITT, Tom, 1899-1970
HEWITT, Martha, No Dates
HEWITT, Mrs. E., 1869-1943
HEWITT, E., 1867-1952
HEWITT, Thomas E., Co. C., 4th Miss. Inf., C. S. A., No Dates
HOLLON, Ruth, dau. of Mr. & Mrs. Sam, 5-19-1905 8-11-1906
HOLLON, Paul, son of Mr. & Mrs. Sam, 8-22-1907 6-6-1910
HOLLON, Myrtle PAYNE, 1887-1969
HOLLON, Sammie H., 1882-1954
JACKSON, Byron, 1888-1934
JACKSON, Beatrice E., 1860-1944
JACKSON, Parish G., 1855-1906
ALDRIDGE, Mrs. L. J., 1-5-1841   11-18-1928
ALDRIDGE, J. R., 8-4-1829   2-6-1907
SIMS, Elizabeth, 4-16-1915   6-23-1935
SIMS, Edgar, 4-9-1904   3-11-1947
HAWKINS, Ora L., 1890-1973
HAWKINS, Joe W., 1888-1971
THOMPSON, Arminda, 1850-1903
SHERRILL, Lucy, 1881-1953
SHERRILL, W. W., 1869-1929
SHERRILL, Robert, 1904-1905
WHEELER, William J., 1868-1923
WHEELER, Beulah A., 1871-1945
WHEELER, Herbert, 1896-1977
WHEELER, Eugenia R., 1898-No Date
WHEELER, Helen, 1899-1909
TAYLOR, William Harey, 1924-1924
BRYANT, John W., Okla., Pfc., Btry C., 50 Arty, CAC, W. W. I.
                              6-12-1894 7-14-1959
BRYANT, Emily BENNETT, 2-23-1898 5-4-1968
BRYANT, William W., Tex., Tec-5, 9222 Tech. SVC, Unit, W. W. II,
                              9-30-1922 5-15-1961
CHEATHAM, J. R., 9-10-1878   11-15-1913
CHEATHAM, Willie, 1885-1954

TAYLOR, Balma C., 1903-No Date
TAYLOR, Walter E., 1897-1973
PRICE, William C., Sgt., Co. F., 22 Tex. Cav., C.S.A., No Dates
PRICE, Elizabeth, No Dates
WHEELUS, Bess C., 1906-1974
HALL, Ruben Milton, 1881-1964
HALL, Alice Inez HOLLON, 1884-1956
HOLLON, W. Z., 8-12-1858 9-16-1907
                Commander of Camp # 317, W. O. W.
HOLLON, Mrs. W. Z., 7-15-1860 4-20-1920
BROTHERS, Audine, 8-13-1929 2-3-1930
BROTHERS, Hence, 1861-1929
WILLIAMS, Mary Joe, 1928-1928
WILLIAMS, James Edgar, 1930-1930
BROTHERS, Clarence E., son of H. & Maggie, 12-21-1886 10-5-1911
WRIGHT, Virginia Lee, 2-12-1913 2-19-1913
WRIGHT, Larry Wayne, 8-23-1941 12-14-1941
WRIGHT, Minnie Lee, 3-15-1887 1-11-1964
WRIGHT, Henry M., Sr., 8-17-1881 8-16-1963
WRIGHT, Mary L., 1916-1979
NOLAND, Isa, Dau. of W. T. & Rena, 7-2-1901 9-18-1915
SHIPLEY, Lou NEAL, 12-23-1888 No Date
SHIPLEY, William V., 2-19-1879 3-3-1942
SHIPLEY, Raymond Ellis, 12-22-1911 2-12-1912
REEDER, Priscilla, 1874-1960
REEDER, John W., 1860-1910
REEDER, John Lester, Sr., 1897-1970
REEDER, Annie LEMON, No Dates
SMITH, Inf. dau. of H. H. & Laura, born and died 10-10-1903
SMITH, H. H., 5-29-1872 1-10-1940
SMITH, Laura A., 9-18-1870 2-23-1913
NEWMAN, Jacob C., 1904-1975
NEWMAN, Olivia H., 1882-1971
NEWMAN, Samuel C., 1873-1939
MANTOOTH, Daisy B., 1903-1969
MANTOOTH, Leonard L., 1900-No Date
MANTOOTH, Lizzie, 12-15-1898 9-13-1913
MANTOOTH, Lucy, 4-4-1872 1-2-1928
MANTOOTH, Joe, 3-24-1864 12-11-1942
MANTOOTH, Landon, 3-11-1907 7-30-1938
HEMSELL, William, 1842-1922
HEMSELL, Malinda, 1844-1920
HEMSELL, M. L., 1875-1914
JONES, Retia, 1872-1952
JONES, R. P., 1870-1935
HARRIS, Isabelle, 1861-1947
HARRIS, John M., 1854-1938
SHEPHERD, Gertrude, 1911-1938
SHEPHERD, Ervin, 1912-1966
SHEPHERD, Etter, 1875-1969
                married 11-25-1900
SHEPHERD, J. W., 1875-1956
HOOVER, Edgar W., 1892-1954
CORNELIUS, Dora A., 1879-1951

CORNELIUS, John P., 1872-1910
NELSON, Mary A., 1847-1937
CORNELIUS, Mrs. M. E., 7-10-1849 3-6-1924
CORNELIUS, Dewitt E., 1895-1958
UTLEY, Lillian C., 1889-1976
UTLEY, W. H., 1886-1959
UTLEY, Infant, died 5-7-1909
HART, Sterling Price, Jr., 1908-1910
HART, John Francis, 2-21-1902 12-15-1940
HART, Sterling Price, 1873-1960
HART, Tillie Etta, 1880-1945
MAULDIN, Elizabeth J., 6-8-1854 5-13-1912
DEARING, Geneva Evon, 8-3-1913 7-23-1914
HANSON, Floyd A., 1903-1979
DEARING, Elzie Alvin, 1-27-1885 9-11-1970
DEARING, Iva Lee, 8-17-1889 8-30-1956
WHITLEY, Mary Virginia BURT, 3-16-1890 9-11-1968
WHITLEY, Dr. Thomas R., 10-16-1882 8-6-1915
LITTLE, Hal, 11-25-1900 1-24-1970
LITTLE, Frances W., 4-14-1909 No Date
LITTLE, Hal, Tex., Pvt., U.S. Army, W. W. I & II., 1900-1970
BOUNDS, Trafton Bernard, son of T. B. & Lee Ola, died 9-17-1914
MARTIN, Infant, No Dates
MARTIN, William Chester, 2-1-1887 9-21-1964
MARTIN, Jessie A., 5-29-1888 8-14-1966
PATE, J. A., 1st. Sgt., Co. B., 28 Ga. Inf., C. S. A., No Dates
PATE, Mary A., 1868-1963
PATE, Robert A., 1897-1962
NEAL, Tennie M., 4-13-1864 4-9-1919
NEAL, William B., 7-7-1855 4-9-1919
NEAL, Annie Laura, 12-15-1895 4-16-1933
NEAL, Robert R., 1890-1977
KNIGHT, Samuel T., 4-7-1905 4-20-1975
KNIGHT, Amos, 7-17-1879 7-17-1961
KNIGHT, Fannie C., wife of Amos, 12-23-1879 2-25-1913
KNIGHT, Kathleen, dau. of Amos & F. C., 9-20-1910 6-4-1913
KNIGHT, William C., 10-7-1908 No Date
              married 12-20-1941
KNIGHT, Eva G., 8-9-1915 No Date
SPEED, Mary 6-8-1856 7-15-1910
SPEED, John, 2-24-1852 9-12-1918
SPEED, Lessie, 6-13-1897 No Date
SPEED, Julius William, Tex., Pfc., 32 Balloon Co. Air, SVC, W. W. I.,
                    8-19-1895 12-14-1961
SPEED, Daila J., 11-10-1886 1-2-1973
SPEED, Thomas Bemon, 1-14-1886 10-21-1941
ALLEN, Sarah J., 1839-1914
              (She Gave Me My WIFE, W. L. Harrison)
HARRISON, Alice, 10-9-1860 3-8-1919
HARRISON, W. L., 9-5-1855 5-14-1933
DE BUSK, William Clark, 7-27-1900 7-29-1953
DE BUSK, Virginia Annette, No Dates
DE BUSK, Gussie, 1894-1919
DE BUSK, Mrs. Clifford, died 1-25-1952

DE BUSK, W. N., 1864-1933
PATILLO, _____, died 1960 (Funeral Marker)
POER, John Wesley, 4-9-1838 6-20-1914
MARTIN, Jonny, 1898-1916
VICKERS, Harold, 1921-1938
VICKERS, J. D., 1911-1924
VICKERS, Mary, 1915-1915
VICKERS, J. A., 1885-1941
PRATT, Eleanor KELLY, 12-24-1906 1-14-1978
KELLY, Evelyn SCARBOROUGH, 8-27-1885 1-30-1969
KELLY, Henry Jackson, 7-20-1875 7-20-1946
KELLY, Charles Jackson, 4-5-1913 1-11-1915
KNOX, Mae Ella, 1883-1955
KNOX, Henry G., 1883-1950
BYOUS, John Delbert, 10-9-1907 10-9-1965
BYOUS, Ruby Gladys, 5-10-1906 No Date
ROTENBERRY, James G., 10-1-1857 12-20-1928
JAMES, Clemlee C., and Infant, died 1917
CARTER, Frank, III., 1918-1918
JANES, Joe C., Tex., Pfc., Co. H., 58 Inf., W. W. I
                              7-25-1888 10-28-1959
COLLINS, Mollie ORR, 1872-1943
FULLER, Earl H., 1891-1914
MILLICAN, Carl, 1904-1913
HAISLIP, Leila CLIFTON, 4-20-1867 12-29-1923
CLIFTON, Rev. W. L., 1836-1911
CLIFTON, Laura J., 1845-1912
CLIFTON, Fayt, 5-31-1902 6-2-1968
CLIFTON, Daisy M., 9-12-1877 2-15-1946
CLIFTON, Edgar B., 4-8-1870 4-9-1915
ANDERS, Thomas D., 11-8-1880 4-10-1939
ANDERS, Viola A., 1-1-1893 11-15-1918
ADAMS, Mrs. M. J., 1850-1924
ADAMS, J. F., 1839-1915
ADAMS, Carl F., W. W. I, Veteran, 3-23-1899 10-23-1940
ADAMS, John S., 1-23-1874 7-30-1941
ADAMS, Loulie A., 7-2-1882 7-4-1967
FARROW, Charles Emerson, 1885-1956
FARROW, Alma ADAMS, 1886-1969
ADAMS, Robert Carl, 1889-1975
ADAMS, Nina APPERSON, 1892-1969
HANES, Addie, 9-19-1896 3-3-1934
HANES, Herman, 10-2-1893 12-2-1916
HANES, Robert O., 2-2-1870 6-10-1962
ROBERTS, John H., 1908-1940
ROBERTS, Martha Frances, 1871-1963
ROBERTS, Willis Hawkins, 1857-1915
REES, Kathleen Grace ROBERTS, died 3-17-1968
FRANKLIN, William W., 1886-1940
HARRISON, Georgia Mae, 1883-1964
HARRISON, William Romer, 1880-1969
SHEPPEARD, Jack, 12-9-1900 10-13-1974
HENDERSON, M. O., 2-3-1886 10-24-1918
HENDERSON, Mary S., 12-16-1857 10-17-1932

HENDERSON, J. C., 9-30-1888 7-26-1910
MC KITTRICK, W. J., 3-10-1865 10-21-1950
MC LAIN, Nancy PERKINS, 1933-1968
MC LAIN, Georgia Lynne, died 8-20-1962
MC LAIN, Martha Frances, died 8-18-1961
ARMISTEAD, Jimmie, 4-15-1884 12-10-1951
ARMISTEAD, Bunchie, 11-27-1888 10-10-1955
BERG, Perter N., 1891-1976
BERG, Lida, 1898-1926
MC LEOD, Laura, 10-29-1893 10-11-1978
MC LEOD, George Donald, Jr., 1913-1928
MC LEOD, George Donald, Sr., 1890-1954
MC LEOD, Richard Roderick, 6-30-1915 10-30-1915
WATSON, Ella B., 1876-1964
WATSON, Richard, 1868-1947
MARSHALL, Mable H., 1881-1963
MARSHALL, Mack H., 1876-1941
MOON, John Wesley, 1871-1916
MOON, Fannie MARSHALL, 1874-1943
PADDOCK, Alan Eastman, 1892-1948
MEISSNER, Ava, PADDOCK, 1901-1962
PRITCHARD, Bamah Elaine, 1921-1931
PRITCHARD, Oliver Frank, 1924-1925
PRITCHARD, Ruth, 10-1-1899 NO Date
PRITCHARD, Frank L., 10-19-1899 3-7-1977
STEPHENS, John Harvey, 12-2-1891 10-27-1926
DUNN, W. B., 1862-1916
DUNN, Maggie, 1874-1951
FERGUSON, Myrtle B., 1-19-1891 5-24-1976
FERGUSON, C. W., 8-20-1884 7-6-1955
REID, Walter, 1880-1951
REID, Marcia D., 1881-1975
PRIM, Clara, 8-20-1916 No Date
PRIM, Kenneth, 2-1-1917 7-5-1958
CLINTON, Mary Frances, wife of W. J., 1871-1916
PRIM, Kenneth, Tex., Pvt., Co. L., 116 Inf., W. W. II., BSM-PH,
                          2-1-1917 7-5-1958

ADAMS, Hal A., 7-9-1910 6-23-1954
ADAMS, Jim A., 4-28-1873 2-15-1943
ADAMS, Dora M., 3-10-1881 5-6-1974
ADAMS, Howard, 1905-1935
MARSHALL, Newton, 1838-1915 C.S.A. Marker
ADAMS, Z. T., 1847-1925
                  Co B., 63rd. Ala. Inf., C. S. A.
COODY, Eula May MARSHALL, 8-7-1882 3-19-1936
MARSHALL, M. B., 7-17-1871 10-1-1914
LARD, Adlyn Lois, 9-10-1902 6-20-1972
NUNN, Junior B., 1871-1928
NUNN, Asbury T., 1856-1935
COODY, Gelon, 1887-1935
SCRUGGS, Katherine, 1886-No Date
SCRUGGS, Joe F., 1877-1964
1 - Funeral Marker, No Name or Dates
YARBROUGH, Daniel H., 3-9-1882 8-21-1918

YARBROUGH, Cordia M., 11-17-1887 6-6-1931
HEATH, Hannah P., 1852-1935
ABERNATHY, Flora B. BAILEY, 5-25-1861 4-28-1955
ABERNATHY, John B., 6-20-1859 11-29-1917
FOLLIS, Georgia Ethel, 3-31-1893 10-2-1918
ABERNATHY, Mary, 1887-1971
ABERNATHY, Claude, 1887-1971
SAYLE, William E., Jr., 1883-1918
SWEAT, Robert H., Tex., Cpl., 2 Marine Air Controls Sq., W. W. II.,
                          6-16-1926 3-26-1960
GORMAN, Homer O., 1892-1957
GORMAN, A. Edna, 1894-1979
ERWIN, Mrs. Lillian, 1886-1966
OLIVER, Martha V., 10-23-1918 10-27-1918
OLIVER, J. S., 1876-1951
OLIVER, Allie F., 1884-1963
SIMPSON, Mary Ellen, 1-15-1910 No Date
                married 11-5-1939
SIMPSON, Samuel Earl, 2-6-1898 9-30-1965
BEAULAC, Edna R., 1903-No Date
BEAULAC, Joseph L., 1900-1965
WEST, Annie L., 7-25-1894 No Date
WEST, Horace H., 5-17-1886 8-7-1960
STEWART, Myrtle V., 5-20-1889 7-26-1975
STEWART, Samuel M., 12-28-1882 3-30-1960
DIXSON, W. .A., 9-24-1850 No Dates
CORNISH, Clinton Wheeler, 9-30-1918 10-16-1918
CORNISH, Ina E., 1876-1935
CORNISH, Henry N., 1875-1936
CLARK, J. H., 11-4-1839 11-22-1919
CLARK, Mrs. Sarah E., 2-3-1841 2-14-1913
CLARK, Edna, 1883-1969
CLARK, R. W. "Dick", 1866-1937
NICHOLS, William Loyd, 8-22-1898 11-5-1936
COX, W. Bryan, 7-20-1897 10-1-1977
COX, Lucille, 10-20-1900 3-20-1979
BIGGERS, James Bruce, 1902-1921
BIGGERS, Kellye Ann, 1883-1962
BIGGERS, James Henry, 1871-1955
STOCKTON, Ann BOGGESS, 1916-1965
BOGGESS, Irma A., 1890-1977
BOGGESS, L. O., 1893-1933
WINN, Laura Lilly, 1870-1938
BOWERS, John N., Co. I., 142 Inf., 36 Div., U. S. Army, Wounded in Action
                died in France, 1-26-1899 11-22-1916
DOUGLAS, Belle S., 12-20-1876 11-28-1970
DOUGLAS, William H., 2-16-1876 10-4-1948
DOUGLAS, Henrietta, 1-21-1845 3-7-1924
DOUGLAS, S. B., 3-26-1841 6-26-1921
DOUGLAS, Catharine, 4-17-1891 9-16-1968
DOUGLAS, Eugene, 6-2-1884 1-17-1962
DOUGLAS, Walter S., 10-13-1871 8-9-1937
PORTERFIELD, Texas P., 8-16-1865 5-12-1921
CLIFTON, Eva, 4-18-1900 1-7-1940

CLIFTON, Kelly, 1-30-1900 6-5-1939
RASOR, Laura, 1-22-1879 3-31-1961
RASOR, W. P. "Pete", 11-2-1872 3-14-1961
RASOR, Otis O., 1898-1934
KING, Gene, 1928-1934
HAMILTON, Gertrude, 8-28-1901 3-31-1971
HAMILTON, Fred, 3-12-1899 11-10-1978
HAMILTON, J. T., 2-22-1851 1-29-1921
HAMILTON, Lurena L., 1-1-1856 7-1-1938
PATTERSON, Samuel Thomas, 1868-1932
PATTERSON, Cora, 1872-1936
PATTERSON, Ira Eugene, 1906-1928
MILLIKAN, Helen E., (Granddaughter of S. T. & Cora HAMILTON), 1919-1920

SECTION "C"

MC DONALD, James Ivan, 1-14-1891 2-8-1905
CRAIG, Gladys E., 6-29-1892 12-6-1972
CRAIG, William Robert, 1888-1951
CRAIG, Billy, 1917-1919
BLASSINGAME, Vicie, 1893-1966
BLASSINGAME, Pauline, 1917-1918
BLASSINGAME, George, 1889-1956
BLASSINGAME, Infant, born & died 1906
MUSGROVE, Orlena JERNIGIN, 1875-1935
MUSGROVE, Bush W., 1863-1928
MUSGROVE, Sarah E., 1825-1915
HALL, Mammie Augusta, 1881-1967
HALL, Minnie M., 1854-1933
HALL, John A., 1853-1908
HALL, Mary A., 1-17-1825 5-13-1906
PEERCE, Margriete C., 1904-1906
PEERCE, Charles J., 1891-1911
PEERCE, Francis V., 1896-1916
MANN, Marie PEERCE, 1898-1947
ENGLAND, E. S., 1-15-1838 10-19-1912
JACKSON, Frances Jane, 1842-1925
WELCH, Robert C., 1861-1941
WELCH, Ida LINDLEY, 1865-1942
EDWARDS, Joe Earl, 9-7-1902 4-17-1919
EDWARDS, Gracie Joe, 5-3-1883 2-12-1906
LINDLEY, Henry Carl, 12-8-1880 5-27-1946
FREEZE, Fred E., 5-4-1899 3-23-1918
FREEZE, Jessie Mae, 1873-1957
ROBINSON, Douglas, 1893-1938
AMACKER, Lelia M., 1855-1941
MEURER, Cleo BLASSINGAME, 5-29-1913 5-16-1968
2 - Markers (Stone) No Names or Dates
MC DONALD, Thomas V., 11-18-1866 7-9-1947
MC DONALD, Marieta C., 8-19-1873 1-16-1958
ACKER, Walter L., 10-11-1898 12-18-1974
HORTON, Dora Elizabeth, 11-12-1870 11-17-1906
HORTON, Robert Dale, 3-11-1866 4-19-1940
HUDSON, Alberta, 10-23-1876 8-8-1948

HUDSON, Tom C., 2-12-1876 11-2-1949
OWENS, Isaac N., 3-23-1855 4-16-1935
OWENS, Lou E., 2-23-1864 5-21-1912
SHEELY, W. M., 5-10-1821 1-28-1912
SHEELY, Mary L., 5-3-1843 3-28-1910
HILL, Sarah N., 6-6-1830 6-7-1909
HILL, Brode O., 2-20-1886 12-9-1940
HILL, Emma Alice, 11-19-1858 4-26-1931
HILL, C, O., 9-1-1854 9-9-1939
SMALLWOOD, W. O., 4-23-1880 8-8-1960
COX, Charlie B., 11-7-1877 3-23-1917
GUTHRIE, Zethreau, 7-29-1908 5-11-1910
META, No Name or No Dates
FORTENBURY, Ollie M., 11-21-1887 7-11-1977
FORTENBURY, Edgar D., 11-2-1885 8-15-1955
SHOOK, Percie Lee, 9-18-1889 8-30-1963
SHOOK, Charlie F., 1-24-1881 No Date
MILLER, Maggie J., 1893-1957
MILLER, Lebert E., 1892-1968
BRACKEEN, Edna L., 6-23-1902 No Date
BRACKEEN, S., 1-16-1897 12-30-1957
SHOCKLEY, Esther M., 9-19-1894 4-18-1958
COX, Liddie B., 10-4-1906 5-23-1914
BARTLETT, Leslie Kate, 5-23-1884 8-22-1959
BARTLETT, George W., 10-28-1875 4-18-1960
HARRIS, Thurman R., 1888-1961
HARRIS, Bernice HALL, 8-13-1889 10-22-1955
REED, Roy W., Sgt., Medical Dept. Texas, W. W. II.,
                         9-8-1905 12-6-1950
HUDSON, Icie Lena, 10-4-1874 3-4-1958
HORTEN, Henry Clark, 1901-1928
ACKER, Allie Stella, died 9-5-1924
ACKER, Ollie H., 1875-1941
ACKER, John B., 1875-1960
ACKER, Infant, died 6-1910
GAYLON, W. E., 1879-1953
CARROLL, Naomi May, 4-23-1896 10-16-1966
CARROLL, Homer John, 9-3-1897 2-26-1968
LINDLEY, Mrs. Bess L., 1889-1936
CARROLL, J. P., 9-17-1859 7-28-1912
CARROLL, Mrs. J. P., 7-15-1857 10-12-1910
OWENS, Robert G., HA-1, Texas, U. S. Navy, W. W. I., 12-29-1902 3-12-1971
OWENS, Ray Lynn, 1-23-1909 6-25-1913
DURHAM, Maggie, 1862-1951
DURHAM, John L., 1860-1942
LYONS, Flora Bell, 1870-1953
FAIN, Julia, 10-4-1859 1-14-1944
FAIN, Samuel A., 3-18-1858 2-5-1919
SHADDEN, Rebecca A., 1845-1914
JENKINS, Sarah E., 9-9-1892 12-12-1972
JENKINS, Elgan T., 3-23-1888 6-9-1968
JENKINS, Mary, 6-7-1851 7-15-1913
WADE, Jacob B., 9-12-1910 7-16-1963
WADE, Lilly Mae, 1882-1912

WADE, L. F. "Luke", 1876-1924
SMITH, Clyde, 1911-1912
SMITH, Pearl, 10-7-1878 10-10-1962
SMITH, Walter, 3-8-1878 11-4-1934
SMITH, Lucy, 1849-1912
SMITH, Lee, 1849-1927
DUNCAN, Bud, 1887-1926
DUNCAN, Lizzie, 1872-1962
LYNCH, Elizabeth, 1-28-1843 11-25-1926
SHIFLET, Artie Mae, 5-2-1889 2-4-1964
SHIFLET, Thomas Buel, 7-6-1887 10-22-1960
JOHNSON, Roberta, 1898-No Date
JOHNSON, Ross Earl, 1895-1960
ARNOLD, Rosamond H., PFC., 102 Signal Const. BN. W. W. II, Texas.,
                              8-26-1913 5-27-1969
ARNOLD, Sadie B., 1892-1979
ARNOLD, Paul A., 1888-1947
HEATH, Glady J., 1898-1909
TUTTLE, Louisa, 1852-1952
TUTTLE, J. A., 1853-1909
PICKLE, Walter F., 12-6-1881 1-7-1940
HARGRAVE, Marilyn, 1929-1930
HARGRAVE, Georgia Ann, 1858-1934
HARGRAVE, Miles Butler, 1852-1915
JOHNSON, Ross Earl, Tex., Pfc., Co. C., 315 Field Sig. BN W. W. II, PH
                          1-29-1895 8-31-1960
ALLARD, Jessie HOLLON, 12-8-1893 11-13-1974
ALLARD, Charles Benton, 4-5-1893 9-21-1976
HENDERSON, Milton Ray, 1916-1917
MILLER, Mildred, 1910-No Date
MILLER, R. E. "Doc", 1892-1979
PRIM, Leta MILLER, 1905-1951
WYNN, Frances, 1868-1939
PERRY, James, 1867-1939
CHAPMAN, Mattie E., 1895-1974
CHAPMAN, Thomas J., 1886-1974
CHAPMAN, Effie STEVENS, 1894-1919
CHAPMAN, Maggie, 1850-1915
MARTIN, Mozelle, 1914-1914
MARTIN, Mary Emma, 1880-1942
MARTIN, B. E., 1885-1969
CHAPMAN, Thomas Burton, died 1917
ROSE, Mack, 3-17-1874 2-27-1945
ROSE, Blanche, 4-11-1882 4-11-1930
PITTS, Amanda, 5-9-1852 9-10-1925
JANES, Jessie TUTTLE, 2-1-1884 1-2-1930
JANES, John Wesley, 8-13-1884 6-22-1961
HARGRAVE, Willie HALL, 6-16-1892 7-9-1969
HARGRAVE, Dennis Neal, 12-1-1888 1-27-1940
ALLARD, Marion HENDERSON, 1917-1958
ALLARD, Charles Manson, 1923-1926
MOXLEY, Ocie MILLER, 9-28-1899 No Date
MOXLEY, Jess E., 9-31-1883 9-25-1966
MOXLEY, William Perry, 4-7-1924 9-3-1963

ALEXANDER, Infant, 1949-1952
MARTIN, Johanna, 1858-1922
MARTIN, J. H., 1866-1946
LYTLE, John J., 1865-1946
LYTLE, Jennie, 1868-1917
LYTLE, Ruth V., 9-15-1905 No Date
LYTLE, Vernie R., Pvt., U. S. Army, W. W. I, 1896-1978
DUPREE, John H., Co. D., 1st. Ark. Inf., C. S. A., No Dates
DUPREE, Sallie TERRY, 9-15-1847 4-3-1926
DUPREE, Verda Lee, 1884-1947
DUPREE, Pink M., 1880-No Date
EUDY, Emma J. L. DUPREE, 6-8-1877 12-13-1954
EUDY, Arthur M., 7-19-1880 1955, aged 73 yrs.
                    married 8-6-1904
THOMPSON, Grace, 1883-1963
THOMPSON, John A., 1883-1959
THOMPSON, Rev. E. B., 8-8-1840 1-17-1917
THOMPSON, Frances C., 8-20-1845 9-7-1925
GIBSON, Rev. A. W., 8-15-1847 2-16-1924
GIBSON, Mattie Alice, 7-18-1862 6-21-1939
GIBSON, William Meade, 1888-1928
WEBB, Lemay G., 1890-1968
MOODY, Welcome D., 5-10-1903 10-22-1920
MOODY, William S., 1-8-1884 11-5-1947
MOODY, Nannie L., 1-23-1860 1-17-1926
MOODY, S. E., 9-16-1852 7-22-1916
BAXTER, Mildred C., 1890-1965
BAXTER, Russell L., 1887-1959
BAXTER, James Russell, 1915-1917
LILLY, James A., 1859-1947
LILLY, Alice, 1874-1914
LILLY, George Homer, Tex., Pfc., Co. L., 133 Inf., W. W. I.,
                    9-9-1892 6-25-1971
BRECHEEN, Robert L., 3-28-1889 7-25-1914
BRECHEEN, Virgil M., 8-2-1862 7-14-1929
BRECHEEN, Catherine LILLY, 3-30-1861 7-9-1952
RICHARD, J. P., 12-2-1871 8-3-1909
SPEED, Pearl, 1883-1943
BISHOP, Mary, 1852-1928
BREECHEEN, Dorothy, 7-21-1886 11-5-1951
LEONARD, Waite B., 7-10-1891 6-27-1969
LEONARD, William Edwin B., 8-5-1879 3-20-1958
LEONARD, J. M., No Dates
LILLY, Curtis Anders, Tex., Pfc., 14 Field Hospt., W. W. II.,
                    8-27-1905 3-24-1973
LILLY, Verna C., 11-30-1899 11-20-1974
LILLY, Robert E., 1-28-1895 10-17-1972
1 - Marker (Stone) No Dates or Names
LITTLE, James Emmett, 1-16-1890 7-13-1937
LITTLE, Larry M., died 9-16-1925
LITTLE, Vernie Mae, 9-20-1924 9-21-1924
DUPREE, Golden, 1-1-1909 1-1-1918
MOODY, Bert D., 3-5-1894 4-15-1972
MOODY, Willie, 11-23-1871 5-7-1947

MOODY, Hugh H., 10-3-1860 7-10-1932
HOLLIS, Rev. R. R., 3-23-1857 7-2-1915
PEMBERTON, Beaulah R., 12-31-1909 No Date
PEMBERTON, Joe S., 3-6-1888 9-12-1961
BRIGANCE, Gertrude, No Dates
BRIGANCE, John H., 11-7-1885 10-2-1968
BRIGANCE, Nancy L., 2-8-1861 11-1-1958
BRIGANCE, Edgar, 7-28-1895 7-25-1917
FAIN, Charlie L., 1887-1949
FAIN, Nancy V. DEBLENPORT, 1866-1944
FAIN, Gabriel A., 1861-1918
UNDERWOOD, Jennie, 9-29-1884 8-1-1965
UNDERWOOD, Dan, 5-18-1886 10-26-1960
THURMAN, J. M., 1851-1930
THURMAN, Lueisa, 1857-1917
STIDHAM, Joseph Alexandria, 5-19-1917 9-22-1917
STIDHAM, Kittie, 10-3-1858 2-2-1936
WARD, Wesley Clark, 1855-1938
WARD, Nancy Elizabeth, 1859-1941
WILKINS, Maude F., 1886-1952
WILKINS, George Garrison, 1877-1917
HARTWELL, E. L., 1883-1946
HARTWELL, Clarinda, 1845-1918
HARTWELL, George W., 1845-1928
HARTWELL, L. D., 6-18-1881 4-11-1968
PALMER, Helen H., 2-1-1915 10-23-1872
1 - Funeral Marker (No Name or Dates)
COX, James W., Tex., Mus. 3, C., Co. L., 359 Inf., W. W. I.,
8-14-1894 1-4-1966

COX, Lugenia, 11-17-1895 No Date
MIMS, John M., died 1962
MIMS, Mrs. John M., died 1978
MIMS, Infant, died 9-29-1916
PEMBERTON, Roy Bruce, 3-29-1916 7-25-1916
BLYTHE, Carl V., 7-20-1916 6-29-1966
BLYTHE, Beatrice G., 11-18-1918 No Date
WELCH, Clarence C., 6-26-1885 8-17-1969
WELCH, Myrtle G., 12-28-1895 4-30-1964
EVANS, Sarah A., 2-17-1872 2-28-1912
KELLY, Charles Wesley, 2-16-1912 11-4-1956
KELLY, Ethel S., 1892-1954
KELLY, James C., 1888-1950
ADAMS, Mary Ida, 12-12-1915 4-4-1978
ADAMS, John C., 1-1-1909 No Date
KELLY, Alice Elizabeth, 8-30-1913 7-16-1916
RUSSELL, Thomas Robert, died 1-26-1970
CAPERTON, Mary Ellen, 1939-1978
MULKEY, J. E., 12-28-1916 1-21-1917
JOHNSTON, Eula Mae, 12-26-1905 No Date
JOHNSTON, Jack Arlee, 9-16-1909 8-8-1971
GREEN, Jessie, 11-23-1895 4-4-1979
GREEN, Willie A., 2-6-1896 6-19-1937
GREEN, Nannie J., 10-25-1857 4-5-1919
GREEN, W. L., 1-26-1855 1-8-1900

CUNNINGHAM, Arjeree G., 6-26-1920 No Date
CUNNINGHAM, Clarence W., 1-5-1918 8-6-1971
ALTON, Barbara Elaine, died 11-2-1941
JOHNSON, Nannie MEADOR, 1859-1940
O'NEIL, Lottie, 1879-1955
O'NEIL, Tom, 1879-1943
MALONEY, Plen E., 1868-1926
MALONEY, Grace, 1876-1929
MALONEY, Dan E., 1989-1918
BROWNING, Henrietta, 1866-1948
BROWNING, John R., 1860-1947
BROWNING, Roy J., 1906-1936
O'NEAL, Belle, 1883-1966
LANDS, Allie, 6-6-1890 4-19-1972
LANDS, Floyd, 6-29-1889 9-20-1963
WALKER, Mrs. Dora, 6-17-1888 1-11-1918
RHODES, Tullie G., 1885-1979
RHODES, Omer A., 1883-1951
BEARDEN, Mary V., 12-1-1846 11-27-1935
BEARDEN, Willia C., Co. H., 31st. Tex. Cav., C. S. A., (No Dates)
DRODEN, Benjamin Jones, Pfc., U. S. Army, W. W. I.,
                            9-28-1899 1-1-1966
WILLIAMS, Sallie BRECHEEN, 1867-1934
WILLIAMS, Wesley Weems, 1859-1934
WILLIAMS, Bruce Brecheen, Yeoman 3rd. Class, U. S. Navy, 10-5-1894 12-7-1917
            [First member of the Crew of the U. S. S. Montana to lost his
            life on Active Duty in the War with Germany.
            This monument is erected to his memory by the Officers and
            Crew of the Montana]

MANGUM, J. C., 1886-1968
MANGUM, D. J., 1-12-1856 12-21-1936
MANGUM, W. E., 5-17-1844 11-27-1921
TURNER, William O., 6-18-1895 11-11-1918
PRICE, Samuel, 10-31-1875 1-29-1921
PRICE, Myrtle, 11-9-1885 6-4-1969
SISK, Susan PRICE, 1873-1960
PERKINS, Uneeta STEPHENS, wife of Dewey, 10-4-1901 11-2-1920
STEPHENSON, Jo Samuel, Jr., 1862-1946
STEPHENSON, Nora V., 1888-1970
STEPHENSON, Willie Amos, 1889-1972
O'NEIL, Homer A., 1892-1967
O'NEIL, Kathryn G., 1892-1968
DRAPER, Zelma Clare, 10-5-1919 10-23-1919
DRAPER, Eugenia, 1880-1975
DRAPER, Charles N., 1880-1951
MOORE, Nannie E., 1874-No Date
MOORE, Cord H., 1874-1945
MOORE, Porter, Sgt. Co. B., 3rd. Mo. Inf. C. S. A., (No Dates
PHILIPS, F. G., 3-11-1884 8-7-1926
PHILIPS, Margaret B., 1-12-1873 2-29-1952
GUTHRIE, James Felix, 12-13-1887 6-4-1945
GUTHRIE, Myrtle, 7-23-1895 No Date
MARTIN, Lula Ann, 4-25-1870 8-1-1954

MARTIN, Alvin, 10-20-1867 12-23-1953
TEEL, Gila E., 1907-1959
TEEL, Fulton W., 1906-1972
LOVE, Ida Bell, 1869-1950
LOVE, John R., 1869-1963
CLIFTON, Eva Lanie, 3-7-1872 6-18-1918
LEAFORD, J. H., 6-8-1850 6-27-1918
PALMER, Ethel E., 1890-1971
PALMER, Joseph H., 1892-1977
HAM, Clyde, 10-13-1882 9-15-1919
O'NEAL, John, 1876-1918
O'NEAL, H., 1879-1951
ZIMMERMAN, Nita M., 10-17-1913 No Date
ZIMMERMAN, Raymond, Sgt. Air Force, W. W. II.,
                                    8-4-1918 10-21-1972

O'NEIL, Norah, 1889-1971
O'NEIL, Michael, 1877-1941
O'NEIL, Maggie, 1848-1921
O'NEIL, John, 1847-1921
WINN, Homer, 2-8-1879 12-15-1936
WINN, Laural, 7-30-1879 9-1-1918
SALMON, Grace, 1897-No Date
SALMON, Frank, 1890-1977
CLIFTON, Hellman P., 12-17-1872 4-3-1924
CLIFTON, Pauline, 9-25-1877 3-18-1919
ADAMS, Pauline CLIFTON, 12-24-1912 6-30-1956
ANDERSON, Janice, 1901-1918
ANDERSON, Laura W., 5-6-1874 8-29-1946
ANDERSON, John B., 9-2-1906 7-31-1962
WATT, Catherine, 1915-1964

                        SECTION "D"

THOMPSON, Mary, 1873-1949
THOMPSON, Ben, 1872-1903
THOMPSON, Leah, 1875-1911
THOMPSON, T. S., 1825-1908
HUTCHISON, Ann, 1849-1929
NEAL, H. F., 12-28-1890 2-21-1933
NEAL, Mattie R., 6-5-1852 11-6-1912
NEAL, J. H., 5-22-1835 12-15-1903
MITCHELL, Wade D., Tex., Sgt., HQ Co., 144 Inf., W. W. I.,
                                    10-12-1893 6-20-1966

MITCHELL, Bettie W., 1865-1939
MITCHELL, John W., 1851-1904
LILLY, Ann W., 1840-1924
LILLY, Robert W., 1824-1904
O'NEIL, Lou Ellen, 1888-1971
O'NEIL, Harry Henry, 1885-1948
O'CONNOR, Katie Rose O'NEIL, 1875-1905
O'CONNOR, Infant son of F. F. & Katie, died 1-12-1905
HOGUE, Lillie I., 1881-1974
1 - Metal Marker, No Name or Dates
CAMERON, Nancy Belle, 2-2-1890 2-7-1973

CAMERON, Justus Brown, 8-5-1887 8-4-1963
MOODY, Thomas B., 1879-1919
CALDWELL, Hallie E., 1883-1960
EASTMAN, H. P., 10-8-1858 2-11-1905
1 - stone Marker, No Name or Dates
Moody, Infant, 5-3-1910 6-15-1910
HARRISON, Gleoda U., dau. of W. G. & Hallie, 2-18-1905 11-7-1906
3 - Stones with the following only: G. H.; A. T. E.; I. B. M.
DONAVAN, Winifred Rose, 11-6-1876 7-12-1972
LILLY, Ive, died 1968
LILLY, A. W. "Jack", died 1968
LILLY, Jackie, 1929-1934
Funeral Marker with J. W. M. only
FUNERAL MARKER with B. W. M.
SMITH, Gretchen M., 1898-1973
MITCHELL, John Donald, 3-9-1895 5-14-1969
MITCHELL, Alma Dell RUSSELL, 8-10-1905 3-24-1978
1-STONE Unreadable
1-FUNERAL MARKER with T. S. T. only
MALONEY, Harry, 1874-1915
4- MARKERS with A.H.T.; L.T.; B.T.; M.T., only
MALONEY, Cornelia, 1877-1962
ANDERS, Glynn, 1902-1904
ANDERS, Mozelle, 1900-1904
ANDERS, Lola, 1876-1925
ANDERS, Curtis L,, 1874-1935
DRIVERS, Mary R., 1876-1957
DRIVERS, Joseph M,, 1867-1937
BROWN, Ann Ellen, W.A.A.C., W. W. II., 1904-1977
LILLY, Arthur Jack W., Tex., Pvt., U. S. Army, W. W. I.,
                              7-13-1886 5-4-1968

DRIVERS, Eva, No Dates
THOMAS, Floyd William, 1909-1960
PECK, Mrs. Belle, 1846-1930
PECK, William M., 3-8-1845 2-12-1906
WRIGHT, Nettie Belle, 10-25-1884 1-3-1971
WRIGHT, Virgil Calvin, 10-12-1878 4-13-1966
WRIGHT, Weldon, 2-19-1914 2-20-1914
WRIGHT, Thomas L., 9-23-1915 9-27-1915
WARD, Oma Oscar, 1893-1933
WARD, Mary Teresa, 1899-1973
WARD, Jessie Garish, 6-5-1860 10-2-1914
WARD, Ella RAY, 12-29-1869 7-31-1931
GRUNK, Jimmie, 10-6-1896 7-25-1909
GRUNK, Sallie Almeda, 1877-1961
GRUNK, Hiram Edgar, 1873-1959
WILLIAMS, Mrs. J. W., 3-4-1850 5-25-1905
WOFFORD, M. E., 10-19-1867 5-1-1944
WOFFORD, B. E., 8-22-1857 8-9-1927
HAMILTON, Robert, 1833-1916
THOMPSON, Ella Rebecca, 1-16-1919 1-18-1919
WARD, Byron, 1892-1944
WARD, Stella, 1899-1940
WRIGHT, Thomas E., 1852-1923

WRIGHT, Martha J., 1856-1946
HOLLIS, Noah E., 1895-1960
ROUNDTREE, Margaret B., 1879-1939
ROUNDTREE, David S., 1873-1941
NAYLOR, Margaret Merle, 7-26-1904   7-1-1905
NAYLOR, Blanche Cason, 10-8-1914   3-5-1915
ANDERS, Thomas B., 1852-1919
ANDERS, Mary Sue, 1854-1919
STEPHENSON, Mary Kate, 11-27-1897   6-7-1973
LAYNE, J. T., Jr., 1902-1905
LAYNE, Beulah, 1886-1928
LAYNE, Leslie H., 1874-1966
LAYNE, Arrie M., 1886-1969
JONES, J. W., Jr., 1912-1912
JONES, Fannie M., 1912-1912
JONES, Berth L., 1906-1954
HULING, J. A., 1839-1907
HULING, Dora C., 1845-1913
FIEMAY, E. F., 2-15-1889   5-18-1909
LINDSEY, A. D., 2-12-1876   11-27-1906
FERGUSON, Ira J., 8-27-1886   4-1-1911
FERGUSON, Laura A., 4-6-1854   4-8-1911
FERGUSON, John, No Dates
FERGUSON, Floyd M., 1894-1940
FERGUSON, Tip Monroe, 5-3-1859   11-2-1923
FERGUSON, Martha ROBERTs, 1-10-1863   6-24-1910
STAPP, Josie, 7-18-1887   7-7-1915
STAPP, Hubbard R., 7-13-1888   11-4-1918
STUCKEY, Sallie M., 1860-1936
HOPKINS, Josephine C., 12-26-1853   12-9-1908
HOPKINS, Thomas T., 2-1-1849   10-28-1922
PHIPPS, Bernice, 9-30-1899   9-12-1905
1 - Metal Marker
IRVIN, Royd Gene, 9-20-1925   No Date
IRVIN, Sara Sue, 8-21-1929   2-25-1970
DENTON, Paul R., 10-4-1904   4-15-1979
DENTON, Ruby F., 9-21-1905   No Date
BARKER, Gertrude STUCKY, 1885-1972
STAPP, Mary Sue, 1861-1934
STAPP, John C., 1860-1937
GIST, Ernest S., 1888-1927
BRADDY, Kate, No Dates
BRADDY, Ellen, No Dates
2 - Markers, No Names or Dates
JONES, J. W., Sr., 1876-1952
LAYNE, Mattie E., 1854-1946
LAYNE, J. T., 1845-1911
ESTES, Hettie ROSCOE, 1867-1944
ESTES, Dewitt Dillard, 1860-1939
ELROY, Joe S., Jr., 1909-1977
ELROY, Beaulah, 1906-1977
SLAYTER, Cora Lena, 1879-1955
SLAYTER, William S., 1875-1954
LAWRENCE, Mary, 1857-1945

LAWRENCE, J. M., 1858-1932
FAIRES, Margaret Rose, 2-25-1912 8-11-1913
FAIRES, Infant, died 7-1925
FAIRES, Ellie O'NEIL, 12-13-1888 5-29-1964
FAIRES, Thomas F., 1-5-1873 11-25-1965
THORNTON, Emma Itura, 9-7-1883 12-18-1925
BARKER, Ruth NEILL, 1889-1965
BARKER, W. P., 1888-1953
BARKER, Mollie DOWNING, 1853-1929
BARKER, Henry Clay, 1851-1913
LINDLY, Francis Lee, 1866-1911
FERRIER, Maurine LINDLEY, 4-20-1903 5-10-1929
YATES, Irene B., 12-22-1909 No Dates
YATES, Jessie B., 8-14-1899 3-25-1969
MORGAN, Mattie A., 4-26-1852 3-11-1923
MORGAN, Dan H., 4-29-1849 1-24-1924
MORGAN, Infants of John & Mamie Morgan, No Dates
STERLING, Pansy Lee, 1-11-1910 10-20-1911
BARKER, Claude Neal, 1895-1952
MAY, Leonard Lee, 5-3-1911 5-1-1968
Meier, Edwin J., 1884-1922
ESTES, Gladys, 1891-1965
LAYNE, Walter L., 1872-1936
LAYNE, Rosa M., 1873-1954
LAYNE, Fay DOUGLAS, 8-15-1906 8-6-1913
MORGAN, Martin Luther, Pvt., U. S. Army, W. W. I., 1893-1978
MORGAN, Tobe Bice, 1886-1954
DILLINGHAM, Thomas A., died 1922
DILLINGHAM, Sarah, died 1950
DILLINGHAM, Tom A., died 1953
SMITH, Margaret Lois, 3-23-1915 11-26-1977
SMITH, Manly L., 4-21-1907 No Date
SMITH, Mary Lou, 12-26-1875 10-8-1950
SMITH, Walter T., 9-22-1876 7-21-1934
HOGAN, Michael F., 8-25-1858 7-20-1910
LINLEPAGE, Bessie W., 1899-1979
WORLEY, George M., 8-31-1863 7-10-1910
WORLEY, Lady Clara, 7-18-1878 No Date
O'NEAL, Mrs. Allie, 11-6-1882 12-19-1966
CLAY, Kathryn MAXWELL, 11-6-1875 7-23-1950
MAXWELL, Mrs. M. L., 1860-1934
MAXWELL, Dr. M. L., 1865-1939
MAXWELL, David Emmett, 9-28-1861 7-10-1920
MAXWELL, Kate P., 6-9-1840 7-3-1910
BAGWELL, Sarah, died 1912
BAGWELL, Kimbrell, 1908-1924
BAGWELL, Ruby RIDLEY, 1884-1974
BAGWELL, Boyd R., 1879-1936
WATSON, Ella A., 8-31-1886 1-7-1959
WATSON, Lawrence E., 7-24-1874 1-28-1935
WATSON, Mahala C., 1-15-1878 1-17-1911
GARLAND, Rosa Belle WATSON, 2-12-1906 5-16-1975
LOUIS, Archibald Buford, 4-11-1907 8-1-1907
LAKE, C. A., 7-13-1883 12-9-1959

1 - Stone Marker, No Name or Dates
CAGLE, William W., 1895-1960
CAGLE, Aileen F., 1901-No Date
HOGAN, Henry P., 1896-1974
SMITH, Gussie C., 8-3-1909 7-23-1910
SMITH, Prebble Ann, died 3-22-1941
SMITH, Harry E., 9-1-1926 10-23-1926
LANGSTON, C. A., 12-6-1890 6-1-1907
HESTER, Lola REID, 1-6-1896 11-11-1918
ADAMS, Mary C., 12-17-1879 7-25-1967
ADAMS, Homer F., 5-6-1876 8-5-1913
HAYSLIP, Del U., 3-22-1912 8-23-1918
MOBERLY, Ralph L., Okla., Major, U. S. Air Force, W. W. II.,
                         5-5-1919 10-11-1969
BENNETT, Mary CORNELIUS, 2-13-1893 3-2-1970
CORNELIUS, E. C. HAGLER, 1859-1928
CORNELIUS, Frank D., Co. I., 34 Tex. Cav., C. S. A., No Dates
MALONE, Edna COWAN, 5-10-1902 11-9-1970
MALONE, John B., 10-9-1896 1-27-1962
EVANS, Pearl COWAN, 3-30-1878 10-6-1960
COWAN, Walter, 2-14-1873 7-23-1912
WILLIAMS, Jessie Isaac, 1858-1935
WILLIAMS, Manervy, 1862-1932
WILLIAMS, William Isaac, 5-27-1896 4-18-1911
BRECKEEN, Lillian GRAVES, 4-15-1877 7-22-1961
BRECKEEN, Leslie B., 5-25-1876 7-29-1929
BRECKEEN, William T., 4-6-1851 2-9-1933
BRECKEEN, Preston M., died 12-9-1949
BRECKEEN, Lizzie SPITE, 1856-1908
BRECKEEN, Beatrice, died 12-9-1949
BRECKEEN, Rudolph, Tex., Sgt., 78 AAF Base Unit, W. W. II.,
                         7-22-1921 9-21-1948
WILLIAMS, Jess, 1891-1930
WETSEL, William Cecil, 7-14-1889 3-17-1977
WETSEL, Winnie CORNELIUS, 5-14-1891 8-11-1966
WETSEL, Thomas Edgar, Tex., MAM-3, U.S.N.R., W. W. II, Korea.,
                         1-19-1927 6-26-1967
JACKSON, W. J., 11-29-1865 1-3-1946
JACKSON, Naomi S., 1875-1955
GEORGE, Mary Ann., 5-2-1935 9-5-1935
LAKE, William B., Tex., Pvt., 6 MTR Co., 90 Div., W. W. I.,
                         5-20-1887 4-17-1959
LANGSTON, Emly Rena, 3-26-1893 11-8-1918
LANGSTON, Infant, died 11-8-1918
LANGSTON, Addie Overtra, 8-21-1916 12-7-1918
WRIGHT, Maurine, 1904-No Date
WRIGHT, Cecil, 1905-No Date
PERKINS, Mollie B., died 3-12-1909
PERKINS, J. B., died 8-3-1944
DOBBINS, Andrew J., 11-4-1859 7-7-1931
WILLIAMS, J. Boone, 10-17-1884 7-16-1912
WILLIAMS, Ethel, 6-20-1887 11-27-1969
FULLER, Amelia, 9-10-1869 11-29-1953
FULLER, Seth, 1-19-1910 3-23-1910

FULLER, C. D., 7-28-1873 1-28-1943
WALDEN, Mrs. R. C., 8-20-1837 11-22-1923
WALDEN, R. C., 8-17-1854 3-15-1912
MASON, Robert H., 9-26-1882 3-6-1924
KNIGHT, Martin, 6-27-1878 11-28-1910
COCHRAN, Joseph, 1831-1908
COCHRAN, Roberta Estelle, 10-10-1870 2-4-1928
COCHRAN, Joseph B., 1907-1977
HUEY, Cleo, No Dates
HUEY, J. D., No Dates
WILLIAMS, Katheryn, 7-6-1911 5-1-1912
MITCHELL, Edwin J., 4-9-1909 3-12-1971
MITCHELL, Inez W., 4-28-1910 No Date
PERKINS, Belle DRENNAN, 9-22-1887 11-5-1972
WILLIAMS, J. T., Co. F., 18th Miss. Cav., C. S. A., NO DATES
BAKER, Robert E., 9-20-1896 6-28-1971
BAKER, Gussie Lee, 9-2-1897 2-27-1961
MABRY, Grace C., 1900-1970
MABRY, T. L. "Tom", 1901-1962
KELLY, C. W., No Dates
MORRISON, Paralee, 5-6-1872 4-11-1939
MORRISON, William, 1876-1951
KELLY, Joe William, 9-17-1890 4-13-1962
KELLY, Carrie P., 1-3-1870 7-28-1956
KELLY, Jim Franklin, 8-8-1862 10-18-1928
NUNN, Mattie M., 9-21-1886 7-17-1925
KELLY, Ida DAY, 1862-1939
KELLY, J. H., 4-9-1853 7-4-1909
O'NEAL, Christelle, 7-24-1908 10-14-1908
O'NEAL, Emma Lou, 2-15-1882 1-8-1943
O'NEAL, Emmett C., 2-18-1876 3-29-1965
O'NEAL, Bessie EVANS, 10-29-1877 8-24-1965
O'NEAL, George W., 9-7-1871 4-16-1955
O'NEAL, Ida E., 1872-1910
O'NEAL, Mary C., 5-17-1910 5-18-1910
THURMAN, Horace P., 9-22-1903 3-30-1977
THURMAN, Artie Y., 2-20-1904 No Date
RODGERS, Charles L., 7-26-1873 2-16-1908
HIRE, Lewis, No Dates
ROSE, Billy, No Dates
PEDIGO, Daisy Belle, 1877-1934
PEDIGO, Willis Albert, 1874-1928
ROSE, Mary PEDIGO, 8-3-1905 5-21-1974
ROSE, Thomas Leeman, Sr., 10-16-1898 3-17-1976
JERNIGAN, Woodrow W., 1912-1950
PEDIGO, Mary M., 9-2-1901 1-13-1924
PEDIGO, J. M., 4-15-1901 No Date
MC DANIEL, Mary Ann., 1858-1929
BOTTOMS, David W., Co. H., 2nd. Ark. Inf., Sp. Am. War.,
                                7-4-1874 11-8-1936
O'NEAL, W. A., 1844-1921
O'NEAL, Mary J., 1848-1918
SMITH, R. N., 8-29-1867 6-14-1955
SMITH, Anna O'NEAL, 5-18-1882 1-22-1974

SMITH, John, died 9-5-1923
KELLY, Kate M., 6-3-1898   2-17-1923
KELLY, Grant W., 6-5-1897   2-4-1946
GOSSETT, Ada L. KELLY, 4-14-1902   4-22-1972
ANTHONY, J. H., 12-6-1880   3-16-1907

SECTION "E"

SEARS, Jim Mc Clinton, 12-12-1897   12-7-1919
MC CLINTON, James H., 1849-1937
MC CLINTON, Nannie V., 1856-1941
GALYON, Hester O., 3-31-1906   8-28-1931
GALYON, John J., 12-8-1882   2-8-1960
ARNOLD, John, 3-20-1878   12-18-1966
ARNOLD, Galden, 1-9-1900   4-8-1971
ARNOLD, Betty, 1856-1939
SMITH, James Emmett, 6-4-1872   6-6-1950
SMITH, Rosa Ella, 12-19-1879   3-3-1963
SMITH, Weldon A., Tex., Pvt., 1 CC QM Corps, died 3-9-1941
SMITH, Virginia, 6-27-1924   1-8-1943
SAYLE, Margaret K., 6-13-1911   11-8-1919
SAYLE, Robert R., Pvt. 3rd. Tex. Inf., Spanish American War, No Dates
SAYLE, Hattie Belle, 1-21-1879   5-16-1951
POMMERING, Heaman H., 10-30-1891   10-3-1921
CWALTNEY, John T., 1-13-1847   4-23-1922
JONES, Jessie B., 10-13-1880   7-22-1956
SELF, Mike, died 3-18-1926
LITTLE, James H., 4-18-1896   5-30-1924
LITTLE, Charles M., 1867-1940
LITTLE, Lola, 1872-1952
SHOEMAKE, Edward D., 1874-1949
SHOEMAKE, Altie W., 1880-1974
BARROW, Albert, 2-12-1893   4-28-1919
BARROW, George G., 10-4-1851   5-14-1923
CARVER, Mattie C, 11-5-1855   2-13-1921
CARVER, W. J., 5-16-1851   7-22-1935
SMITH, Lewis I., Jr., 6-11-1918   4-29-1974
SMITH, Mary PERRY, 6-18-1889   3-21-1958
SMITH, Lewis Ingram, 10-28-1886   12-7-1952
BRICKLEY, Gertrude E., No Dates
YANCY, Maurine, 4-17-1904   11-15-1952
YANCY, Alonzo, Tex., 93 Balloon Co. Air SVC, 3-29-1895   10-29-1963
SHAY, Bettie C., 1894-1938
SHAY, John B., No Dates
SHAY, Mary Jane, 7-7-1874   7-7-1953
OWEN, John A., 1890-1923
OWEN, Bates F., Tex., Cpl., 65 Depot Brig., died 7-25-1923
MASON, Marion A., 1866-1942
MASON, William, 1863-1935
WOOSLEY, Billie, 6-11-1856   4-20-1926
SALMON, Billie, 12-29-1922   12-29-1925
SALMON, Lorine A., 1888-1926
SALMON, Will Hampton, 1880-1966
SIDNEY, James, 12-28-1857   12-8-1928

DANIEL, Ara Lou, 10-6-1915 6-18-1927
DANIEL, Elsie A., 4-12-1892 6-27-1927
ALEXANDER, Evart M., 10-20-1885 6-3-1966
ALEXANDER, Mary V., 10-14-1886 3-24-1957
HARRIGAN, Dennis, 1845-1920
HARRIGAN, Mary, 1853-1932
HARRIGAN, Joseph, 1877-1953
HARRIGAN, John F., 1875-1966
BRYANT, Winifred HARRIGAN, 1883-1960
REAVES, Wilford R., 12-21-1870 7-9-1936
REAVES, Emma A., 12-31-1841 4-23-1920
SITZ, Cara, 12-31-1874 10-24-1933
SPARKS, S. W., 1886-1934
SPARKS, Eliza F., 1851-1925
SPARKS, Gertrude, wife of S. W., 1891-1957
POLK, R. M., 1872-1935
POLK, William S., Cpl., 359 Inf., 90 Div., died 9-5-1921
POLK, Evelyn May, 9-19-1927 6-27-1934
STERLING, V. W., 1847-1924
STERLING, A. H., 1851-1934
STERLING, Delia, 1871-1933
STERLING, Harry, 1880-1940
HOBBS, J. W., 1887-1952
HOBBS, Florence Lou., 2-6-1885 7-2-1934
ASSITER, Ira Pierce, 11-28-1880 12-29-1953
ASSITER, Willie T., 9-5-1895 No Date
FREEMAN, W. M., 1887-1954
FREEMAN, Ethel M., 1888-1968
FERGUSON, Payton Mosley, 1871-1967
FERGUSON, Lillie Maude, 1861-1954
HALL, Claude V., 1874-1954
HALL, Ethel A., 1883-No Date
RODGERS, Hazel Z., 2-11-1901 No Date
RODGERS, James Berry, 8-9-1889 6-1-1978
MC CLUSTER, P., 5-29-1899 6-26-1934
MC CLUSTER, Joseph M., 1-29-1874 6-29-1936
RAGAN, Mattie C., 12-17-1879 2-28-1964
RAGAN, Walter C., 11-2-1879 5-24-1956
CARGILE, Freeman, 1910-1979
CARGILE, Louie, died 8-21-1935
SHARP, R. V., 1915-1934
CONDER, Billy Joe, 1922-1925
CONDER, Cleo, 1897-1954
PRATER, Opal CONDER, 1918-1938
ACKERSON, E. D., 1891-1963
            married 7-22-1916
ACKERSON, Rose, 1895-1977
JONES, Luice Alice, 1883-1972
JONES, Curtis Leroy, 1880-1972
BRADFORD, Lewis Bryan, 8-13-1923 9-14-1923
BRADFORD, Odis Lee, 8-13-1923 9-21-1923
BRADFORD, Mildred LEE, 1898-1961
BRADFORD, Odis Bryan, 1899-1971
JERNIGAN, Russell,C., Tex. Lt. Col., U. S. Army, W.W. I & II, Korea., 9-7-1896
                                                                    4-8-1974

JERNIGAN, Jeff D., 11-23-1859 9-2-1923
JERNIGAN, Zona, 9-30-1871 8-10-1958
CARR, Zachery T., 5-23-1848 10-31-1944
CARR, Mary G., 3-12-1851 4-26-1942
CARR, Orna, 1-2-1879 4-16-1942
WEBB, Robert J., 9-8-1878 9-5-1939
WEBB., Ernestine C., 8-28-1880 10-6-1975
JOHNSON, J. Bothwell, 9-13-1899 No Date
JOHNSON, Acenith N., 4-7-1900 No Date
JOHNSON, Joseph O., 1865-1945
JOHNSON, Marg., V., 1868-1933
SHIPP, Amma Low, 1900-1924
MC CURDY, Emma Jane, 8-17-1891 9-16-1941
MC CURDY, Rev. A. C., 10-28-1885 8-31-1954
MC CURDY, Bascum, 8-20-1910 1-26-1925
BRYAN, Bernice, 7-9-1919 3-6-1939
MOORE, Luther, 2-16-1883 10-2-1971
MOORE, Emma L., 4-14-1885 1-10-1968
MOORE, Harold E., 7-2-1923 7-28-1932
MOORE, Lydia J., 12-6-1910 4-16-1936
SANDERS, J. C., 2-10-1849 7-29-1925
SANDERS, Rufus H., 1891-1979
LEDFORD, James Edgar, 7-27-1880 9-23-1967
LEDFORD, Bertha Alice, 2-7-1900 2-4-1926
ERWIN, Myra E., 1867-1938
ADAMS, Jean W., 2-23-1926 11-6-1969
ADAMS, Alice May, 7-27-1912 9-24-1948
CRUSE, Jessie Rose, 10-31-1880 6-19-1947
CRUSE, John William, 11-24-1877 2-8-1963
CRUSE, Rosie Etta, 1-5-1904 5-12-1927
CRUSE, Johnnie B., 1-23-1915 1-13-1972
BRYANT, Anna C., 1889-1935
BRYANT, George L., 1886-1941
PIERCE, Will, Tex., Pvt., 1 CL., 115 AW 7 W 10 Div., 1-19-1914 No Date
MATTHEWS, Terry Delane, 2-29-1944 3-1-1949
ECHART, Thomas Vester, 4-2-1904 9-2-1962
ECHART, Faye C., 6-8-1910 No Date
ECHART, Thomas Vester, Jr., 6-4-1932 2-21-1934
CARGILE, Ernest C., 1887-1934
CARGILE, Odessa, 1892-1975

SECTION "F"

TURNER, Mattie, 3-24-1858 2-2-1939
TURNER, J. B., 9-12-1853 11-23-1918
KELLY, Jane, 12-27-1846 12-5-1925
KELLY, C. H., 1890-1940
PERKINS, Myrtis Marie, 10-10-1904 4-29-1876
PERKINS, Dewey Lee, 3-26-1899 No Date
PERKINS, Bill Lee, Tex., Pfc., 4 Inf., 2-29-1928 7-10-1969
COLTON, Mrs. M. A., 1857-1940
OWENS, Ottie MILLER, 12-29-1886 3-17-1966
MILLER, Thomas L., 5-22-1875 1-7-1919
OWENS, Levi G., Tex., Pvt., 67 Inf., 9 Div., 9-1-1926 No Date

THOMAS, Rebecca, 3-4-1880 2-10-1974
THOMAS, Henry W., 5-11-1875 1-6-1960
THOMAS, Infant of H. W. & R., died 4-16-1919
SCAFF, J. Allen, son of A. J. & Nettie, 1901-1918
SCAFF, Nettie ALLEN, wife of A. J., 1878-1933
SCAFF, Jas. R., 1869-1935
SCAFF, R. Jack, son of A. J. & Nettie, 1917-1942
BALLARD, Sidney D., 3-5-1895 10-3-1968
BALLARD, Cleo, 4-17-1908 No Date
MILLER, David Howard, 1884-No Date
2-FUNERAL MARKERS, Unreadable
BALLARD, A. A., 9-18-1868 11-23-1918
MARSHALL, Lloyd, 12-2-1910 1-19-1975
MARSHALL, Essie E., 1892-No Date
MARSHALL, Horace G., 1885-1961
MARSHALL, Pat. H., La., Pvt., Co. B., 12 Regt. Miss. Cav., C. S. A.
                          1-22-1845 11-3-1918
LOONEY, Millie, 3-1-1868 1-11-1959
LOONEY, Edwin C., 12-7-1897 11-27-1918
LOONEY, Armilda, wife of L. Z. STUTEVILLE, 4-26-1893 2-20-1920
STUTEVILLE, L. Z., 6-2-1890 1-18-1961
LOONEY, E. Ervin, 12-31-1860 11-15-1940
STEWARD, Dan F., 12-8-1884 9-10-1919
STEWARD, Bernice, 5-5-1905 8-17-1920
MC COMBS, Lee E., 1889-1962
MC COMBS, Ninnie L., 1892-1974
COX, J. P., 1st. Ark. Cav., C. S. A., No Dates
COX, Clemmie P., 1859-1935
CHUMLEY, Pearl COX, 8-1-1881 12-3-1954
COX, J. P., Jr., 1910-1919
CROCKETT, Mrs. Davis H., 7-11-1892 11-4-1919
CROCKETT, Bret H., 1-5-1890 8-8-1930
CROCKETT, Cornelia Jane, 11-5-1864 3-25-1950
1 - FUNERAL MARKER
MARTIN, G. B., 8-13-1841 12-27-1919
MARTIN, Melba Jo, 1924-1933
MARTIN, Joe W., 1892-1975
MARTIN, Mildred, 6-15-1910 12-5-1923
LINDLEY, R. Claude, 1892-1957
LINDLEY, Nannie C., 1897-1975
LINDLEY, R. C., Jr., 3-8-1920 3-11-1920
MOORE, Tommie Ann, 12-4-1882 No Date
MOORE, Marcus M, 8-18-1875 2-12-1921
MOORE, Sarah Veatrice, 2-18-1906 10-12-1936
HADDOCK, Virginia, 4-1-1849 1-24-1937
HADDOCK, Calvin, 12-7-1845 2-28-1927
HADDOCK, Nunie M., 9-10-1905 11-29-1967
HADDOCK, William D., 11-22-1887 12-11-1948
HARRIS, J. T., 7-18-1852 1-2-1920
HARRIS, Ida M., 1857-1937
COWAN, Lillian HARRIS, 1888-1923
GREEN, Annie O., 1857-1921
GREEN, P. M., 1854-1938
DICKERSON, Mamie L., 1885-1920

JOHNSON, Casey WILLIAMS, 10-11-1877 10-13-1928
WILLIAMS, Susie F., 1858-1920
WILLIAMS, Dr. Henry, 1857-1921
STRANGE, Maggie L., 1868-1946
STRANGE, Dawson M., 1864-1922
TAYLOR, Era Mae, 1892-1966
                    married 6-9-1918
TAYLOR, William W., 1897-No Date
HARRISON, William Mark, 1881-1952
HARRISON, Annie, 7-29-1889 6-20-1920
EDGE, John W., 6-2-1867 7-10-1944
EDGE, Bulah SHELL, 5-16-1881 6-15-1922
RAINBOLT, N. Faye, 1911-1942
FOOSHEE, Lana Joan, 1-23-1942 2-6-1943
PATTERSON, Vicki Lynn, 1951-1951
THOMAS, Ora, 1-11-1890 12-12-1960
THOMAS, M. A., Sr., 12-31-1882 10-6-1946
WEATHERBEE, J. D., No Dates
WEATHERBEE, Infant, No Dates
WEATHERBEE, Mother, No Dates
WEATHERBEE, Father, No Dates
WEATHERBEE, Mother, No Dates
PITCHARD, Inf. son of M. L. & M. E., died 5-25-1921
PITCHARD, Ruth, 4-9-1918 7-13-1939
PITCHARD, Mandred "Buck", 2-16-1907 9-24-1956
PITCHARD, Mary Elizabeth, 1-18-1887 1-26-1968
PITCHARD, Martin Luther, 1-26-1885 4-20-1958
KERBY, Virginia PITCHARD, 6-5-1914 3-11-1944
ALLEN, Thomas H., Co. A., 37th. Tenn. Inf., C. S. A., No Dates
ALLEN, Thomas E., 6-29-1886 4-24-1961
ALLEN, Robert E., 9-20-1883 6-29-1932
ALLEN, Eva TUNE, 10-24-1884 6-3-1961
MULLINS, Joel R., 1880-1926
MULLINS, John C., 10-19-1855 1-31-1939
MULLINS, Cordie, 3-1-1863 3-15-1942
MULLINS, Emmett M., 1892-1973
PATTERSON, Earl Gene, 10-14-1935 10-22-1973
COMER, L. Berry, 1868-1945
BROWN, Henry Walter, 1872-1921
BROWN, Mary Sue, 3-25-1877 1-9-1965
BROWN, Walter Oran, 3-22-1901 10-16-1974
FAUGHT, Carrie C., 10-20-1863 4-28-1922
FAUGHT, James Wylie, 5-14-1855 6-1-1925
RHODES, Vesta WILKINS, 1-26-1888 5-12-1971
                    married 12-15-1908
RHODES, Conrad Brooks, 11-3-1886 3-4-1962
WILKINS, Alice T., 4-3-1858 7-4-1922
WILKINS, David, 2-13-1849 7-5-1928
WILKINS, Nannie, 1876-1955
WILKINS, Lon, 1873-1954
BICKLEY, Iris W., 6-16-1885 3-4-1971
BICKLEY, Eugene P., 9-7-1881 11-5-1969
BRYANT, Samuel B., 10-6-1876 7-15-1922
O'CONNOR, Charles S., 1860-1926

O'CONNOR, Samantha J., 1868-1957
PETERS, Bettie, 10-23-1837 2-8-1931
2-ROCKS
CLARK, James L., 4-14-1884 9-3-1967
CLARK, Annie Maude, 6-27-1884 9-24-1958
WHITLEY, John Edward, son of John E. & Olga M., 10-31-1929 9-9-1933
WHITLEY, Dr. E. R., 9-21-1870 3-26-1923
WHITLEY, John Evan, 2-18-1905 10-21-1971
ROLATER, Olga M. WHITLEY, 2-24-1907 No Dates
FAIRCHILD, Pearl WHITLEY, 9-26-1881 5-18-1963
FAIRCHILD, Newton Wise, 2-5-1873 1-28-1959
MC DOWELL, James Dwight, 1899-1937
MC DOWELL, Norma Dwayne, Inf. dau. of Mr. & Mrs. J. D., 6-28-1922 6-29-1922
BLY, Sarah Emma, 5-30-1865 3-20-1923
BLY, Paul Gerald, Tex., Aviations Corps, USNR, W. W. II.,
                                        4-19-1924 5-18-1952
FREEMAN, William Webb, Jr., 1-1-1920 No Date
BLY, Lois Jean FREEMAN, 8-31-1924 No Date
BLY, Homer Becker, 5-16-1921 No Date
SCOTT, R. N., 1867-1923
ONEY, Mary Cleone, wife of Harold W. NICHOLS, 7-19-1907 7-24-1939
ONEY, Ida Mae, 1880-1970
ONEY, William Noah, 1876-1962
ONEY, Martha H., 1-6-1911 No Date
ONEY, W. E. "Bill", 7-13-1910 12-31-1968
LEEMAN, Lucile V., 1-22-1883 11-12-1958
LEEMAN, James R., 8-18-1869 7-2-1943
MC COLLUM, Infant son of Mr. & Mrs. D. F., died 9-14-1923
THOMAS, Margie, 11-16-1896 2-17-1959
THOMAS, J. B., 8-16-1890 1-31-1964
RAINBOLT, Louis A., 1887-1960
RAINBOLT, Mamie E., 1893-1976
GILL, Thomas Matcher, 1843-1923
GILL, Mary Ellen, 1860-1932
SALMON, Wenna GILL, 1899-1934
GILL, Charles W., 7-29-1885 9-10-1961
GILL, Bettye M., 5-4-1902 11-29-1973
PARKER, Mary Molly, 4-1-1867 2-3-1932
PARKER, Cocoa, No Dates
CROW, Hartzell R., Tex., Pfc., Med. Corps., W. W. I, 11-1-1893 8-27-1967
CROW, H. R. "Skutter", Jr., 4-7-1923 8-31-1925
CROW, Hattie Belle, 12-27-1901 No Date
PARKER, George Lewis, Tex., Pvt., Co. B., 198 Engrs., W. W. I,
                                        9-3-1888 2-8-1968
HANNAH, Dellar, 3-28-1892 7-31-1925
ENGLAND, Frank, 10-9-1860 11-5-1949
ENGLAND, Annie, 11-27-1870 10-20-1939
MULKEY, Oliver C., 1864-1942
MULKEY, Jennie O., 7-18-1868 7-16-1965
MULKEY, E. F., 1841-1925
MULKEY, Mary D., 1843-1926

GODWIN, Ethel R., 1892-No Date
GODWIN, Arthur E., 1888-1957
HART, Virgene GODWIN, 4-2-1923 12-25-1969
GODWIN, Thomas A., 1921-No Date
RAY, Emma F., 1866-1930
RAY, Robert N., 1859-1922
RAY, John R., 7-22-1895 12-27-1931
SALMON, Dessa L., 6-19-1898 12-3-1977
SALMON, John M,, 2-23-1882 5-17-1961
SPARKMAN, Robert Lewis, 1924-No Date
SPARKMAN, Lynn Max, 1925-1931
SPARKMAN, Alma L., 1904-1977
SPARKMAN, L. A. "Chig", 1898-1959
SPARKMAN, John R., 10-20-1857 11-30-1938
SPARKMAN, Lula WILLIS, 12-15-1868 2-22-1959
SPARKMAN, William Arvell, 5-8-1895 7-7-1954
CLONINGER, Eli F., 2-3-1871 2-17-1939
CLONINGER, Dovie, 1-18-1883 8-6-1957
WILLIAMS, Maud D., 1875-1950
WILLIAMS, Dewey C., 1898-1923
SMITH, Thomas L., Sgt., U. S. Army, W. W. II., 1912-1977
SMITH, Velma N., 1911-No Date
HUMPHRIES, Jim Ed., 9-23-1868 10-25-1973
DISMUKE, Ada ERWIN, 2-19-1884 7-28-1959
ERWIN, W. C., 1877-1924
HAMILTON, Paul A., Tex., SFC. Co. C., 2 BN., 1 TNG Regt, W. W. II, Korea.,
                    5-31-1918 2-8-1959
HAMILTON, Vernia C., 8-1-1915 8-18-1930
BRACKIN, Mary A., 1863-1953
RHUDE, Claudine, 6-25-1914 7-15-1961
RHUDE, William, 12-27-1902 No Date
MISPAH, N. Jane MOODY, 5-4-1861 10-15-1924
JOHNSON, Perry C., 2-19-1929 10-13-1948
RHEW, Nara M., 1-30-1893 5-31-1973
CARPENTER, Mary Elizabeth, 11-25-1869 7-22-1939
CARPENTER, Joseph D., 5-17-1901 1-19-1923
MONROE, J. M., 5-20-1871 12-30-1921
MONROE, Mrs. J. M., 5-2-1874 No Date
MITCHELL, Ruth, 4-8-1901 1-9-1922
LANE, Ira F., Tex. Cpl., 359 Inf., 90 Div., died 5-14-1937
DOUDNEY, James Edward, Tex., Cpl., U. S. Army, W. W. II., 5-31-1928 10-16-1957
BARRETT, _____, 1888-1945
CASTEEL, Viola B., 1875-1965
CASTELL, Joseph W., 1874-1950
FULLER, Lester Elwood, 12-19-1879 4-28-1951
FULLER, Rose M., 3-6-1883 9-14-1964
FULLER, Horton Elwood, 4-25-1907 4-7-1962
FULLER, Jacob Lester, 10-24-1913 2-4-1969
FULLER, Sallie DAY, 2-11-1852 3-15-1924
BALLARD, Jeff D., 1861-1929

BALLARD, Nancy, 1866-1948
BALLARD, J. D. "Dave", 12-18-1904 3-5-1973
KENNEDY, Mattie B., 7-18-1888 2-10-1970
KENNEDY, John M., 1884-1936
WOOSLEY, Robert Glen, MM-3, U. S. Navy, W. W. II., 1924-1976
GAY, Johnny, 1911-1973
GAY, Jimmie, 6-7-1909 9-6-1957
GAY, Ada P., 8-28-1877 12-3-1924
GAY, Amzi H., 11-4-1870 2-19-1947
STIDHAM, Eulishes, 6-8-1897 12-31-1974
ALLEN, Mrs. Rosa Belle, 2-24-1877 9-14-1958
HOLLEY, Mary Esterlee, 3-15-1871 1-8-1953
CHADWICK, Effie Irene, 9-4-1891 11-28-1972
CHADWICK, Wayne Harrison, 10-18-1889 1-31-1953
CHADWICK, Jerry Wayne, Tex., Capt., 9407 Recovery Sq., A. F.,
                                4-22-1934 7-16-1964
PHARR, Ellen, 5-9-1950 7-8-1970
HART, Luther A., Tex., Pfc., 29 Air Depot, G.P., A. A. F., W. W. II
                                6-28-1909 11-5-1962
HART, John T., 1903-1924
HART, Andrew J., 1853-1926
HART, Nancy L., 1874-1942
ROBERTSON, Ruth, 1899-No Date
ROBERTSON, N. Hunter, 1900-1978
SMITH, Henry, 1846-1924
SMITH, Lizzie, 1878-1961
SMITH, Merritt, 1877-1950
MAYES, Elza, 1909-1978
MAYES, Charles, 1878-1964
MAYES, Stella, 1879-1975
MAYES, Johnie, 9-26-1913 1-15-1924
MAYES, Mary E., 1855-1941
MAYES, Crofford S., Pvt., Co. E., 13th. Ga. Cav., C. S. A.,
                                5-29-1840 12-20-1928
GALYON, Gertrude MAYES, 1887-1965
GALYON, Danmayes, 1-27-1922 4-24-1931
GALYON, Infant, No Dates
SANDRIDGE, George W., 11-22-1854 6-16-1926
SANDRIDGE, Era E., 2-16-1877 5-2-1955
SANDRIDGE, Emma Lee, 11-27-1900 10-22-1971
SANDRIDGE, Raymon C., 7-20-1903 9-22-1974
JOHNSON, Georgia A., 9-17-1878 5-7-1966
JOHNSON, Bertha Lee, died 6-30-1971
DAUGHTRY, Augustus H., 1856-1941
DAUGHTRY, Lilly Belle, 1876-1946
MATTINGLY, William, 12-7-1872 9-16-1935
MILLER, Eula Mae, 1909-No Date
MILLER, Clarence C., 1907-1943
MILLER, Kenneth J., died 9-28-1939
NICHOLS, Olyn N., Pfc., U. S. Army, W. W. I & II., 10-10-1895 12-17-1977
                        married 2-6-1935
NICHOLS, Willie M., 8-15-1910 No Date
HOUSE, Robert W., 1920-No Date
HOUSE, Esther H., 1921-1977

HOOD, J. H., 1-8-1864 1-3-1929
THORNHILL, Amy Everia, 2-17-1900 No Date
THORNHILL, Bart L., 3-16-1893 7-13-1971
WILLIAMS, Emmett, 2-8-1901 12-26-1977
WILLIAMS, Sarah Maud, 12-16-1928 1-23-1930
SHAW, Oscar Samuel, Tex., Pvt., 1-CL, 359 Inf., 90 Div., died 9-30-1932
BALLARD, Leora A., 1877-1946
BALLARD, Stephen G., 1860-1935
DUNN, Victor Gordon, 1900-1979
HUMPHRIES, Melba, 1919-1967
HUMPHRIES, Gay, 1916-No Date
HUMPHRIES, Tilly, 10-2-1939 10-13-1939
LOVELACE, John 1882-1932
LOVELACE, H. M., 1858-1935
1 - FUNERAL MARKER
KELLUM, Beulah BUTLER, 1894-1966
KELLUM, Wylie Jackson, 1882-1958
ALFRED, Fannie GAYLOR, 9-14-1891 1-15-1975
ALFRED, George W., 4-2-1886 4-22-1930
MARTIN, J. W., "Jim", Sr., 6-3-1877 6-26-1962
MARTIN, Amy K. HAYNES, 10-7-1885 8-19-1932
KING, Lucy, 1871-1930
KING, William Edgar, 1871-1931
SMITH, Lt. Clyde, 1921-1943
ROBERTS, L. Pearl, 12-2-1882 2-21-1973
ROBERTS, J. T., 2-20-1880 7-17-1930
MORGAN, Fred C., Pfc., Army Air Force, W. W. II., 1906-1976
MORGAN, Walter T., 4-17-1871 4-27-1929
THOMAS, W. M. "Mack", 3-7-1884 3-26-1931
MARSHALL, Raymond W., Tex., Pfc., U. S. Army, W. W. II., 12-23-1918 11-15-1957
CLINTON, Linnie M., 1897-No Date
            married 1917
CLINTON, William L., 1893-1973
THOMAS, Willie, 1-31-1889 No Date
THOMAS, Dock, 4-7-1886 3-11-1932
MOORE, Mae, 1896-1952
MOORE, L. C., 1890-1967
SPEIGHT, Ollie, 1914-No Date
SPEIGHT, Willie Mae, 1918-No Date
GILBERT, Mary Delia, 12-20-1878 12-7-1955
GILBERT, James Sanford, 6-12-1880 12-22-1931
ATKINS, Miles Thomas, 1890-1943
ATKINS, Sarah Elizabeth, 1866-1937
ATKINS, George James, 1856-1925
ROBINSON, Edna, 1882-No Date
ROBINSON, T. E., 1876-1959
KELLUM, Gale Lynn, died 5-3-1960
PORTER, Aubrey L., 1907-1958
PORTER, Juanita, 1910-No Date
KELLUM, James Weldon, S-2, U. S. Navy, W. W. II., 1928-1975

KELLY, W. L., 5-24-1896 5-6-1926
HUTCHERSON, William B., 1880-1957
HUTCHERSON, Ruby R., 1891-1958
HINDMAN, Mrs. T. P,, 1872-1937
HINDMAN, T. P., 1870-1931
BROWN, Mosley, 1852-1935
MARTIN, Annie MILLER, 5-2-1874 12-19-1940
MARTIN, Jerome Brandon, 11-19-1858 11-24-1937
CRAMER, Samuel P., 1860-1934
CRAMER, Addie Belle, 1874-1953
PERKINS, Everett Peyton, Pvt., U. S. Army, W. W. I., 3-18-1894 12-5-1976
PERKINS, Tabor CRAMER, 12-1-1909 No Dates
CRAMER, Noveline, 2-11-1908 7-21-1959
HAMONDS, Ada Hazel, 1916-1944
LOVELACE, Minnie Ida, 1878-1954

SECTION "G"

PART 3

THOMAS, B. B., 4-13-1867 5-19-1944
THOMAS, Irene, 2-20-1876 12-28-1958
MC CURDY, Virgie Annie, 5-13-1888 7-15-1971
MC CURDY, Edward Clide, 5-27-1883 7-10-1944
MC CURDY, Edward Delaney, 4-21-1901 5-7-1962
CAPERTON, Clara Clyde, 2-10-1891 8-20-1974
CAPERTON, Eddie Lee, 1-18-1880 1-3-1945
BURT, Lydia WALLS, 3-26-1906 No Date
BURT, Henry Daniel, 12-6-1904 3-15-1945
SCOTT, Alfonso, 1903-1945
MAINARD, A. C., 3-7-1868 4-22-1952
MAINARD, Lou, 10-20-1883 4-21-1945
PROFFER, P. P., 4-5-1870 1-30-1953
PROFFER, Fannie, 10-6-1881 7-11-1960
SURRATT, Catherine J., 11-25-1892 No Date
                married 10-7-1934
SURRATT, Arthur A., 2-10-1884 6-3-1977
SURRATT, Mattie MILLER, 6-7-1866 2-4-1951
SURRATT, William J., 8-30-1861 2-8-1948
MATTINGLY, Lorene, 8-24-1918 No Date
                married 3-3-1940
MATTINGLY, Roy, Tex., CCM U. S. Navy, W. W. II., 3-26-1915 4-30-1970
HANES, Leona May, 1883-1947
HANES, Bill, 1870-1954
WILSON, Willie Mae, 10-12-1900 2-16-1975
WILSON, Jess G., 7-29-1885 7-22-1947
FLOWERS, Della, 1-27-1868 11-27-1969
FLOWERS, William Parker, 11-14-1868 11-8-1946
WALKER, Mary Nell, Tex., A.S., W. R. U. S. C. G. R., W. W. II,
                4-10-1927 8-19-1946
PAXTON, William C., 1944-1945
BISHOP, Wyatt C., Tex., Pfc., QM Corps, W. W. I., 5-12-1897 12-15-1958
NEWELL, Donnie Lee, 1945-1947
STEPHENSON, Ethel M., 3-7-1879 12-18-1971

STEPHENSON, Charlie J., 7-21-1871   12-4-1945
SHIPP, Lydia CORBIN, 3-8-1889 1-24-1978
SHIPP, Henry Walter, 1-21-1886 6-13-1965
TRACY, Maudine E., 5-31-1913   No Date
MYERS, Robert Samuel, son of Larry & Marlene, died 5-9-1975
TREDWELL, Sallie, 1870-1951
TREDWELL, Dock, 1869-1947
HYMAN, Dianne, Infant dau. of C. J. & Annie, died 10-31-1947
HYMAN, Tommie, 8-1952 10-24-1952
GAYLOR, R. T., Tex., Sgt., 38 Inf., 2 Inf. Div., W. W. II.,
                                7-3-1921 7-28-1944

GAYLOR, Josephine, 1888-1976
GAYLOR, Walter T., 1886-1974
MOODY, J. H., 4-1-1854 11-7-1953
MOODY, Mrs. Martha, 10-11-1857 4-15-1910
MOODY, Ida Mae, dau. of J. H. & M. N., 7-22-1884 1-8-1894
HANES, Argie Mae, 10-13-1887   11-18-1973
HANES, Albert Sidney, 12-23-1882 6-8-1949
BERRY, Opal, 1931-1954
SCOTT, Betty Sue, 4-2-1932 10-5-1949
ARNOLD, Larnce Leslie, Tex., Pvt., 328 Areo Sq., W. W. I.,
                                3-27-1891 1-31-1950
HEFNER, Wilda F., 10-5-1949- No Date
HEFNER, Russell L., "Rusty", 7-18-1947 4-29-1977
MARR, Lillie Bell, 11-24-1894 1-9-1973
MARR, James A., 4-13-1881 11-23-1969
WALKER, Betty Jewell, 6-30-1924 7-24-1973
              married 6-6-1947
WALKER, E. Dale, 1-10-1930 No Date
WALKER, Thomas W., 1-13-1897 3-19-1965
LANDS, Liston Doris, 6-27-1917 2-6-1967
VENUS, Artie W., 5-14-1871 5-5-1956
JONES, Gertrude VENUS, 1898-No Date
              married 1-16-1916
JONES, Johnie Thomas, 1893-1978
BRAMLETT, Thomas Earl, 5-25-1951 5-26-1951
BRAMLETT, W. Earl, 8-6-1930 2-19-1979
WATKINS, Vera HENRY, No Dates
WATKINS, Frederick Raymond, 1886-1950
MOORE, Cynthia RAY, 1949-1961
WALLACE, James Bennie, died 10-15-1976 aged 72 yrs.
WALLACE, Ollie, 4-1-1884 10-13-1971
WALLACE, J. Newton, 11-9-1882 1-12-1950
HARBOUR, Donald W. "Donnie", 11-2-1939 10-16-1948
HARBOUR, J. E., 5-22-1906 6-16-1972
YOUNG, Melvin, 1874-1947
MYERS, Myrtle, 1894-No Date
MYERS, Marshall, 1895-1949
MARTIN, Daisy B., 9-1-1891   No Date
MARTIN, William C., 10-1-1887 11-12-1947
SCOTT, Annie LOVE, 1872-1968
SCOTT, G. Dudley, 1859-1952
SCOTT, Nina Virginia, died 10-27-1966
CLARK, Samuel P., 5-7-1898 7-26-1973

CLARK, Lelia Mae, 8-22-1897 1-29-1948
RATLIFF, Hardin A., Tex., Capt., 143 Inf., W. W. II., 3-30-1921 11-22-1943
SPENCER, Evelyn, 10-17-1952 11-18-1977
TREADWELL, Jerry, 9-10-1936 4-9-1950
TEEL, Blettress L., 1906-1954
TEEL, John, 1904-No Date
TICE, Della, 5-25-1893 6-24-1972
TICE, Marlin R., 7-29-1889 2-27-1967
FULFER, Bertie E., 1894-No Date
FULFER, William T., Tex., Pfc., Co. D., 133 MG-BN, W. W. I.,
                           4-23-1891 9-28-1972
RIFFLE, Carl F., 1-18-1922 2-18-1979
RIFFLE, Lillie, 5-25-1885 7-25-1962
GARZA, Thomas Lynn, died 8-1-1970
SPARKS, Ruby Lera, 1905-No Date
SPARKS, James Corley, 1907-1958
TEEL, H. R., 1882-1968
TEEL, Pearl O., 1889-1958
ALEXANDER, Mary Pearl, 1879-1961
ALEXANDER, Lee Roy, 1874-1955
SHEFFIELD, Jewell, 1901-1963
SHEFFIELD, Bill, 1896-1970
WEEMS, H. Jack, PHM-1, U. S. Coast Guard, 5-29-1924 5-12-1974
WEEMS, Zuma, 1889-1968
WEEMS, Mary S., 8-16-1903 No Date
WEEMS, Odis E., 4-18-1902 4-1-1964
WEEMS, Frances, 1862-1950
WEEMS, W. E., 1859-1930
WEEMS, Verda, 8-17-1899 11-17-1967
WEEMS, Eugene W., Tex., Pvt., 30 Co., 165 Depot Brigade, W. W. I.,
                           3-19-1895 5-12-1957

MC COOL, James L., 1921-1949
KELLEY, Carolyn Virginia, 1938-1947
KELLEY, Virginia Dare, 1911-No Date
KELLEY, Cecil Ray, 1908-1978
TRAWEEK, Charlie Bee, 1902-1970
TRAWEEK, Mary Colleen, 7-18-1939 6-11-1949
ROARK, Virgie, 1-10-1889 4-29-1978
ROARK, Marlin, 12-18-1890 3-14-1964
NOWLIN, Tom, 12-22-1879 2-9-1967
MARTIN, Allie G., 1886-1969
MARTIN, Isaac M., 1879-1951
ALLEN, F. M. "Buddy", 3-22-1914 4-25-1965
ALLEN, C. M., 10-9-1885 5-17-1961
ALLEN, Blanch, 10-21-1885 4-15-1952
DAVIS, Jess, 1869-1954
DAVIS, Willie B., 1884-1952
ANDERS, Deborah A., 4-17-1954 4-19-1954

SECTION "G"

PART 4

MIDDLEBROOK, Pearl L., 9-16-1882 9-5-1947

MIDDLEBROOK, Dee W., 10-31-1875 10-7-1950
ATKINS, Wade Mc Combs, 6-25-1900 12-26-1973
ATKINS, William H., Tex., Pfc., U. S. Army, W. W. I., 4-5-1891 11-3-1972
ATKINS, Samuel W., Tex., Master Sgt., 10 AAF Resecue Sq., W. W. II.,
                        2-28-1922 8-15-1947
CRAMER, Fred C., 1886-1949
CRAMER, Samuel W., Tex., Pfc., 38 Inf. Div., W. W. II.,
                        12-20-1922 7-31-1944
ATHA, Quincy L., Missouri, Lt., U. S. N. R., W. W. II.,
                        7-26-1911 2-18-1966
NICHOLD, Edith, 9-27-1949 9-14-1979
SULLIVAN, Jessie Mae, 1-25-1893 9-5-1966
SULLIVAN, Clifford Weir, 7-18-1889 9-6-1973
SMITH, Jessie Venner, 8-19-1888 2-28-1970
SMITH, Talmage Austin, 7-24-1889 5-2-1973
JENKINS, Jeffie Lee, 6-9-1917 3-26-1955
            married 11-25-1931
JENKINS, George Albert, 4-26-1909 No Date
CANNADAY, C. Verde, 7-9-1897 8-27-1957
CLAYTON, Tressie Mae, 9-23-1909 No Date
            married 12-4-1928
CLAYTON, Osie J., 8-12-1906 No Date
GILLHAM, C. J., Jr., Tex., S-1, U. S. N. R., W. W. II.,
                        10-27-1922 4-3-1954
DEES, Sarah, 1884-1962
DEES, Joe, 1884-1963
TICE, Ann G., 1-4-1912 No Date
TICE, Hiram F., 5-19-1913 7-28-1976
EARWOOD, Dollie Sue, 1902-No Date
EARWOOD, John T., 1899-1965
JONES, Terry Dean, son of E. A. & Mamie, 12-1-1951 10-19-1954
ALEXANDER, Nora Bell, 4-22-1899 No Date
ALEXANDER, Bertie L., 2-7-1897 5-16-1967
MILLER, Vergie Mae, 1908-No Date
MILLER, Thadys K., 1905-1976
PRICE, Ruth O., 11-9-1903 8-13-1971
PRICE, Dallis H., 12-10-1904 No Date
BURROW, Pauline, 9-24-1917 5-24-1978
            married 6-1940
BURROW, Robert C., 5-14-1910 12-28-1978
WOODWARD, Howard F., 11-20-1900 No Date
WOODWARD, Dorothy N., 11-8-1905 6-10-1978
FRANCIS, Oza Lee, 1910-1971
SHUPING, Amlee MILLER, 1883-1967
MILLER, Robert Garvin, Tex., Cpl., 369 Engr., A. M. PH., SPT., Regt.
                        5-1-1931 8-14-1952
MILLER, Mae VENUS, 3-18-1901 8-19-1976
            married 12-24-1920
MILLER, Claude Lee, 7-8-1895 12-10-1971
VENUS, Willie Mae, 10-13-1911 No Date
VENUS, Thomas Weldon, 5-16-1910 6-25-1973
VENUS, Jerry Glenn, 11-12-1939 4-25-1975
NOWLIN, Lillian M., 8-17-1913 No Date
NOWLIN, Floyd Treat, 4-27-1908 9-15-1977

NOWLIN, James A., 1944-No Date
SCHMITZ, Fannie "Missie", 8-13-1877 1-20-1955
WEATHERBEE, Gerald E., 1933-1955
WEATHERBEE, Nancie E., 1908-No Date
WEATHERBEE, Reuben E., 1908-1978
WEATHERBEE, Ara I., 12-24-1906 No Date
              married 7-7-1923
WEATHERBEE, Henderson M., 11-12-1900 8-27-1973
MASTERS, Walter Franklin, Lt., J.G., U. S. Navy, W. W. II., 1911-1978
MASTERS, Elma A., 1912-No Date
RAUPHELI, Clay Alan, 8-25-1978 8-29-1978
ROSEBURE, Fred O., 11-5-1896 No Date
ROSEBURE, Maude L., 9-9-1907 No Date
GARZA, Rhonda Elaine, (Infant), died 9-17-1973

SECTION "H"

THOMPSON, T. W., 1-3-1870 11-3-1945
THOMPSON, Rockie A., 6-20-1872 7-26-1952
THOMPSON, Thomas W., Tex., 1st. Lt., U. S. Navy, W. W. II.,
              11-14-1909 4-3-1972
YORK, Hagan L., 1881-1934
CLARK, Jennie YORK, 1881-1969
BOSWELL, Allie I., 1911-No Date
BOSWELL, Ray R., 1911-1976
WELCH, Florence, 1894-1960
HALE, William M., 1864-1934
HALE, Sue E., 1876-1965
COWLING, Lee, 1862-1934
COWLING, Nancy, 1866-1946
COWLING, Martha, 1883-1964
COWLING, Halton, 1887-1956
COWLING, Annie Lee, 1888-1975
LANTRIP, Mary, 1855-1937
TANTON, Essie Viola, 12-3-1896 5-7-1937
CURRIN, Albert J., 2-9-1898 8-18-1940
SANDERS, Cordelia, 3-25-1866 1-23-1944
ARNOLD, Maurice Hugh, 4-14-1924 7-25-1968
ARNOLD, John Hugh, 8-13-1888 5-8-1970
ARNOLD, Lena L., 4-13-1893 No Date
BARNES, Mealia, 1-2-1877 6-13-1944
BARNES, J. W., 9-13-1872 9-13-1954
BARNES, Billie Clatus, 7-31-1929 8-22-1971
NABERS, Bervenia V., 1867-1962
NABERS, B. F. "Dink", 1864-1944
NABERS, Hugh, 6-11-1908 No Date
NABERS, John H., 10-19-1899 10-27-1948
HENDRIX, O. Faye, 9-26-1917 No Date
HENDRIX, James R., 11-24-1913 11-26-1978
HENDRIX, John M., Jr., Tex. Pvt., Air Corps, W. W. II., 1-30-1924 7-1-1945
HENDRIX, Ruth A., 9-17-1882 2-6-1944
HENDRIX, James R., T-Sgt., U. S. Army, W. W. II., 1913-1978
FOX, Etress Delbert, 1903-1959
FOX, Laura Belle, 1905-No Date

HENDRIX, John M., 1880-1979
VERNER, Myrtlie M., 5-5-1876 8-14-1957
VERNER, John W., 12-25-1870 10-3-1942
VERNER, Claudet T., 9-11-1893 1-11-1946
ROBERTS, David A., Tex., 129 Motor Trans. Co., OMG., 8-20-1893 7-13-1955
RHODES, Mary W., 1864-1942
RHODES, Asa A., 1851-1930
RHODES, T. C., 7-16-1897 7-26-1977
WATSON, Dee W., Tex., Cpl., 255 Base Unit, AAF, W. W. II., 12-25-1900 1-1-1958
RHEW, Eugene H., 11-12-1893 1-19-1952
RHEW, Elsie Geneva, 5-11-1896 4-10-1942
GOLDSWORTHY, Emma MORLOCK, 12-13-1866 2-13-1936
GOLDSWORTHY, William Wills, 2-18-1862 5-5-1932
LONG, Mack, 1914-1940
LONG, Mack B., 1881-1933
1-FUNERAL MARKER
WOOSLEY, Jefferson D., 8-13-1867 3-19-1930
WOOSLEY, Anna J., 3-28-1874 8-1-1926
WALL, Imogene, born & died 6-6-1926
WALL, J. B., 3-2-1881 4-17-1928
WALL, Thomas H., Tex., Cpl., U. S. Army, W. W. II., 4-25-1914 3-27-1968
MATLOCK, Coy E., Tex., Pvt., 520 QM Railhead Co., W. W. II.,
                                          8-2-1909 1-25-1962

EASLEY, Ruby Nell, 7-18-1952 12-15-1971
WALKER, Bertha Lee, 6-3-1896 6-8-1958
WALKER, Mary Caroline, wife of Pink, 4-27-1876 3-22-1926
WALKER, Pink, 3-27-1869 3-11-1959
WALKER, Walter Loyd, Ala., MeWC, U.S.N.R., W. W. II., 1-1-1904 9-26-1959
WALLS, Earl, 12-2-1901 12-17-1960
WALLS, Johnnie Sue, 11-16-1911 No Date
BOYER, Mamie D., 1894-No Date
BOYER, Joseph D., 1887-1926
DIXON, Ada, 1873-1931
DIXON, Gilbert, 1863-1944
BOYER, Joe D., Tex., Pvt., 184 Milt. Police BN, W. W. II., 1-21-1918 2-24-1971
SISSEL, Charles B., 1883-1942
SISSEL, Lona E., 8-9-1898 No Date
SISSEL, Dorothy Ann., 12-27-1919 12-6-1926
ESSARY, J. C., 1860-1928
ESSARY, Mrs. Mary, 1866-1927
ESSARY, Infant, died 7-5-1930
GILLHAM, Oliver V., Pvt., U. S. Navy, 10-13-1890 10-16-1974
ESSARY, J. Welton, 1898-1954
ESSARY, L. Pauline, 1906-No Date
TALLEY, Thelma, 1913-No Date
TALLEY, Lee, 1910-1968
ODOM, Lillian FITZGERALD, 11-12-1890 1-3-1965
ODOM, John William, 9-30-1885 11-18-1962
BREAKIRON, Thomas P., SN, U. S. Navy, Vietnam, 1952-1975
BRANCH, Rev., J. C., 3-9-1877 5-12-1956
HALE, Era M., 1893-No Date
HALE, Melvin B., 1892-1955
LANTRIP, Kittie KNIGHT, 1-5-1896 7-29-1973
LANTRIP, Joseph Malachi, 9-16-1882 7-27-1955

NOLEN, Samuel A., 1865-1953
DEARING, Thelma, 1908-No Date
DEARING, Waylon, 1908-No Date
KELLY, Thomas B., 1855-1932
PATTERSON, Ruth, 1893-1945
PATTERSON, Sidney E., 1879-1952
DAVIS, Mary Louise, 1922-1968
DAVIS, Robert T., 1911-No Date
PORTER, Nora R., 2-2-1906 No Date
PORTER, Cleo C., 11-13-1905 No Date
NABERS, Jewell, 1906-No Date
NABERS, Gus., 1904-No Date
MC COMBS, Minnie O., 1893-1977
MC COMBS, Henry M., 1889-1974
MC COMBS, Lena Nadine, 10-15-1913 10-25-1916
JOHNSTON, Alton James, 7-15-1948 7-17-1948
STOOKSBERRY, Effie Sudie, 9-7-1884 6-4-1948
STOOKSBERRY, John Rusk, 4-18-1878 5-19-1973
2 - FUNERAL MARKER
STOOKSBERRY, Easton, 1919-1973
STOOKSBERRY, Lela E., Tex., S-Sgt., U. S. Army, W. W. II., 4-6-1919 4-17-1973
SWINEY, Irene POWERS, 7-22-1920 8-2-1957
SWINEY, Kenneth Glenn, 8-15-1940 8-3-1957
POWERS, Joe L., 12-17-1861 6-7-1947
POWERS, Amanda C., 7-3-1880 12-26-1956
HARRIS, Docia E., 4-6-1889 1-4-1963
HARRIS, John M., 7-26-1874 4-15-1946
TURLEY, Martin, 5-15-1894 6-8-1970
1 - FUNERAL MARKER
OWENS, Andrew T., 3-15-1857 8-12-1935
OWENS, Martha L., 6-19-1862 12-12-1929
WILSON, Wiley, died 4-23-1956
1 - FUNERAL MARKER
OWENS, Hoyt L., 6-15-1893 1-26-1964
OWENS, Mary Myrtle, 12-7-1889 11-23-1971
WYLIE, Annie P., 1878-1960
WYLIE, Robert N., 1872-1949
WALL, Mrs. Frances, 10-16-1843 1-18-1929
MONTGOMERY, Zelma F., 6-12-1927 7-20-1928
MONTGOMERY, Carl M., 9-7-1921 12-3-1927
BRYANT, Frances, 11-4-1907 8-31-1967
BRYANT, Fred A., 12-4-1900 1-19-1972
GRISHAM, Z. D., 1852-1927
MC FADDEN, Fannie GRISHAM, wife of Z.D. GRISHAM, 1875-1952
SANDS, Nannie Pearl, 6-3-1915 1-31-1961
                married 11-5-1940
SANDS, Lee A., 2-3-1912 4-14-1975
PETTIT, Harold S., Tex., 2nd. Lt., A. A. F., W. W. II., PH.,
                        12-23-1923 6-19-1946
PETTIT, Edward Tennis, 4-1-1892 1-10-1962
PETTIT, Ruby YORK, 8-1-1897 9-7-1968
PETTIT, Edward T., Tex., Pvt., U. S. M. C., W. W. I., 4-1-1892 1-10-1962
WATTENBARGER, Edith M., 1893-No Date
WATTENBARGER, Edgar, 1889-1972

MYERS, John H., 11-13-1863 11-12-1951
MYERS, Laura A., 5-29-1865 12-5-1940
MYERS, Oscar, 2-12-1878 3-10-1927
LINDLEY, Mattie MYERS, 9-29-1882 10-26-1965
RAGLAND, Brode D., 9-8-1896 11-17-1960
HILL, Joseph B., 3-10-1890 6-22-1957
HILL, Eula L., 1-6-1894 1-16-1927
RAINEY, Laura A., 3-6-1861 9-13-1945
RAINEY, William C., 9-3-1848 9-5-1927
RAINEY, Price B., 10-17-1898 12-13-1960
PRIGMORE, Lydia E., 7-22-1893 10-13-1967
PRIGMORE, Clarence L., 10-3-1888 2-27-1963
BROWNING, H. W., 9-27-1874 12-26-1927
BROWNING, Fannie, 12-7-1879 12-26-1927
FONTAINE, William F., Sgt., A.A.A., 3-27-1920 10-24-1944
ABERNATHY, Elsie BROWNING, 1-13-1904 No Date
ABERNATHY, Francis Bailey, 8-7-1902 5-6-1971
COATS, William M., 9-2-1906 4-14-1974
COATS, William James, 9-11-1938 11-3-1938
BLEDSOE, Edna Frances, 11-22-1886 6-18-1928
BLEDSOE, James Marcus, 11-27-1876 10-6-1948
CLIFTON, Stanley C., 2-26-1903 6-20-1928
CLIFTON, George W., 11-9-1879 6-3-1938
CLIFTON, Georgia E., 3-21-1915 10-6-1972
CLIFTON, Petricia, 8-18-1925 4-7-1930
SWANN, James F.., 1857-1928
GREGORY, Mary SEAY, 1863-1940
SWANN, Mitt Almus, 1889-1956
SWANN, Ida SEAY, 1903-1961
MATHERLY, Surber L., 11-7-1878 6-2-1951
MATHERLY, Mattie Belle, 2-10-1878 9-8-1958
MATHERLY, Joe G., 3-17-1900 12-10-1947
GADD, Madaline MATHERLY, 10-13-1898 10-20-1928
1 - FUNERAL MARKER
WILLIS, John Freely, 1913-1932
WILLIS, Cenia Bell, 1883-1953
WILLIS, James F., 1875-1959
FREEMAN, L. L., 1876-1935
FREEMAN, Edna Pearl, 1885-1951
FREEMAN, Clark, 1906-1934
FREEMAN, Doyle Leroy, 7-10-1901 6-17-1959
WILLIS, Pearl, dau. of Charles & Elizabeth LAKE WILLIS, 2-7-1890 6-1952
SNODGRASS, Nelly Pearl, 1903-1977
SNODGRASS, Zona, dau. of Charles & ELizabeth LAKE WILLIS, 1875-1947
LAKE, James S., 9-30-1892 10-26-1969
LAKE, Harriett M., 10-12-1899 No Date
WALKER, Nora H., 1880-1958
WALKER, L. M., 1880-1949
CLARK, John D., Tex., Cpl., 193 Tank BN, W. W. II., 11-12-1922 4-27-1945
CLARK, John W., 1-7-1895 10-25-1957
CLARK, Druecilla, 1-12-1899 10-13-1957
RAY, Horace L., 1909-1962
RAY, Gladys I., 1919-No Date
MC COOL, Clarence W., Tex., Pfc., 321 Inf., 81 Inf. Div., W. W. II., 11-21-1916
                                                                      9-24-1944

MC COOL, Jackson H., 3-15-1884 1-19-1953
MC COOL, Lou Ella, 11-21-1887 1-31-1953
HAMMONS, M. Z., 11-23-1905 No Date
HAMMONS, Ruby G., 5-5-1907 6-28-1946
HUFFMAN, Edwin Ray, 1930-1934
REX, Mattie Lee, 4-21-1891 4-10-1972
REX, Willie J., Tex., Pvt., U. S. Army, W. W. I, 7-16-1896 9-22-1971
REX, Ida E., 4-29-1867 9-27-1943
REX, Ed, 1-13-1864 11-19-1949
REX, Edel, 1929-1929
REX, Jimmie, 1927-1929
REX, Gorman, 1931-1931
MILLER, Annie Lee, 1870-1952
LAKE, James Marion, 1926-1929
LAKE, Della, 1893-1959
LAKE, W. W., 1890-1960
LAKE, Wesley H., Tex., 2nd. Lt., U. S. Army, W. W. II., 2-12-1919 10-22-1967
HAYNES, Nina, 10-14-1928 10-14-1928
HAYNES, Kathleen Elaine, 1-25-1945 3-13-1947
ADAMS, Drucilla, 6-12-1895 7-17-1951
HAYNES, Alva Etta, 12-7-1883 6-26-1971
HAYNES, John J., 9-30-1879 12-13-1949
SANDERS, Mrs. Annie B., 7-27-1889 11-5-1968
CORNELIUS, Stella D., 1882-1928
CORNELIUS, Walter F., 1875-1936
CORNELIUS, Harold D., Tex., 1st. Lt., U. S. Army, W. W. II.,
                      9-20-1904 6-3-1963
STRICKLAND, Areda, 5-8-1894 11-19-1936
YOWELL, Tennie P., 4-13-1860 1-30-1939
YOWELL, James A., 1-30-1861 10-19-1928
REX, Ruth I., 4-5-1905 No Dates
                married 4-28-1922
REX, Ira H., 6-29-1903 6-26-1970
WYNN, I. B., 10-3-1898 9-13-1928

SECTION "I"

ERWIN, Mrs. Roy, 10-31-1893 2-29-1936
CROOM, Bennie L., 7-6-1876 1-10-1965
MC WHIRTER, William S. "Bill", 1-11-1897 10-16-1973
MC WHIRTER, Julia HORN, 3-2-1898 No Date
ELLIOTT, Evelyn CROOM, 3-6-1907 No Date
ELLIOTT, Harry Ray, 12-17-1905 8-10-1978
GRAY, Kathleen, 1-27-1926 7-1-1971
WHITE, Vennie Mae, 1903-No Date
                married 4-19-1925
WHITE, Marshall, 1902-1966
WHITE, Lilla W., 1880-1935
WHITE, Weldon, 1910-1944
WHITE, Charlie W., 1878-1968
HURT, Gus, No Dates
HURT, Jim, NO Dates
HURT, Frances, No Dates
ROBERTS, Audrey, No Dates

CROW, Lovell, No Dates
MALONEY, Alpha Telula, 1863-1939
MALONEY, William David, 1856-1935
ORREN, Daniel Eli, 1883-1938
ORREN, Frances E., 1883-1943
ESTES, W. Neal, Sr., 11-12-1907 12-23-1970
ESTES, Mary Lou, 9-21-1899 2-27-1972
ESTES, Marion, 2-12-1912 12-14-1934
ESTES, J. G., 9-11-1865 11-5-1931
ESTES, Della Loy, 7-16-1874 6-6-1960
ESTES, L. Dillard, 8-31-1894 2-10-1943
THURMAN, George, 6-25-1878 3-21-1945
KELLEY, George, 1880-1931
KELLY, Annie Maude, 1882-1975
CORLEY, Alfred P., 12-13-1868 4-2-1930
CORLEY, Mattie J., 5-1-1875 4-24-1968
BLOUNT, Mary Etta CORLEY, 6-15-1896 2-10-1964
ABLOWICK, Alfred A., 2-7-1872 3-14-1953
ABLOWICK, Gertrude E., 1-13-1888 5-15-1979
ABLOWICK, Cornelia L., 4-5-1848 4-9-1929
ABLOWICK, Abraham, 7-6-1886 10-9-1931
CLAYTON, Harry G., 1876-1946
CLAYTON, Cornelia B., 1886-1971
LESTER, Hannah H., 1849-1928
SCOTT, Ed H., 9-9-1865 7-20-1941
SCOTT, Alice T., 3-2-1867 3-29-1955
BRADDY, John W., 10-5-1879 2-13-1934
BRADDY, Infant Son of Mr. & Mrs. H., No Dates
HARTSOOK, Lena BRADDY, 8-22-1881 12-14-1969
HARTSOOK, Warren D., 2-14-1886 8-25-1954
KANTZ, Samuel D., 1921-1930
KANTZ, William Paul, 1879-1934
TURNER, Myrtle Lou, 1-20-1892 7-1-1961
            married 2-20-1910
TURNER, John Wiley, 10-17-1885 10-11-1954
TURNER, Leon J., 10-21-1912 7-14-1930
ADAIR, Crate, 7-18-1908 12-29-1955
HATHAWAY, William Chester, Jr., 1918-1931
HATHAWAY, Mabel , 5-10-1894 5-17-1978
            married 10-7-1915
HATHAWAY, William Chester, Sr., 4-10-1893 3-24-1970
MABRY, Billy Wray, 7-7-1935 1-10-1936
TICE, Wessie WRAY, 2-22-1915 2-5-1976
POSTON, Janie Judy, 1884-1964
POSTON, J. W., 4-5-1875 2-27-1932
HILL, Leota, 1901-1960
HILL, Johnny P., 1892-1937
HILL, R. O. "Thell", 1889-1971
GROVE, William Joseph, 11-2-1930 2-10-1973
GROVE, Nelle, 3-13-1897 No Date
GROVE, Joseph G., 8-13-1888 3-12-1971
GROVE, Nettie, 2-19-1898 No Date
FLING, Capt. Roy, 1921-1944 (Lost near Antwerp, Belgium, 9-9-1944)
FLING, Tommie M., wife of H. H., 8-1-1881 8-15-1957

FLING, H. H., 3-15-1874 4-22-1961
EASTLAND, Thelma Jane, wife of J. M., 8-21-1908 10-7-1934
HALL, Sidney P., Tex., Pvt., 93rd. Balloon Co., W. W. I.,
6-6-1895 9-8-1970
HALL, Myrtle M., 9-24-1900 No Date
HALL, J. K., 10-8-1860 10-5-1932
HALL, Mary, 1880-1959
HALL, Tom, 1875-1958
POE, Samuel J., 1867-1961
POE, Minnie ROAN, 1883-1967
CARVER, Mollie M., 1890-1932
CARVER, Hugh, 1887-1939
FIFE, Bobbie D., 1931-1932
MILLER, Mary Isadora WYNN, wife of James O., 1-28-1862 7-5-1932
MILLER, James O., 8-5-1858 1-30-1942
MILLER, Morris, 12-12-1903 8-13-1932
MILLER, Mary BOONE, 12-19-1876 1-24-1963
MILLER, Robert M., 4-27-1873 8-27-1949
MILLER, Capt. John, 6-6-1894 10-7-1957
WHITE, Grace MILLER, 3-9-1896 1-21-1979
WATSON, Isabel MILLER, 7-14-1911 7-29-1979
WHITLEY, Samuel Henry, 9-1-1878 10-2-1946
WHITLEY, Lucie LOVE, 3-25-1880 5-3-1973
WHITLEY, Robert Love, P.H.D., 9-26-1905 1-20-1933
MARTIN, Matt W., 1885-1967
MARTIN, Ethel L., 1892-No Date
NOWELL, T. Hicks, 1847-1936
ANDERSON, S. R., 7-10-1868 3-15-1948
ANDERSON, Martha Ann, No Date,
JACKSON, Curtis W., Sgt., U. S. Army, 6-13-1911 8-29-1973
JACKSON, Maerita H., 10-5-1911 No Date
HUMPHRIES, Marion Riely, 7-26-1889 11-16-1973
HUMPHRIES, Bertha B., 9-1-1887 10-17-1976
LOVEL, C. S., 1891-1934
LOVEL, Hesta, 1892-1966
ELLISON, Eva F., 1872-1958
ELLISON, Thomas D., 1856-1935
BRILEY, Inf. son of Ray & Edna, died 12-23-1946
DAVIS, Tom., 1877-1949
DAVIS, Susie M., 1882-1934
BRADDOCT, Esta, 4-21-1854 10-23-1935
JACKSON, W. E., 1869-1935
JACKSON, Mary H., 1883-1967
MORRIS, William C., Tex., S-Sgt., died 6-4-1937
MORRIS, Charlotte, 1898-1937
BRADFORD, Dora A., 1886-1936
BRADFORD, Henry B., 1869-1950
SHIVE, Glynice M., 1915-1960
GEORGE, Linda C., 1880-1949
GEORGE, John L., 1874-1935
SMITH, Wadie R., 1876-1955
SMITH, Thomas H., 1872-1951
PRITCHARD, Lafayette, 1856-1932
PRITCHARD, Nancy C., 1857-1946

YOUNG, James T., 1892-1931
YOUNG, Fred L., BTL., U. S. Navy, W. W. I & II., 1899-1932
YOUNG, Carrie., 1877-1941
YOUNG, James O., 1872-1936
LILLY, Grace POTTER, 1896-1967
POTTER, Mattie M., 1867-1933
POTTER, Catherine, 1890-1967
POTTER, Dorthy, 1920-1951
POTTER, George H., 1893-1932
POTTER, Albert, 1863-1957
CARY, Johanna POTTER, 1896-1964
MC DANIEL, Emory Neal, 12-22-1884 3-15-1976
           married 12-20-1909
MC DANIEL, Kate NEAL, 11-9-1885 1-24-1978
WRIGHT, Lucille A., 3-8-1901 1-9-1978
BRYANT, Addie, 1867-1936
ANDERSON, Vesta Mae, 11-13-1891 2-3-1951
ANDERSON, J. E., 1-31-1887 4-23-1934
ASHWORTH, George L., 1906-1955
ASHWORTH, Irene, 1896-No Date
ASHWORTH, Beulah, 1879-1968
ASHWORTH, J. T., 1871-1940
ANDERSON, Vallie, 6-7-1879 10-26-1940
ANDERSON, James N., 12-23-1879 6-7-1948

SECTION "J"

PARKS, Marie, 7-15-1910 1-14-1970
HOBBS, James T., Tex., CM-2, U. S. Navy, W. W. II., 9-24-1906 11-12-1967
CAMERON, Kate, 10-6-1894 12-23-1948
           married 4-4-1917
CAMERON, Noah, 12-24-1892 1-22-1962
ARTHUR, Noble A., 8-26-1903 9-22-1973
ARTHUR, Willie BROOKS, 11-27-1898 3-15-1974
BROOKS, Effie, 1866-1929
DAVIS, Homer Lee, Sgt., Co. G., 387 Inf., W. W. I., 10-8-1891 1-7-1966
DOBBINS, Margery R., 8-31-1898 7-5-1943
DOBBINS, W. E., 1-17-1895 5-16-1930
HOLLEY, C. FOREST, 3-30-1906 2-3-1957
HENDERSON, Nell, 9-1-1905 4-2-1974
HENDERSON, Rosa, 5-7-1898 5-19-1970
HENDERSON, Elizabeth, 6-25-1896 4-26-1964
HENDERSON, Mary A., 10-29-1869 6-13-1949
HENDERSON, J. T., 7-22-1848 4-23-1930
HENDERSON, J. T., 3-29-1920 1-23-1936
HENDERSON, Maude St. CLAIR, 8-24-1900 6-3-1970
FEATHERSTONE, Jessie ROAN, 6-14-1904 No Date
FEATHERSTONE, Patrick Earl, 10-11-1902 3-15-1976
FEATHERSTONE, Blanch Dean, 4-10-1900 9-8-1976
FEATHERSTONE, Michael, 1865-1929
MOORE, Infant Son, died 10-13-1913
MOORE, Infant Son, died 8-26-1929
MOORE, Nora DAVIS, 11-28-1891 9-6-1973

MOORE, Stephen Louis, 9-16-1888 9-12-1964
GUTHRIE, Ada, 8-16-1883 4-7-1964
GUTHRIE, W. N., 10-27-1874 7-4-1929
ALLARD, Lilas, 1896-No Date
ALLARD, Claude, 1897-1979
HICKERSON, Jack, 1st. Lt., Killed in Africa, 11-16-1916 5-11-1943
HICKERSON, Bertie B., 2-7-1890 3-7-1930
HICKERSON, Dan, 8-22-1910 5-16-1929
HICKERSON, Jewel T., 8-27-1889 7-21-1932
HORTON, Dearlee HICKERSON, 12-10-1894 4-9-1956
HORTON, R. Clyde, 6-20-1896 9-18-1965
BUTLER, David C., 11-19-1899 No Date
BUTLER, Maurine G., 11-2-1902 No Date
SPARKS, Stella F., 4-12-1891 12-2-1977
          married 12-22-1913
SPARKS, J. Walter, 12-21-1884 3-31-1968
HAMMONS, James Earl, Tex. Sgt. 5th Armored Div., 4-5-1931 6-16-1967
SPARKS, Hattie O., 1-24-1873 12-26-1956
SPARKS, J. A., 2-23-1877 2-3-1952
BROWNING, Mary Lee, 1890-1936
BROWNING, Chester O., 1884-1930
TRAUGHBER, Clark R., 1901-1975
TRAUGHBER, Leona, 1878-1972
TRAUGHBER, Will E., 1871-1930
LEDFORD, Nina, 9-16-1903 No Date
          married 6-2-1928
LEDFORD, Bee, 11-11-1904 11-15-1976
LEDFORD, Jessie Lou, 1916-1934
LEDFORD, Jessie S., 1879-1937
LEDFORD, M. E. (Ed), 1873-1957
BLANKENSHIP, Alva CARRUTH, 1886-1959
BLANKENSHIP, Albert S., 1880-1975
BRADY, Thomas Harold, 12-21-1877 5-26-1969
BRADY, Dona HARGROVE, 4-12-1878 3-6-1948
LUNDY, Della H., 4-28-1884 12-16-1929
HALL, Claude V., 5-22-1905 11-27-1959
          married 4-9-1927
HALL, Ethel Emma, 6-13-1907 No Date
SMIDDY, Mary Elmina, 1-26-1879 9-22-1959
SMIDDY, J. W., 11-14-1869 11-24-1929
SCOTT, Max, 2-22-1898 6-26-1968
SCOTT, Roger, 1918-1972
SCOTT, Roger Q., 10-28-1895 9-16-1929
OWENS, Florine R., 7-12-1910 3-14-1977
OWENS, Henry Grady, 6-16-1895 5-19-1968
OWENS, Mertie, 8-26-1895 1-30-1970
RHODES, Roy R., 1890-1962
RHODES, Grace D., 1898-No Date
POTTS, William B., 1896-1974
POTTS, Viola G., 1908-No Date
BRANCH, Jerry J., 9-13-1935 12-4-1974
BRANCH, Clifton, 8-13-1913 No Date
BRANCH, Doll, 7-2-1904 No Date
MATTHEWS, Edgar, 11-24-1918 No Date

WILLIAMS, Zuma HAWES, 1895-1975
SHEPHERD, Dave W., 8-17-1905   10-5-1975
SHEPHERD, Mable K., 2-28-1911   No Date
WATERS, Elizabeth H., 1901-1978
MENTE, George H., Pvt., U. S. Army, W. W. II., 1-4-1918   5-28-1976
NOLEN, Mary E., 8-8-1917   5-3-1973
   married 4-11-1942
NOLEN, Albin R., 12-17-1918   No Date
GARRETT, Hattie B., 9-13-1895   11-26-1975
   married 2-12-1912
GARRETT, Lee R., 8-14-1888   10-5-1971
HORTON, Cynthia H., 1907-No Date
HORTON, T. R. (Bob), 1904-No Date
HORTON, Billie W., 11-25-1938   1-16-1970
WHITLEY, Francis L., 1901-1970
WHITLEY, J. Lawrence, 1900-1953
WHITELY, Billy Wayne, 1935-1937
HARMON, Mary C., 1871-1963
HARMON, Thomas E., 1873-1943
FITZPATRICK, Ruby HARMON, 1900-1959
YOUNG, Elva H., 1898-1974
YOUNG, Rex R., 1898-1969
YOUNG, Ollie H., 1886-1953
YOUNG, Carl D., 1884-1934
SWEAT, Willie N., Tex., Pvt., U. S. Army, W. W. II., 12-11-1898   1-9-1964
ADAMS, James V., 1892-1954
ADAMS, Vera R., 1893-1931
EASTER, Modena, 1-5-1906   9-16-1930
ALLEN, Clarance G., 1891-1959
ALLEN, James G., 1868-1941
ALLEN, Esther MORRIS, 1871-1891
RANDOLPH, Wiley E., 1861-1930
RANDOLPH, Clara, 1867-1933
JEFFCOAT, Nannie RANDOLPH, 8-3-1899   No Date
JEFFCOAT, E. Herman, 1-24-1900   No Date
TRANTHAM, L. R., No Dates
TRANTHAM, R. S. Olga, 1879-1964
SAYLE, Mrs. Willie, 1877-1955
BISHOP, Guy, 4-29-1906   10-7-1931
BISHOP, A. B., 10-1-1878   11-15-1954
BISHOP, Lois, 1-15-1881   9-26-1956
MARTIN, Martha BISHOP, 8-18-1910   3-19-1979
BRACKEN, Leve, Jr., 1934-1936
SPARKS, John Wesley, Pvt., U. S. Army, W. W. I., 5-1-1889   10-19-1972
SPARKS, Zera, 10-20-1901   11-15-1971
BROADFOOT, William A., Jr., Lt., W. W. II., 12-27-1920   2-23-1944
BROADFOOT, Emma Ruth, 2-14-1925   4-26-1942
LYTLE, Joe H., 4-6-1894   3-1-1962
LYTLE, Thelma, 9-28-1903   9-6-1967
HALE, Basil, Tex., F-1, U. S. Navy, W. W. I., 6-25-1897   8-3-1960
HALE, Beulah WOMACK, 12-14-1903   1-7-1969
LYTLE, Anna J., 9-28-1937   1-15-1978
TURNER, Joe L., Tex., M-Sgt., U. S. Marines, W. W. II & Korea
       2-26-1924   12-21-1969

TURNER, Burline R., 7-16-1927 No Date
YATES, Charles L., Tex., Pfc., U. S. Army, W. W. II., 3-24-1919 5-5-1970
YATES, Bessie May, 1892-No Date
SAMS, Joe, 1898-1971
          married 2-28-1920
SAMS, Anna L., 1900-1979
DAVIS, Hubert, 4-20-1901 No Date
DAVIS, Bessie B., 7-11-1902 9-15-1970
WRIGHT, Ernest E., 7-12-1895 7-31-1975
WRIGHT, Eva Faye, 2-28-1895 No Date
WRIGHT, Donald E., Cpl., U. S. Marines, W. W. II., 12-25-1929 7-25-1970
FELLEY, Cameron, 8-9-1916 7-28-1976
OWENS, Emmett Lee, 8-23-1938 6-29-1977
ROUNDTREE, Carl, 1901-1977
BROWN, Virgil Perry, Cpl. U. S. Marines, W. W. II., 1-30-1923 9-8-1974
LATSON, William Richard, 1922-1977
PRIGMORE, William W., Jr., 12-6-1946 8-25-1974
WHITE, Charles M., 1901-1977
LOWMAN, Evelyn Clara, 11-29-1915 1-24-1978
MC GUYER, Dorothy F., 11-30-1900 5-25-1974
SCOTT, Kinsey Lee, 10-5-1955 12-29-1973
MANGELS, Edward Scott, Sgt., U. S. Army, W. W. II., 1907-1977
MC WHIRTER, Robert Paul, SN., U. S. Navy, Vietnam, 1950-1978
GRAHAM, Maggie O., 1893-1973
GRAHAM, John Eli., 1878-1969
GIBSON, Burley I., 10-31-1911 5-14-1972
PARKER, Henry N., Tex., Pvt., Co. A., 703 TD BN., W. W. II.,
                    9-14-1920 1-19-1973
FINDLEY, Ronald C., Wyoming, Pvt., U. S. Army, 3-21-1949 6-3-1966
ATTRED, Infant, died 10-09-1973
KING, Melissa Ann, died 7-23-1973 (Infant)
KING, Eunie OLIVER, 11-22-1902 1-21-1974
KING, Ada L., 9-15-1904 3-17-1960
MC CURDY, Etta, 7-25-1883 1-1-1954
MC CURDY, David, 6-27-1877 3-22-1941
FOX, Kate E., 1887-1977
FOX, James D., 1883-1960
WHITE, Joe E., 11-23-1905 5-14-1965
MOORE, Grace, 1910-1977
SWEAT, Ruth FOLLIS, 3-10-1914 6-26-1978
SWEAT, Billie G., 10-16-1928 3-24-1972
DANIEL, Donna Marie, 9-26-1961 2-9-1963
WAITBEY, Anne, 11-10-1877 2-8-1955
WAITBEY, James G., 9-25-1877 5-9-1948
TALLEY, Claude, 12-17-1887 1-4-1966
TALLEY, Dezie M., 11-2-1890 10-18-1939
WALLACE, Roy Lee, 2-27-1918 7-24-1939
WALLACE, Alpha A., 10-31-1887 10-6-1944
WALLACE, James H., 1-28-1881 10-4-1944
FOWLER, Robert D., 1904-1970
MICHELS, Genenieve W., 2-13-1910 9-27-1967
MICHELS, Kenneth W., 6-26-1913 9-27-1967
DENSON, Katie L., 1885-1970
DENSON, William L., 1878-1967

GIBSON, Irvin, Pvt., U. S. Army, W. W. I., 1894-1976
GIBSON, Grady, Tex. Pfc., Batry A., 344 Field Arty, W. W. I.,
            3-5-1896 4-4-1968

SECTION "K"

HOBBS, Ben. F., Jr., 4-19-1937 5-15-1937
HOBBS, Sallie C., 11-30-1874 4-25-1960
HOBBS, Ben. F., 1-8-1860 11-24-1941
BRUCE, Thelma TITTLE, wife of Dr. Grady, 8-14-1909 12-19-1937
DRAKE, Mary Etta, 1875-1964
DRAKE, William Clifton, 1875-1966
DRAKE, Leila Victoria, 1886-1958
DRAKE, W. Cleveland, 1885-1974
DRAKE, Julia D., 1886-1978
DRAKE, George B., 1883-1936
HEAD, Mary S., 1884-1970
HEAD, W. A., 1871-1937
ANDERSON, Daisy B., 1877-1962
ANDERSON, Walter E., 1876-1936
KNIGHT, Ira Joe, 11-16-1922 10-24-1939
KNIGHT, Hattie M., 3-26-1884 3-29-1936
KNIGHT, Ira L., 10-5-1881 11-1-1976
JORDAN, Mary Anna, 10-29-1888 2-15-1970
JORDAN, Wendell J., 8-22-1886 3-9-1936
LISTON, Clarance, 1902-1936
LISTON, Elizabeth, 1877-1968
LISTON, William T., 1869-1939
LISTON, Ella, 2-2-1906 No Date
LISTON, Cleo, 2-6-1905 8-17-1978
ARRINGTON, Mae L., 1898-No Date
ARRINGTON, William P., 1892-1973
WALLER, Dr. Leroy T., 1874-1953
WALLER, Mattie A., 9-28-1875 8-27-1972
WALLER, Louis O., 1913-1937
MOORE, Alma, 6-27-1894 4-15-1970
MOORE, Joe J., 12-30-1891 8-3-1962
MOORE, Charles Edward, 8-28-1934 11-12-1936
RICH, Linda S., 5-8-1941 3-8-1974
PENN, Marcus R., 1880-1938
PENN, Eula S., 1882-1937
RENWICK, Annie F., 9-28-1920 No Date
RENWICK, Woodrow W., 7-24-1918 4-22-1962
CORNISH, Mollie, 1897-1937
CORNISH, Roi Harding, 1889-1975
CORNISH, Ruby BURGESS, 1889-1974
KELLEY, Leta Frances, 1-16-1922 6-27-1937
KELLEY, Floyd Sims, 8-2-1902 1-11-1975
KELLEY, John T., 12-23-1870 12-14-1950
KELLEY, Dora M., 4-28-1883 4-29-1959
DILLINGHAM, Ethel, 1878-1958
DILLINGHAM, James, 1871-1937
WILLIAMS, James Davis "Uncle Jimmy", 5-7-1872 1-30-1938
WILLIAMS, Boyd Ella, 6-8-1885 12-9-1977

JACKSON, Lula, 8-8-1881 7-10-1960
JACKSON, Bascomb, 8-27-1875 2-12-1958
JACKSON, Eula Faye, 11-16-1910 5-27-1937
JACKSON, Keith, died 7-2-1938
BRUNER, Carolyn Ann, 1948-1976
MAGRANS, Berta M. REY, 1918-1976
HENDRIX, Ora J., 1894-1979
SIMS, Clyde C., 7-31-1913 1-16-1979
PORTER, Jessie Estelle, 1-8-1912 No Date
                 married 1-14-1932
PORTER, Joe Olin, 4-28-1910 No Date
PORTER, Rosalie G., 1911-No Date
PORTER, T. Omer, 1903-1977
FORD, Laura L., 1899-No Date
FORD, Charles R., 1895-No Date
TIPPETT, Anna L., 1892-1978
TIPPETT, Tom B., 1885-1955
TIPPETT, Darlene, 8-28-1923 No Date
TIPPETT, Loyd A., 7-11-1912 3-29-1976
TIPPETT, Gene, 1922-1937
TUCKER, Lovella T., 12-24-1904 No Date
TUCKER, Seth Cuyler, 9-17-1902 1-27-1971
TAYLOR, Ida L., 3-28-1888 3-22-1966
TAYLOR, William H., 10-24-1881 10-20-1969
WINNIFORD, Everett D., 9-16-1903 No Date
WINNIFORD, Elsie L., 2-17-1907 5-3-1979
ROBERTS, Oscar R., 1869-1939
ROBERTS, Clara S., 1877-1937
KEYS, A. N., 3-7-1865 6-17-1939
ALLMON, Florence, 1885-1961
ALLMON, De Witt Clinton, 7-27-1875 10-28-1947
JACKSON, Bert John, Sr., 2-28-1888 2-10-1952
JACKSON, Jerry Dale "Butch", 5-28-1942 4-28-1946
JACKSON, Lowell, 1-20-1911 10-4-1953
DAVIS, Louise, 1914-1965
DAVIS, Albert, 1914-1937
ALLEN, Effie Evelyn, 3-18-1886 3-31-1959
ALLEN, Albert Homer, 3-4-1878 12-8-1937
MURPHY, Gladys E., 1901-No Date
MURPHY, Clarence D., 1898-1971
ALLEN, John C., 1877-1937
ALLEN, Carrie, 1884-1947
VERNON, Sidney A., Tex., Pvt., 2nd. Co. Conv. Center, W. W. I, PH.,
                          12-25-1891 12-5-1959
VERNON, Leola ALLEN, 9-1-1902 No Date
VERNON, Addie Lee, 6-3-1927 1-5-1975
VERNON, S. M. "Jack", 7-25-1920 No Date
HAWKINS, No Name or Dates
SHAW, Belvie E., 4-3-1890 6-19-1960
SHAW, Noah J., 5-26-1884 8-18-1959
FREEMAN, Cliff M., 1881-1937
FREEMAN, Claude L., 1882-1958
ROGERS, Ruby H., 12-19-1897 7-4-1965
ROGERS, James R., 4-17-1887 4-25-1968

SPEARMAN, Nancy J., 1862-1939
SPEARMAN, Robert T., 1859-1955
WOOD, George, 7-19-1887 7-10-1947
WOOD, Velma, 3-18-1889 No Date
WOOD, Donal, 8-13-1921 5-1-1938
REYNOLDS, Nellie FERGUSON, wife of W. H., 1880-1938
REYNOLDS, William H., 1876-1955
PARSONS, Viola H., 1891-1941
HUFFSTULTER, Tracy L., III, born & died 6-8-1938
SMITH, Florence, 10-10-1874 1-20-1941
SMITH, Tom, 8-3-1868 6-11-1938
SMITH, John Roy, 12-24-1900 2-13-1967
JONES, Donnie, 3-27-1892 12-13-1974
MC DONNOLD, Vibo M., 1-12-1896 7-19-1966
MC DONNOLD, Lela, 4-18-1874 4-14-1941
MC DONNOLD, P. T., 6-26-1861 8-26-1938
MC DONNOLD, Ollie Ray, 5-25-1903 1-30-1975
BUCHANAN, Clarence Otis, 10-16-1889 10-14-1938
BUCHANAN, Vertie Viola, 4-30-1888 2-27-1958
PICKETT, Howard, 1911-1939
BRUCE, Ann REED, 12-1-1865 9-17-1943
BRUCE, Thomas Jefferson, 9-20-1861 1-7-1944
BRUCE, Bert H., 1900-1939
HORN, R. O., 10-14-1862 4-3-1943
HORN, Mrs. Laura Francis, 7-24-1877 6-23-1939
HORN, G. D. "Dub", 6-15-1903 11-30-1962
HILL, George C., 6-2-1875 9-7-1945
HILL, Jessie L., 6-20-1880 7-26-1939
HILL, Avis JOHNSON, 4-6-1913 No Date
          married 3-30-1933
HILL, William A. "Doc", 1-26-1898 4-10-1979
JOHNSON, Grace, 1-10-1905 3-24-1950
JOHNSON, Curtis J., 2-15-1900 2-23-1969
NICHELS, J. W., 1866-1940
NICHELS, Ellen, 1869-1947
HAMILTON, Wade, 8-18-1893 3-6-1976
HAMILTON, Kerdeen, 1916-1978
MC BEE, Marion R., 1-10-1923 1-21-1948
MC KINNEY, John Franklin, 9-23-1899 11-10-1940
HOLLOWELL, J. I. "Slim", 6-23-1895 3-13-1941
CREAMER, Annie L., 1867-1960
CREAMER, M. W., 1858-1941
RAGAN, Mary MILLS, 10-8-1884 11-18-1941
RAGAN, Olen Reece, 4-5-1909 11-5-1966
O'NEAL, David Alden, 1-10-1963 2-5-1963
COX, William Homer, 10-5-1900 12-11-1940
COVINGTON, Mae B., 1910-No Date
COVINGTON, Robert Frank, 1904-1974
MC WHIRTER, Mary Annie, 6-2-1877 7-25-1961
MC WHIRTER, Thomas Haynes, 3-10-1877 3-16-1946
PIERCE, Luzelle "Pete", 1907-No Date
PIERCE, Carol "Dock", 1903-1972
DUNHAM, Edith M., 1908-No Date
DUNHAM, Jules V., 1909-1968

DUNHAM, Sadie, 1888-1943
DUNHAM, John J., 1885-1955
VEAL, Ras B., 3-7-1881 2-10-1943
VEAL, Mary, 11-18-1890 3-21-1975
DRUMMOND, Marion Rat, 1-31-1943 2-3-1943
DRUMMOND, William Delvin, 4-19-1903 6-16-1970
WAGES, Sallie T., 10-26-1877 11-12-1972
WAGES, William H., 1-21-1873 10-31-1943
WAGES, Thomas C., 1-16-1902 10-6-1970
MC CLAIN, May K., 1883-1943
MC CLAIN, Torvns M., 1887-No Date
MC CLAIN, J. Melvin, 1910-1945
HENSLEY, Winnie Lee, 7-10-1891 4-11-1976
          married 8-5-1912
HENSLEY, Marion Elwood, 7-21-1890 No Date
HENSLEY, Betty Jean, dau. of Geo. & Jean, 3-9-1942 8-2-1942
JOHNSON, Nellie, 7-21-1885 1-20-1975
JOHNSON, Ben, 3-29-1880 9-25-1956
JOHNSON, Graham Madden, son of Mr. & Mrs. G. M., died 1942
FIELDS, Samuel H., Tex., Pvt., 143 Inf., 36 Div., died 10-27-1940
CASEY, Myrtle, 1894-1978
CASEY, Jessie F., 1911-1944
BRENNAN, Esther R., 6-13-1895 11-16-1977
          married 1-24-1918
BRENNAN, Charles C., 4-17-1884 8-6-1944
KILLINGSWORTH, Mary V., 11-8-1915 No Date
KILLINGSWORTH, Robert L., 3-12-1910 12-28-1973
KILLINGSWORTH, Michael, died 2-8-1945
MC CLENDON, William H., 6-13-1894 4-10-1966
BELL, Claude, 9-26-1876 2-20-1961
BELL, Lila K., 4-10-1875 12-26-1954
BELL, Claude J., Tex., S-1, U. S. Navy, W. W. I., 9-9-1898 7-16-1970
COLLEY, Vida M., 1903-1952
STEWART, William Henry, 1886-1953
STEWART, Mary Dee., 1896-1968
DAVIS, Nelle S., 1917-No Date
DAVIS, Haskell H., 1914-1971
JACKSON, Doyle, 11-9-1912 11-11-1951
BENSON, Lillie Mae, 1900-No Date
BENSON, Porter, 1884-1965
VAUGHAN, John P., 1-13-1864 6-15-1950
STEVENS, Charles J., Tex., Pvt., 3706 AAF Base Unit, W. W. II.,
          2-17-1927 3-5-1946

SECTION "1"

(Oldest Part of the Cemetery)

FIELDER, F. Annie, 1841 7-7-1909
1- Stone Unreadable
DILLARD, Ella, 6-27-1862 8-12-1913
RILEY, Mary F., dau. of F. & J. H., 4-8-1885 12-7-1896
REILLY, Peter, 6-21-1841 5-27-1896
ZIMMERMAN, Virginia GUTHRIE, 8-17-1927 5-11-1976

WHISTLER, Charles Franklin, 1-9-1929 7-24-1975
WHISTLER, Bessie Nell, 6-28-1897 No Date
WHISTLER, Frank A., 10-24-1894 10-12-1978
TOWLES, Georgia, 8-6-1892 9-17-1973
JONES, Herrman Michael, son of Mr. & Mrs. J. E. Jones, 8-3-1899 11-4-1901
BRANTLEY, Cynthia D., 8-31-1970 12-16-1978
NELSON, Gladys E., 9-11-1926 11-12-1934
MENDENHALL, Leita KNIGHT, 1895-1978
JACKSON, George Douglas, 2-12-1906 9-26-1940
ADAMS, Oscar C., 1910-1978
SPARKMAN, Myrtle Lee, 11-7-1897 2-10-1972
SPARKMAN, R. Lawrence, 8-30-1893 No Date
KNIGHT, Jefferson, 5-10-1890 12-23-1890
KNIGHT, Calvin C., 3-1-1886 5-31-1900
KNIGHT, J. T., 12-4-1840 3-29-1907
KNIGHT, Susan E., 10-4-1845 3-13-1909
KNIGHT, Larra Ellar, 9-12-1870 4-1-1948
KNIGHT, Infant Daughter, died 12-21-1893
KNIGHT, John, 9-15-1861 5-20-1959
KNIGHT, Ella Virginia, 3-29-1870 12-1-1936
KNIGHT, Howard Wayne, 3-12-1905 9-5-1964
THOMPSON, Aldo C., Tex., Pfc., Co. D., 47 Inf., W. W. I.,
                          6-20-1894 4-25-1961
THOMPSON, Ara B., 7-25-1896 No Date
1 - Funeral Marker Unreadable
PRESLEY, Larkin W., Co. D., 18th Ala. Inf., C. S. A., No Dates
PRESLEY, Lou Ella, 6-25-1850 9-27-1922
MORRISON, Anna Bell, 2-13-1878 8-13-1962
CARR, Andrew J., 1866-1955
CARR, Hettie A., 1872-1951
DILLINGHAM, Inf. Dau. & Son of J. A. & Ada,
                  Daughter, died 1898
                  Son, died 1902
SLADE, Catherine, wife of S. D., 11-17-1881 4-22-1901
HOGAN, Ruth K., 1903-1971
HOGAN, Jack P., 1894-1960
BOREN, Charlie A., 12-7-1910 11-23-1968
BOREN, Howard J., Tex. Pvt., 1911 Service Comd. Unit, W. W. II.,
                  10-25-1908 1-27-1963
GUTHRIE, Lula W., 4-14-1901 NO Date
GUTHRIE, J. Frank, 7-24-1901 12-17-1973
HOLLON, Elbert, 1893-1961
HOLLON, Bertha, 10-24-1888 1-15-1961
SLAUGHTER, Mary Lorene, 1927-1940
BALLARD, Lottie Frances, 9-30-1898 No Date
BALLARD, John William, Sr., 11-10-1884 3-9-1963
JACKSON, John T., No Dates
JACKSON, Sam H., No Dates
HUNDLEY, Lucy, dau. of C. J. & C. J., 10-25-1893 5-1-1898
HUNDLEY, C. G., 1-1-1876 9-8-1907
HUNDLEY, Dr. C. J., 6-28-1837 9-17-1913
HUNDLEY, Mrs. C. J., 12-1-1844 3-1-1921
SPEIGHT, Ada Lee BARTO, 9-17-1912 4-23-1933
GRIFFIN, Ethridge L., No Dates

GRIFFIN, "Father", No Dates
GRIFFIN, "Mother", No Dates
GRIFFIN, Jess, No Dates
MARS, Freda Glyn, dau. of W. W. & S. E., 3-28-1890 10-17-1891
SIMPSON, Mack, died 1957
SIMPSON, Mamie, died 1966
REDMON, Edna, 12-10-1908 7-13-1935
CROWDER, Laura E., wife of H. R., 9-4-1858 9-28-1892
                              married 11-22-1883
THOMAS, Earl R., Tex., Pfc., 1876 Inf., W. W. II., 3-14-1923 1-4-1961
1 - Stump
CONEY, Roy Leon, 3-12-1913 8-1-1942
1 - Stump
HOGAN, Hortense, 1888-No Date
HOGAN, Frank, 1886-1950
PELL, Edward R., son of W. T. & E. T., 5-5-1881 11-11-1899
PELL, Harry, son of W. T. & E. T., 8-4-1877 11-22-1906
PELL, Elizabeth T., 1-26-1855 10-30-1914
PELL, W. T., 1855-1924
ANTHONY, Lona Gene, 9-24-1901 10-20-1901
HARTWELL, Daisy PELL, 1883-1930
PELL, Tim W., 1879-1931
1 - Funeral Marker Unreadable
HOGAN, George P., Tex., Pvt., Co. C., 717 RY ORB, BN, TC., W. W. II
                              6-29-1913 3-25-1970
CONEY, Leon Josphus, 9-5-1870 10-2-1966
CONEY, Ida Augusta, 10-21-1874 12-12-1960
JENKINS, Canzada, 2-28-1884 2-19-1965
JENKINS, William Lee, 2-15-1880 12-6-1957
MURPHY, B. L., 1848-1928
MURPHY, Bedora, 1846-1916
COMMANDER, Bob, died 1952
COMMANDER, Martha, died 1956
BARTO, Earl, 8-21-1889 No Date
                  married 11-12-1911
BARTO, Molly D., 8-7-1896 9-6-1978
ENGLAND, Sallie, wife of C. T., 2-22-1880 9-6-1941
ENGLAND, Carlton T., 12-26-1879 10-11-1954
HUNDLEY, J. W., 11-15-1871 6-22-1913
JACKSON, Josiah Hart, 4-4-1821 3-13-1892
JACKSON, Sallie A., 9-26-1824 7-14-1887

"HISTORICAL MARKER"
"Jackson, Josiah Hart, 1821-1892, Texas Ranger. Born in Kentucky,
came to Texas 1839 and in 1850's opened Jackson's Store, 1 mile
Northeast of here. Starting "Cow Hill", a village with Race Track,
Blacksmith Shop, other Stores. He became Postmaster and Renamed
Place Ashland, 1873. But moved Post Office here to Commerce, at
City's Birth. Married Sara A. Maddox in 1841. Had 6 Children.
After Her Death married Elvira Jeringan. Recorded 1967.

EUBANKS, Lurah, 7-23-1885 12-24-1942
RUSH, Charles William, born Lincoln Co., Mo., 3-17-1844 6-12-1905
DUNN, Jerry Glenn, 1937-1978

RUSH, Charles Forrest, born Warrenton, Mo., 9-18-1874 4-30-1900
RUSH, Mrs. Lucy E., wife of C. W., 5-20-1851 2-7-1927
POSTON, Frances E., 8-30-1909 No Date
POSTON, Clyde C., 12-12-1906 10-24-1967
GANT, Edith D., 6-14-1894 12-13-1970
                    married 4-6-1915
GANT, Isaac B., 11-24-1882 12-7-1974
WEBB, Mahala Jane MC CRAW, GALES, ZUNDEL, 11-2-1859 1-16-1928
VOYLES, Nettie Lee, 11-22-1871 2-13-1960
VOYLES, Charles W., 11-5-1872 12-9-1930
BUSEY, B. F., Husband of M. C., 4-10-1827 Ky., 10-20-1893 Commerce, Texas.
WILSON, Docia, 1-26-1896 No Date
WILSON, Louis, 12-17-1899 9-26-1976
BEAVER, Ada S., 9-3-1869 12-25-1894
PRESTON, Warren T., 2-26-1878 3-5-1895
PRESTON, Mary D., 7-12-1825 11-27-1896
WHITE, Edna B., 12-20-1899 6-24-1976
ARNSPIGER, Clyde, 1896-1971
ARNSPIGER, Fay, No Dates
FARROW, John Adam, 1853-1928
FARROW, Edna Mae, 1870-1940
FARROW, Ellen, wife of J. A., 9-13-1857 9-24-1890
MC DILL, Flora, 3-27-1847 3-31-1926
MC DILL, Calvin, 6-6-1849 5-17-1926
DUNN, Jerry Glynn, 3-31-1937 8-15-1978
INGRAM, Troy Hardee, 5-18-1925 2-23-1959
FARROW, Lucy W., 2-13-1813 1-2-1902
FARROW, Dr. W. W., 11-20-1815 9-4-1890
FARROW, Joe E., 2-15-1853 5-22-1887
FARROW, Bertha, dau. of J. A. & Ellen E., 12-11-1887 5-29-1889
BANKS, Hallie B., 6-3-1892 1-7-1969
BANKS, Rufus A., 5-17-1884 3-28-1953
RAGLAND, William Fletcher, 4-5-1850 2-10-1900
RAGLAND, Nellie Myrtle, 9-19-1867 12-1-1882
RAGLAND, Mrs. W. F., 6-13-1862 12-6-1939
RAGLAND, W. F., 4-5-1850 2-10-1900
PHILLIPS, Martha F., 7-13-1825 8-4-1900
OVERSTREET, Winnie M., 1890-1927
OVERSTREET, George L., 1884-1952
MC FARLAND, Evelyn Raye, 4-18-1914 11-26-1974
MC FARLAND, A. E., Jr., 5-31-1912 No Date
MOORE, Ethel M., 12-20-1910 No Date
                    married 1-25-1940
MOORE, Aubrey L., 2-8-1916 No Date
GOFF, Claudy, son of G. W. & M., 11-19-1888 5-1-1891
MASHBURN, Fed F., Tex. Pvt., Co. C., 744 Milt. Police BN, W. W. II.,
                    4-26-1904 10-26-1957
HAIR, Sally A., wife of John V., 1890-1965
HAIR, Sadie E., wife of John V., 6-19-1879 1-14-1933
1 - Broken Stone by Large Tree
HILL, Annie Lee, 1883-1895
BOWMAN, Oma HILL, 1887-1914
HILL, R. G., 1856-1930
HILL, Mrs. R. G., 1866-1935

CLINTON, Lottie CLAXTON, 1892-1928
CLINTON, Walter A., 1889-1977
HARRINGTON, Samuel L., 1-5-1848 1-18-1897
HARRINGTON, Mary B., 6-29-1855 3-14-1912
HARRINGTON, Frances C., 12-25-1818 1-6-1905
HARRINGTON, Owen B., 12-26-1886 6-22-1921
POPE, Martha A., 6-4-1869 9-29-1950
POPE, Alen H., 3-3-1871 1-18-1929
GARRETT, Loler POPE, 7-24-1896 8-5-1933
PATTERSON, Charles S., 1880-1960
PATTERSON, Sallie MURRAH, 7-16-1853 4-29-1920
PATTERSON, George Fleming, 9-14-1834 12-19-1897
HARRINGTON, Chester A., Chief Gunners Mate, U. S. Navy,
                              12-9-1883 4-4-1933
HARRINGTON, Richard O., 12-2-1895 3-8-1978
HEDGES, Mrs. Vitula, 6-3-1889 10-19-1918
ST. CLAIR, J. Robert, 1868-1904
ST. CLAIR, Celia N., wife of J. M., 10-28-1833 No Date
ST. CLAIR, J. M., 2-22-1822 12-10-1897
HUGHES, Vernon Ray, son of Vernon & Bess, 7-5-1926 3-17-1928
MASHBURN, Nancy Ann., 1-10-1878 1-14-1964
MASHBURN, Joseph R., 2-26-1869 4-17-1943
RAGLAND, Evan L., 12-3-1816 7-14-1890
OVERALL, Barbara Ann, born & Died 4-24-1948
COVINGTON, Kate I., 6-14-1885 12-20-1916
RUTLAND, Kittie I., 6-14-1885 1-13-1904
RUTLAND, William Watson, 1851-1922
RUTLAND, Chloe Tilda, 1851-1926
RUTLAND, Virgie, dau. of W. M. & A. E., 12-30-1884 8-28-1888
ARNOLD, John Jeffery, 8-3-1963 8-4-1963
DISMUKE, A. J., 4-6-1879 7-8-1948
DISMUKE, Mrs. A. J., 8-1-1883 11-9-1928
HUNT, James, 10-10-1816 10-21-1891
HUNT, Mary Jane, wife of J. T., 3-6-1838 5-9-1891
ATKINS, D. Lee, 1908-1970
FOWLER, Jack D., 9-5-1901 11-5-1927
JONES, Sibyl L., 7-27-1898 11-8-1973
JONES, Paul C., 1-3-1891 5-1-1978
                    Co. A, 16th M.G. Balt., 6th Div., W. W. I.
JONES, Charlie, died 7-15-1893
JONES, Beulah, died 1-17-1898
JONES, Annie E., 12-7-1861 8-19-1940
JONES, Joe, 11-26-1851 6-10-1926
JONES, George D., 3-6-1853 2-10-1899
COX, Lora Belle, 1908-No Date
            married 10-2-1926
COX, C. W., 1906-1977
DAVIS, Mary Ann., 1874-1971
DAVIS, Ben M., 1871-1933
JANES, Ethel E., 1881-1979
JONES, Elizabeth CARTER, 5-23-1840 8-28-1895
FOWLER, Willis, 1875-1941
FOWLER, Fannie, 1880-1947
BRYER, Bernice WILLIAMS, 2-4-1912 No Date

married 11-15-1929
BRYER, John, 9-2-1900 6-4-1971
CURTIS, Cora Lee, 1929-1969
MATLOCK, Joe, No Dates
BRACE, Lemora, wife of F. H., 2-3-1837 8-21-1883
MILFORD, Rhode, No Dates
CAMP, Oscar, 1891-1906
CAMP, Cora DAVID, 1871-1963
CAMP, Thomas Wesley, 1861-1906
NEFF, H. Drue, 1857-1943
NEFF, Carson C., 1852-1928
DODD, Lizzie, 1910-No Date
DODD, Jim, 1890-1969
DAY, Mary Stella, 10-2-1900 No Date
DAY, Robert Byron, 11-30-1897 3-10-1973
MADDEN, John F., 8-1-1887 5-13-1905
MADDEN, Charles, 8-10-1850 3-13-1909
HOLLEY, Mary E., 7-6-1856 6-17-1945
HOLLEY, Jas. P., 6-7-1849 9-12-1927
MASHBURN, Howard L., 7-14-1911 5-21-1972
TILFORD, Calvin, son of W. R. & A. L., 8-30-1898 2-3-1899
TILFORD, Leta Mae, 11-11-1905 2-3-1925
TILFORD, Mrs. W. R., 12-22-1876 1-3-1936
TILFORD, William Reed, 9-21-1872 12-8-1942
MORELAND, Will R., 6-30-1875 10-30-1941
MORELAND, Mabel LONG, 11-19-1878 5-1-1972
NORSWORTHY, Sophia, 1-31-1882 6-6-1901
HOLLEY, Addison R., 4-6-1885 9-5-1951
HOLLEY, Mary I., 3-29-1886 10-20-1975
MILLSAP, Maud, 3-23-1879 9-2-1955
MILLSAP, Jack, 6-11-1877 10-20-1968
FERGUSON, Minnie DEVANEY, 10-26-1882 3-12-1961
DEVANEY, Jas. L., 12-2-1879 5-1-1920
DAVIS, L. H. "Cotton", 6-13-1903 10-4-1964
married 7-5-1930
DAVIS, Lois BICKLEY, 8-16-1911 No Date
TODD, James Major, Jr., died 1913
PYLE, Mary Ann, died 1934
1 - Marker No Name or Dates
BLIZZARD, Fred Ganor, 9-25-1917 4-25-1970
BLIZZARD, Allie Norma, 3-16-1919 No Date
TALLEY, Jeana Gail, died 4-11-1970
NABERS, Homer, 10-22-1897 11-20-1969
JERNIGAN, Jesse M., 1882-1926
JERNIGAN, Bertha, 1884-1888
JERNIGAN, W. A., 11-14-1847 3-19-1889
JERNIGAN, John Felix, 1856-1927
JERNIGAN, Emaline S., 1858-1934
REEDER, Sarah, 1834-1889
MILLS, Alpha, 1864-1893
ROGERS, Robert W., 1-13-1866 3-24-1926
ROGERS, Annie E., 12-18-1872 8-6-1949
JAGGAR, James Douglass, 8-12-1862 2-19-1892
WEATHERBEE, Nadine, 1920-1964

WEATHERBEE, Ellis, 1924-1962
CULVER, Jacob N., 8-2-1849 1-30-1900
RECTOR, J. Henry, 7-22-1858 5-27-1907
RECTOR, Louisa Ann, 12-22-1859 5-29-1945
RECTOR, C. Jack, 11-30-1885 3-24-1898
RECTOR, William Albert, 8-17-1883 11-1-1926
MYERS, Rena J., 11-26-1912 No Date
                    married 9-16-1930
MYERS, Dennis E., 4-15-1912 6-24-1977
COX, Etta May, 8-15-1900 11-5-1900
HUTCHERSON, Tollie W., 11-15-1876 10-22-1946
SHOEMAKE, Maud HUTCHERSON, 1890-1950
SHOEMAKE, Howard L., 1885-1958
SPEIGHT, Kim Elaine, 12-1-1959 4-24-1960
DE HOYOS, Reyes Longoria, 7-5-1924 9-15-1963
MC ALISTER, Carrie ROGERS, 6-8-1892 5-9-1931
MALONEY, George Leslie, 10-12-1863 1-20-1895
JERNIGAN, Marie, 4-20-1904 No Date
JERNIGAN, Joe, Tex., Pvt., 1st. Casual Co., W. W. I.,
                    2-27-1895 4-28-1960
SCOTT, Effie THOMAS, 6-22-1893 3-29-1969
SCOTT, Oliver M., 8-19-1889 4-12-1976
JERNIGAN, Robert, 1886-1960
JERNIGAN, James H., 1889-1941
NEAL, Elizabeth C., (Dates Unreadable, Broken Stone)
THOMPSON, Verdell, 4-18-1911 3-7-1978
DUNN, J. Florence, 1880-1965
DUNN, W. Anderson, 1872-1942
HALL, Lou, wife of Lee H., 1-7-1842 5-23-1891
HACKNEY, Walter L., 1869-1926
HACKNEY, Cordie, 1881-1959
CHANEY, E. Frank, 1894-1979
CHANEY, Frances KNIGHT, 1902-1979
CHANEY, Frank Knight, 1st. Lt., U. S. Army, W. W. II., 1922-1977
SHIPMAN, Eunice, wife of V. E., 1896-1927
FOSTER, Alvia ALEXANDER, 12-30-1895 8-16-1970
MURRAY, Dewey, son of A. P. & Lizzie, 4-13-1898 9-24-1899
RECTOR, Clarance, died 1912
RECTOR, Oneda, 1910-1915
RECTOR, Jack, Jr., 1916-1923
BARNETT, William N., 1856-1929
BARNETT, Cynthia E., 1871-1954
MYERS, Della M., 8-24-1893 No Date
MYERS, Ivor D., 3-4-1890 7-25-1960
ELLINGTON, Kate THORNTON, 8-6-1885 2-20-1909
THORNTON, Guy, son of L. B. & N. P., 1-9-1900 8-19-1900
THORNTON, Eva, dau. of L. B. & N. P., 2-6-1891 10-1-1900
THORNTON, Nancy Paralee, wife of L. B., 9-20-1858 4-2-1901
THORNTON, Mamie May, dau. of L. B. & N. P., 10-6-1894 8-8-1895
THORNTON, Dewey, son of L. B. & N. P., 7-18-1898 8-4-1909
HINES, B. F. "Frank", 3-4-1906 8-8-1973
                    married 2-24-1939
HINES, Daisy Jane, 4-16-1914 No Date
PINGLETON, Lillie, 8-11-1896 8-5-1972

PINGLETON, Luther, 4-2-1887 9-19-1967
MULLINS, Viola DUNN, 1899-No Date
MULLINS, Ollie Norman, 1886-1968

SECTION "2"

SAYLE, Bettie, 1-24-1873 10-29-1917
SAYLE, Stella A., 5-25-1887 10-5-1888
SAYLE, Durward A., 2-15-1892 2-22-1895
SAYLE, Mary A., 11-25-1851 3-27-1912
SAYLE, William E., 1842-1924
WILLIAMS, James, 4-14-1862 5-18-1889
SPANN, Polly, 9-2-1867 3-5-1960
SPANN, Tessie L., dau. of W. W. & Polly, 7-22-1904 10-17-1926
KNIGHT, Thomas L., 1865-1952
KNIGHT, Viola E., 1870-1940
KNIGHT, Annie Lee, dau. of T. L. & V. E., 12-7-1899 5-18-1901
KNIGHT, Ima May, dau. of T. L. & V. E., 5-7-1898 5-27-1899
1 - Stone Unreadable
FALLS, Eva Faye, 1910-No Date
FALLS, William T., 1910-1971
HANEY, Corpl. Newton, Co. H., 8th. Tenn. Inf., C. S. A., No Dates
CANNON, Lelia A., wife of Lee, 1882-1940
HILL, Walter S., 1871-1926
BOND, Ada HILL, 1883-1967
BOND, J. William, 1882-1947
SAYLE, Robert Adams, 1909-No Date
MATTHEWS, Sam L., 2-19-1879 9-27-1970
MATTHEWS, Mae E., 4-10-1883 5-29-1965
MATTHEWS, Buster, 9-1-1905 No Date
WHITE, Minnie HYMAN, 12-5-1901 No Date
ADAMS, Ella, 5-28-1859 11-19-1898
ADAMS, Isam L., 4-13-1851 6-3-1933
JOHNSTON, James E., Pfc., U. S. Army, W. W. II., 9-18-1927 11-27-1971
NEWLAND, Pearl, 1904-1977
NEWLAND, Willis G., 1902-No Date
TAYLOR, G. W., 1868-1949
TAYLOR, James M., 3-4-1862 6-29-1939
TAYLOR, Lula, 11-29-1868 3-29-1957
1 - Funeral Marker
WILBURN, Mary E., 1880-1977
ADAIR, Melvin Jodie, 1935-1979
SMITH, Claudine, 2-22-1932 3-22-1976
HARDEMON, Rev. Eddie, 1902-1972
ROBERTS, David, 1910-1973
THOMAS, Olga May, 1898-1900
JOBE, Earl, 7-18-1906 4-20-1929
WITCHER, Monroe L., 1875-1936
WITCHER, Sarah Jane, 1874-1942
POMMERENING, Johnnie J., 1885-1974
POMMERENING, R. A. A., "Pom", 1883-1961
CARMACK, James R., 6-30-1884 4-6-1900
                    Buried at Bristol, Tenn.
ACKER, George W., 1884-1905

ACKER, William G., 1871-1895
ACKER, Will Hile, Tex. Pvt., STV., U. S. Army, TNG Corps, W. W. I.,
                          12-17-1899 7-28-1951
ACKER, Pearl, 1876-1968
ACKER, Walter, 1874-1920
ACKER, Sarah A., 1852-1934
ACKER, G. W., 1846-1926
MALONEY, Mylie A., 1878-1973
MALONEY, Edgar E., 1870-1934
SURRATT, Clarance E., 9-29-1907 11-22-1964
SURRATT, Nora Etta, 2-1-1870 11-24-1947
SURRATT, J. W., 12-6-1859 3-9-1944
SURRATT, Winnie, 9-21-1881 11-19-1891
HELTON, Gladys, 12-31-1901 7-26-1928
MYERS, Isaac, Tex., Pvt., 127 Field Artillery, W. W. I.,
                          7-19-1893 10-19-1960
MYERS, Dove, 1895-1954
BLEDSOE, Lontis M., 1905-1926
BLEDSOE, Vera, 1884-1975
BLEDSOE, James H., 1881-1951
JERNIGAN, Cordlia, 1851-1936
JERNIGAN, J. H., 1840-1906
ANDERS, Lucy M., 1889-1963
ANDERS, Naaman C., 1884-1958
ANDERS, Mrs. J. H., 5-5-1845 7-8-1932
ANDERS, J. B., White's Co., Giddings Bn., Tex. Cav., C. S. A.,
                          5-15-1848 3-27-1916
ANDERS, Sarah, wife of David, born in Benton Co., Tenn., 11-29-1816
                          6-16-1891 aged 74 yrs. 6 mos. 18 days
ANDERS, David, 1-18-1814 1-7-1890
LONG, M. V., died 7-5-1897 aged 57 yrs.
LONG, Mary E., wife of M. V., 2-24-1830 9-14-1881
NEWMAN, Jacob, 1848-1909
NEWMAN, Mattie A., 1852-1899
NEWMAN, John R., 1887-1889
NEWMAN, Sadie A., 1889-1891
NEWMAN, Lena Mertice, 1891-1909
NEWMAN, Bulah Edna, 1885-1912
NEWMAN, Nancy M. WORK, 1878-1942
CHAPMAN, Fannie A., 1930-1965
CHAPMAN, John F., 1877-1927
RIDDLES, Mrs. T. A., 4-2-1877 No Date
RIDDLES, T. A., 9-11-1870 2-9-1929
RIDDLES, Lydia J., 3-8-1886 3-26-1944
RIDDLES, Bob, 6-13-1901 No Date
WAGGONER, Daniel N., 1841-1931
WAGGONER, Ann C., 1843-1934
WAGGONER, Clifford R., 1881-1898
PRITCHARD, Andrew J., 1857-1935
PRITCHARD, Ollie, wife of A. J., 6-6-1866 12-18-1909
PRITCHARD, Andrew J., son of A. J. & O. A., 12-5-1890 4-20-1911
BRYANT, John N., 3-14-1879 12-12-1927
BRYANT, Hattie Mae "Dollie", 4-20-1879 10-22-1968
CROW, Audrey D., dau. of M. L. & R. L., 10-4-1908 4-9-1911

KYLE, Florence A., wife of J. B., 5-28-1867   9-4-1899
KYLE, Leon, son of J. B. & Florence, 4-14-1889   10-4-1890
APPERSON, Willie F., son of W. F. & M. M., 11-11-1893   1-5-1901
APPERSON, Martha M., 1871-1959
APPERSON, Will F., 1866-1942
APPERSON, Dorothy, 2-3-1918   9-27-1918
BRIGHAM, Bertha Mae, 1914-1978
ROBINSON, Sallie, 1875-1979
JOHNSON, Bedie, 1922-1978
CARRETT, W. L., son of F. L. & M. J., 12-13-1882   7-23-1902
CARRETT, R. E., dau. of F. L. & M. J., 12-26-1884   1-1-1904
BROOKS, E. Amanda, wife of J. L., 4-5-1847   5-23-1900
PATRICK, Miles G., 1859-1953
JAMES, J. Middleton, 1848-1929
JAMES, Eliza J., 1853-1930
BROOKS, Thurman, 1893-1898
BROOKS, Mary Frances, 1873-1907
BROOKS, Daniel D., 1874-1907
MAYO, William Leonidas, Jr., son of W. L. & Etta BOOTH MAYO, died 3-1901
MAYO, Etta BOOTH, wife of W. L., 12-20-1869   9-4-1918
MAYO, Douglas, dau. of W. L. & Etta BOOTH MAYO, 2-1895   8-26-1902
MAYO, Booth, son of W. L. & Etta, 12-9-1896   8-6-1898
ROREX, Ola GREGORY, born in Shelbyville, Tenn., 4-16-1869   9-11-1954
MARSHALL, Earl Patterson, 1896-1897
MARSHALL, Freda Mae, 1909-1910
MARSHALL, Paralee B., 1846-1894
MARSHALL, Bama, 1873-1938
MARSHALL, O. P., 1869-1953
JOHNSON, Jeff, 1868-1934
JOHNSON, Lura, 1870-1925
POWELL, Mittie E., 10-17-1805   8-22-1901
ROGERS, W. K., 1-4-1831   2-27-1906
ROGERS, Amanda, 4-9-1840   12-29-1899
HARRIS, Dovie J., dau. of C. W. & L. E., Dates Unreadable
WRIGHT, James M., 10-17-1916   6-27-1973
WRIGHT, Emma Clyde, 3-29-1890   7-17-1956
WRIGHT, Jim M., 11-10-1883   11-27-1960
KEMP, Frances WHITFIELD, 1861-1893
ANGLIN, Eula, dau. of G. M. & S. L., 5-31-1889   8-6-1890
KETNER, Fay Maxine, 1-26-1934   7-11-1973
          married 9-24-1949
KETNER, E. E. "Pee Wee", 4-17-1929   No Date
KETNER, Bernia, 11-10-1897   8-23-1960
          married 10-2-1920
KETNER, Joe O., 9-3-1903   4-27-1973
APPERSON, F. Lee, 1898-1900
APPERSON, Geo. W., 1856-1931
APPERSON, Martha E., 1862-1918
APPERSON, Paul, 1894-1894
APPERSON, Buris H., 1886-1967
APPERSON, Carl C., 1885-1947
BYARS, Thelma, 3-8-1930   9-10-1934
HORTON, Robert E., 1851-1936
HORTON, Henrietta E., 1863-1950

APPERSON, Carl Cleveland, Jr., 12-3-1908 7-4-1977
APPERSON, Faynell KILGORE, 7-26-1915 No Date
SPITLER, Alven, 9-17-1900 8-5-1976
SPITLER, Pauline, 1-16-1904 No Date
RAZNIAK, Stephen, 10-27-1906 3-14-1977
RAZNIAK, Sophie M., 9-27-1907 9-2-1972
MC COOL, Frank A., Sgt., U. S. Army, W. W. II., 1919-1977
HAMM, Allean, 1910-1972
HAMM, W. G., 1909-1979
MC COOL, Pearl P., 1920-No Date
MC COOL, Frank A., 1919-1977
ELHUFF, George H., (Teacher at East Texas Normal College), 8-17-1874
              12-22-1898; Original Stone Erected by His Students,
              Fellow Teachers and Friends
BOOTH, H. C., 8-16-1836 4-9-1923
BOOTH, Fannie D., 8-12-1835 2-15-1910
WHITFIELD, Addie, wife of W. H., 3-11-1860 12-5-1899
WHITFIELD, W. H., 1859-1930
STAPP, J. HUgh, 4-30-1885 11-4-1918
2 - Funeral Markers Unreadable
HARWELL, Wash., 1870-1947
HARWELL, Laura A., wife of G. W., 3-6-1868 7-10-1901
1 - Funeral Marker Unreadable
HICKERSON, James T., 12-23-1859 8-26-1943
HICKERSON, Mary E., 11-25-1867 2-28-1925
HICKERSON, Horace H., 2-21-1887 8-16-1900
ROWE, Lera, wife of Odis, 1-26-1905 7-19-1941
ROWE, Odis Ennis, BKR-2, U. S. Navy, W. W. II., 1910-1976
HEVRON, Emma, 1865-1957
HEVRON, J. W., 1858-1944
HAWLEY, B. F., Sr., 1852-1916
BULLS, Myrtle H., 1-1-1889 1-14-1956
BULLS, Demps J., 11-3-1873 7-22-1957
POWELL, Laura Etta, 1874-1959
POWELL, John Wesley, 1871-1961
PENN, Robert, 1919-1929
MC COMBS, Gertrude, wife of Quitman, 1-19-1896 No Date
MC COMBS, Quitman, 7-22-1895 12-10-1927
YOUNG, Gwen, 1893-1974
YOUNG, Frank L., 1891-1974
HODGEMAN, _____, 1891-1962
SHERWIN, Christopher, 1st. Lt., Co. A., 3rd. Tenn. Cav., C. S. A., No Dates
NEAL, Mary Ella, dau. of J. T. & M. J., 9-1-1875 10-8-1895
NEAL, Mary J., 8-27-1835 5-11-1908
NEAL, John T., husband of Mary J., 5-12-1823 9-12-1898
NEAL, Gladys, 9-1-1880 4-30-1957
NEAL, Robert H., 4-21-1881 7-9-1949
BISHOP, Myrtle Louise, 6-3-1879 11-22-1950
BISHOP, A. L., 7-7-1877 11-1-1929
MC COMBS, Aunt Frue, 4-21-1891 8-5-1972
MC COMBS, Molly H., 4-5-1858 2-10-1941
MC COMBS, John L., 4-1-1857 6-21-1928
RUTLAND, Leon W., Tex., 2nd. Lt., U. S. Army, W. W. I.,
                          4-13-1895 3-17-1974

RUTLAND, Lula MALONEY, 9-29-1872 3-5-1954
RUTLAND, Lawrence W., 10-11-1867 1-12-1955
RUTLAND, Donette, died 3-27-1941
BRECHEEN, Ava Lee, 1889-No Date
BRECHEEN, J. Cameron, 1887-1965
BRECHEEN, John C., Tex., S. Sgt., U. S. Army, W. W. II.,
                    7-22-1917 1-13-1974
CREDILLE, Willie A., wife of Dr. H. P., 8-18-1861 3-8-1895
CREDILLE, Dr. H. P., 1848-1910
CREDILLE, A. B., 1852-1920
BAILEY, Dr. H. L., 7-29-1872 6-3-1899
WALKER, James F., 1-15-1864 9-27-1948
WALKER, Addie Lou, 11-15-1870 6-29-1967
WALKER, F. W., 9-9-1901 9-13-1939
WALKER, J. F., Jr., 12-12-1892 12-23-1937
DE JERNETT, W. B., 3-30-1859 1-31-1942
DE JERNETT, Kathryne, 11-29-1900 3-16-1977
DE JERNETT, Lee Lindsey, 11-25-1868 12-2-1950
DE JERNETT, Alice Agnes, 10-28-1896 3-13-1898
DE JERNETT, Rene'e, 3-10-1929 5-25-1970
DE JERNETT, Brodie E., 6-2-1902 5-7-1932
DE JERNETT, Eugene L., Sgt., 4th Co., 3rd. Regt. A.S.M., 8-7-1891 10-19-1918,
                A Volunteer in France, he died for his Country.
DE JERNETT, Warren Eugene, 11-30-1925 5-27-1929
DE JERNETT, Marion R., Tex., S-2, U. S. Navy, W. W. I., 9-24-1898 11-18-1956
WHEATLEY, Martin Jewell, 2-7-1896 7-30-1898
WHEATLEY, Mary Peart, 6-15-1897 7-30-1898
WHEATLEY, Thelma Adell, 6-24-1907 8-10-1922
WHEATLEY, Dee, 6-24-1867 11-1-1939
WHEATLEY, Lou, 10-21-1875 5-10-1948
JACKSON, James Cullen, 3-24-1899 11-16-1961
MC DANIEL, Mary Louise, 1918-1918
WHEATLEY, Robert Eugene, 3-28-1930 4-16-1930
WHEATLEY, Dee, Jr., 1-21-1904 2-5-1951
GREEN, Maggie L., dau. of G. C. & A. A., 8-26-1899 10-9-1900
GREEN, John C., husband of Addie A., 11-8-1868 12-21-1902
MC CLELLAND, Edward Monroe, 7-23-1874 6-16-1941
MC CLELLAND, Mary Leatha, 6-20-1877 6-13-1943
RIDDLE, Claude, 8-11-1899 11-11-1965
MC ALISTER, Edward, 9-12-1890 4-18-1971
MC ALISTER, Chloe, 2-8-1893 12-6-1973
ELKINS, Harriet R., 1905-1963
ELKINS, John Marion, Pvt., U. S. Army, W. W. I., 1898-1976
ENGLAND, Robert L., 1871-1951
ENGLAND, Jessie A., 1878-1954
CONNER, Sarah Elizabeth, 1883-1943
CONNER, Edward Neal, 1872-1957
BROWN, Leona, 1913-1940
BARNES, Mollie J., 1880-1923
APPERSON, Roy, No Dates
APPERSON, Violet, No Dates
MC DANIEL, James Madison, 1892-1963
LINDSEY, Alice A., 9-15-1843 2-23-1929
LINDSEY, Capt. George, 3-25-1844 1-19-1923

GOBER, Cpl. Arvle G., RA25925410, Co. B., 23rd. Inf. Regt., 2nd. Div.,
11-6-1932 9-23-1951
RUSH, Lydia, 2-10-1891 No Date
RUSH, James A., 4-4-1884 7-21-1960
RAY, W. H., 1841-1923
RAY, Martha Jane, 1842-1911
RAMARO, Margaret D., 1904-1957
DEBENPORT, Allie MARTIN, 1869-1945
DEBENPORT, C. J., 1864-1949

SECTION "2" PU

HARLOW, William C., 10-24-1874 2-2-1944
HARLOW, Maude S., 11-3-1877 8-1-1960
GAITHER, Joseph Elmer, 2-18-1891 11-11-1970
GAITHER, Maurine HARLOW, 1-3-1907 3-30-1974
MALONEY, Percy W., 3-20-1877 7-29-1944
MALONEY, Minnie T., 8-24-1886 4-15-1956
MARTIN, J. J., 6-5-1878 2-26-1944
MARTIN, Florence E., 7-27-1886 4-4-1968
MARTIN, James Frank, Inf. son of Maurice & Jane, 5-25-1951 5-29-1951
MARTIN, Harold Ray, 1st. Sgt., U. S. Army, W. W. II., 9-23-1919 2-10-1978
MARTIN, Edith L., 2-21-1896 1-16-1972
MARTIN, J. O., 3-23-1892 8-13-1945
OLD, Montie Jay, 11-5-1958 4-9-1977
OLD, Harlon J., 4-30-1933 1-13-1973
1 - Marble Stump
HAMMONDS, Sara Ellen, 1880-1945
MILLICAN, Homer C., 1899-1971
MILLICAN, Laura L., No Dates
LONG, No Name or Dates
NEWTON, Daniel M., Tex. Pfc., Co. H., 21 Engrs., W. W. I,
8-9-1893 4-29-1965
NEWTON, Jessie Mae, 8-3-1898 No Date
LONG, Harry G., 4-28-1887 12-21-1947
SHUMATE, Cora, No Dates
SHUMATE, Roy, 6-1-1891 5-29-1946
RICHARDSON, Ernest Ligon, 2-4-1880 5-16-1959
RICHARDSON, Eula GOROUTTE, 3-28-1887 3-19-1968
BROWNING, James A., 9-6-1864 2-6-1949
HOLLEY, Willie O., 12-5-1880 10-8-1961
HOLLEY, John H., 2-12-1878 8-27-1959
KIBLER, Cleo A., 1901-No Date
KIBLER, George, 1898-1977
HOLLEY, Mavis Dean, 1920-1946
CONNER, Toledo D., 3-22-1901 4-24-1949
CONNER, Ida E., 9-7-1869 5-24-1957
HOBBS, Lema J., 1881-1945
HOBBS, Elizabeth, 1886-1955
BLACKBURN, William L., 3-4-1908 10-11-1944
BOYDSTON, R. F., 1898-1965
1 - Marble Marker
LAFFERTY, Thomas O., 1884-1968
LAFFERTY, Tennie E., 1891-1944

MOLDER, Thomas J., 1-11-1897 6-6-1966
MOLDER, Jessie R., 1-26-1903 7-10-1976
LAFFERTY, Emma F., 1-31-1890 7-23-1965
ROGERS, John Lee, 9-28-1884 3-27-1943
ROGERS, Mildred M., 8-12-1883 2-17-1953
POPE, L. Hubert, 7-25-1909 4-16-1944
POPE, Luther C., 4-22-1880 3-14-1955
POPE, Martha A., 12-18-1891 2-23-1960
ADAIR, Bloomer C., 7-10-1904 1-18-1969
ADAIR, Ollie L., 7-19-1902 No Date
FLEETWOOD, John D., 1876-1953
FLEETWOOD, Elizabeth L., 1879-1961
STONE, William Bradly, 8-17-1881 1-7-1943
STONE, Catherine WRIGHT, 4-17-1865 3-17-1958
STONE, Lester Monroe, 12-28-1884 5-26-1977
STONE, Leafy Lee Clifton, 8-23-1899 12-2-1934
MORAN, James E., 3-7-1877 10-10-1960
MORAN, Karrie L., 9-30-1883 9-10-1979
PRESLEY, Barney F., 1874-1956
HARRINGTON, Roy, 10-22-1881 9-9-1971
HARRINGTON, Lela, 11-4-1892 11-6-1974
PRATT, Robert V., 1854-1950
PRATT, Melvina, 1857-1942
PRESLEY, William H., Tex. Pvt., 143 Inf., 36 Div., died 12-26-1941
O'NEAL, Emmett M., 1905-1963
MEFFER, J. O., Sr., 1885-1970
MEFFER, Paulia, 1886-1940
MEFFER, J. O., Jr., 1923-1977
SAYLE, Dr. W. A., 12-17-1904 3-2-1944
SAYLE, Dorothy, 3-10-1906 10-11-1974
SAYLE, Dr. Upton, 3-4-1910 6-11-1941
SAYLE, Ethel G., 3-29-1888 2-18-1954
SAYLE, George E., 8-10-1885 8-31-1961
GILES, Virgil, 3-3-1884 12-17-1888
GILES, Barney, 10-24-1890 10-31-1890
GILES, Mollie, 12-25-1900 1-21-1973
GILES, Upton J., 1-11-1898 4-26-1949
GILES, Agnes, 5-17-1860 11-12-1935
GILES, W. S., 1-21-1851 6-7-1930
CAMPBELL, Leota G., 7-9-1881 6-30-1958
CAMPBELL, Frank R., 4-4-1879 2-16-1963
PATMAN, Charles H., 1871-1944
PATMAN, Lula, 1876-1957
CLARK, James Ray L., 2-4-1907 6-1-1957
MILLER, Floyde E., 1896-1971
MILLER, Jewell M., 1899-No Date
MILLER, Otray Allenby, 11-15-1918 5-11-1927
MOODY, Mitchell T., 8-7-1861 10-12-1948
MOODY, Martha E., 9-13-1868 3-17-1933
MOODY, J. R., 7-3-1893 4-8-1966
RAINEY, Edna E., 1896-1948
WILKENS, William David, 5-1-1893 4-30-1961
WILKENS, Golda Fannie, 12-8-1896 1-10-1978
WILKENS, Lloyd Don, 7-25-1939 3-7-1947

CARTER, Othello T., 1882-1948
HICKY, Ernest L., 9-10-1875 10-4-1947
TURLEY, Arthur, 10-24-1880 1-20-1952
TURLEY, Minnie J., 2-24-1878 6-27-1947
1 - Marble Stone Unreadable
WILLIAMS, B. H., 8-5-1882 6-23-1947
WILLIAMS, Maude D., 7-2-1883 9-26-1972
SHEELY, Forrest T., 3-2-1910 11-7-1953
WILLIAMS, Charles, 12-31-1899 9-22-1952
MULLER, Chester J., 1-6-1882 11-26-1946
MULLER, Lora B., 11-12-1884 10-29-1959
LINDLEY, Eugene, 3-7-1872 10-6-1964
SLAVEN, Charlie M., 12-19-1886 9-13-1951
RAYNES, William T., Tex., Flight Officer, AAF., 12-25-1920 1-19-1945
MC MINN, Fred Gordon, 8-3-1886 8-23-1956
MC MINN, Katherine Irene, 8-14-1895 5-7-1978
CRUMP, Etta, 1869-1944
JOHNSON, D. B., 1872-1953
JOHNSON, Harriett V., 1877-1949
WHEELER, Dan W., 1870-1950
WHEELER, Mary V., 1874-1952
MC MILLAN, Bonnice W., 1903-1969
MC MILLAN, Bryan, 1896-1972
SHEELY, F. N., 3-14-1879 3-5-1940
SHEELY, Elza D., 1-5-1885 8-8-1971

SECTION "3" PU

BICKLY, Charles B., 7-24-1912 7-23-1939
BICKLY, Jack C., 12-3-1910 2-5-1959
BICKLY, Gussie, 1-17-1881 5-30-1967
BICKLY, Harold K., 9-12-1907 5-4-1974
ARNOLD, J. A., 8-14-1907 12-21-1951
ARNOLD, William Haskell, 11-29-1908 9-17-1942
ARNOLD, I. Modie, 9-1-1878 3-14-1949
ARNOLD, Ora, 2-13-1885 2-9-1970
RILEY, W. A., Sr., 3-24-1882 9-23-1959
RILEY, Ens. W. A., Jr., 2-3-1920 8-25-1942
RILEY, V. V., 6-6-1907 3-4-1971
MC CRARY, James W., Tex., Capt., U.S.A.F.R., W. W. II., 4-21-1893 10-30-1972
MC CRARY, John Easton, 1st. Lt., U.S.M.C.R., BA, MS, 3-16-1910 11-27-1943
CAMPBELL, Della SEARS, 3-25-1877 10-31-1972
TURRENTINE, M. J., 1884-1970
TURRENTINE, Ethel, 1891-1968
ASHWORTH, Wheeler, 1901-1978
ASHWORTH, Gertrude, 1905-1969
ETHRIDGE, Odell STAFFORD, 1892-1978
ETHRIDGE, Annanias Grant, 1894-1954
GOSSETT, Ida LIVINGSTON, 1870-1951
GOSSETT, Mrs. Elsie Louise, 1903-1946
HEATH, Michael Patrick, 6-11-1971 6-28-1971
HAMMOND, C. B., 6-20-1888 4-23-1947
HAMMOND, Ruby B., 3-12-1890 3-14-1966
LANCASTER, Jamie Ann, 3-14-1947 3-24-1947

PEEK, William T., 11-11-1873 6-11-1957
PEEK, Clara, 6-11-1881 10-31-1960
LANGLEY, Norma June, 6-27-1936 7-10-1936
LANGLEY, Ernest Leon, 6-1-1931 6-3-1931
HAMMONDS, Robert W., Tex. S-Sgt., 3rd. Div., W. W. II.,
                                10-19-1923 4-15-1944
HAMMONDS, Robert, 12-23-1900 No Date
HAMMONDS, Ruby, 3-11-1904 6-12-1970
MITCHELL, Lucy M., 3-10-1901 No Date
MITCHELL, Hugh B., 1-3-1885 1-5-1964
CALHOUN, Joe N., 4-28-1898 9-25-1963
CALHOUN, Christine L., 9-5-1917 No Date
DEONIER, Carl A., 1891-No Date
DEONIER, Bertha E., 1892-1964
FERGUSON, James A., 1865-1949
FERGUSON, Dovie A., 1873-1958
NASH, Walter C., 1896-1964
NASH, Lola Pearl, 1898-No Date
STRINGER, No Name or Dates
MELBO, Winnie, 1910-1949
ALEXANDER, Myrtle, 3-1-1895 8-4-1975
ALEXANDER, Carrie T., Tex., Pfc., Gaines Regt. SVC, W. W. I.,
                                5-17-1891 7-2-1970
NASH, Walter Clifton, Tex., HA-1, U. S. Navy, W. W. I.,
                                9-15-1897 3-25-1964
MC DOWELL, Della H., 1881-1971
MC DOWELL, W. Clyde, 1881-1948
HOLLON, Dan B., 8-21-1898 12-24-1965
WEBB, Daisy, 10-11-1904 4-1-1948
BARRETT, Debbie G., No Dates
HUFFMAN, Ocie May, 3-16-1886 9-4-1963
GIST, Fred, 1892-1947
GIST, Elsie, 1894-1949
MULLINS, George, 11-12-1888 10-23-1957
MULLINS, Ellie, 6-30-1897 5-12-1970
JOHNSON, W. H., 7-5-1873 6-20-1948
JOHNSON, Delanio, 7-7-1875 10-23-1967
BROWNE, John W., 1894-1959
BROWNE, Ibah Lee, 1896-No Date
MULLINS, Gerald D., Sgt., W. W. II, 10-24-1917 10-10-1944
MATHERLY, James V., 2-19-1902 11-12-1947
PEEK, Adolphus, died 11-21-1978
MILFORD, Tula, 1895-1973
MILFORD, Annie L., 1869-1948
CLAYTON, J. D., 7-9-1911 11-9-1968
CLAYTON, Thelma A., 12-10-1911 No Date
KETRON, Clara B., 12-17-1927 2-4-1965
BULLARD, James A., 1906-No Date
BULLARD, Lois A., 1912-No Date
BULLARD, Mary E., 2-9-1947 2-24-1947
WINTON, Martha Sue, 8-30-1934 8-30-1946
NICHOLSON, Frank M., 1880-1954
NICHOLSON, Lector A., 1878-1946
TAYLOR, No Name or Dates (Funeral Marker)

MC ANN, Janice, 1-9-1929 11-25-1945
BONHAM, Charles A., 4-21-1876 11-10-1958
BONHAM, Sallie, 11-14-1878 2-4-1969
COBB, James O., 11-8-1871 11-9-1959
COBB, Annie E., 8-4-1877 11-14-1955
PRATT, Stephen W., 8-17-1877 7-28-1946
PRATT, Birdie, 9-9-1881 11-17-1966
JUMPER, Clint C., 1913-No Date
JUMPER, Ollie C., 1911-No Date
LANDERS, Virginia C., 7-18-1911 7-4-1973
LANDERS, Larkin B., 1-22-1911 No Date
PRATT, Marie, 2-2-1905 5-17-1967
ECHART, Lee Herbert, 5-14-1902 1-10-1969
GOODWIN, John L., 1880-1957
GOODWIN, Clota, 1885-1974
ECHART, Thomas A., 1874-1946
ECHART, Virginia E., 1880-1963
STUBBLEFIELD, Susan, 12-19-1945 12-20-1945
YARBROUGH, Fannie F., 9-25-1888 5-6-1972
ROBERTSON, Verbal COWEN, 1904-1945
RUSHING, Charles "Bill", 9-25-1906 3-1-1979
RUSHING, Audrey Faye, 2-6-1910 No Date
HILLIARD, Walter A., 1871-1945
HILLIARD, Mattie L., 1879-1964
RUSHING, J. W., 1868-1945
RUSHING, Mattie T., 1874-1959
YOUNG, Edith, 9-28-1913 2-22-1944
SMITH, Charles M., 12-1-1876 12-5-1968
SMITH, Lucy P., 4-3-1880 7-3-1947
SHUMATE, Clyde, 1923-1945
SHUMATE, Willie Mary, 1881-1959
SHUMATE, Rubert Walter, 1872-1962
OPPEL, John E., 1874-1912
OPPEL, Frederick J., 1862-1943
MILLER, Maggie B., 1880-1944
MILLER, Eli T., 1875-1956
FISHER, Lawrence W., 1938-1944
RAYNES, Daisy, 1878-1959
RAYNES, William, 1869-1952
OPPEL, Betty, 12-29-1893 10-27-1975
OPPEL, Lizzie, 4-6-1900 No Date
WINTON, Varney, 1891-1939
WINTON, Mamie, 1892-1962
MC ALLISTER, Blake, 1898-1945
MC ALLISTER, Ruth, 1898-1940
WATSON, Jerry Sue, 9-4-1933 1-16-1943
WATSON, Jerline R., 11-8-1897 4-3-1960
WATSON, E. H., 8-16-1887 9-16-1960
BERRY, Christopher M., 1884-1941
BERRY, Irene, 1888-1965
GEORGE, W. M., 1-11-1871 3-12-1953
GEORGE, Emma, 1876-1978
BROWN, Fithian J., 1881-1958
BROWN, P. Dell, 1884-1967

DILLINGHAM, Dick D., 1883-1963
BARSON, H. J., 12-19-1872 3-25-1942
BARSON, Helen MC COOL, 7-12-1877 4-10-1965
PATTERSON, H. M., 8-26-1885 9-4-1955
PATTERSON, Lera, 1-14-1940 No Date
MITCHELL, Margaret, 1918-1924
JUNIGER, Flora K., No Dates
JUNIGER, Margaret M., No Dates
HUNDLEY, William M., No Dates
HUNDLEY, Olma RAY, No Dates
HOLDERNESS, Mary Ellen, 1870-1951
HOLDERNESS, Lt. J. Russell, 1894-1941
HOLDERNESS, Dr. G. W., 1862-1945
PHILLIPS, Vee, 1905-1939

SECTION "3" PU

NELSON, Faunda F., 8-10-1924 No Date
BLALOCK, Joseph Ewell, Tex., Cook., 50 Field Arty., 17 Div., W. W. I.,
                                7-8-1888 10-26-1946
BLALOCK, Clara Belle, 9-9-1890 7-31-1970
1 - Metal Marker No Name or Dates
SWEARINGIN, Lucy, 3-2-1904 8-20-1964
SWEARINGIN, Alice M., 11-1-1876 9-11-1970
SWEARINGIN, B. Lee., 10-14-1872 2-8-1949
ROAN, Charlie F., 3-15-1870 12-11-1953
ROAN, Maggie A., 3-30-1876 8-30-1953
CAMERON, Oscar, 7-31-1890 11-1-1974
CAMERON, Ruth, 11-19-1892 No Date   Married 8-3-1913
POE, James M., 2-20-1860 4-30-1944
POE, Susan Emily, 5-18-1864 2-12-1963
POE, Thomas Franklin, 3-16-1898 8-18-1968
THOMAS, Pat, 1933-1975
FINDLEY, Paul A., Tex., Pvt., 1-CL, 220 Armed Engrs., 8-19-1925 8-20-1945
GENTRY, Sue Ethel, 1887-1974
GENTRY, Joseph John, 1884-1975
GENTRY, Murray O., 1911-1973
THURMAN, Walter W., 1878-1961
THURMAN, Eva R., 1883-1949
LAGRONE, C. W., 1881-1970
LAGRONE, Truda GOUGH, 1889-1952
DONNER, Leonard A., 8-22-1889 7-9-1973
DONNER, Sue E. POE, 8-1-1892 No Date   married 12-22-1912
OWENS, Laura Belle, 1923-1944
OWENS, Thomas E., Sr., 1883-1949
OWENS, Laura E., 1894-No Date
LILLY, John Edward, 5-21-1874 3-22-1953
LILLY, Lora Lee, 4-8-1877 5-15-1949
LILLY, Bob Thomas, Capt., U. S. Army, W. W. II., 3-19-1904 5-21-1978
PATRICK, Benjamin Linus, 10-26-1902 2-8-1964
PATRICK, Mrs. Lorene L., 10-7-1902 2-20-1979
MC DOWELL, Mamie, 1870-1946
LONGSHORE, Otis, Tex., Pvt., Co. C., 21 Machine Gun, BN., W. W. I.,
                                11-2-1895 12-6-1946

LONGSHORE, Mary, 1867-1960
CARRUTHERS, William S., M.D., 3-16-1872 1-21-1944
CARRUTHERS, Bessie S., 7-30-1879 1-11-1968
MC GILL, Margaret, 1-8-1893 10-13-1946
MC GILL, Mary MC CORMACK, 10-7-1866 6-26-1945
MC GILL, Mary, 11-24-1894 7-18-1951
KING, Molly, 1-27-1972 1-28-1972
KING, Phillip Thomas, 4-30-1947 10-23-1958
KING, Doris S., 1-17-1918 No Date
KING, Newell T., M. D., 10-26-1913 5-28-1978
RENFRO, Marvin M., 10-8-1880 1-13-1969
RENFRO, Prudy E., 12-7-1885 5-15-1962
RENFRO, Melville B., 3-12-1909 6-12-1968
CHAPMAN, Dewey S., 1901-No Date
CHAPMAN, Mildred K., 1903-1975
BARRIER, Nora K., 1881-1949
BARRIER, W. M. T., 1877-1949
SWINDELL, Will M., 8-10-1953 1-20-1967
SWINDELL, William A., 10-21-1922 2-14-1961
MYERS, Yvorn C., 2-3-1904 5-11-1945
BROWN, T. Taylor, 9-14-1884 1-7-1976
BROWN, Lutie LONG, 4-28-1888 3-3-1976
BROWN, Patricia, 5-25-1930 7-1-1945
BROWN, Erskin Long, 10-25-1918 7-3-1925
HANES, M. T., 1900-1979
HANES, Annie L., 1901-1977
HOLLON, Hilda, 1901-1956
HANES, Henry Grady, 1898-1965
HANES, Martha Elizabeth, 1873-1956
THOMAS, Carl Filmore, 1905-1950
O'NEAL, Hal, 10-4-1905 8-8-1973
O'NEAL, Emmett Benton, o2-5-1896 6-27-1970
MOODY, Charles A., 1892-1953

SECTION "4" PU

OWEN, Victor L., Jr., Tex. Lt., U.S.N.R., W. W. II., 12-19-1916 5-8-1950
NEU, Johnie Marshall, 9-20-1885 5-9-1975
NEU, Charles Ternay, 2-18-1885 5-8-1950
OLIVA, Simon, Tex., Pfc., 127 Gen. Hospt., W. W. II, 10-28-1922 6-2-1949
OLIVA, Luz G., 1889-1969
FREEZIA, A. Arnold, 5-24-1895 10-9-1948
FREEZIA, Henrie B., 8-20-1896 1-30-1978
MEYER, Kittie J., 12-23-1877 8-22-1966
STARK, Thomas K., 3-10-1881 No Date
STARK, Elmer Scott, 1917-1979
RATLIFF, Lela C., 3-27-1897 9-29-1949
RATLIFF, Joseph E., 1-31-1897 3-7-1972
STARK, Ed S., 1886-1949
STARK, Kate MORGAN, 1885-1957
HURSE, Rufus W., Tex. Pvt., 308 Cav., W. W. I., 3-4-1896 2-13-1950
WHITE, M. L., Pfc., U. S. Army, W. W. I., 10-21-1895 4-20-1979
HURSE, Foy SHUMPERT, 10-16-1893 6-5-1968
HURSE, Charlie, Miss., Pvt., Co. C., Conv. Center, W. W. I., 10-19-1891 8-13-1960

WHITE, M. L., 1895-1979
WHITE, Jewel, 1902-No Date
WALKER, Ralph L., Tex., Pfc., 35 Inf., W. W. II., 8-23-1923 2-8-1945
IVEY, Eleanor, N. J., Pfc., 1852 Service Command Unit, W. W. II.,
                                    1-23-1921 10-26-1948

MORGAN, Jesse J., 1890-1968
MORGAN, Ruth CLINTON, 1895-1964
MORGAN, John D., 1880-1951
PEARING, Mamie MORGAN, 1888-1969
PORTER, Omer Don, 1932-1949
CLINTON, Jmaes Monroe, 1-1-1891 10-4-1949
CLINTON, Bessie May, 2-21-1899 10-24-1961
MORGAN, Rex E., 5-25-1915 2-16-1967
PORTER, T. L., 1864-1951
PORTER, Mary Nelia, 1871-1962
TERRY, James Robinson, 1880-1967
TERRY, Sarah Ellen, 1889-1950
MC CANN, Alvie E., 1907-1949
CLARK, Charlie R., 1911-No Date
CLARK, P. J. "Buddie", 1907-No Date
FARMER, Raymond Lee, 1-27-1938 8-21-1949
FARLER, J. N. "Jim", 8-6-1878 12-1-1856
FARLER, Martha K., 7-22-1878 3-25-1948
FARLER, Jess F., Tex., Pfc., 6 M. Cav., RCN Sq., W. W. II,
                                    3-4-1918 1-9-1945

OLIVER, Ulysses E., 11-8-1889 9-7-1953
OLIVER, Mae VON LOOSDON, 7-17-1894 1-28-1976
BROOKS, Rena LOVE, 1880-1951
HARRISON, Roy N., Tex., Staff Sgt., 331 Inf., 83 Div., W. W. II.,
                                    11-24-1916 1-13-1945

GRADY, Maud, 1883-1954
GEORGE, Clark H., 1886-1957
OLIVER, John Rayford, died 1-15-1920 (Infant)
OLIVER, Rumah, 7-25-1885 7-5-1967
OLIVER, Laura Inez, 6-9-1887 10-10-1949
LOVE, Jeffie, 1885-1974
LOVE, Etta V.,,1891-1956
JONES, Autna B., 1904-No Date
          married 6-3-1923
JONES, Homer P., 1899-No Date
HODGES, Hester Bernice, 1913-No Date
HODGES, Ralph Weldon, 1914-1977
YOUNG, David A., 1-3-1869 10-21-1949
GOFF, Rosalee N., 1887-No Date
GOFF, Paul W., 1890-1970
BLOUNT, William A., 1889-1949
BLOUNT, Feebbie May, 1893-1978
FAGAN, Willie May, 9-6-1913 7-19-1966
TOLES, Billie Dove PRESSLEY, 8-8-1927 10-23-1949
PRESSLEY, Carlos Ray, 9-27-1922 5-28-1979
          married 11-29-1955
PRESSLEY, Gladys Lou, 6-27-1936 No Date
HATHAWAY, Milton D., Tex., Cpl., 11 Prcht & Maint. Co., 10-12-1927 1-14-1961
WILLIAMS, Charlie A., 7-15-1889 1-19-1955

WILLIAMS, Berdie M., 11-4-1893 10-25-1973
JONES, Belle, 1895-1951
JONES, Clark, 1896-1961
SIMS, William Jasper, 11-27-1908 1-18-1965
PRESLEY, Stella D., 12-27-1887 11-22-1964
PRESLEY, Mert W., 3-2-1886 10-13-1955
CARRINGTON, L. S., 9-4-1887 8-6-1949
CARRINGTON, Lawrene, 3-20-1887 9-16-1975
JONES, John, Georgia, Pvt., 157 Depot Brig., W. W. I.,
                              2-6-1894 11-17-1949
ROGERS, Claude W., Tex., Wagr. Hq. Co., 345 Mil. BN, 90 Div.,
                              12-23-1892 3-12-1953
VERNER, Charles Harold, 10-21-1926 No Date
VERNER, Kathryn Marie, 9-5-1927 No Date
PARKER, L. V. "Pat", 1892-1953
APPLE, Eltha, 1907-1978
APPLE, Clarance, Jr., 1929-1953
WINTERS, Clemmie G., 1925-1950
MC CAULEY, Eva M., 1-22-1877 4-27-1950
MC CAULEY, Cyrus A., 2-13-1876 8-23-1949
TAYLOR, Anne, 12-3-1952 12-6-1952
BINION, Warren T., Jr., Tex., Sgt., 315 Engrs., 90 Div., W. W.I.,
                              1-24-1893 9-24-1949

BINION, Beula B., 9-20-1894 No Date
SMITH, T. C., 5-17-1904 2-14-1955
WEST, Oscar D., 6-1-1877 11-3-1954
WEST, Stella C., 4-1-1884 4-20-1963
BRECKEN, Wert C., died 6-1-1955
PERKINS, Milton W., 1876-1951
ISAACS, Virginia Lou, 1-27-1934 7-1-1953
JOHNSON, Pierce. 1901-1960
FOSTER, Velma Effie, 1-3-1898 5-29-1973
FOSTER, Mattie J., 12-10-1870 1-10-1961
SHUMATE, Birdie M., No Dates
SHUMATE, Lon, 8-10-1879 2-4-1950
ROBINSON, Kelsie Lee, 2-2-1893 No Date
ROBINSON, T. Viola, 3-31-1896 10-2-1953
ADAIR, Jim C., 1-30-1873 4-28-1951
ADAIR, Margaret M., 9-8-1875 10-12-1955
SIMPSON, Calvin P., 1883-1951
SIMPSON, Mary SEAY, 1890-No Date
HILL, L. C., 1891-1953
HILL, Mittie, 1894-1962
CREEKMORE, John R., 1872-1952
CREEKMORE, Hattie L., 1878-1973
OWENS, Mertie E., 1892-No Date
OWENS, Cicero, 1891-1952
DAVIS, Exie M., 1899-1954
DAVIS, Horace E., 1893-1971
NICHOLSON, Lizzie, 1880-1974
NICHOLSON, Albert, 1878-1952
WILLIAMS, Pearle E., 11-13-1891 11-15-1970
WILLIAMS, James M., 3-5-1889 1-9-1952
MORRISON, Hattie E., 2-7-1880 1-14-1952

MORRISON, John T., 4-17-1880 9-3-1960
PERKINS, John Fletcher, 1878-1967
PERKINS, Effie HOLLON, 1881-1953
FOSTER, James T., 5-22-1907 1-9-1954
FOSTER, Jewell B., 2-13-1912 No Date
BIGGERSTAFF, A. Mae, 1881-1953
FORTENBERRY, Dewey C., 1907-1954
FORTENBERRY, Johnnie, 1911-1967
FORTENBERRY, James H., 1880-1953
FORTENBERRY, Evelyn S., 1882-1970
NEWMAN, Allie B., 1891-No Date
NEWMAN, Eugene R., 1885-1967
HEURON, Carl William, Tex., S-1, U. S. N. R., W. W. II.,
                         6-27-1914 5-26-1963
HEURON, Oma Mae, 12-31-1919 No Date
HANNABAS, Eurette S., 1901-1964

                    SECTION "5" PU

RAGLAND, Clark Asher, 7-1-1878 4-30-1957
PATTERSON, Ava Lee, 6-17-1903 7-6-1957
HARRISON, Morris T., 10-10-1875 6-5-1954
HARRISON, Ida SMITH, 9-11-1882 3-4-1973
NELSON, Ronnie L., 4-9-1943 8-19-1962
HORN, Harold H., 3-1-1927 No Date
          married 12-17-1951
HORN, Mildred E., 3-30-1924 No Date
LYTAL, Ada, 1884-1975
LYTAL, Noah, 1879-1960
BLACK, Raymond L., 6-23-1908 No Date
BLACK, Ayline L., 3-27-1906 No Date
MOONEYHAM, Leona, 2-10-1886 2-22-1969
MOONEYHAM, Roy L., 10-14-1880 8-1-1954
HURSE, Evelyn LYTAL, 1903-1950
HURSE, Frank Lee, Miss., Pfc., Batry. F., 183 Field Arty, W. W. I
                         3-15-1894 11-23-1955
HURSE, Mae LYTAL, 1905-No Date
HURSE, Ruben M., 1899-1956
MC COMBS, Rufus Hammond, 2-10-1895 3-10-1965
MC COMBS, Alice Beatrice, 12-21-1895 9-5-1955
SIMMS, Myrtlee, 3-31-1886 7-8-1954
RAGAN, Charles Clarence, 1908-1963
SIMMS, Neva Nell, 9-1-1917 No Date
SIMMS, Harry Lester, 12-20-1911 9-19-1970
INGLE, Jerry A., Seaman, U. S. Navy, 12-17-1896 10-8-1974
INGLE, Alvin Earl, 4-28-1908 No Date
PARKER, Sidney, Tex. OM-2, U. S. Navy, W. W. II., 2-20-1894 1-29-1960
PARKER, Elizabeth, 3-1-1902 No Date
INGLE, Sarah, 2-15-1879 1-29-1965
INGLE, R. J., 11-16-1872 1-20-1956
TURNER, Charlotte Lea, 11-17-1954 11-19-1954
BRANOM, Ethel Clarine, 9-12-1904 7-21-1979
GAROUTE, Mary Ethel, 9-17-1882 10-10-1971
GAROUTE, James Merit, 6-29-1882 5-28-1956

                         163

JOHNSON, Hattie, 1874-1957
ALLARD, Martha Ann, 5-1-1943 10-22-1955
ALLARD, Ernest W., 1-4-1902 No Date
ALLARD, Bonnie Kate, 11-9-1901 1-18-1978
YOW, Frank L., 2-13-1890 3-27-1961
YOW, O. G., 1-19-1889 11-15-1976
SANSING, Winfred H., 6-3-1912 11-28-1954
SANSING, Eula, 2-2-1910 No Date
PATTERSON, Madge S., 1889-1974
LUMPKIN, Julia F., 1893-1962
LUMPKIN, Tom F., 1883-1954
WISE, Hettie Dana, 1893-1968
WISE, Francis Elbert, 1886-1956
MERRELL, Ruth A., 1917-No Date
MERRELL, Audrey E., 1914-1956
COWELL, Roland R., 3-28-1887 10-24-1954
COWELL, Georgia, 4-2-1892 4-16-1969
NICHOLSON, Bertha May, 1902-1955
NICHOLSON, Willie R., 1901-No Date
LAWSON, Joseph H., 1883-1960
LAWSON, Mora Lee, 1884-1905
ROLLEN, Mollie M., 1-15-1871 10-6-1957
ROLLEN, George W., 6-23-1887 8-3-1967
PETTY, Nettie FORD, 1889-1975
FORD, William D., "Sam", 1886-1956
PULDER, Mertie W., 3-28-1887 1-5-1974
                married 12-14-1903
PULDER, Sam Harvey, 9-21-1882 3-4-1960
SPEIGHT, Vina Sue, 1908-1955
MOORE, Joseph Edgar, 1873-1955
MOORE, Fannie L., 1882-1967
BEDFORD, Walter, 2-1-1878 11-24-1956
BEDFORD, Lola E., 4-14-1886 No Date
KNIGHT, Homer David, 12-12-1898 3-3-1957
KNIGHT, Lurline MAJORS, 6-17-1901 No Date
SPARKS, Lorene, 1906-No Date
SPARKS, Merlin C., 1903-1975
KNIGHT, Claude C., 7-11-1896 6-2-1960
CLEMONS, Effie, 1-8-1887 8-31-1960
CLEMONS, Joe D., 2-21-1888 9-6-1967
DUNN, Reba T., 8-23-1907 No Date
DUNN, Henry A., 1-29-1902 12-28-1956
BREWER, J. Raymond, 4-21-1907 10-24-1957
SPARKS, Charles H., U.S.A.F., W. W. II., 1912-1961
SPARKS, Katherine, 1913-No Date
MANTOOTH, Harvey, 1896-1962
MANTOOTH, Leah, 1895-1976
ANDERSON, Thad H., 12-27-1895 No Date
ANDERSON, Margaret E., 7-28-1902 1-15-1974
DAVIS, Jane ANDERSON, 9-10-1921 4-3-1966
JACKSON, Eunice M., 1896-1979
JACKSON, Wilburn G., 1888-1963
JOHNSON, Jim Bob, 1930-1963
STRICKLEN, Harvey Glenn, 9-9-1904 7-4-1963

GEORGE, William Dewitt, 4-12-1894 No Date
          married 12-29-1923
GEORGE, Myrtle May KELLEY, 4-6-1900 7-2-1974
STRINGER, Arthur B., 4-23-1891 1-9-1967
STRINGER, Millie PRATT, 6-19-1890 6-17-1976
WRISNER, Cleburn C., 4-5-1907 9-7-1966
          married 4-5-1942
WRISNER, Jean, 8-7-1922 No Date
JOHNSON, Estelle G., 6-12-1915 No Date
JOHNSON, Robert, 11-4-1910 6-28-1967
SIMS, Emma, 8-23-1896 10-28-1978
MOORE, Johnnie I., Tex., Pfc., 405 Inf., 105 Inf. Div., BSM, W. W. II.,
          8-8-1922 8-30-1964
KING, Jane HAZLEWOOD, 1915-No Date
KING, Weldon B., 1910-1977
FERGUSON, Arthur Clinton, 1876-1973
FERGUSON, Claire RUSH, 1880-1975
SMITH, Emily Claire, 1913-1973
SMITH, Harry Clinton, 1912-No Date
ROBERTSON, James W., 4-23-1883 5-24-1965
ROBERTSON, Western, 5-3-1888 7-25-1977
ISAACS, I. E. "Ike", 1903-1967
PETTY, Henry, Ark, Pvt., U. S. Army, W. W. I., 5-24-1894 9-10-1967
JOHN, Robert L., Missouri, Sgt., Co. A., 18th. Inf., W. W. I.,
          2-5-1896 2-16-1965
CHENAULT, Rudith Marie, 7-29-1964 1-26-1965
SHOEMAKE, Aubrey T., Tex., Pvt., U. S. Army, W. W. II.,
          3-23-1913 12-10-1965
MARCUM, Bennie O., 4-1-1904 No Date
MARCUM, Henry L., 8-4-1900 11-30-1965
NEWMAN, Rosa ALLEN, 5-5-1926 9-17-1965
NEWMAN, Lewis Edward, 1-21-1916
SURRATT, Ella, 1-9-1887 10-28-1970
SURRATT, Johnnie A., 2-24-1883 7-3-1965
BEAVERS, John E., 1900-1966
BEAVERS, Ida C., 1898-1975
WOFFORD, Haskell E., 1911-1966
WOFFORD, Edith L., 1912-No Date
ECHART, Clarance A., 11-20-1899 12-31-1976
          married 12-24-1924
ECHART, Olga M., 5-29-1902 No Date
FULFER, Boyd E., 9-28-1904 1-13-1968
          married 3-8-1940
FULFER, Ione LADD, 9-29-1907 No Date
WATTENBARGER, Bernice JOHNSON, 5-31-1902 No Date
WATTENBARGER, Milburn L., Tex., Pvt., 359 Inf., W. W. I.,
          9-18-1894 6-29-1969
YATES, Fannie Ann, 12-31-1902 4-26-1978
YATES, J. M. "Jim", 11-26-1896 No Date
WITCHER, Margrette C., 1909-No Date
WITCHER, James H., 1911-No Date
ROUNDTREE, Lawrence Wheeler, 1896-1968
ROUNDTREE, Clysta Grace, 1899-1976
JOHNSON, Herbert Hugh, 11-18-1896 3-9-1973

JOHNSON, Callie SURRATT, 1-6-1898 No Date
MORELAND, James Ralph, Tex., Sgt., Co. E., 58 Inf., BN., W. W. II.,
                                    11-25-1907 1-14-1971
MORELAND, Lena M., 1-23-1905 5-29-1978
MORELAND, Otis Kyle, Tex., M-Sgt., U.S.A.F., W. W. II.,
                                    6-16-1920 3-20-1968
RUDOFF, Rachel, 12-1967 5-1968

SECTION "6" PU

BROWN, Ira M., 1897-1971
BROWN, Lucy P., 1899-No Date
MILLER, Reginia Dawn, 1970-1971
MILLER, Eugenia Denise, 2-5-1968 2-8-1968
SCOTT, Lelah, 1893-No Date
SCOTT, Norphlett, 1908-No Date
MC NAMEE, Frances Mary, 6-16-1949 8-9-1969
POMPA, Julia Losa, 1888-1960
POMPA, Damian GUERRERO, 1886-1961
CLAYTON, Martha Etta, 1-22-1896 4-12-1969
CLAYTON, Elmer E., 8-21-1896 No Date
WHISTLER, Myrtle LEE, 4-12-1891 5-28-1970
WHISTLER, Joel Lonzo, 7-25-1888 4-18-1969
ANDERSON, R. Hampton, 1884-No Date
ANDERSON, Della D., 1886-1969
WEDDLE, Edith GEORGE, 1915-No Date
WEDDLE, Martin Everett, 1909-1970
NANNEY, Thelma GEORGE, 1913-No Date
NANNEY, Meade Marshall, 1892-1969
PRATT, Louie Arthur, Tex., 1st. Lt., AAF., W. W. II, DFC-Am & OLC.,
                                    3-20-1920 9-8-1972
GRIFFITTS, Hida CATE, 1900-No Date
GRIFFITTS, C. Roscoe, 1896-1978
ANDERSON, Deedie, 1909-No Date
ANDERSON, Alvin E., 1905-1970
SIMS, Wilma, 1902-1975
SIMS, Ira O., 1897-1972
TARTER, Gladys, 10-28-1924 2-22-1976
TARTER, Sarah G., 1896-No Date
TARTER, Brent C., 1893-1970
KENNEMER, Jewel David, 1908-1969
KENNEMER, Dorothy MORGAN, No Dates
SPARKS, Claud C., 1885-1978
SPARKS, Mamie SHOEMAKE, 1887-1971
STANDEFER, Era ROSS, 1901-1978
STANDEFER, Cecil Willard, 1898-No Date
PILGRIM, Herman Lee, 6-13-1913 7-13-1973
PILGRIM, Emma Jewel, 6-19-1917 No Date
CAMPBELL, Elbert R., 4-25-1909 6-14-1971
CAMPBELL, Stella E., 3-16-1910 No Date
PHILLIPS, T. R., Jr., 1-3-1904 3-29-1978
EVANS, Alice R., 1-3-1904 3-29-1978
EVANS, Audra C., 12-6-1899 6-8--1971
PRATT, Robert P., 1889-1973

VAUGHAN, Lena O., 1918-No Date
VAUGHAN, Charles E., 1914-1969
POLK, Mary Allie, 6-20-1904 No Date
POLK, Robert Clyde, 7-27-1904 3-3-1970
OWENS, Thelma, 2-25-1918 No Date
OWENS, Cecil, 5-4-1910 12-24-1978
FARLER, Thelma W., 10-4-1904 No Date
FARLER, George E., 9-6-1906 2-23-1975
EVANS, Frances Gypsy, 2-14-1921 11-4-1977
EVANS, John Sam, 12-22-1916 No Date
BIGGERSTAFF, Aletha Marie, 2-28-1910 6-1-1972
BIGGERSTAFF, Marion C., 11-24-1904 No Date
HILL, Lewis Earl, Tex., CMM, U. S. Navy, W. W. II., 2-27-1916 10-5-1972
HILL, Mary M., 5-22-1920 No Date
CAIN, Kathryn H., 1917-No Date
CAIN, Louie T., 1907-1976
WEDDLE, Shirley, 7-12-1944 7-11-1975
ROBERTSON, William A., Sgt., U. S. Army, W. W. II., 8-27-1913 6-21-1975
SMITH, Sammie H., 5-19-1901 3-28-1974
SMITH, Opal MITCHELL, 11-8-1905 No Date
YOUNGER, Robert Carroll, 1-26-1928 No Date
YOUNGER, Camille Sue, 3-23-1928 No Date
WINDELL, Frankie H., 1904-No Date
WINDELL, John S., 1903-1973
JOHNSON, Christine S., 12-30-1922 1-20-1974
JOHNSON, Ross E., Jr., 1-17-1920 No Date
WILLIAMS, Ramona, 5-14-1935 8-14-1974
FORTENBURY, Burton, PFC., U. S. Army, W. W. II., 10-27-1914 7-29-1975
COMPTON, Tommy R., 1-25-1903 2-17-1972
MEHAFFEY, Maynona Edith, 1893-1971
HESTER, Buford Lee, 11-2-1926 4-12-1969
HESTER, Gerta Lou, 12-2-1926 No Date
TEAGUE, Melvin N., Tex., AS-U. S. Army, W. W. II., 10-6-1919 7-13-1973
TEAGUE, Nita M., 12-26-1920 No Date
TEAGUE, Ollie, 4-22-1895 No Date
TEAGUE, W. P., 6-21-1892 9-17-1970
SIMS, Christine B., 5-1-1893 No Date
SIMS, Harvey C., 3-28-1887 12-16-1975
REGAN, Alma, 1906-No Date
REGAN, Earl, 1906-No Date
YOUNG, Dorothy J., 1919-No Date
YOUNG, Sidney S., 1910-1975
LANDS, Ruby E., 5-21-1912 No Date
LANDS, Carl W., 4-19-1910 No Date
RAINEY, Hilda W., 1910-No Date
RAINEY, Russell H., 1905-1978
MATTHEWS, Oma Allene, 9-21-1920 10-5-1969
MATTHEWS, Roy Lee, 4-27-1911 No Date

SECTION "7" PU

BURT, Zora L., 9-5-1895 No Date
BURT, Willie E., 1894-1979
TALLEY, David S., 1959-1979

SURRATT, Homer P., 7-19-1910 5-10-1979
SHANNON, Jeffery O., 1963-1979
MC KENZIE, Joseph O., 1894-1979
MC KENZIE, Jessie H., 1902-No Date
BELL, Jewel Frank, 1908-1979
    married 1-9-1935
BELL, Reba Odena, 1912-No Date
THOMPSON, Bill, 3-25-1908 3-25-1979
    married 5-10-1930
THOMPSON, Marie, 9-28-1910 No Date
COOK, Henry H., Tex., Pvt., 130 Inf., 11-3-1936 No Date
COOK, John W., 4-26-1918 4-12-1964
ADAMS, Joseph C., S-2, U. S. Navy, 1-25-1929 8-28-1974
PHILLIPS, Ira Dees, 3-8-1913 2-14-1917
PHILLIPS, Robert C., 10-13-1904 10-24-1904
PHILLIPS, Emma, 2-22-1897 6-22-1898
URBING, Girl Baby, 7-16-1979 7-17-1979
JENNINGS, Stephen David, 5-8-1979 7-28-1979
ROWLEY, John J., died 6-3-1898
PETTIS, David, 1907-1918
BRITT, _____, 1885-1960
HASLEY, Ruby Bell NORMAN, 1903-1942
BOREN, George W., 6-22-1874 9-16-1958
WALKER, Willie Louise, 1921-No Date
WALKER, John H., 1915-1976
SMALLEY, Jackson Kermit, son of S. K. & Cynthia, 1911-1969
RAMIREZ, Carlos Hernandez, 9-22-1957 12-4-1977
SIMPSON, Milinda, 8-27-1903 9-7-1978
PARKER, John Thomas, 7-17-1924 8-8-1979
WALKER, Patsy Lou, dau. of John & Lou., 10-13-1938 10-14-1938
BARTON, James Henry, Pvt., Regt., Tex. Inf., C. S. A.,
        1-14-1836 12-3-1890
KRAUSE, Judy Marie, dau. of Derrile & Delma, died 12-18-1970
SANDS, Kenneth Ray, son of Kenneth & Martha, died 10-8-1975
STEPHENS, John, Tex., Pfc., U. S. M. C., W. W. I.,
        6-25-1923 11-27-1957
STEPHENS, Elizabeth, 8-3-1898 11-22-1978
STEPHENS, George O., 1-21-1894 9-27-1975
STEPHENS, Nellie, 1908-No Date
STEPHENS, Marcus C., 1885-1962
KEY, Billie George, 10-20-1957 3-17-1958
CARTER, _____, 10-9-1910 2-11-1978

END OF CEMETERY

" HISTORY OF ROSE MOUND CEMETERY ASSOCIATION "

The Odd Fellows first sponsored the Cemetery, then consisting or named old part North of the then gate entering between Block A and old part, the main drive.

Uncle Si Jackson's wife was the first burial in the Cemetery. Later the City took it over and couldn't handle it alone, so a group of young women sponsored it from 1904 to 1906. Miss Mary Thompson, president, Daisy (Pell) Hartwell, secretary, Ethel Janes, treasurer.

In 1906 the present Rose Mound Cemetery Asso., was organized:

    Mrs. Claud Randle- President
    Miss Bettie Sayles-Vice President
    Mrs. Tom Lindsey- First Vice President
    Mrs. W. W. Sherrell-Recording Secretary
    Mrs. Bob Sayles-Corresponding Secretary
    Ethel Janes-Treasurer
    Mrs. John Farrow-Treasurer
    Mrs. E. K. Freeze-Treasurer

A State Charter was issued to this Association on March 16, 1907 for a period of 50 years. Charter was filed in the office of the Secretary of State on July 19, 1909 by W. B. Townsend.

All through the years the City has helped the organization in work and some money to put over many projects. The Funeral Homes have always cooperated and helped in every way they could.

An Advisory Board of some of the leading business men, have through the years been a source of sound advice and help.

In 1909 a fence fund was started and the ladies kept working until the iron fence was completed.

Mrs. C. W. Rush and Mrs. John Heath were appointed to see about buying more land south. Four acres were bought from W. E. Mangrum in 1916. In 1924 more land was needed and 4 more acres were bought from W. E. Mangrum east of the other 4 acres. Two more acres were bought from Mrs. H. H. England, known as the triangle entrance south and west of present land. The Gate was moved west about 300 yards making a new entrance to the Cemetery. In 1938, 2 acres was bought from O. P. Marshall and Wayne Chadwick, north across main drive between the 2 plots.

In 1932 in Commemoration of the Bi-Centennial many shrubs and trees were set out being financed by the Federated Clubs, Mrs. W. B. Dejernett, Chairman.

Due to the untiring efforts of Mrs. Harry O'Neil and Aubrey Gough and their committee a walk from the Railroad to the Cemetery was built and the drives graveled. Many $.50 dinners and ice cream suppers were given to make money along with special donations.

In 1938, the Permanient Upkeep Plot was opened on the triangle previously bought. In the fall of 1940, O. P. Marshall, a true and helpful friend of the Association gave the cemetery a new gate of two beautiful columns of white pressed brick in Memory of his wife, Bama Marshall.

On November 11, 1951, the President, Mrs. J. A. Adams called a meeting in the home of Mrs. L. T. Walker for the purpose of selecting a Board of Directors to sponsor the work of the Cemetery since the work had gotten too much for the women. A motion was made and carried to elect A. W. Lilly, O. P. Marshall, Gene Bickley, Dick Dillingham and Mayor Ferguson as Board to assume the responsibility of carring on the Association.

Friday, December, 1951, the president called a meeting of the Association and these Directors together and read the resolutions formulatied by the following Committee., Mrs. J. A. Adams, Miss Ethel Janes and Mrs. Romer Harrison.

Be it resolved that the maintenance of Rose Mound Cemetery Association be delegated to a Board of Directors as provided by in the Constitution and By-laws. The present officers resign and turn over all bonds and money to the elected Board, provision being made for a supervisior to direct the work and workers.

W. Y. Goff was appointed by the Board. This Board functioned about ten years when at a called meeting a new Board was elected:

Mary Lou Whitley-President
Elizabeth Henderson-Secretary
J. W. Cox-Supervisor

NEW BOARD

Herbert Wheeler
Romer Harrison
L. G. Dixon
Gene Bickley
W. T. Arrington

This group has accomplished many needed projects:

1. Taking down old worn out fences.

2. New Culverts draining the entire cemetery.

3. New Markers designating the different plots.

4. Painting and enlarging the tool house.

5. Dirt to level all low places.

6. Needed gravel for repairing the drives.

7. Enlarging the mowing area.

This History covers the period up to 1960.

by Mrs. J. A. Adams

ROSEMOUND CEMETERY RECORDS

COMMERCE, TEXAS

Collected

by

Mrs. J. A. Adams, President

ROSEMOUND CEMETERY ASSOCIATION

and

Mrs. S. H. Whitley, Genealogist

Captain Charles Croxall Chapter of the
Daughters of American Revolution

Commerce, Texas

1941

48779

18487

TABLE OF CONTENTS

This copy of Rosemound Records, compiled by Mrs. J. A. Adams and Mrs. S. H. Whitley was typed from a copy in the Library at East Texas State University. The Supplement, also prepared by Mesdames Adams and Whitley, was taken from a second book of records in E. T. Library.

ROSEMOUND CEMETERY

COMMERCE, TEXAS

Located about one-half mile east of the city. It is owned by Rose-mound Cemetery Association. It is laid off in blocks and is kept up by annual dues. Functions under State charter.

<u>Copyist</u>: Mrs. J. A. Adams, Mrs. S. H. Whitley
(Pres. Cem. Asso.)

<u>Donated by</u>: Captain Charles Croxall Chapter, D. A. R.
Commerce, Texas

<u>Records Follows</u>:

<u>Block-Old Part.</u>

FELDER LOT
1. Fannie FIELDER -- b. 1844   d. July 7, 1909

H. G. HOLCOMB LOT
2. Elizabeth N. Holcomb-- b. July 6, 1852 d. 7-24-1891
3. Hervey G. Holcomb -- d. December 20, 1927--Aged 75 yrs. 8 mos.

BOB DILLARD LOT
4. Ella Dillard--b. June 27, 1862 d. August 12, 1913

BOB NELSON LOT
5. Gladys E. Nelson--b. September 11, 1926 d. December 12, 1934

PETER REILLY LOT
6. Mary F. Reilly--b. April 8, 1895 d. December 7, 1896
7. Peter Reilly--b. June 21, 1841 d. May 27, 1897
8. Herman Michael, Johns--b. August 3, 1899 d. November 4, 1901

GEORGE H. MC LEOD LOT
9. R. W. Gilley, d. February 16, 1920--Aged 62 yrs. 10 mos. 20 days

HENRY COOK LOT
10. Henry H. Cook--Pvt. 13 U. S. Inf.--died November 3, 1936

TEEL LOT
11. Juanita F. Teel--b. January 9, 1938 d. February 19, 1938

FLINT LOT
12. Carl G. Flint--d. February 7, 1931--Aged 22 yrs., 2 mos., 20 days

GEORGE D. JONES Lot
13. George D. Jones--b. March 6, 1853--d. February 10, 1899
14. Ben Moody Davis--d. September 7, 1933--Aged 62 yrs., 7 mos., 5 days.

JOE JANES LOT

15. Joe Janes--b. November 26, 1851 d. June 10, 1926
16. Annie Elizabeth Janes--d. August 19, 1940--aged 78 yrs. 8mos. 12 days.

JACK D. FOWLER LOT

17. Jack D. Fowler--b. September 5, 1901 d. November 5, 1927

J. C. HUNT & A. G. BARNS

18. Mary Jane Hunt--b. March 6, 1838 d. May 9, 1891
       wife of J. T. Hunt
19. James Hunt--b. October 20, 1816 d. October, 1891

A. J. DISMUKE LOT

20. Mrs. A. J. Dismuke--b. August 1, 1883 d. November 9, 1928

H. M. BALL LOT

21. Virgie Ball--b. December 30, 1884 d. August 26, 1888
        Daughter of H. M. & A. E. Ball

W. W. RUTLAND LOT

22. William Watson Rutland--b. 1851 d. 1892
23. Chloe Tilda Rutland--b. 1851 d. 1926
24. Kate I. Covington--b. June 14, 1885 d. December 20, 1916
25. Kittie I. Rutland--b. June 14, 1885 d. January 13, 1904

W. A. JERNIGIN LOT

26. W. A. Jernigin--b. November 14, 1842 d. March 19, 1889

A. M. NEAL LOT

27. Elizabeth C. Neal--b. April 10, 1886 d. September 23, 1888

J. F. JERNIGIN LOT

28. J. F. Jernigin--d. February 17, 1887--Aged 70 yrs., 10 mos., 17 days.

R. W. ROGERS LOT

29. R. W. Rogers--d. March 21, 1926--Aged 60 yrs., 2 mos., 11 days.

J. G. JAGGAR LOT

30. James Douglass Jaggar--b. August 12, 18__ d. February 19, 1892

JACOB REEDER LOT

31. George Leslie Maloney--b. October 12, 1893 d. January 20, 1895

W. L. HACKNEY LOT

32. W. L. Hackney--d. July 22, 1928--aged 57 years

J. J. ELMS LOT

33. Sarah Francis Elms--d. January 31, 1937--aged 70 years

J. N. CULVER LOT

34. Jacob N. Culver--b. August 2, 1840   d. January 30, 1900

L. B. THORNTON LOT
35. Kate Ellington, Nee Thornton--b. 8-6-1885   d. September 30, ____
36. Nancy Parelee--b. September 30, 185_   d. April 2, 1901
37. Guy Thornton--b. January 9, 1900   d. August 19, 1900
38. Eva Thornton--b. February 6, 1891   d. October 1, 1900
39. Mamie May Thornton--b. October-_, 1896   d. August 8, 1895
40. Dewey Thornton--b. July 18, 1898   d. August 4, 1899

A. B. MURRAY LOT
41. Dewey Murray--b. April 19, 1898   d. September 24, 1899

J. H. & ALBERT RECTOR LOT
42. Clarence Rector--d. 1912
43. Omega Rector--b. 1910   d. 1915
44. Jack Rector, Jr.,--b. 1915   d. 1923
45. Etta May Cox--d. 1900
46. Albert Rector--b. 1885   d. 1926
47. Jack Rector--b. 1885   d. 1903
48. Henry Rector--b. 1858   d. 1907

GEO. ANGLIN LOT
49. Lula N. Anglin--b. May 31, 1889   d. Augsut 6, 1890

G. W. APPERSON LOT
50. G. W. Apperson--b. 1856   d. 1931
51. Martha E. Apperson--b. 1862   d. 1918
52. Fitzhugh Lee Apperson--b. November 27, 1898   d. June 9, 1900
53. Paul Apperson--b. July 10, 1894   d. July 26, 1894

MRS. THELMA BYARS LOT
54. R. E. Horton--b. December 9, 1851   d. March 18, 1926
55. Thelma Byars--b. March 8, 1930   d. September 9, 1934

H. C. BOOTH LOT
56. H. C. Booth--b. August 16, 1838   d.
57. Fannie D. Booth--b. August 19, 1835   d. February 15, 1919
58. George H. Elhuff--b. August 17, 1874   d. December 22, 1989

OLD PART (CONT.)   4

F. L. GARRETT LOT
1. Mrs. Lola Garrett--d. August 5, 1933--age 37
2. Mrs. Sallie Patterson & husband--No Record

S. L. HARRINGTON LOT
1. Chester Albert Harrington, World War Veteran C. H. F. -- Gunners Mate
   U. S. Navy--d. April 4, 1933
2. Samuel Harrington, father, b. Jan. 6, 1848, Jan. 18, 1897
3. Vitula Hedges, dau., b. June 3, 1889   d. Oct. 19, 1918

J. W. ST. CLAIR LOT
1. J. M. St. Clair, b. Feb. 22, 1822   d. Dec. 10, 1897

2. Celia N. St. Clair, wife of J. M., b. Oct. 26, 1833 No Date of Death
3. Robert St. Clair, son, born 1868 died 1904

R. C. HILL LOT

1. R. C. Hill--b. 1856 d. 1930
2. Mrs. R. C. Hill--b. 1866 d. 1935
3. Oma Bowman, dau., b. 1887 d. 1914
4. Annie Lee Hill, dau., b. 1883 d. 1895

ROY HUGHES LOT

No Records

J. V. HAIR LOT

1. Sadie E. Hair, wife of J. V., b. June 19, 1879 d. Jan. 4, 1933

G. L. OVERSTREET LOT

No Records

S. M. CASTEEL & RAGLAND LOT

1. William Fletcher Ragland, b. April 5, 1850 d. February 10, 1900
2. Nellie Myrtle Ragland, b. September 19, 1887 d. December 1, 1892
2. Martha B. Philipson--b. July 13, 1825 d. August 4, 1900

W. W. FARROW & RUSH LOT

1. Joe E. Farrow--b. Feb. 15, 1853 d. May 25, 1887
2. Dr. W. W. Farrow--b. Nov. 15, 1815 d. 1890
3. Lucy W. Farrow, wife of W. W.--b. Feb. 13, 1813 d. June 2, 1902

G. W. GOFF LOT

1. Claudie, son of G. W. & M. Goff--born Nov. 19, 1888 d. Nov. 4, 1891

OLD PART (CONT.)   5

H. B. CROWDER LOT

1. Laura, wife of H. B. Crowder--b. in Henderson Co., Ky., Sept. 4, 1856
   married H. B. Crowder Nov. 22, 1888. d. in Hunt Co., Sept. 28, 1892

W. E. SAYLE LOT

1. Stella, dau. of W. E. & Mary Sayle, b. May 25, 1887 d. Oct. 5, 1888
2. Durwood, son of W. E. & Mary Sayle, b. Feb. 15, 1892 d. Feb. 22, 1895
3. Mary A. Sayle, wife of W. E., b. Nov. 25, 1851 d. Mar. 27, 1913
4. W. E. Sayle, No Dates
5. Bettie Sayle, No Dates

JAMES WILLIAMS & SPANN LOT

1. James Williams--b. Mar. 14, 1862 d. Nov. 12, 1889
2. Tessie L. Spann, dau. of W. W. & Pollie Spann--b. July 22, 1904
                                            d. Oct. 17, 1926

W. T. ROAN LOT

1. Mrs. W. T. Roan, No Dates

T. I. KNIGHT LOT

1. Viola E. Knight--b. 1870 d. 1949

2. Annie Lee, Dau., b. Dec. 7, 1899 d. May 18, 1901
3. Ima May, Dau., b. May 7, 1895 d. May 27, 1899

J. D. MC DADE & WALTER HILL LOT

1. Infant of J. D. & E. M. Mc Dade--b. July 3, 1895 d. July 11, 1895
2. Corp. Newton Haney, Co. H., 8th Tenn. Inf. N. H.
3. Lilia A., wife of Lee Cannon--b. 1882 d. 1940
4. Walter S. Hill--b. 1871 d. 1926

I. L. ADAMS LOT

1. Ella, wife of I. L. Adams--b. May 28, 1859 d. Nov. 19, 1898
2. I. L. Adams--No Dates

W. F. APPERSON LOT

1. Willie, son of W. F. & M. U. Apperson--b. Nov. 11, 1890 d. Jan. 3, 1901

J. B. KYLE LOT
1. Florence, wife of J. B. Kyle--b. May 28, 1867 d. Sept. 4, 1899

D. M. CROW LOT
1. Audrey, dau. of W. L. & R. L. Crow--b. Oct. 4, 1908 d. Apr. 9, 1911

J. N. BRYANT LOT
1. J. N. Bryant--b. 1897 d. ?

OLD PART (CONT.)   6

W. W. FARROW & C. W. RUSH LOT
1. Charles William Rush--born in Lincoln Co., Mo., b. Mar. 17, 1884
                                                    d. June 12, 1885
2. Charles Forest Rush, son, born in Warrenton, Mo., b. June 12, 1896
                                                    d. Apr. 30, 1900
3. Mrs. Lucy E. Rush, wife,,b. May 20, 1857 d. Feb. 7, 1927

JAMES WILLIAMS LOT
No Records

J. A. FARROW LOT
1. Ellen, wife of J. A. Farrow--b. 1857 d. 1890
2. John A. Farrow, no Marker
3. Bertha, dau., b. Dec. 11, 1887 d. Sept. 16, 1940
4. Mrs. Edna Ward Farrow, second wife of J. A., b. 1871 d. May 29, 1889

G. G. MC DILL LOT
1. Flora Mc Dill--b. Mar. 27, 1847 d. Mar. 31, 1926
2. Calvin Mc Dill--b. June 6, 1840 d. May 17, 1926

W. H. HARRIS LOT
No Record

G. Z. WEBB LOT
1. Mahala Jane McGraw Webb, married Gale Zendoll Webb, b. 11-2-1859 d. 1-16-1928

GEO. D. FOWLER & VOYLE LOT
1. C. W. Voyles, d. 12-9-1930 age 58

M. C. POSEY LOT
1. M. C. Posey--born Bowling Green, Ky., Apr. 10, 1827 d. 10-29-1893
2. Mrs. E. E. Thatten-dau., d. Nov. 25, 1935
3. E. E. Tatten, no record

W. A. CLINTON LOT
No Records

J. T. PRESTON LOT
1. Warren T. Preston, b. Feb. 26, 1873 d. Mar. 5, 1895
2. John Preston, No Record

ROWLEY LOT IN POTTERS FIELD
1. John W. Rowley, d. June 3, 1893

OLD PART (CONT.)   7

A. J. PRITCHARD LOT
1. Andrew Jr., son of A. J. & O. A. Pritchard--b. Dec. 5, 1890 d. Mar._____
2. Ollie, wife of Andrew J. Pritchard--b. Jan. 6, 1866 d. Dec. 8, 19__
3. Andrew J. Pritchard--b. 1857 d. 1935

D. N. WAGGONER LOT
1. Clifford R. Waggoner--b. 1881 d. 1898
2. Daniel N. Waggoner--b. 1841 d. 1931
3. Anne C. Waggoner--b. 1843 d. 1934

A. C. RIDDLE LOT
1. Mrs. T. A. Riddle--b. Sept. 11, 1870 d. Feb. 9, 1929

JOHN CHAPMAN LOT
1. John F. Chapman--b. 1877 d. 1909

J. C. NEWMAN LOT
1. Jacob Kreth Newman--b. 1848 d. 1909
2. Mattie A. Newman--b. Aug. 28, 1852 d. Apr. 24. 1899
3. Sadie A. Newman--b. Dec. 16, 1889 d. Sept. 9, 1891
4. John D., son--b. Mar. 8, 1887 d. May 11, 1895
5. Lena Newman, dau.,--b. 1891 d. 1909

J. T. NEAL LOT
1. John T. Neal, husband of Mary J. Neal--b. May 12, 1823 d. Sept. 12, 1898
2. Mary J. Neal--b. Aug. 27, 1835 d. May 11, 1908
3. Mary Ellen, daughter--b. Sept. 1, 1875 d. Oct. 8, 1895

J. L. MC COMBS LOT
1. John L. Mc Combs--b. April 1, 1857 d. June 21, 1928

C. C. SHERWIN LOT
1. Christopher Sherwin--Co. A., 3rd. Tenn., Col., C. S. A.

QUITMAN MC COMBS LOT

1. Quitman Mc Combs, Jr., b. July 22, 1895 d. Dec. 10, 1927

J. T. HICKERSON LOT

1. Horace Hickerson--b. Feb., 1857 d. Aug. 18, 1900

G. W. HARWELL LOT

1. Laura A., wife of G. W. HARWELL--b. Aug. 6, 1868 d. July 10, 1901

OLD PART (CONT.)   8

F. H. BRACE LOT

1. Lenora Brace, wife of F. H., born Knox Co., Ill., Feb. 3, 1857
                                          d. Aug. 31, 1888

J. MADDEN LOT

1. John F. Madden--b. Aug. 1, 1887 d. May 13, 1905
2. James L. Devaney--b. Dec. 3, 1879 d. May 1, 1920
3. Charles Madden--b. Aug. 10, 1850 d. Mar. 13, 1909

HOLLY LOT

No Record

J. W. BARNUP LOT

No Record

W. R. TILFORD LOT

1. Mrs. W. R. Tilford--b. Dec. 22, 1876 d. Jan. 3, 1936
2. Lea Mae Tilford--b. Nov. 11, 1885 d. Feb. 3, 1935
3. Calvin, son, b. Aug. 30, 1898 d. Feb. 3, 1899

W. W. NORSWORTHY LOT

1. Sophia Norsworthy, dau.--b. Jan. 8, 1892 d. June 6, 1901

JOHN WOODRUFF LOT

1. Mrs. M. M. Woodruff--b. Aug. 27, 18__ d. Aug. 8, 1938

JOHN PAINTER LOT

1. Rosa Painter, dau.--b. Aug. 16, 1900 d. Mar. 2, 1918

JOHN ROAN LOT

1. John Roan--d. April 10, 1937-aged 77 yrs.

M. N. MC ALISTER LOT

1. M. N. MC Alister--b. Jan. 7, 1871 d. Nov. 27, 1938

TOM LINDSEY & CORMACK LOT

1. James R. Cormack--b. June 20, 1834 d. April 6, 1900

G. W. ACKER LOT

1. G. W. Acker--b. 1846 d. 1926
2. Sarah A. Acker, wife--b. 1859 d. 1934
3. William G. Acker, son--b. 1871 d. 1895
4. George W. Acker, son, no dates

5. Walter Acker--b. 1874 d. 1920

W. H. WHITFIELD LOT
59. W. H. Whitfield--b. 1859 d. 1930
60. Addie Whitfield--b. Mar. 11, 1860 d. Dec. 5, 1899
61. J. High Stapp--b. April 30, 1885 d. Nov. 4, 1918

J. H. JACKSON LOT
62. Sallie Jackson--b. Sept. 26, 1824 d. July 14, 1887
63. J. H. Jackson--b. April 4, 1821 d. March 15, 1892

C. J. HUNDLEY LOT
64. Mrs. C. G. Hundley--b. Jan. 1, 1876 d. Sept. 8, 1907
65. Dr. C. J. Hundley--b. June 28, 1837 d. Sept. 17, 1917
66. Mrs. C. J. Hundley--b. Dec. 1, 1844 d. Mar. 1, 1921
67. J. W. Hundley--b. Nov. 15, 1871 d. June 22, 1913
68. Lucy Hundley--b. October 25, 1869 d. March 11, 1890

W. W. MARS LOT
69. B. L. Murphy--b. 1848 d. 1928
70. I. Murphy--b. 1846 d. 1916
71. Freda Glynn Mars--b. 1890 d. 1891

J. T. KNIGHT SR. LOT
1. Jefferson, son of J. T. Knight--b. May 10, 1890 d. Dec. 23, 1900
2. Calvin Cleveland Knight--b. Mar. 1, 1886 d. May 31, 1900
3. J. T. Knight, Sr., --b. Dec. 4, 1840 d. Mar. 29, 1907
4. Susan, wife of J. T. Knight--b. Oct. 4, 1845 d. Mar. 13, 1909

J. L. SLAUGHTER LOT
1. Mrs. J. L. Slaughter, wife of J. L., No Dates
2. Mary Louise, granddaughter--d. June 30, 1940

JOHN KNIGHT LOT
1. Infant son of J. & E. V. Knight--d. Dec. 21, 1898
2. Mrs. Jno. Knight--b. Mar. 29, 1870 d. Dec. 1, 1936

L. W. PRESLEY LOT
1. Larkin W. Presley--No Date--Ala., Inf., C. S. A.
2. Lou Ella Presley, wife--b. June 25, 1850 d. Sept. 27, 1922

S. D. SLODE LOT
1. Catherine, wife of S. D. Slode--b. Nov. 17,1861 d. April 22, 1901

J. L. PHILIPS LOT
1. Joe Philips--No Dates
2. Gertrude Philips--b. Dec. 15, 1894 d. Apr. 26, 1919
3. Ira Dee Philips--b. Mar. 8, 1913 d. Feb. 14, 1917
4. Robert C. Philips--b. Oct. 13, 1904 d. Oct. 24, 1904
5. Emma I. Philips--b. Feb. 22, 1897 d. June 22, 1892
          (Children of Mr. & Mrs. Tom Philips)

EDGAR MALONEY LOT
1. E. E. Maloney--b. 1870 d. 1934

L. W. TRAYLOR & J. W. SURRATT
1. Winnie, dau., b. Sept. 21, 1887 d. Nov. 19, 1891

J. H. BLEDSOE LOT
1. Dante Bledsoe--b. 1905 d. 1926

J. R. JERNIGAN LOT
1. Cordelia, wife--b. June 21, 1861 d. March 18, 1937

M. V. LONG & D. ANDERS LOT
1. Mary E. Long, wife of M. V.,--b. Feb. 21, 1830 d. Feb. 11, 1899
2. M. V. Long--d. July 5, 1897--aged 57 yrs.
3. David Anders--b. Jan. 18, 1814 d. Jan. 27, 1899
4. Sarah, wife of David--b. Nov. 29, 1816 d. June 16, 1891
5. J. B. Anders--Whites Company--Texas Calv., C. S. A.--No Dates

W. R. ROGERS LOT & JEFF JOHNSON
1. W. R. Rogers--b. Jan. 4, 1831 d. Mar. 27, 1906
2. Amanda Rogers--b. Apr. 9, 1840 d. Dec. 29, 1899
3. Nettie E. Powell, dau.--b. Oct. 17, 1865 d. Aug. 22, 1901
4. James, son of Nettie; No Dates

O. P. MARSHALL LOT
1. Paralee B. Marshall, Mother of O. P., wife of Newton Marshall--
                         b. Feb. 22, 1846 d. Oct. 19, 1894
2. Bama Marshall, wife of O. P., Dau. of Z. Y. Carr & Wife; b. 1873 d. 1938
3. Earl Patterson Marshall, son--b. 1896 d. 1897
4. Freda Mae, dau.--b. 1909 d. 1910

W. L. MAYO LOT
1. Wife and Children on Lot--No Dates

J. L. BROOKS LOT
1. Amanda, wife of J. L.--b. Apr. 5, 1847 d. May 23, 1900

JOHN GREEN LOT
1. John Green--b. Nov. 8, 1868 d. Dec. 21, 1902
2. Maggie, dau.--b. Aug. 25, 1899 d. Oct. 9, 1900

SAM R. BROWN LOT
1. Mrs. Sam R. Brown--d. July 27, 1940--aged 26 yrs.

D. WHEATLEY LOT
1. D. Wheatley--b. June 24, 1867 d. Nov. 31, 1939
2. Thelma, dau--b. June 24, 1907 d. Aug. 10, 1932
3. Martha Jewel, dau.--b. Feb. 7, 1896 d. July 30, 1898
4. Mary Pearl, dau.--b. June 15, 1897 d. July 30, 1895

DR. W. B. DEJERNETT LOT

1. Eugene, a son, World War Veteran, Sgt. 4th. Co., 3rd. Regt. A.S.M.
            b. Aug. 7, 1891 d. Oct. 19, 1916 A Volunteer in
         France--He died for his Country
2. Brode Evertt, a son, No Dates

J. F. WALKER LOT

1. J. F. Walker, Jr.,--b. Dec. 12, 1892 d. Dec. 23, 1937
2. T. W. Walker--b. Sept. 9, 1901 d. Sept. 13, 1930

DR. H. P. CREDILLE LOT

1. Dr. H. P. Credille--b. 1842 d. 1910
2. Willie A. Credille, wife--b. Aug. 18, 1851 d. May, 1895
3. Alice Bailey Credille, second wife--b. 1852 d. 1920
4. Dr. H. L. Bailey, son--b. July 29, 1872 d. June 3, 1899

G. G. LINDSEY LOT

1. G. G. Lindsey--Co. E., 117th Inf., C.S.A.

W. H. WHITFIELD LOT

1. Addie Whitfield--b. Mar. 11, 1860 d. Dec. 5, 1899
2. W. H. Whitfield--b. 1859 d. 1920
3. Hugh Stapp--b. April 30, 1885 d. Nov. 4, 1918

BLOCK A   12

G. W. FOWLER LOT

1. Evah C. Fowler--b. May 28, 1881 d. June 11, 1904
2. Mintie A. Fowler--b. Jan. 13, 1860 d. Jan. 12, 1912

J. J. SMITH LOT

3. J. J. Smith--b. Jan. 24, 1875 d. Dec. 6, 1908

AUBREY H. GOFF LOT

4. Julia Gregory--b. May 25, 1825 d. Jan. 31, 1912
5. Aubrey H. Goff--b. Oct. 7, 1884 d. Mar. 25, 1932

W. Y. GOFF LOT

6. W. Y. Goff--b. Dec. 13, 1860 d. July 10, 1909

GEORGE L. MALONEY LOT

7. George L. Maloney--b. Jan. 12, 1848 d. Oct. 24, 1906
8. Lelia Maloney--b. Apr. 19, 1857 d. Feb. 2, 1916

JESSE BRYANT LOT

9. F. G. Bryant--b. June 28, 1839 d. Sept. 25, 1909
10. Jesse Bryant--b. April 16, 1833 d. May 14, 1914

SAM PRICE LOT

11. Frieda Virginia Price--b. 1903 d. 1923
12. Jack Taylor Price--b. 1917 d. 1918
13. Melba Melissa Price--b. Jan., 1908 d. June, 1908
14. Lucinda Stephens--b. Mar. 1, 1836 d. Sept. 27, 1903

JIM SIMS LOT
15. Leila C. Sims--b. Jan. 19, 1885 d. Dec. 4, 1901
16. Two Graves unmarked--Jim Sims, wife, Charlie Sims, Darwin Sims, Will Sims

W. F. GARNER & BROWNING LOT
17. Dora Browning--b. 1888 d. 1912
18. One unmarked grave--Child

JOE FREEMAN & NORSWORTHY LOT
19. F. W. Norsworthy--b. 1872 d. 1929--son
20. Mother--b. 1848 d. 1918
21. Father--b. 1848 d. 1918

BLOCK A (CONT.)   13

G. E. JONES LOT
22. Mary F. JOnes--b. Jan. 9, 1849 d. Oct. 1, 1908
23. Henrietta Jones--b. Jan. 28, 1871 d. Sept. 21, 1912

T. M. SCANTLEN LOT
24. R. F. Mc Kinney--b. Dec. 7, 1836 d. Mar. 20, 1909
25. T. M. Scantlen--b. April 20, 1866 d. March, 1909

JOHN SALMON LOT
26. Mrs. Laura Salmon--b. Jan. 23, 1877 d. Feb. 7, 1906

R. B. LONG LOT
27. R. B. Long--b. Nov. 7, 1852 d. Sept. 3, 1925
28. Annie Conroe Long--b. Feb. 19, 1859 d. Dec. 20, 1908

H. H. SMITH LOT
29. H. H. Smith--b. May 29, 1872 d. Jan. 10, 1940
30. Laura A. Smith--b. Sept. 18, 1870 d. Feb. 23, 1913

R. J. MC DONALD LOT
31. Mrs. R. J. Mc Donald--b. Sept 4, 1843 d. Jan. 8, 1913
32. R. J. Mc Donald--b. _____   d. _____

D. T. PRATT LOT
33. D. T. Pratt--M. D.,--b. 1866 d. 1929
34. Maude P. Pratt--b. 1871 d. 1912
35. Delaney T. Pratt--b. 1898 d. 1918

W. L. PIPPEN LOT
36. Melba L. Pippen--b. 1907 d. 1909
37. Dr. W. L. Pippen--b. 1878 d. 1938 (Dentist)

EZRA TRAYLOR LOT
38. Margaret Ann Traylor--b. July 13, 1880 d. May 29, 1909
39. Two unmarked graves

R. E. L. MC CARTER LOT
40. R. Edward Lee Mc Carter--b. 1866 d. 1934
41. Nora Jane Mc Carter--b. 1867 d. 1940

42. T. C. White--b.   d.

JAMES H. BULLS LOT
43. James H. Bulls--b. Oct. 15, 1845 d. Dec. 18, 1912
44. Mrs. J. H. Bulls--b. Dec. 3, 1848 d. May 20, 1921
45. Jewell Abernathy--b. Nov. 21, 1891 d. Feb. 11, 1919

JAMES H. HINER LOT
46. James H. Hiner--d. June 1, 1928
47. Amie A. E. Hiner--No Dates
48. Charles Melvin Fields--b. Oct. 31, 1883 d. Aug. 23, 1907
49. Samuel C. A. Fields--b. Nov. 10, 1839 d. Feb. 23, 1934
50. Charlottie S. Fields--b. Mar. 20, 1849 d. Mar. 18, 1923

JOHN BULLS, JR. LOT
51. Mamie Patrick Bulls--b. Jan 19, 1897 d. Jan. 25, 1924
52. Doris Jean Bulls--b. Aug. 4, 1921 d. Mar. 31, 1923

LUTHER F. NORFLEET LOT
53. Luther F. Norfleet--b. Dec. 22, 1884 d.
54. Jessie B. Norfleet--b. Feb. 24, 1891 d. Sept. 9, 1912
55. Sarah C. White--b. Aug. 9, 1834 d. Oct. 20, 1914

J. A. STEPHENS LOT
56. J. A. Stephens--b. 1869 d. 1921
57. Voncile Stephensb. 1912--baby

JOE MAGEE LOT
58. J. C. Roberts--b. 1835 d. 1913

BILL HANES LOT
59. Harry B. Hanes--b. 1909 d. Sept. 5, 1940
60. Mrs. Mary A. Bruster--d. December 9, 1935--aged 32 yrs., 2 mos., 2 dys.
61. One unmarked grave

R. P. BUSBY LOT
62. Ophelia R. Busby--b. May 10, 1866 d. May 29, 1931
63. S. E. Busby--b. Dec. 19, 1883 d. Oct. 31, 1918
64. Jesse Busby Jones--d. Feb. 11, 1911--aged 24 years.

W. J. SALMON LOT
65. Andrew Jackson Salmon--b. Oct. 27, 1854 d. Dec. 19, 1902
66. Mary J. Salmon--b. Sept. 13, 1852 d. Aug. 15, 1903
67. Clarence Wayne Winn--b. Aug. 3, 1905 d. June 24, 1906
68. Nannie Evans--d. Jan. 6, 1936--aged 79 yrs., 3 mos., 3 days

G. L. MALONEY LOT
69. James M. Maloney--b. Sept. 14, 1839 d. Sept. 10, 1902
70. Martha A. Maloney--b. Aprl. 27, 1845 d. Mar. 8, 1906

T. P. GRIFFETTS LOT
71. R. P. Bell--b. 1868 d. 1940

72. C. E. Bell--b. 1847 d. 1927
73. Nancy Bell--b. 1847 d. 1926
74. T. P. Griffetts--b. 1866 d. 1928
75. Maurine Griffetts--b. 1903 d. No Date

N. D. INGRAM LOT
76. Earl Ingram--b. Mar. 28, 1902 d. Mar. 2, 1903

S. W. RANDLE LOT
77. S. W. Randle--b. Dec. 14, 1868 d. Aug. 10, 1908

H. U. OLIVE LOT
78. H. U. Olive--b. Jan. 8, 1869 d. July 28, 1903
79. Richard Rengold--b. 1869 d. 1918

WM. D. NUNN LOT
80. William D. Nunn--b. June 25, 1858 d. Feb. 28, 1938
81. Ray Nunn--No Dates
82. Mrs. Wm. D. Nunn--No Dates

W. J. TAYLOR LOT
83. W. J. Taylor--b. 1846 d. 1934
84. Melissa Taylor--b. 1846 d. 1914
85. John M. Taylor--b. 1880 d. 1914
86. Beatrice Price--d. 1907--Daughter of S. C. & Jessie Price

G. E. WATSON LOT
87. George M. Vaden--b. Oct. 2, 1901 d. Dec. 13, 1901
                son of N. L. & Georgia Vaden
88. Dr. Guy Watson--No Dates
89. Mrs. Guy Watson--No Dates

L. L. KNIGHT LOT
90. Alton H. Knight--b. June 7, 1904 d. Aug. 12, 1905
                son of L. L. & Dollie Knight

EDD YOUNG LOT
91. J. E. Young--b. 1909 d. 1909
92. J. E. Young, Sr.,--b. 1882 d. 1928
93. Samuel Young--b. 1842 d. 1916

FRANK H. DELANEY LOT
94. Frank H. Delaney--b. 1857 d. 1934
95. Fannie M. Madison--b. 1850 d. 1933

CLIFF JAMES LOT
96. Infant of C. C. & L. L. James--b. Nov. 15, 1913 d. Jan. 3, 1914

O. N. HARRIS LOT
97. Annie E. Harris--b. Jan. 22, 1851 d. June 21, 1912

E. E. TRAYLOR LOT
97b. Mrs. E. E. Traylor--b. July 28, 1834 d. Nov. 5, 1919

HOMER R. HINKIE LOT
98. Mrs. Lula Hinkie--b. Nov. 18, 1880 d. Jan. 19, 1911

J. L. BOSTICK LOT
99. John P. Kinselow--b. 1889 d. 1938

MILTON H. TERRY LOT
100. Hubert M. Terry--b. May 3, 1906 d. May 7, 1907
101. Ollie Margaret Terry--b. May 5, 1910 d. May 11, 1911
             daughter of H. M. & N. A. Terry
102. Milton H. Terry--b. 1851 d. 1931

G. A. MC ADAMS LOT
103. G. A. Mc Adams--b. Aug. 5, 1880 d. Sept. 18, 1907
             Commerce Camp # 317

R. E. STRINGER LOT
104. Sophia Stringer--b. 1846 d. 1906
105. Ruben E. Stringer--b. 1837 d. 1930

DR. W. W. LEMMON LOT
106. Laura Maurine Lemmon--b. 1900 d. 1903

JOSEPH P. GOODMAN LOT
107. Joseph P. Goodman--b. Dec. 22, 1862 d. May 6, 1936
108. Edna R. Goodman--b. Dec. 30, 1867 d. Aug. 26, 1901

G. W. LYON LOT
109. Clarence W. Lyon--b. Feb. 8, 1866 d. Sept. 4, 1906
110. Lillie M. Lyon--b. May 25, 1872 d. Feb. 1, 1903

G. E. JONES LOT
111. Myrtle Jones--b. Jan. 13, 1892 d. May 8, 1907
             daughter of G. E. & W. E. Jones

REV. R. B. MORELAND LOT
112. Mary Emma Moreland--b. Mar. 26, 1875 d. Nov. 26, 1911

J. H. GARMANY LOT
113. J. H. Garmany--d. April 26, 1931
114. Mrs. E. M. Lasater--b. 1841 d. 1935
115. Mrs. R. F. Prim--b. 1867 d. 1934
116. C. F. Prim--b. 1857 d. 1931
117. Maudie Prim--b. 1888 d. 1907

BLOCK B   17

W. W. SHERRILL LOT
1. W. W. Sherrill--b. 1866 d. 1929
2. Robert Sherrill--b. 1904 d. 1905

SIMS LOT
1. Elizabeth Sims--b. April 16, 1915 d. June 23, 1935

J. R. ALDREDGE LOT
1. J. R. Aldredge--b. Aug. 4, 1829 d. Feb. 6, 1907
2. Mrs. J. L. Aldredge--b. Jan. 2, 1841 d. Nov. 18, 1928

SAM HOLLON LOT
1. Ruth Hollon--b. May 19, 1905 d. Aug. 11, 1906
2. Paul Hollon--b. Aug. 22, 1907 d. June 6, 1910

E. HEWETT LOT
1. Thomas E. Hewett, Veteran, Company C-4, Miss. Inf., C. S. A. No Dates

R. N. & WILL JOHNSON LOT
1. R. N. Johnson--b. Nov. 3, 1848 d. April 1, 1908
2. Kate Smith--b. Feb. 24, 1882 d. July 17, 1910
3. S. R. Johnson, wife of R. N.,--b. Dec. 18, 1839 d. Aug. 1, 1906
4. Sarah Emma Johnson--b. Feb. 27, 1875 d. Sept. 17, 1923

D. M. FINLEY LOT
1. D. M. Finley--b. May 20, 1848 d. Feb. 22, 1917
2. Phebe Finley--b. Aug. 28, 1848 d. Dec. 23, 1928

KNOX CRAIG LOT
1. Knox Craig--b. Aug. 13, 1853 d. June 23, 1906

TOM NEAL LOT
1. Tom Neal--b. November 2, 1858 d. Mar. 16, 1904

JOHN SPEED LOT
1. John Speed--b. Feb. 24, 1852 d. No Date
2. Mary Speed--b. June 8, 1856 d. July 15, 1910

JOE MANTOOTH LOT
1. Martha Elizabeth--b. Dec. 15, 1888 d. Sept. 13, 1913
2. Lucy Mantooth--b. April 4, 1872 d. Jan. 2, 1928

BLOCK B (CONT.)   18

WILLIAM HEMSELL LOT
1. William Hemsell--b. 1842 d. 1922
2. Malinda Hemsell--b. 1844 d. 1920
3. R. P. Jones--b. 1870 d. 1935

JOHN M. HARRIS LOT
1. John M. Harris--d. May 15, 1938

JOHN P. CORNELIUS LOT
1. Gertrude Shepherd--b. 1911 d. 1938
2. John P. Cornelius--b. Nov. 28, 1872 d. April 19, 1910
3. Mrs. M. M. Cornelius--b. July 10, 1849 d. March 6, 1924

S. P. & JOHN HART LOT

1. John Hart--b. March 22, 1902 d. December 15, 1940 aged 38 years

C. S. & ELIZABETH MAULDIN LOT
1. Elizabeth Mauldin--b. June 8, 1854 d. May 16, 1912

E. A. DEARING LOT
1. Geneva Era Dearing--b. Aug. 3, 1913 d. July 23, 1914

M. B. MARSHALL LOT
1. M. B. Marshall--b. July 17, 1871 d. Oct. 1, 1914
2. Mrs. Eula Marshall--b. 1882 d. March 19, 1936
3. Gelon Coody--b. 1871 d. 1928
4. Junior B. Nunn--b. 1871 d. 1928
5. Asbury Nunn--b. 1856 d. 1933

J. A. ADAMS LOT
1. Howard Adams--b. 1905 d. 1938
2. Z. T. Adams, Veteran--b. 1847 d. 1925
3. Isaac Newton Marshall--b. March, 1838 d. March, 1915

W. J. CLINTON LOT
1. Mary Francis Clinton--b. 1871 d. 1916

W. B. DUNN LOT
1. W. B. Dunn--b. 1862 d. 1916
2. J. N. Stephens--b. 1872 d. Oct. 27, 1926

FRANK PRITCHARD LOT
1. Elaine Pritchard--b. No Date d. May 16, 1931

R. WATSON LOT
1. Lida Watson Berg--b. 1898 d. 1926
2. Two Unidentified graves

BLOCK B (CONT.)   19

J. W. MOON LOT
1. J. W. Moon--No Dates

REV. W. L. CLIFTON LOT
1. Rev. W. L. Clifton--b. 1836 d. 1911
2. Laura J. Clifton--b. 1845 d. 1913
3. Leila Clifton--b. April 20, 1867 d. December 29, 1923
4. Carl Millcan--b. 1904 d. 1913
5. Edgar B. Clifton--b. April 8, 1870 d. April 9, 1915

CARTER & FULLER LOT
1. Earl H. Fuller--b. 1891 d. 1914
2. W. Frank Carter--d. 1939

J. A. VICKERS LOT
1. Francis Harold Vickers--b. Jan., 1882 d. May 7, 1898

JACK KELLEY LOT

1. Charles Jackson Kelley--b. April 15, 1913   d. Jan. 1, 1915

A. G. PATILLO LOT
1. John Wesley Poer--b. April 9, 1838   d. June 28, 1914
2. Winifrield Patillo--d. Sept. 11, 1940

W. L. HARRISON LOT
1. W. L. Harrison--b. Sept. 5, 1855 d. May 14, 1933
2. Sarah J. Allen--b. 1839   d. 1914
3. Wm. N. Debusk--b. 1864   d. 1933
4. Gussie Debusk--b. 1894   d. 1919

G. W. WOOSLEY LOT
1. Lizzie Woosley (his wife)--No Dates

DANIEL H. YARBROUGH LOT
1. Daniel H. Yarbrough--b. March 9, 1882   d. August 21, 1918
2. Cordie M. Yarbrough--b. November 17, 1887   d. June 6, 1931
3. Hannah P. Heath--b. 1852   d. 1935

J. B. ABERNATHY LOT
1. J. B. Abernathy--b. June 20, 1858   d. Nov. 29, 1917

J. F. FOLLIS LOT
1. Georgia Ethel Follis--b. March 31, 1893   d. Oct. 2, 1918

WILLIAM E. SAYLE, JR. LOT
1. William E. Sayle, Jr., --b. 1883   d. 1918

BLOCK B (CONT.)   20

J. F. OLIVER LOT
1. Martha V. Oliver--b. Oct. 23, 1918   d. Oct. 27, 1918

H. L. BLAINE LOT
1. H. Blaine--No Dates

W. A. DIXSON LOT
1. W. A. Dixson--b. Sept. 24, 1850   d. No Date

HENRY N. CORNISH LOT
1. Clinton Wheeler Cornish--b. Sept. 30, 1918   d. Oct. 16, 1918
2. Ina E. Cornish--b. 1876   d. 1935
3. Henry N. Cornish--b. 1875   d. 1936

J. H. CLARK LOT
1. J. H. Clark--b. Nov. 4, 1839   d. Nov. 22, 1919
2. Mrs. Sarah E. Clark--b. Feb. 5, 1841   d. Feb. 14, 1918
3. Richard W. Clark--b. 1886   d. 1937

DR. THOMAS B. WHITLEY LOT
1. Dr. Thomas B. Whitley--b. Oct. 16, 1882   d. Aug. 6, 1915

J. A. PATE LOT
1. J. A. Pate--b. 1846   d. Jan. 7, 1916

AMOS KNIGHT LOT

1. Fannie C. Knight--b. Dec. 23, 1879 d. Feb. 25, 1913
2. Kathleen Knight--b. Sept. 20, 1910 d. June 4, 1913

J. C. HENDERSON LOT

1. J. C. Henderson--b. Sept. 30, 1888 d. July 26, 1910
2. Mary S. Henderson--b. Dec. 16, 1857 d. Oct. 17, 1932
3. M. O. Henderson--b. Feb. 3, 1886 d. Oct. 24, 1918

W. W. FRANKLIN LOT

1. W. W. Franklin--b. May 5, 1886 d. July 31, 1940

JOHN H. ROBERTS LOT

1. Willis H. Roberts--b. July 4, 1857 d. Oct. 11, 1915
2. John H. Roberts--b. 1908 d. 1940

J. O. HAYNES LOT

1. Addie Haynes--b. Sept. 19, 1896 d. March 3, 1934
2. Herman Haynes--b. Oct. 2, 1893 d. Dec. 2, 1916

BLOCK B (CONT.)   21

J. F. ADAMS LOT

1. Mrs. M. J. Adams--b. 1850 d. 1924
2. J. F. Adams--b. 1839 d. 1915
3. Carl F. Adams--b. May, 1899 d. Oct. 23, 1940

TOM D. ANDERS LOT

1. Viola A. Anders--b. Jan. 1, 1893 d. Nov. 15, 1918
2. Tom D. Anders--b. 1881 d. April 10, 1939

SAM PATTERSON LOT

1. Cora Knight Patterson--b. Oct. 17, 1870 d. Dec. 11, 1936
2. Samuel Thomas Patterson--b. 1868 d. 1932
3. Iva Eugene Patterson--b. 1906 d. 1928

J. T. HAMILTON LOT

1. Helen E. Millikan--b. 1919 d. 1920
2. J. T. Hamilton--b. Feb. 22, 1851 d. Jan. 29, 1921
3. Gene King--b. April 4, 1928 d. Oct. 2, 1934
4. Otis O. Rasor--b. December 3, 1899 d. Aug. 17, 1934

OWEN BOGGESS LOT

1. Mrs. H. W. Winn--b. Jan. 27, 1871 d. May 3, 1938

JAMES B. BIGGERS LOT

1. James B. Biggers--b. April 20, 1902 d. August 25, 1921

LOYD NICHOLS LOT

1. Willie Loyd Nichols--b. August 17, 1898 d. November 5, 1936

BLOCK C   22

F. G. PHILLIPS LOT

191

1. F. G. Phillips--b. March 11, 1864 d. August 7, 1926

STEPHENSON LOT

1. Uneeta Stephenson, wife & infant of Dewey Perkins, October 4, 1901
                                                    November 2, 1920

PERRY PRICE LOT

1. Samuel Perry Price--b. July 31, 1875 d. Jan. 29, 1921

WILLIAM JIM TURNER LOT

1. William Jim Turner--b. June 18, 1895 d. Nov. 11, 1918

W. E. MAUGUM LOT

1. D. J., wife of W. E. Maugum--b. Jan. 12, 1856 d. Feb. 21, 1936
2. Capt. W. E. Maugum, b. May 17, 1844 d. Nov. 21, 1921

J. B. ANDERSON LOT

1. Janice Anderson--b. 1901 d. 1918

H. P. CLIFTON LOT

1. Pauline, wife of H. P. Clifton--b. Sept. 26, 1877 d. March 18, 1919

HOMER W. WYNN LOT

1. Laura I. Wynn--b..July 30, 1878 d. Sept. 17, 1918
2. Homer W. Wynn--b. Feb. 8, 1879 d. Dec. 15, 1936

JOHN ONEAL LOT

1. John Oneal--1847-1921
2. Maggie Oneal--1848-1921

JOHN ONEAL JR. LOT

1. John Oneal, Jr., 1876-1918

J. K. LEDFORD LOT

1. Clyde Ham--b. Oct. 13, 1882 d. Sept. 15, 1919
2. J. K. Ledford--b. June 6, 1850 d. June 27, 1918

H. L. CLIFTON LOT

1. Era Larrie, wife of H. J. Clifton--b. March 7, 1872 d. June 17, 1918

G. G. WILKINS LOT

1. G. G. WIlkins--d. April 2, 1917 aged 39 years

BLOCK C (CONT.)   23

WESLEY CLARK WARD LOT

1. Wesley Clark Ward--b. 1855 d. 1938

JIM STIDHAM LOT

1. Mrs. Elizabeth Stidham--b. Oct. 3, 1848 d. Jan. 2, 1938
2. Joseph Alexandred, infant son of Jim--No Dates
3. Allie Stidham--b. May 19, 1917 d. Sept. 22, 1917

J. M. THURMAN LOT

1. J. M. Thurman--b. 1851 d. 1930
2. Lucisa, his wife--b. 1857 d. 1917
3. W. M. Thurman, d. July 25, 1935 aged 25 yrs.

GABE FAIN LOT
1. Gabreal A. C. Fain--b. Dec. 3, 1861 d. Jan. 10, 1918

M. L. BRIGARIC LOT
1. Edgar Bregarice, b. July 28, 1895 d. July 25, 1917

J. W. EVANS LOT
1. Sarah A. Evans--b. Feb. 17, 1872 d. Feb. 28, 1912
2. Billie Bob Welch--b. No Date d. June 21, 1932--aged 18 days
3. Ima Jean Sweat--d. Mar. 29, 1931--Aged 1 yr., 22 days

J. E. MULKEY LOT
1. J. E. Mulkey--b. Dec. 28, 1916 d. Jan. 21, 1917
2. Mrs. S. E. Moody--d. March, 1926--Aged 65 yrs., 11 mos., 22 dys.

W. L. GREEN LOT
1. Willie A. Green--b. Feb. 6, 1896 d. June 19, 1937
2. Nannie J. Green--b. Oct. 25, 1857 d. Apr. 5, 1919
3. W. L. Green--b. January 26, 1855 d. Jan. 3, 1900

TOM ONEAL LOT
1. Mrs. Nannie E. Johnson--d. May 28, 1940--Aged 80 yrs., 10 mos., 22 days.

PLEN E. MALONEY LOT
1. Plen E. Maloney--b. 1868 d. 1926
2. Grace Maloney--b. 1875 d. 1923
3. Dan E. Maloney--b. 1898 d. 1918

ROY J. BROWNING LOT
1. Roy J. Browning--b. 1906 d. 1936

DORA WALKER LOT
1. Dora Walker--b. June 17, 1888 d. Jan. 11, 1918

M. V. BEARDEN LOT
1. Mrs. M. V. Bearden--b. Dec. 1, 1847 d. Nov. 28, 1935
2. Willis C. Bearden--No Dates

W. W. WILLIAMS LOT
1. Sallie Brecheen Williams--b. 1857 d. 1934
2. Wesley Weems Williams--b. 1859 d. 1934
3. Bruce Breecheen Williams--b. Oct. 5, 1894 d. Dec. 7, 1917

J. J. LYTLE LOT
1. E. J. Lytle --b. June 8, 1868 d. Mar. 2, 1917

BLOCK C (CONT.)   24

S. E. MOODY LOT
1. Welcome D. Moody--b. May 10, 1903 d. Oct. 22, 1920

2. Nannie L. Moody--b. Jan. 23, 1860 d. Jan. 17, 1926
3. S. E. Moody--b. Sept. 16, 1852 d. July 22, 1916
4. Hugh H. Moody--b. Oct. 3, 1860 d. July 10, 1932

R. L. BAXTER LOT
1. James Russel Baxter--b. 1915 d. 1917

ELENOR LILY LOT
1. Elenor Lily--d. Sept. 26, 1931--aged 2 days
2. Robert L. Brecheen--b. Mar. 28, 1889 d. July 25, 1914
3. V. M. Brecheen--d. June 14, 1929 -- Aged 66 yrs. 10 mos.
4. J. P. Richard--b. Dec. 2, 1871 d. Agu. 3, 1909

ROBERT D. HORTON LOT
1. Robert D. Horton--b. Mar. 11, 1866 d. Apr. 14, 1940
2. H. C. Horton--d. Aug. 23, 1929--Aged 28 yrs. 7 mos., 11 days

W. M. SHEELY LOT
1. I. N. Owens--d. Apr. 16, 1935--Aged 80 yrs. 24 days
2. Lou E. Owens--b. Feb. 23, 1864 d. May 21, 1912
3. W. M. Sheely--b. May 10, 1831 d. Jan. 28, 1912
4. Mary L. Sheely--b. May 3, 1843 d. Mar. 28, 1910

C. O. HILL LOT
1. Sarah N. Hill--bJune 6, 1830 d. June 7, 1909
2. Brode O. Hill--d. Dec. 9, 1940--aged 54 yrs., 9 mos., 17 days
3. Emma Alice Hill--b. Nov. 19, 1858 d. April 26, 1931
4. C. O. Hill--b. Sept. 1, 1854 d. Sept. 9, 1939

C. C. COX LOT
1. Charles Vernon Cox--b. Jan. 17, 1936 d. Jan. 17, 1936

T. V. MC DONALD LOT
1. Billy Craig--b. 1917 d. 1919
2. James Ivan Mc Donald--b. Jan. 14, 1894 d. Feb. 8, 1905

SARAH E. MUSGROVE LOT
1. Infant Daughter of Mr. & Mrs. Bush W. Musgrove--b. 1906 d. 1906
2. Orlena Jernigan Musgrove--b. 1875 d. 1935
3. Bush W. Musgrove--b. 1863 d. 1928
4. Sarah E. Musgrove--b. 1825 d. May 13, 1915

JOHN A. HALL LOT
1. Minnie M. Hall--b. 1854 d. 1933
2. John A. Hall--b. 1853 d. 1908
3. Mary A. Hall--b. Jan. 17, 1825 d. May 13, 1906

E. K. FREEZE LOT
1. E. S. England--b. Jan. 15, 1838 d. Oct. 19, 1912
2. E. K. Freeze--b. Mar., 1867 d. Sept. 4, 1937
3. Fred E. Freeze--b. May 4, 1899 d. Mar. 23, 1918

BLOCK C (CONT.)   25

H. M. SATCHER LOT

1. Frances Jane Jackson--b. 1842 d. 1925
2. H. M. Satcher--d. Mar. 29, 1940--Aged 79 yrs.

REV. R. HOLLIS LOT

1. Roy Bruce Prim--No Dates
2. Rev. R. Hollis--b. Mar. 23, 1857 d. July 2, 1916

J. A. TUTTLE LOT

1. Jessie Tuttle, wife of J. A.--b. Feb. 1., 1884 d. Jan. 2, 1930
2. J. A. TUTTLE--b. Apr. 28, 1853 d. May 29, 1909

WALTER F. PICKLE LOT

1. Walter F. Pickle--b. Dec. 6, 1881 d. Jan. 7, 1940

DENNIS NEAL HARGRAVE LOT

1. Marylyn Hargrave--b. 1929 d. 1930
2. Dennis Neal Hargrave--b. Dec. 1, 1888 d. Jan. 27, 1940
3. George Ann Hargrave--b. 1858 d. 1934
4. Dennis Miles Butler Hargrave--b. 1832 d. 1915
5. Frances Wynn Miller--b. 1868 d. 1939
6. James Perry--b. 1867 d. 1939

WILLIAM G. SMITH LOT

1. Lucy Smith--b. Apr. 22, 1849 d. Feb. 29, 1912
2. William G. Smith--b. Sept. 16, 1911 d. Mar. 16, 1912

L. E. LUKE LOT

1. Lillie Mae Wade--b. 1882 d. 1912
2. L. E. Luke--b. 1876 d. 1924

SAMUEL A. FAIN LOT

1. Rebecca A. Shadden--b. 1846 d. 1914
2. Samuel A. Fain--b. Mar. 18, 1858 d. Feb. 5, 1919

W. O. LYNN LOT

1. Ray Lynn, son of W. O. & Cordie --b. Jan. 18, 1909 d.June 25, 1913
2. J. P. Carrol--b. Sept. 17, 1859 d. July 28, 1912
3. Mrs. Bess L. Lindley--b. 1889 d. 1936

T. V. MC DONALD LOT

1. James Ivan Mc Donald--b. Jan. 14, 1894 d. Feb. 8, 1905

BLOCK D   26

J. D. HUEY LOT

1. J. D. Huey--1907

MARTIN KNIGHT LOT

1. Martin Knight--b. June 27, 1878 d. Nov. 28, 1910

R. C. WALDEN LOT

1. R. C. Walden--b. Aug. 17, 1854 d. Mar. 15, 1912
2. Mrs. R. C. Walden--b. Aug. 20, 1857 d. Nov. 22, 1923

CLAUD FULLER LOT
1. Seth Fuller--b. Jan. 19, 1910 d. Mar. 23, 1910

J. T. WILLIAMS LOT
1. J. T. Williams--No Dates

C. A. LANGSTON LOT
6. C. A. Langston--b. Dec. 6, 1890 d. June 1, 1907
7. Addie Langston--b. Aug. 21, 1916 d. Dec. 7, 1918
8. Emily Rona Langston--b. Mar. 26, 1893 d. Nov. 8, 1918

J. B. REID LOT
1. Lola Reid Hester--b. Jan. 6, 1896 d. Nov. 11, 1918

HOMER P. ADAMS LOT
10. Homer P. Adams--b. May 6, 1876 d. Agu. 5, 1913
11. Mary Ann George--b. May 2, 1936 d. Sept. 5, 1936

DAN HAYSHIP LOT
12. Doyle Hayship--b. Mar. 22, 1913 d. Aug. 23, 1913

FRANK D. CORNELIUS LOT
13. Frank D. Cornelius--b. Aug. 23, 1842 d. Jan. 4, 1913
14. E. C. Hagler Cornelius--b. 1859 d. 1928

WALTER COWAN LOT
15. Cleron Decatur Evans--d. Jan. 23, 1919--aged 2 yrs., 2 mos., 23 days
16. Paul J. Evans--d. July 11, 1922
17. Emma Cleva Evans--d. Mar. 29, 1932--aged 12 yrs.
18. Walter Cowan--d. July 28, 1912--aged 39 yrs.

ISAAC WILLIAMS LOT
19, Isaac Williams--b. 1858 d. 1935
20. Manarvy Williams--b. 1862 d. 1932
21. William Isaac Williams--b. May 27, 1895 d. Apr. 11 1917

LIZZIE SPITE BRACHEEN LOT
22. Lizzie Spite Bracheen--b. 1856 d. 1908
23. Tommie Sue Waller--b. 1881 d. 1932

DAN H. MORGAN LOT
24. Dan H. Morgan--b. Apr. 29, 1849 d. Jan. 24, 1924
25. Mattie A. Morgan--b. Apr. 26, 1852 d. Mar. 11, 1923

PANSY LEE STERLING LOT
26. Pansy Lee Sterling--d. Oct. 2, 1911--Aged 1yr., 9 mos.

BLOCK D (CONT.)   27

JOHN LINDLEY LOT
27. Frances Lee Lindley--b. 1866 d. 1911

H. C. BARKER LOT
28. H. C. Barker--b. Nov. 7, 1851 d. Mar. 27, 1913

29. Mrs. H. C. Barker--d. Oct. 21, 1939--aged 76 yrs., 6 mos., 20 days

JOHN THORNTON LOT
30. Emma Itura Thornton--b. Sept. 7, 1883 d. Dec. 18, 1925

TOM FAIRES LOT
31. Margaret Rose Faires--b. Feb. 25, 1912 d. Aug. 11, 1913
32. Rev. J. M. Lawrence--d. Mar. 19, 1932--aged 73 yrs.
33. Edwin J. Meier--b. 1884 d. 1922

W. L. LANE LOT
34. Dewitt Dillard Estes--b. 1860 d. 1939
35. Fay Douglas Layne--b. Aug. 15, 1906 d. Aug. 6, 1913

THOMAS B. ANDERS LOT
36. Glynn ANders--b. 1902 d. 1904
37. Mozelle Anders--b. 1900 d. 1904
38. Lola Anders--b. 1876 d. 1935
39. Thomas B. Anders--b. 1852 d. 1919
40. Mary Sue Anders--b. 1854 d. 1919
41. Curtis L. Anders--b. 1874 d. 1935

MARGARET B. ROUNDTREE LOT
42. Margaret B. Roundtree--b. 1879 d. Dec. 20, 1939

W. M. PECK LOT
43. Mrs. Bell Peck--b. 1846 d. 1930
44. W. M. Peck--b. Mar. 3, 1815 d. Feb. 12, 1906

J. G. WARD LOT
45. Mrs. Byron Ward--b. Jan. 9, 1899 d. Mar. 10, 1940

H. E. CRUNK LOT
46. Jimmie Crunk--b. Oct. 6, 1896 d. July 25, 1909

B. E. WOFFORD LOT
47. B. E. Wofford--b. Aug. 22, 1857 d. Aug. 9, 1927
48. Mrs. M. J. Williams--b. Mar. 4, 1850 d. May 25, 1905

T. B. EASTMAN LOT
49. Infant of T. B. & Hallie Moody--b. May 3, 1910 d. June 15, 1910
50. Cleon Harrison--b. Feb. 18, 1905 d. Nov. 7, 1906
51. Thomas B. Moody--b. 1879 d. 1919
52. Amanda Tennessee Eastman--b. Oct. 8, 1858 d. Feb. 11, 1905

BLOCK D (CONT.)   28

J. W. MITCHELL LOT
1. Mrs. Bettie Wade Mitchell--d. Apr. 28, 1939--aged 74 yrs.
2. John Wilson Mitchell--d. Nov. 21, 1904--aged 53 yrs.

F. F. CONNER LOT
1. Kate Rose, wife of F. F. Conner--b. June 10, 1875 d. Jan. 16, 1905
2. Infant son of F. F. & Kate Rose Conner--b. & D. Jan. 12, 1905

JAMES PERRY HOGUE LOT
1. James Perry Hogue--d. Dec. 29, 1939--aged 66 yrs.
2. Mrs. Geneive Wimberly--d. June 2, 1930--aged 22 yrs.

PERMANENT UPKEEP LOT
1. F. N. Sheely--b. Mar. 14, 1879 d. Mar. 5, 1940
2. Mrs. Jim Wheeler--d. Nov. 12, 1940--aged 54 yrs.
3. Charles B. Beckley--b. July 24, 1912 d. July 23, 1939
4. Vee Phillips--b. 1905 d. 1939
5. Barney Winton--b. 1891 d. 1939
6. Ruth Malister--b. Sept. 15, 1898 d. Sept. 30, 1940

W. A. ONEAL LOT
1. W. A. Oneal--b. 1844 d. 1921
2. Mary G. Oneal--b. May 17, 1910 d. May 18, 1910
3. Ioa E. Oneal--b. 1872 d. 1910
4. Mary J. Oneal--b. 1848 d. 1918
5. Christelle Oneal--b. July 24, 1908 d. Oct. 14, 1908

J. H. KELLEY LOT
1. J. H. Kelley--b. Apr. 9, 1858 d. July 4, 1909
2. Ida Day Kelley--b. 1862 d. 1939
3. Mattie M. Nunn--b. Sept. 31, 1886 d. July 4, 1925

J. H. ANTHONY LOT
1. J. H. Anthony--b. Dec. 9, 1880 d. May 16, 1907
2. Mrs. Parelee Harrison--b. May 5, 1872 d. Apr. 11, 1939

C. W. KELLEY LOT
1. C. W. Kelley--b. Oct. 22, 1844 d. Dec. 22, 1905

W. A. PEDIGO LOT
1. W. A. Pedigo--d. Jan. 11, 1934 -- Aged 56 years

CHARLES F. RODGERS LOT
1. Charles F. Rodgers--b. July 26, 1873 d. Feb. 16, 1908
2. David Bottom--Co. H., 2nd. Ark. Inf., Spanish Amer. War. No Dates

KIMBELL BAGNELL LOT
1. Kimbell Bagnell--b. 1908 d. 1924
2. Boyd Bagnell--b. 1879 d. 1936

BLOCK D (CONT.)   29

HUBBARD R. STAPP LOT
1. Josie Stapp--b. July 18, 1887 d. July 7, 1915
2. Hubbard R. Stapp--b. July 3, 1888 d. Nov. 4, 1918

TIP FERGUSON LOT
1. Tip Monroe Ferguson--b. May 3, 1859 d. Nov. 2, 1923
2. Martha Robert Ferguson--b. Jan. 10, 1863 d. June 24, 1910
3. Floyd M. Ferguson--d. Dec. 19, 1940--aged 46 yrs.

JOHN F. FERGUSON LOT

1. John F. Ferguson--d. Mar. 7, 1931 ==aged 79 years
2. Laura A., wife of John F.,--b. Apr. 6, 1854 d. Apr. 8, 1911
3. Ira J., son of John & Laura--b. Aug. 27, 1886 d. Apr. 1, 1911

L. D. LINSEY LOT
1. Effie May, wife of L. D. Linsey--b. Feb. 15, 1889 d. May 14, 1909

J. A. HULING LOT
1. J. A. Huling, 1839-1907
2. Cora C. Huling--1845-1913

J. T. LAYNE LOT
1. Beaulah Lane--1886-1928
2. J. T. Layne--1845-1911
3. J. T. Layne, Jr.,--1902-1905

T. S. THOMPSON LOT
1. Ben Thompson--1872-1903
2. Leah Thompson--1875-1911
3. Ann Hutchinson, wife of T. S. Thompson--1844-1929
4. T. S. Thompson--1825-1908
5. Harry Malmey--1874-1915

J. H. NEAL LOT
1. J. H. Neal--b. May 22, 1835 d. Dec. 15, 1903

WALTER T. SMITH LOT
1. Harry E. Smith--b. Sept. 1, 1926 d. Oct. 23, 1926
2. Gussie C. Smith--b. Aug. 3, 1909 d. July 23, 1910
3. Walter T. Smith--b. Sept. 22, 1876 d. July 21, 1934

MICHAEL F. HOGAN LOT
1. Michael F. Hogan--b. Aug. 25, 1858 d. July 20, 1910

GEORGE M. WORLEY LOT
1. George M. Worley--b. Aug. 31, 1863 d. July 10, 1910

DAVID EMMETT MAXWELL LOT
1. David Emmett Maxwell--b. Sept. 28, 1861 d. July 10, 1920
2. KateP., wife of H. M. Maxwell--b. June 9, 1840 d. Jly. 5, 1910

BLOCK D (CONT.)   30

L. E. WATSON LOT
1. G. Mahala Watson--b. June 15, 1878 d. Jan. 17, 1911

P. B. LEWIS & TONGSTON LOT
1. Archibold Buford, son of P. B. & B. E. Lewis--b. Apr., 1909 d. Aug. 1, 1909

B. L. PHIPPS LOT
1. Bernice Phipps--b. Sept. 30, 1899 d. Sept. 12, 1906

T. T. HOPKINS LOT
1. Josephine C. Hopkins--b. Dec. 26, 1853 d. Dec. 9, 1908

2. Thomas Hopkins--b. Feb. 1, 1849 d. Oct. 28, 1922

FRED STUCKEY LOT
1. Sallie M. Stuckey--b. 1860 d. 1936
2. Mary Sue Stapp--d. Oct. 14, 1934 --aged 72 yrs.
3. John C. Stapp--d. Dec. 20, 1937--aged 71 yrs.

BLOCK E   31

W. J. CARVER LOT
1. Mammie L. Carver--b. Nov. 5, 1855 d. Feb. 13, 1921
2. W. J. Carver--b. May 16, 1851 d. July 22, 1935

L. I. SMITH LOT
1. Infant of Mr. & Mrs. L. I. Smith--d. Aug. 21, 1926

JOHN B. SHARP LOT
1. Gertrude Estelle Sharp--b. July 21, 1897 d. Apr. 5, 1920
2. Bertie C. Sharp--b. Nov., 1894 d. Mar. 5, 1936
3. John B. Sharp--b. Oct. 12, 1864 d. May 20, 1938
4. Bates Franklin Owens, Jr.,--d. July 25, 1923

W. M. MASON LOT
1. W. M. Mason--b. Oct. 2, 1863 d. Nov. 8, 1935
2. Martha Crutchfield Woosley--b. June 11, 1853 d. Apr. 20, 1920

D. HARRIGAN LOT
1. Dennis Harrigan--b. 1845 d. 1920
2. Mary Harrigan--b. 1853 d. 1932

CORA SITZ LOT
1. Emma A. Reaves--b. Dec. 31, 1841 d. Apr. 23, 1920
2. Cora Sitz--b. Dec. 31, 1874 d. Oct. 2, 1933
3. W. R. Reaves--d. July 9, 1936---aged 65 yrs., 6 mos., 18 days

S. W. SPARKS LOT
1. S. W. Sparks--b. 1886 d. 1934

R. M. POLK LOT
1. R. M. POLK--b. 1872 d. 1935
2. Evelyn May Polk--b. Sept. 19, 1927 d. June 27, 1934
3. William S. Polk--d. Sept. 5, 1921

V. W. STERLING LOT
1. V. W. Sterling--b. 1847 d. 1924
2. A. H. Sterling--b. 1851 d.
3. Delia Sterling--b. 1871 d. 1933
4. Harry L. Sterling--b. 1880 d. 1940

G. W. BARROW LOT
1. George G. Barrow--b. Oct. 4, 1851 d. May 14, 1923
2. Albert A. Barrow--Pvt. Med. Corps--b. Feb. 12, 1893 d. Apr. 18, 1919

BLOCK E (CONT.)   32

J. H. LITTLE LOT

1. Arnold Little--No Dates
2. Mrs. C. M. Little--b. Sept. 25, 1867 d. July 8, 1940

J. T. G. WALTNEY LOT

1. John T. G. Waltney--b. Jan. 13, 1847 d. Apr. 28, 1922

R. SAYLE LOT

1. One Grandchild--No Name or Dates

J. A. ARNOLD LOT

1. J. A. Arnold--b. Aug. 15, 1853 d. Sept. 5, 1919

W. E. GALYON & CLINTON LOT

1. James Harrison MC Clinton--d. Jan. 5, 1938 aged 88 yrs.
2. Mrs. Kim Mc Clinton Sears--b. Dec. 12, 1897 d. Dec. 7, 1919

J. W. HOBBS LOT

1. Florence Lou Hobbs--b. May 29, 1879 d. June 26, 1934

J. M. MC CLURE LOT

1. Retter Mc Clure--b. May 29, 1879 d. June 26, 1934

E. ALEXANDER LOT

1. Virginia Alexander--b. Feb. 16, 1915 d. Mar. 6, 1920
2. Two unmarked graves

J. S. ALEXANDER LOT

1. James Sidney Alexander--b. Dec. 28, 1857 d. Dec. 8, 1928
2. Iris R. Alexander--b. Feb. 10, 1865 d. No Date
3. Laurine Alexander Salmon--b. Dec. 29, 1922 d. Dec. 29, 1925

JEFF D. JERNIGEN LOT

1. Jeff D. JERNIGAN--b. Nov. 23, 1859 d. Sept. 2, 1923

Z. T. CARR LOT

1. Robert J. Webb--b. Sept. 8, 1878 d. Sept. 5, 1939

ED ADKINSON LOT

1. Mrs. Maud Jane Adkinson--d. Jan. 20, 1925
2. Mrs. Emily F. Adkinson--d. July 27, 1929

Y. E. FLINT LOT

1. Jack Flint--d. Aug. 13, 1932 -- aged 15 yrs.

BLOCK E (CONT.)   33

G. LEE BRYANT LOT

1. G. Lee Bryant--d. Jan. 17, 1941--gaed 55 yrs.

ERWIN LOT

1. Myra Erwin--b. 1887 d. 1938

LUTER MOORE LOT

1. Lydia Moore--d. April 16, 1936--aged 25 yrs.
2. Harold Moore--d. July 25, 1932--aged 9 yrs.

A. C. MC CURDY LOT

1. Bascum Mc Curdy--b..1910 d. 1925

O. C. MULKEY & MC DOWELL LOT
Norma Wayne Mc Dowell--No Dates
James Dwight Mc Dowell--b. 1899 d. 1937

SAM BRYANT LOT
Sam Bryant--b. Oct. 6, 1876 d. July 15, 1922

DAVE WILKINS LOT
Dave Wilkins--b. Feb. 13, 1843 d. July 5, 1928

J. W. FAUGHT LOT
J. W. Faught--b. 1855 d. 1925
Carrie C. Faught--b. 1863 d. 1922

E. E. LOONEY LOT
E. E. Looney--d. Nov. 15, 1940 aged 81 yrs.
Armida Looney, wife of L. Stutsville, b. Apr. 26, 1893 d. Feb., 1920

DAVE MILLER & BALLARD LOT
Mrs. Margaret Miller, died aged 85 yrs.
A. A. Ballard--b. 1868 d. 1918

H. W. THOMAS LOT
Baby - died April 16, 1919

J. B. TURNER LOT
J. B. Turner--b. Sept., 1853 d. Nov., 1918

JANE KELLEY LOT
Jane Kelley--b. Dec., 1846 d. Dec., 1925
Mattie Turner--b. Mar. 1858 d. Feb., 1939
Charlie H. Turner--d. April 6, 1940--aged 49 yrs.

JACK SCAFF LOT
J. R. Scaff--b. Mar. 24, 1869 d. Oct. 24, 1936

BILL BRANSON LOT
Bertha Branson--d. Mar. 26, 1924--aged 2 yrs.
James Allen Branson--d. Dec. 11, 1932--aged 1 year

P. M. GREEN LOT
P. M. Green--d. Sept., 1938--aged 84 yrs.

MRS. IDA M. HARRIS LOT
Mrs. Ida M. Harris--d. Mar. 8, 1937--aged 79 yrs.
J. T. Harris--b. July 18, 1852 d. Jan. 2, 1920

MART MOORE LOT
Virgie, wife of Calvin Haddock--b. Apr. 1, 1849 d. No Date

C. B. MARTIN LOT
C. B. Martin--b. Aug. 13, 1841 d. Dec. 27, 1919

BLOCK F (CONT.)   35

BERT H. CROCKETT LOT
Bert H. Crockett--b. Jan. 5, 1890 d. Aug. 8, 1930
Mrs. Dorris H. Crockett--b. July 11, 1892 d. Nov. 4, 1919

J. P. COX LOT
J. P. Cox--Ark. Cav., C. S. A.-- No Dates

T. T. STEWART LOT
Bernice Stewart--b. May 5, 1905 d. Aug. 17, 1920
Dan F. Stewart--b. Dec. 8, 1884 d. Sept. 10, 1919

TOM MILLER LOT
Tom Miller--b. May 22, 1875 d. Jan. 7, 1919
Levi G. Owens--d. Sept. 1, 1926
Mrs. M. A. Cotton--b. 1851 d. 1940

JOHN MULLINS LOT
John Mullins--d. Feb. 1, 1939--aged 83 yrs., 3 mos., 13 days

J. H. ALLEN LOT
Robert E. Allen, died June 29, 1932--aged 48 yrs., 8 mos., 9 days
Thomas B. Allen--d. Jan. 10, 1927, --aged 81 yrs.
J. H. ALLEN--d. Sept. 1, 1935--aged 56 yrs., 5 mos., 2 days

L. PRITCHARD LOT
Ruth Pritchard--b. Apr. 9, 1918 d. July 13, 1939

DAWSON M. STRANGE LOT
Dawson M. Strange--b. 1864 d. 1922
Annie Harrison--b. July 29, 1889 d. June 20, 1920

DR. HENRY WILLIAMS LOT
Dr. Henry Williams--b. 1857 d. 1921
Susie F. Williams--b. 1859 d. 1920
CAsey Williams Johnson--b. Oct. 11, 1877 d. Oct. 13, 1928

R. N. SCOTT LOT
R. N. Scott--b. 1867 d. 1923

D. F. MC COLLUM LOT
Infant Son--No Dates

T. M. GILL LOT
Wonna Salmon-Daughter--b. 1899 d. 1934
Mary Helen-I(Mother)--b. 1860 d. 1932

FRANK ENGLAND LOT

Della Hannah England--b. Mar. 28, 1892 d. July 31, 1925

E. H. MULKEY LOT

E. H. Mulkey--b. 1841 d. 1926
Mary Mulkey--b. 1845 d. 1926

BLOCK G   36

JOHN R. RAY LOT

1. John R. Ray--b. Dec. 27, 1931 d. Mar. 7, 1924--Texas, Sgt., 343 M.G.
                                                   B.N. 90 Div.

JOHN R. SPARKMAN LOT

1. Robert L.--son of Mr. & Mrs. L. A. Sparkman--died Mar. 7, 1924
2. John R.--b. Oct. 20, 1857 d. Nov. 30, 1938

E. F. KLONIGER

E. F. Kloniger--d. Feb. 17, 1939

T. E. SMITH & G. W. HAWKINS LOT

1. Mrs. Mattie Smith--d. Mar. 23, 1924
2. T. E. Smith--d. Nov. 6, 1924

J. H. HOOD LOT

1. J. H. HOOD--b. Jan. 8, 1864 d. Jan. 3, 1929

O. S. SHAW LOT

1. Oscar Samuel Shaw--d. Sept. 30, 1934--Pvt., 1 c., 359 SNF 90 Div.

J. M. MONROE LOT

1. J. M. Monroe--b. May 20, 1871 d. Dec. 20, 1921

MRS. M. F. CARPENTER LOT

1. James D. Carpenter--b. May 17, 1901 d. Jan. 19, 1923
2. Mrs. Mary F. Carpenter--b. Nov. 25, 1869 d. July 22, 1939

W. B. MOODY LOT

1. N. Jane Moody--b. May 14, 1861 d. Oct. 15, 1921

A. ARNOLD LOT

1. Joyce Anne Arnold--b. Sept. 1, 1923 d. Sept. 7, 1923
2. John W. Whitington--d. Nov. 26, 1940--aged 87 yrs.

W. C. ERWIN LOT

1. W. C. Erwin--d. Feb. 6, 1924--aged 47 yrs.

BLOCK G (CONT.)   37

J. T. ROBERTS LOT

1. J. T. Roberts--b. Feb. 20, 1880 d. Apr. 26, 1930

G. W. ALFORD LOT

1. G. W. Alford--b. Apr. 2, 1885 d. Apr. 26, 1940

JOHN L. LOVELACE LOT

1. John L. Lovelace--d. Sept. 24, 1932--aged 49 yrs.
2. H. M. Lovelace--d. Oct. 18, 1935--aged 77 yrs.

O. H. HUMPHREY LOT

1. Tillie Farrel Humphrey--d. Oct. 12, 1939--aged 11 days

C. S. MAYES LOT

1. Dan Mayes Galyon--b. Sept. 26, 1912 d. Jan. 15, 1924
2. C. S. Mayes--b. Aug. 29, 1840 d. Dec. 20, 1926

C. M. MAYES LOT

1. Johnnie Mayes--b. Sept. 26, 1912 d. Jan. 15, 1924

W. M. MATTINGLY LOT

1. W. M. Mattingly--d. Sept. 18, 1935

JEFF BALLARD LOT

1. Jeff Ballard--b. 1861 d. 1929
2. John M. Mc Kinney--b. 1884 d. 1936

W. M. THOMAS LOT

1. W. M. Thomas--b. 1884 d. 1931

S. P. CREAMER LOT

1. S. P. Creamer--d. June 10, 1934--aged 73 yrs.

DR. J. B. MARTIN LOT

1. Dr. J. B. Martin--b. Nov. 19, 1858 d. Nov. 24, 1931
2. Mrs. Annie Martin--b. Aug. 7, 1870 d. Dec. 19, 1940

T. P. HINDMAN LOT

1. T. P. Hindman--b. 1870 d. 1931
2. Mrs. T. P. Hindman--b. 1872 d. 1937

W. L. KELLY LOT

1. Willie Lee Kelly--b. May 24, 1898 d. May 6, 1926

BLOCK G (CONT.)   38

LOTS NO DATES

CLARANCE MILLER--E. DAUGHTERY--T. W. JACKSON--GEORGE BRITTON--CLAUD KELLY--
G. W. SANDRIDGE--H. E. SMITH--A. J. HART--T. T. BROWN--A. H. GAY--BEN JOHNSON--
G. J. ADKINS--J. S. GILBERT--C. W. DAMERON--DOC. THOMAS--R. C. PONDERT--WILL
CLINTON--WALTER MORGAN--W. C. DAVIS--J. T. MC CAMEY--L. E. FULLER--B. C. FREE-
MAN--FRANK MITCHEL--IRA LAYNE--MABEL HAMILTON--W. C. ERWIN--LUCY KING--JIM
MARTIN--G. W. ALFORD--S. G. BULLARD--T. E. WILLIAMS--G. W. HAWKINS--MRS. MAUD
WILLIAMS--JOHN SHIRLEY--MRS. SHOEMAKER

BLOCK H   39

ALBERT CURRIN LOT

1. Albert Currin--b. Feb. 9, 1898 d. Aug. 18, 1940

A. H. COWLING LOT

1. A. H. Cowling--No Date

HARREY TANTON LOT

1. Harrey Tanton--No Date

J. F. EDDINS LOT

1. J. F. Eddins--d. 1940--aged 70 yrs.
2. Martha Jane Eddins--died aged 60 yrs.

WILLIAM H. HALE LOT

1. William H. Hale--b. 1864 d. 1934

H. L. YORK LOT

1. H. L. York--b. Dec. 30, 1882 d. June 26, 1936

ESSORY & GILLAM LOT

1. No Names or Dates

LEE TALLEY LOT

1. Mrs. Alma Hill--d. Mar. 13, 1937--aged 22 yrs.

HORACE POWELL LOT

1. Mary Loyola Powell, wife--d. Oct. 24, 1926

PHEBE TURLEY LOT

1. Phebe Turley--d. June 23, 1931

L. L. FREEMAN LOT

1. L. L. Freeman--b. 1876 d. 1935
2. Clark Freeman--b. 1902- d. 1934

FLORA GARTRELL LOT

1. Flora Gartrell--No Dates

A. T. OWENS LOT

1. A. T. Owens--b. Mar. 15, 1867 No Date
2. Martha L., wife--b. June 18, 1862 d. Dec. 12, 1928

BLOCK H. (CONT.)   40

Z. D. GUSHAM LOT

1. Z. D. Gusham--b. 1852 d. 1927

E. E. COLEMAN LOT

1. Edgar Coleman--b. Mar. 18, 1876 d. Nov. 4, 1927

OSCAR MYERS LOT

1. Oscar Myers--b. Feb. 12, 1878 d. Mar. 10, 1927
2. Mrs. John Myers--b. May 23, 1866 d. Dec. 5, 1940

J. B. HILL LOT

1. Mrs. Eula Hill, wife of J. B.,--b. Jan. 6, 1894 d. Jan. 16, 1927

W. C. RAINEY LOT

W. C. Rainey--b. 1848 d. 1927

H. W. BROWNING LOT
1. Herbert Browning--b. Sept. 27, 1874 d. Dec. 26, 1929

J. M. BLEDSOE LOT
Edna Francis Bledsoe--b. Nov. 27, 1886 d. June 18, 1928
William James Coats--b. Sept. 11, 1938 d. Nov. 3, 1938

STANLEY G. CLIFTON LOT
Stanley G. Clifton--d. June 20, 1928
George W. Clifton--b. 1879 d. 1938
Petricia Clifton--b. Aug. 18, 1925 d. Apr. 7, 1930

M. A. SWAN LOT
Mrs. Mary L. Gregory--d. Nov. 4, 1940--aged 77 yrs.

DAVID T. WATSON LOT
Lorene T. Watson--b. Mar. 21, 1910 d. July 8, 1937
A. Watson--d. Nov. 16, 1926--aged 58 yrs., 7 mos., 25 days

W. W. GOLDSWORTHY LOT
Mrs. W. W. Goldsworthy--b. Dec. 13, 1866 d. Feb. 13, 1936
W. W. Goldsworthy--b. Feb. 18, 1862 d. May 5, 1932

MACK LONG LOT
Mack B. Long--b. 1881 d. 1933
Mack Long, Jr.,--b. 1914 d. 1940

JEFFERSON D. WOOSLEY LOT
Jefferson D. Woosley--b. Aug. 18, 1867 d. Mar. 19, 1930
Anna J. Woosley--b. Mar. 28, 1874 d. Aug. 1, 1926

J. B. WALL LOT
Imagene Wall--b. & d. June 6, 1926
W. T. Hamilton--d. Mar. 26, 1937--aged 88 yrs., 3 mos., 4 days
J. B. Wall--b. Mar. 2, 1881 d. Aprl. 17, 1928

P. WALKER LOT
Mary Caroline Walker--b. Apr. 27, 1876 d. Mar. 22, 1926

<u>BLOCK H.(CONT.)</u>   41

MRS. J. F. YOWELL LOT
Mrs. J. F. Yowell--d. Jan. 30, 1939--aged. 78 yrs., 8 mos., 17 days
Mrs. J. C. Strickland--d. Nov. 19, 1936--aged 43 yrs., 6 mos., 11 days.

W. F. CORNELIUS LOT
W. F. Cornelius--b. 1875 d. 1936
Stella D. Cornelius--b. Apr. 16, 1882 d. Sept. 13, 1928

WILL LAKE LOT
James Marion Lake,--d. Jan. 15, 1929--aged 2 yrs., 2 mos., 15 days.

J. E. HUFFMAN LOT
Edwin Ray Huffman--d. April 12, 1934--aged 3 yrs., 6 mos.

MARSHALL WHITE LOT
Mrs. Lillie W. White--d. Oct. 31, 1935--aged 55 yrs., 9 mos., 17 days

AUDREY MAE ROBERTS LOT
Audry Mae Roberts--d. Mar. 3, 1933--aged 40 yrs., 1 mo., 27 days

WILLIAM DAVID MALONEY LOT
William David Maloney--b. 1858 d. 1935
Alpha Betula Maloney--d. Oct. 7, 1939--aged 76 yrs., 9 mos., 1 day

D. E. ORREN LOT
Daniel Eli Orren--b. 1883 d. 1938

B. A. ANDERSON LOT
Bathama Anderson--d. May 28, 1934
Vallie Anderson--b. June 7, 1879 d. Oct. 26, 1940

J. T. ASHWORTH LOT
J. T. Ashworth--b. 1871 d. 1940

ED R. BECKHAM LOT
Ed R. Beckham--d. Mar. 2, 1932

MRS. ADDIE BRYANT LOT
Mrs. Addie Bryant--d. June 22, 1936--aged 68 yrs., 9 mos., 18 days

GEORGE H. POTTER LOT
George H. Potter--b. 1893 d. 1932
Mrs. Mattie Potter--d. Nov. 20, 1933--aged 66 yrs., 3 mos., 2 days

JAMES O. YOUNG LOT
James O. Young--b. 1872 d. 1936
Fred L. Young--b. 1899 d. 1932
James J. Young--b. 1892 d. 1931

LAFAYETTE PRITCHARD LOT
Lafayette Pritchard--b. 1859 d. 1932

CHESTER C. CRAWSON LOT
CHester C. Crawson--b. July 3, 1881 d. April 18, 1935

C. M. CARDEN LOT
C. M. Carden--b. 1888 d. 1932

D. W. FOLLIS LOT
W. T. Follis--d. June 30, 1937

W. C. MORRIS LOT

W. C. Morris--Veteran--Tex. Staff Sgt., Air Service--d. June 4, 1937

S. R. ANDERSON LOT
Mrs. Martha R. Anderson--d. Dec. 9, 1935--aged 63 yrs.

W. E. JACKSON LOT
W. E. Jackson--b. 1860 d. 1935

ESTHER BRADDOCK LOT
Esther Braddock--b. April 21, 1854 d. Oct. 23, 1935

T. P. DAVIS LOT
Susie M. Davis--b. 1882 d. 1934

T. D. ELLISON LOT
T. D. Ellison--b. 1853 d. 1934

C. S. LOVELL LOT
C. S. Lovell--b. 1891 d. 1934

HUGH CARVER LOT
Hugh Carver--d. Apr. 11, 1934 aged 51 yrs.
Mrs. H. Carver--b. 1890 d. 1932

J. M. EASTLAND LOT
Thelma, wife--b. Aug. 21, 1908 d. Oct. 7, 1934
Mizpah on Stone

R. O. HILL LOT
Mrs. Johnnie Hill--b. 1892 d. 1937

J. W. POSTON LOT
J. W. Poston--b. Apr. 5, 1875 d. Feb. 27, 1932

J. W. TURNER LOT
Leon Turner--b. Oct. 21, 1912 d. July 24, 1930

JOHN BRADDY LOT
John Braddy--b. Oct. 5, 1879 d. 1934
Infant son

H. G. CLAYTON LOT
Hannah Lester--b. 1849 d. 1928

DAVE ABLOWICH LOT
Mrs. C. E. Ablowich--d. april 9, 1929 aged 81 yrs.

ALFNA P. CORLEY LOT
Alfna P. Corley--b. Dec. 13, 1865 d. Apr. 2, 1930

GEO. R. KELLEY LOT
George R. Kelley--b. 1888 d. 1931

J. G. ESTES LOT

J. G. Estes--b. Sept. 11, 1865 d. Nov. 3, 1931
Marion Estes--b. Jan. 12, 1912 d. Nov. 14, 1934

BLOCK I (CONT.)

44

DR. WILLIAM MC GLASSON LOT

Dr. Wm. Mc Glasson--b. Feb. 15, 1874 d. Mar. 17, 1935

R. M. MILLER LOT

R. M. Miller--No Dates
Morris Miller--d. Aug. 13, 1937

DR. S. H. WHITLEY LOT

Robert Love Whitley--b. Sept. 26, 1905 d. Jan. 20, 1933

JOHN MULLER LOT

Mrs. M. Tackaberry--b. July 15, 1860 d. Jan. 24, 1939
M. Tackaberry--b. Feb. 7, 1860 d. June 20, 1937

BLOCK J

T. F. SWEAT LOT

1. T. F. Sweat--d. Apr. 25, 1939--aged 78 yrs.
2. Miss Hassie Sweat--d. May 23, 1934--aged 33 yrs.
3. Iva Lou Sweat--d. July 25, 1940--aged 4 yrs

J. R. MC FARLAN LOT

1. J. R. Mc Farlan--d. Apr. 30, 1937 aged 22 yrs.
2. Albert Edwin Mc Farland--d. July 6, 1939

J. W. SMIDDY LOT

1. J. W. Smiddy--b. Nov. 14, 1869 d. Nov. 24, 1929

ROGER I. SCOTT LOT

1. Roger I. Scott--b. Oct. 28, 1895 d. Sept. 16, 1929

GRADY OWENS LOT

1. Mertie Owens--b. Aug. 26, 1895 d. Jan. 30, 1930

C. O. BROWNING LOT

1. C. O. Browning--d. Jan. 1, 1931--aged 46 yrs.
2. Mrs. Mary Browning--d. Mar. 9, 1936--aged 48 yrs.

W. E. TRAUGHBER LOT

1. W. E. Traughber--b. 1871 d. 1930

M. E. LEDFORD LOT

1. Jesse Lois Ledford--d. Mar. 8, 1935--aged 17 yrs.
2. Mrs. Jesse Ledford--d. May 13, 1939--aged 58 yrs.

JEWEL HICKERSON LOT

1. Jewel Hickerson--d. aged 43 yrs.
2. Gertie Hickerson--d. aged 40 yrs.

W. N. GUTHRIE LOT
1. W. N. Guthrie--b. Oct. 27, 1877 d. July 4, 1929

MICHAEL FEATHERSTONE LOT
1. Michael Featherstone--b. 1865 d. 1929

BLOCK J (CONT.)   46

J. T. HENDERSON LOT
1. J. T. Henderson--b. July 22, 1848 d. Apr. 23, 1930
2. J. T. Henderson, II.,--b. Mar. 29, 1920 d. Jan. 23, 1936

W. E. DOBBINS LOT
1. W. E. Dobbins--b. Jan. 17, 1895 d. May 16, 1930
2. Margery R. Dobbins--b. Sept. 31, 1898 d. No Date

MRS. EFFIE BROOKS LOT
No Dates

GUY BISHOP LOT
1. Guy Bishop--b. Apr. 29, 1906 d. Oct. 7, 1931

TOM SAYLE LOT
No Dates

MELTON L. BROWDER LOT
1. Melton L. Browder--d. Sept. 25, 1940--aged 81 yrs.

LEVI TRANTUM LOT
1. Levi Trantum--d. Oct. 23, 1932--aged 65 yrs.

J. R. WALLACE LOT
1. Roy Lee Wallace--d. July 24, 1939--aged 21 yrs.

BLOCK K   47

B. F. BAILEY--d. Dec., 1940

William Homer Cox--d. Dec. 11, 1940--aged 40 yrs.

Mrs. Annie Saunders, wife of Vernon--b. 1928 d. 1940

John H. Mc Kinney--d. Nov. 10, 1940--aged 41 yrs.

Arion Hamilton--b. Oct. 1, 1940 d. Oct. 1, 1940

J. W. Nickles--d. Jan. 5, 1940--aged 73 yrs.

Mrs. Jesse L. Johnston--d. July 27, 1939--aged 59 yrs.

Mrs. Laura F. Horn--b. July 24, 1877 d. June 23, 1939

William T. Liston--b. 1869 d. 1939

Clarence Liston--b. 1869 d. 1936

Dr. L. T. Waller--No Dates

Joe Moore--No Dates

Charles Moore--b. 1934 d. 1936

Marcus R. Penn--b. 1920 d. 1938

Eula S. Penn--b. 1922- d. 1937

Mollie L. Cornish--b. 1897 d. 1937

Leta Francis Kelley--d. June 27, 1937--aged 15 yrs.

J. B. Dillingham--d. May 21, 1937--aged 66 yrs.

BLOCK K (CONT.)   48

J. D. Williams--d. Jan. 30, 1938--aged 65 yrs.

Eula Ray Jackson--d. May 27, 1937

Arta Keith Jackson--d. July 3, 1938--aged 26 yrs.

Bobby Hobbs,--d. May 15, 1937

Billy Frank Turrentine--b. Apr. 30, 1928 d. May 19, 1937

John C. Allen--b. 1877 d. 1937

Albert Homer Allen--b. Mar., 1878 d. Dec., 1937

Albert Davis--b. 1914 d. 1937

Dorothy Jo Jackson--b. Mar. 7, 1865 d. June 17, 1939

A. N. Keys--b. Mar. 7, 1865 d. June 17, 1939

O. H. Roberts--d. Mar. 31, 1939--aged 69 yrs.

Sallie Guthrie Roberts--d. Sept. 23, 1937 aged. 59 yrs.

Gene Tippet--b. 1922 d. 1937

R. T. Spearman-No Dates

Joe D. Wood--b. Aug. 13, 1921 d. May 1, 1933

Tom Smith--d. June,____,--aged 69 yrs.

R. T. Mc Donald--b. June 26, 1861 d. Aug. 26, 1938

J. D. Buchanan--No Date

Howard Picket--b. 1911 d. 1939

W. J. Jordan--b. Aug. 22, 1886 d. May 9, 1936

John L. George--d. Dec. 28, 1935--aged 61 yrs.

Dova Bradford--b. 1867 d. 1936

Walter E. Anderson--b. 1876 d. 1936

W. A. Head--b. 1871 d. 1937

George B. Drake--b. 1823 d. 1936

Thelma Tittle, wife of Dr. Grady Bruce Tittle--b. Aug. 14, 1909 d. Dec. 19, 1937

H. C. BOOTH AND W. L. MAYO LOTS*   49a

1. Frances Avery Booth   b. Aug. 12, 1835
   (Fannie Diane)   d. Feb. 15, 1910

2. Henry Charles Booth   b. Aug. 16, 1836
                                d. Apr. 29, 1923

3. Etta Booth Mayo   b. Dec. 20, 1869
   wife of W. L. Mayo   d. Sept. 4, 1918

4. Booth Mayo, son of   b. Dec. 9, 1896
   Etta Booth and W. L. Mayo   d. Aug. 6, 1898

5. William Leonidas Mayo, Jr.   b. Mar. 15, 1901
   son of E. B. & W. L. Mayo   d. Mar. 15, 1901

6. Douglas Mayo, dau. of   b. Feb., 1894
   Etta Booth and W. L. Mayo   d. Aug. 26, 1902

7. George H. Elhuff   b. Aug. 17, 1874
                                d. Dec. 22, 1898

8. Ola Gregory Rorex   b. Apr. 16, 1869
                                d. Sept. 11, 1954

Lot 8

Rows 13 & 14

* The information on this page was not part of the original study. It has been taken from records in the Commerce Public Library and added to this Study.

                                June, 1975

Adams, J. A.
born April 28, 1873
died Jan. 7, 1943

ATKINS, Miles T.
born Jan. 11, 1890
died June 19, 1943

Bruce, Mrs. Anne
born Dec. 1, 1865
died Sept. 17, 1943

Collins, Mrs. Mollie
born Aug., 1873
died Aug. 26, 1943

Crowder, W. C.
born Feb. 15, 1868
died June 11, 1943

Drummond, Marian Pat
born Feb. 1, 1943
died Feb. 3, 1943

Dunham, Mrs. Sufie
born Sept. 12, 1888
died Dec. 6, 1943

Davis, Margarie Rebecca Holly
born Aug. 31, 1898
died July 7, 1943

Estes, Dillard Loy
born Aug. 31, 1894
died Feb. 10, 1943

Evans, John W.
born Nov. 5, 1873
died Nov. 26, 1943

Fuller, C. D.
born Apr. 20, 1867
died Jan. 28, 1943

Harmon, Thomas E.
born Jan. 1, 1873
died June 10, 1943

Hewitt, Mrs. Anne Reeves
born Apr. 14, 1869
died May 17, 1943

Horn, R. O.
born Oct. 10, 1861
died Apr. 3, 1943

Jackson, Lou Ann
born Mar. 11, 1867
died May 22, 1943

Kelly, Claude
born July 20, 1884
died Apr. 11, 1943

Lands, Virginia
born June 27, 1924
died Jan. 8, 1943

Leeman, J. R.
born Aug. 28, 1864
died July 17, 1943

Mashburn, J. R.
born Jan. 1, 1869
died Apr. 17, 1943

Miller, James Oliver
born Aug. 8, 1856
died Jan. 30, 1943

Miller, C. C.
born 1907
died Sept. 19, 1943

Mc Gary, Lt. John W.
born Mar. 16, 1919
died Nov. 27, 1943

Mc Clellon, Mary Ethel O.
born June 20, 1877
died June 13, 1943

Moon, Mrs. Fannie
born Oct. 12, 1874
died Dec. 22, 1943

O'Neal, Mrs. Emma
born Feb. 15, 1882
died Jan. 8, 1943

O'Neal, Tom
born June 29, 1879
died Mar. 22, 1943

Hickerson, James Thornton
born Dec. 23, 1859
died Aug. 26, 1943

Orren, Mrs. Fannie
born Sept. 27, 1883
died Mar. 21, 1942

SUPPLEMENT (1943) - 2   51

Oppell, _____
born Dec. 18, 1862
died July 17, 1943

Speed, Mrs. Pearl
born Oct. 25, 1882
died Aug. 1, 1943

Painter, John
born Aug. 30, 1860
died Apr. 11, 1943

Veal, R. B.
born Mar. 7, 1881
died Feb. 10, 1943

Rex, Mrs. Ida Ellen
born Apr. 29, 1867
died Sept. 27, 1943

Watson, Jerry Sue
born Sept. 4, 1933
died Jan. 16, 1943

Rainer, Robert L.
born
died Feb. 27, 1943--43 yrs. 6 mos. 8 ds.

Wages, William Haden
born Jan. 1, 1873
died Oct. 31, 1943

Stone, W. B.
born.August 17, 1881
died Jan. 7, 1943

Smith, Lt. Clyde W.,
born Aug. 4, 1920
died Mar. 30, 1943

SUPPLEMENT (1973) - 1   52
BY DUSKIE MYERS

J. T. Knight	1840-1907	
Susan Knight	1845-1909	

Parents of John-Lem-Tom-Ira-Amos

Calvin C. Knight	1886-1900	
Jefferson Knight	1890-1890	
Ellar Knight	1870-1948	

John Knight	1861-1959	
Ella Knight	1870-1936	
Howard Knight	1905-Sept., 1964	

Mrs. C. J. Hundley	1844-1921	Dau. of Si Jackson
Dr. C. J. Hundley	1837-1913	
C. G. Hundley	1876-1907	
J. W. Hundley	1871-1913	
Carlton England	1879-1954	
Sallie England	1880-1941	Granddaughter of Si Jackson

Charles William Rush	1844-1905	
Charlie Forest Rush	1874-1900	
Lucy Rush, wife of C. W.	1851-1927	

J. B. Anders	1848-1916	Son of Dave Anders

Whites Co., Giddens Bn.
Texas Cav.

Sarah Jernigin Anders   Nov. 29, 1816-Bedford Co., Tenn.
          wife of David Anders   June 16, 1891-Commerce, Texas
David Anders   1814-1899

J. H. Jernigin   1840-1906   Mason
Cordelia Jernigin   1851-1936
Mary J. Neal   1835-1908
John T. Neal   1823-1896

SUPPLEMENT (1973) - 2   53

W. A. Jernigin   1848-1889
John Felix   1856-1927
Emeline   1858-1934

Joe Jernigin   1895-1960
Marie   1904-
Robert   1886-1960

James H. Jernigin   1889-1941
Jesse   1882-1926
Bertha   1884-1888

Dr. H. A. Credelle   1848-1910
Willie   1861-1895

SUPPLEMENT (1973) - 3   54

Martha W. Phillips   1825-1900   wife of Reubin Phillips
Mrs. W. F. Ragland   1862-1939   daughter of Reuben Phillips
W. F. Ragland   1850-1900
Nettie Myrtle Ragland   1887-1892   daughter of W. F. Ragland
Evan L. Ragland   Dec. 3, 1816
                                     July 14, 1890

Lee Phillips   1849-1890

J. H. Jackson   Apr. 4, 1821
                                     Mar. 18, 1892
Sallie   Sept. 26, 1824--1887

Fannie Fielder   1844-1908

J. T. Knight   1840-1907
Susan   1845-1909

SUPPLEMENT (1973) - 4   55

Martha F. Phillips   1825-1900   Daughter of Roland Cobb
                                                        Married Reuben Phillips

216

INDIAN BURIAL GROUNDS

This Mound is located Southwest of Campbell, near the Scatter-Branch Cemetery.

BOLES CEMETERY

There were several attempts to located this Cemetery, but it was never located. It is South of the Kingston Cemetery, in the pasture belonging to Boles Homes of Cash, Texas.

FAMILY CEMETERY

The Name of the Family Cemetery is not known, as the Owner of the Pasture will not let anyone enter it. It is said to be located Northeast of Lone Oak, Texas.

INDEX
NAME MAY APPEAR MORE THAN ONCE ON ANY GIVEN PAGE

A.
ABELL, 27;29.
ABERNATHY, 95;102;131; 185;190.
ABEY, 10;11.
ABLOWICK, 133;209.
ACKER, 103;104;149; 150;180;181.
ACKERSON, 116.
ACREY, 30.
ADAIR, 23;133;149; 155;162.
ADAMS, 68;82;100;101; 107;113;117;132;137; 143;149;168;170;171; 172;174;178;189;191; 196;214.
ADAY, 43.
ADDISON, 92.
ADKINS, 205.
ADKINSON, 21;201.
AGEE, 55.
AIKMAN, 59.
ALDRIDGE, 97;188.
ALEXANDER, 37;38;40;51; 83;106;116;126;127;148. 157;201.
ALFRED, 123;204.
ALLARD, 105;136;164.
ALLEN, 19;20;26;46;52; 65;68;84;86;99;119;121; 126;137;140;190;203; 212.
ALLEY, 88.
ALLGEIR, 87.
ALLISON, 22;53.
ALLMON, 140.
ALSOBROOK, 23;63.
ALTON, 108.
AMACKER, 103.
AMES, 46.
AMMONS, 2.
AMONETTE, 39.
ANDERS, 100;110;111; 126;150;191;197.
ANDERSON, 52;76;109; 134;135;139;164;166; 192;208;209;213;215; 216.
ANDREWS, 10;56.
ANGLIN, 151;176.

ANTHONY, 115;144;198.
APPERSON, 100;151;152; 153;176;178.
APPLE, 162.
APPLING, 43.
ARANT, 47.
ARBUCKLE, 55.
ARD, 90.
ARDREY, 55.
AREY, 44;89.
ARMISTEAD, 101.
ARMSTRONG, 4;15;57.
ARNOLD, 31;73;105;115; 125;128;146;156;201; 204.
ARNSPIGER, 145.
ARRINGTON, 139;171.
ARTHUR, 135.
ARUNDALE, 57.
ASBERRY, 32.
ASHBY, 71.
ASHLEY, 48;52;75.
ASHMORE, 49.
ASHWORTH, 135;156;208.
ASKINS, 86;89.
ASSITER, 116.
ATCHISON, 41.
ATHA, 127.
ATKINS, 37;123;127;146; 214.
ATKISSON, 12.
ATTAWAY, 74.
ATTRED, 138.
AUSTIN, 30.
AVEN, 40.
AVERY, 31.
AYERS, 39.

B.
BABB, 89.
BABCOCK, 24.
BACK, 2;34.
BACKUS, 57.
BACON, 59.
BADEN, 30.
BAGGETT, 87.
BAGNELL, 198.
BAGWELL, 8;112.
BAILEY, 47;67;102;153; 183;211.
BAIRD, 19;54.

BAKER, 4;11;34;35;41;47; 66;78;79;114.
BALDRIDGE, 68.
BALDWIN, 34.
BALL, 34;38;171.
BALLARD, 31;60;118;121; 122;123;143;202;205.
BANKS, 55;67;145.
BANTON, 71.
BARBER, 38.
BARCENAS, 77.
BARHAM, 5.
BARKER, 18;29;54;58;111; 112;196;197.
BARKLEY, 14;27;29.
BARLEY, 35.
BARLOW, 21.
BARNES, 128;153.
BARNETT, 148.
BARNES, 175.
BARNUP, 180.
BARR, 31.
BARRETT, 29;48;121;157.
BARRIER, 160.
BARROW, 115;200.
BARRY, 96.
BARSON, 159.
BARTLETT, 104.
BARTO, 143;144.
BARTON, 168.
BATTLE, 73.
BATY, 67.
BAUGHN, 69.
BAUM, 54.
BAXTER, 106;194.
BEALL, 63.
BEAN, 6.
BEANE, 80.
BEASSINGER, 77.
DEARDEN, 3;108;193.
BEAUCHAMP, 30.
BEAULAC, 102
BEAVER, 145.
BEAVERS, 165.
BECKHAM, 208.
BECKLEY, 198.
BECKNELL, 69.
BECTON, 86.
BEDDINGFIELD, 7.
BEDFORD, 164.
BEENE, 7.

DRIVERS, 110.
DRODEN, 108.
DRUMMOND, 142;214.
DUCK, 21;28.
DUFF, 20.
DUGGER, 34.
DUKE, 21;70;85.
DULANY, 8.
DUNBAR, 23.
DUNCAN, 16;19;22;57;
60;79;105.
DUNHAM, 141;142;214.
DUNKIN, 33;38.
DUNLAP, 14;30;34;65.
DUNN, 45;87;101;123;
144;145;148;149;164;
189.
DUPREE, 106.
DURHAM, 104.
DURR, 46.
DURRETT, 91.
DUVALL, 61;82.
DYER, 36;56;63;92.

E.
EARWOOD, 127.
EATON, 44.
EASLEY, 14;129.
EASON, 36.
EAST, 23.
EASTER, 137.
EASTLAND, 134;209.
EASTMAN, 25;110;197.
ECHART, 117;158;165.
ECK, 9.
ECKER, 51.
EDDINS, 206.
EDDLEMON, 63.
EDGE, 119.
EDMONDSON, 52.
EDWARDS, 6;63;81;103.
EICHNER, 63.
EILAND, 5.
ELDRIDGE, 59.
ELEY, 70.
ELHUFF, 152;176;213.
ELKINS, 153.
ELLINGTON, 148;176.
ELLIOTT, 6;21;44;62;
88;132;209.
ELLIS, 20;22;25;41;
60;77;89.

ELLISON, 134.
ELMORE, 40;41;45;77.
ELMS, 175.
ELROY, 111.
EMERSON, 80.
ENDE, 5.
ENGLAND, 19;29;32;103;
120;144;153;169;194;
204;215.
EPPES, 36.
ERWIN, 16;17;28;102;
117;121;132;201;204;
205.
ESSORY, 206.
ESTES, 111;112;129;
133;197;210;214.
ETHRIDGE, 3;156.
EUBANKS, 144.
EUDY, 106.
EVANS, 12;41;42;51;
57;71;94;95;96;107;
113;114;166;167;185;
193;196;214.
EWELL, 54.
EWING, 2;42.

F.
FACTOR, 25.
FAGAN, 161.
FAGG, 30.
FAIN, 25;104;107;193;
195.
FAIRCHILD, 120.
FAIRES, 112;197.
FALLS, 149.
FANT, 55.
FARLER, 161;167.
FARMER, 69;70;161.
FARRELL, 95.
FARRIS, 58.
FARROW, 92;100;145;
169;177;178.
FAUGHT, 119;202.
FAULKNER, 9;10;31.
FEAGIN, 70.
FEATHERSTONE, 135;211.
FELLEY, 138.
FELMET, 81.
FELTS, 47;51.
FERGUSON, 78;70;101;
116;141;147;157;165;
170;198;199.

FERRIER, 112.
FIELDER, 142;174;216.
FIEDS, 95;142;185.
FIEMAY, 111.
FIFE, 134.
FINDLEY, 138;159.
FINLEY, 97;188.
FISHER, 24;25;51;158.
FITCH, 35.
FITE, 77.
FITZGERALD, 5;43;54;81;
82;129;137.
FITZPATRICK, 22.
FITZWATER, 19.
FLEETWOOD, 155.
FLEIG, 51.
FLAMING, 11;43;77.
FLENNIKER, 2.
FLETCHER, 25;57;59;66.
FLEWAHARTY, 82.
FLING, 133;134.
FLINN, 45;77.
FLINT, 174;201.
FLOWERS, 124.
FLOYD, 18;57.
FOLLIS, 52;102;138;190;208.
FONTAINE, 131.
FOSHEE, 119.
FORD, 2;36;51;71;140;164.
FORTENBERRY, 104;163;167.
FOSTER, 2;16;148;162;163.
FOUSE, 10.
FOUST, 39.
FOWLER, 27;28;37;51;63;74;
76;93;138;146;175;179;183.
FOX, 43;77;128;138.
FRANCIS, 127.
FRANK, 25.
FRANKLIN, 100;191.
FRASER, 18.
FRAZIER, 34;66;67.
FREEMAN, 50;77;93;116;120;
131;140;184;205;206.
FREEZE, 103;169;194.
FREEZIA, 160.
FRENCH, 38.
FREY, 19;29.
FRYE, 60.
FRYER, 2;27.
FULCHUM, 27.
FULFER, 126;165.
FUGATE, 31.

NAME MAY APPEAR MORE THAN ONCE ON ANY GIVEN PAGE